A SHORT HISTORY OF THE MIDDLE AGES

A SHORT HISTORY OF THE MIDDLE AGES

BARBARA H. ROSENWEIN
FOURTH EDITION

 UNIVERSITY OF TORONTO PRESS

Library and Archives Canada Cataloguing in Publication

Rosenwein, Barbara H., author
        A short history of the Middle Ages / Barbara H.
Rosenwein. — Fourth edition.

Available in a 2 volume set.
Includes bibliographical references and index.
Issued in print and electronic formats.
ISBN 978-1-4426-0802-3 (bound).—ISBN 978-1-4426-0611-1 (pbk.).—
ISBN 978-1-4426-0612-8 (pdf).—ISBN 978-1-4426-0613-5 (html)

    1. Middle Ages. 2. Europe—History—476-1492. I. Title.

D117.R67 2014   940.1   C2013-906712-4
                                              C2013-906713-2

We welcome comments and suggestions regarding any aspect of our publications—please feel free to contact us at news@utphighereducation.com or visit our Internet site at www.utppublishing.com.

North America
5201 Dufferin Street
North York, Ontario, Canada, M3H 5T8
ORDERS PHONE: 44 (0) 1752 202301
2250 Military Road
Tonawanda, New York, USA, 14150
enquiries@nbninternational.com

ORDERS PHONE: 1–800–565–9523
ORDERS FAX: 1–800–221–9985
ORDERS E-MAIL: utpbooks@utpress.utoronto.ca

UK, Ireland, and continental Europe
NBN International
Estover Road, Plymouth, PL6 7PY, UK

ORDERS FAX: 44 (0) 1752 202333
ORDERS E-MAIL:

Every effort has been made to contact copyright holders; in the event of an error or omission, please notify the publisher.

The University of Toronto Press acknowledges the financial support for its publishing activities of the Government of Canada through the Canada Book Fund.

Printed in Canada

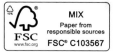

For Sophie

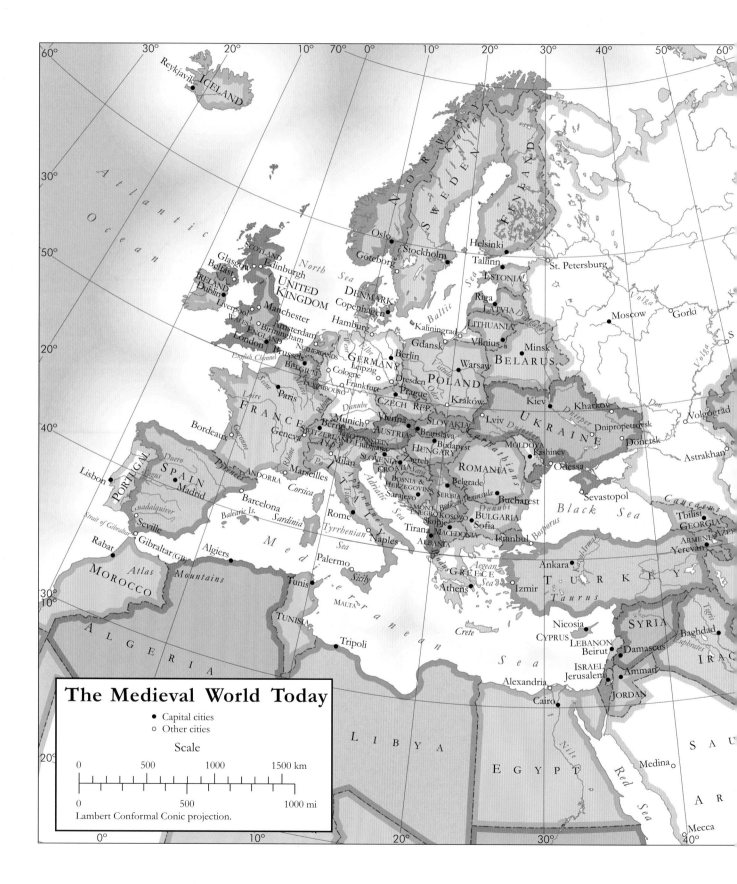

The Medieval World Today

- • Capital cities
- ○ Other cities

Scale

| 0 | 500 | 1000 | 1500 km |

| 0 | 500 | 1000 mi |

Lambert Conformal Conic projection.

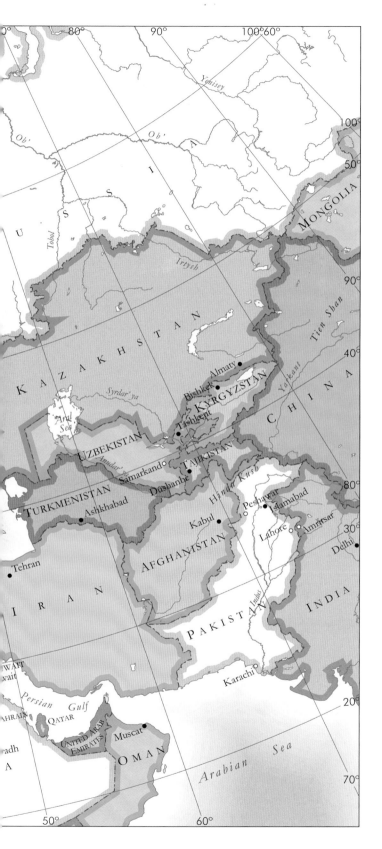

THE UNION of the Roman empire was dissolved; its genius was humbled in the dust; and armies of unknown barbarians, issuing from the frozen regions of the North, had established their victorious reign over the fairest provinces of Europe and Africa.

Edward Gibbon,
The Decline and Fall of the Roman Empire

IT MAY very well happen that what seems for one group a period of decline may seem to another the birth of a new advance.

Edward Hallett Carr, *What is History?*

CONTENTS

MAPS

PLATES

GENEALOGIES

FIGURES

ABBREVIATIONS, DATE CONVENTIONS, WEBSITES

ABBREVIATIONS

c. circa. Used in dates to mean that they are approximate.

cent. century

d. date of death

emp. emperor

fl. flourished. This is given when even approximate birth and death dates are unknown.

r. dates of reign

DATE CONVENTIONS

All dates are CE/AD unless otherwise noted (the two systems are interchangeable). The dates of popes are not preceded by r. because popes took their papal names upon accession to office, and the dates after those names apply only to their papacies.

The symbol / between dates indicates uncertainty: e.g. Boethius (475/480–524) means that he was born at some time between 475 and 480.

WEBSITES

http://www.utphistorymatters.com = The website for this book, which has practice short-answer and discussion questions (with sample answers provided), as well as maps, genealogies, and links to other medieval web resources.

http://labyrinth.georgetown.edu = The Labyrinth: Resources for Medieval Studies sponsored by Georgetown University.

http://www.roman-emperors.org = *De Imperatoribus Romanis*: An Online Encyclopedia of Roman Rulers and Their Families (to 1453).

WHY THE MIDDLE AGES MATTER TODAY

"The past is never dead. It's not even past," wrote William Faulkner in *Requiem for a Nun*. Faulkner was speaking of the past experiences of one human being. Can his statement apply to the historical past? Above all, can it apply to a period so far behind us that it has another name: the Middle Ages? Do the Middle Ages still shape our world?

To be sure! We can say that universities as we know them "began" in the Middle Ages; that medieval representative institutions were forerunners of the US houses of Congress and the Canadian Parliament; and that (giving the question of origins a less positive spin) the idea of making Jews wear a special marker, so important a feature of Nazi Germany in the 1930s, goes back to 1215. Today Neapolitans can walk by the very priory of San Domenico where Thomas Aquinas entered the order of Preachers, the Dominicans, while Americans in Washington, DC, can ogle Washington National Cathedral, built in Gothic style.

So medieval history is relevant today. It helps explain our surroundings and the origins of many of our institutions.

But immediate relevance is not the only reason why the Middle Ages matter. To put it bluntly: they matter because they are past, yet still familiar. The religions that flourished then—Islam, Christianity, Judaism, and the many dissidents within these folds—remain with us, even though they have changed dramatically. This is true as well of many of our institutions—the papacy, royalty, and towns, for example. The problems confronting people in the Middle Ages, not just basic problems such as giving birth, surviving, getting ill, and dying, but sophisticated problems—attempts at thought control, manipulation of markets, outlets and barriers to creativity—are recognizably analogous to our own.

Yet much is *very* different today. This isn't true just at the level of tools—the Middle Ages had nothing that was powered by electricity, no instantaneous communication methods—but also at the level of assumptions about the world. For example, the Middle Ages lacked our ideas and feelings associated with "nationalism." The nation-state, of overriding importance in our time, was unknown in the Middle Ages, even though medieval history became a discipline precisely to prove the reality of nations. (That last fact explains the origins of some of the great medieval primary-source collections undertaken in the nineteenth century, such as the *Monumenta Germaniae Historica*, the Historical Monuments of Germany, whose motto, *Sanctus amor patriae dat animum*, linked "holy love for the Fatherland" with soul, spirit, and inspiration.)

In the end, then, the Middle Ages matter today because they are not so far away as to be entirely foreign, and yet they are far enough away. As the Middle Ages unfolded and became something else (however we may want to define the period that comes next), we can see slow change over time, which we cannot do with our own period. We can then assess what both its stability and its changes may mean for our understanding of human nature, human society, ourselves, and our future.

ACKNOWLEDGMENTS

I would like to thank all the readers, many anonymous, who made suggestions for improving earlier editions of *A Short History of the Middle Ages*. While I hope I will be forgiven for not naming everyone—a full list of names would begin to sound like a roll call of medievalists, both American and European—I want to single out those who were of special help: Eduardo Aubert, Monique Bourin, Elizabeth A.R. Brown, Leslie Brubaker, D.B. van Espelo, Dominique Iogna-Prat, Herbert Kessler, Maureen C. Miller, Eduard Mühle, David Petts, Faith Wallis, Anders Winroth, and Ian Wood. Piotr Górecki supplied me with detailed notes and bibliography and generously critiqued my attempts to write about the history of East Central Europe. Elina Gertsman was a never-ending font of knowledge and inspiration for all matters artistic. Kiril Petkov was a constant and generous resource for matters Bulgarian. Although Riccardo Cristiani was hired simply to check facts, his work for me became a true collaboration. He wrote the questions and answers for the website of this book, compiled the index, and not only corrected many obscurities, infelicities, and errors but also suggested welcome changes and additions. (The mistakes that remain are, to be sure, mine alone.) The people with whom I worked at the University of Toronto Press were unfailingly helpful and efficacious: Judith Earnshaw and Natalie Fingerhut, with whom I was in constant touch, as well as Martin Boyne, Liz Broes, Anna Del Col, Michael Harrison, Matthew Jubb, Beate Schwirtlich, Zack Taylor, and Daiva Villa. I am grateful to the librarians of Loyola University Chicago's Cudahy library—especially Frederick Barnhart, Jennifer Jacobs, Linda Lotton, the late Bonnie McNamara, Jeannette Pierce, David Schmidt, Ursula Scholz, and Jennifer Stegen—who cheerfully fed my voracious hunger for books. Finally, I thank my family, and I dedicate this book to its youngest member, my granddaughter Sophie, born in 2011. May she find much in the Middle Ages to wonder at and enjoy.

ONE

PRELUDE: THE ROMAN WORLD TRANSFORMED (*c.*300–*c.*600)

IN THE THIRD CENTURY, the Roman Empire wrapped around the Mediterranean Sea like a scarf. (See Map 1.1.) Thinner on the North African coast, it bulked large as it enveloped what is today Spain, England, Wales, France, and Belgium, and then evened out along the southern coast of the Danube River, following that river eastward, taking in most of what is today called the Balkans (southwestern Europe, including Greece), crossing the Hellespont and engulfing in its sweep the territory of present-day Turkey, much of Syria, and all of modern Lebanon, Israel, and Egypt. All the regions but Italy comprised what the Romans called the "provinces."

This was the Roman Empire whose "decline and fall" was famously proclaimed by the eighteenth-century historian Edward Gibbon. But in fact his verdict was misplaced. The Empire was never livelier than at its reputed end. It is true that the old elites of the cities, especially of Rome itself, largely regretted the changes taking place around them *c.*250–350. They were witnessing the end of their political, military, religious, economic, and cultural leadership, which was passing to the provinces. But for the provincials (the Romans living outside of Italy) this was in many ways a heady period, a long-postponed coming of age. They did not regret that Emperor Diocletian (r.284–305) divided the Roman Empire into four parts, each ruled by a different man. Called the Tetrarchy, the partition was tacit recognition of the importance of the provinces. Some did, however, regret losing their place in the sun, as happened *c.*400–500, to people still farther afield, whom they called "barbarians." In turn, the barbarians were glad to be the heirs of the Roman Empire even as they contributed to its transformation (*c.*450–600).

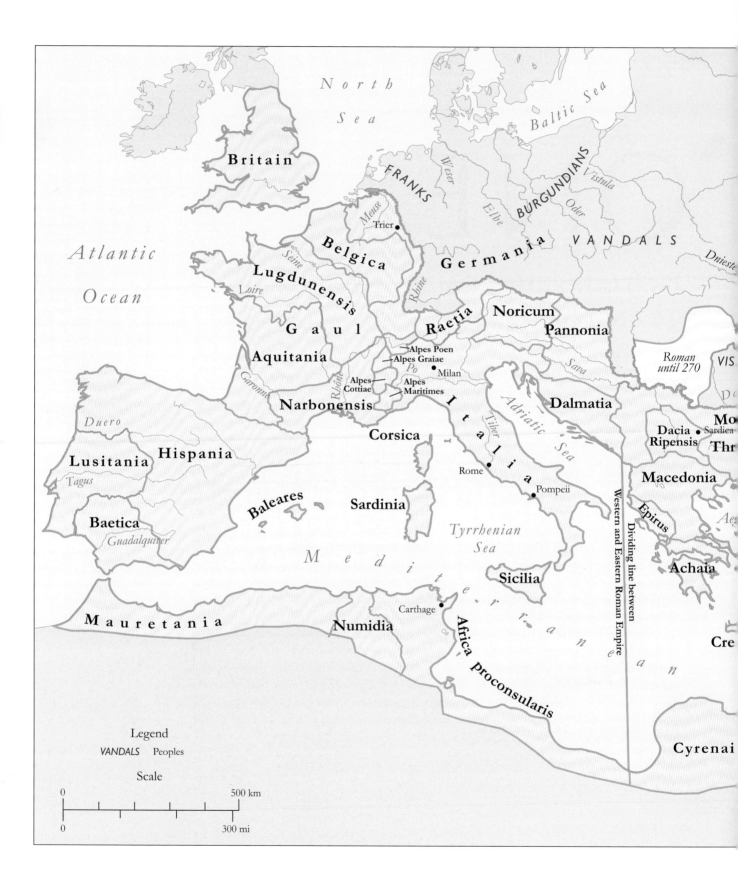

North
Sea

Baltic Sea

Britain

FRANKS

Weser

Vistula

BURGUNDIANS

Elbe
Oder

Germania
VANDALS

Dniester

Atlantic

Ocean

Belgica

Meuse
Trier •

Lugdunensis

Seine

Rhine

Raetia
Noricum

Pannonia

Loire

G a u l

Aquitania

Alpes Poen
Alpes Graiae

Po
Milan •

Roman
until 270

VIS

Sava

Garonne

Alpes
Cottiae
Alpes
Maritimes

Rhône

Narbonensis

Italia

Adriatic Sea

Dalmatia

Duero

Corsica

Tiber

Dacia
Ripensis

• Sardica

Mo

Thr

Hispania

Lusitania

Tagus

Rome •

Macedonia

Baetica

Guadalquivir

Baleares

Sardinia

Pompeii •

Dividing line between
Western and Eastern Roman Empire

Epirus

Aeg

Achaia

M   e   d

Tyrrhenian
Sea

i   t   e   r

Sicilia

M a u r e t a n i a

Numidia

Carthage •

Africa
proconsularis

r   a   n

e   a   n

Cre

Cyrenai

Legend

VANDALS   Peoples

Scale

0

500 km

0

300 mi

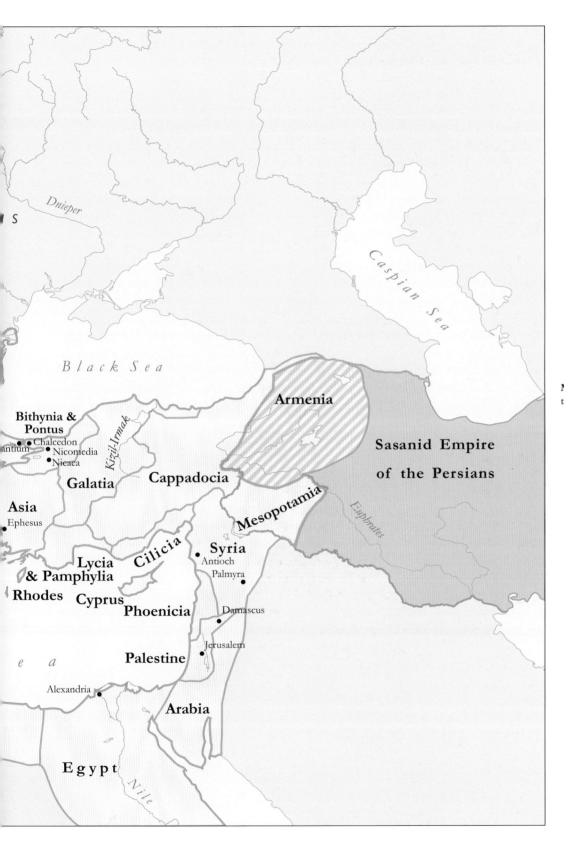

Map 1.1: The Roman Empire in the Third Century

THE PROVINCIALIZATION OF THE EMPIRE (c.250–c.350)

The Roman Empire was too large to be ruled by one man in one place, except in peacetime. This became clear during the "crisis of the third century," when two different groups from two different directions bore down on the frontiers of the Empire. From the north, beyond the Rhine and Danube rivers, came people the Romans called "barbarians"; from the east came the Persians. To contend with these attacks, the Roman government responded with wide-ranging reforms that brought new prominence to the provinces.

Above all, the government expanded the army, setting up new crack mobile forces while reinforcing the standing army. Soldier-workers set up new fortifications, cities ringed themselves with walls, farms gained lookout towers and fences. It was not easy to find enough recruits to man this newly expanded defensive system. Before the crisis, the legions had been largely self-perpetuating. Their soldiers, drawn mainly from local provincial families, had settled permanently along the borders and raised the sons who would make up the next generation of recruits. Now, however, this supply was dwindling: the birthrate was declining, and c.252–267 an epidemic of smallpox ravaged the population further. Recruits would have to come from farther away, from Germania (the region beyond the northern borders of the Empire) and elsewhere. In fact, long before this time, Germanic warriors had been regular members of Roman army units; they had done their stints and gone home. But in the third century the Roman government reorganized the process. They settled Germanic and other barbarian groups within the Empire, giving them land in return for military service.

The term "crisis of the third century" refers not only to the wars that the Empire had to fight on its borders, but also to a political succession crisis that saw more than twenty men claim, then lose with their lives, the title of emperor between the years 235 and 284. (See list on p. 335: Late Roman Emperors; but note that this list names only the most important emperors!) Most of these men were creatures of the army, chosen to rule by their troops. Competing emperors often wielded authority in different regions at the same time. They had little interest in the city of Rome, which, in any case, was too far from any of the fields of war to serve as military headquarters. For this reason Emperor Maximian (r.286–305) turned Milan into a new capital city, complete with an imperial palace, baths, walls, and circus. Soon other favored cities—Trier, Sardica, Nicomedia, and, eventually, Constantinople—joined Milan in overshadowing Rome. The new army and the new imperial seats belonged to the provinces.

The primacy of the provinces was further enhanced by the need to feed and supply the army. To meet its demand for ready money, the Roman government debased the currency, increasing the proportion of inferior metals to silver. While helpful in the short term, this policy produced severe inflation. Strapped for cash, the state increased taxes and used its power to requisition goods and services. To clothe the troops it confiscated uniforms; to arm them it set up weapons factories staffed by artisans who were required to produce a regular quota for the state. Food for the army had to be produced and delivered; here too the state depended on the labor of growers, bakers, and haulers. New taxes assessed on both land and individual "heads" were collected. The wealth and labor of the Empire moved inexorably toward the provinces, to the hot spots where armies were clashing.

The whole empire, organized for war, became militarized. In about the middle of the third century, Emperor Gallienus (r.253–268) forbade the senatorial aristocracy—the old Roman elite—to lead the army; tougher men from the ranks were promoted to command positions instead. It was no wonder that those men also became the emperors. They brought new provincial tastes and sensibilities to the very heart of the Empire, as we shall see.

Diocletian, a provincial from Dalmatia (today Croatia), brought the crisis under control, and Constantine (r.306–337), from Moesia (today Serbia and Bulgaria), brought it to an end. For administrative purposes, Diocletian divided the Empire into four parts, later reduced to two. Although the emperors who ruled these divisions were supposed to confer on all matters, the administrative division was a harbinger of things to come, when the eastern and western halves of the Empire would go their separate ways. Meanwhile, the wars over imperial succession ceased with the establishment of Constantine's dynasty, and political stability put an end to the border wars.

A New Religion

The empire of Constantine was meant to be the Roman Empire restored. Yet nothing could have been more different from the old Roman Empire. Constantine's rule marks the beginning of what historians call "Late Antiquity," a period transformed by the culture and religion of the provinces.

The province of Palestine—to the Romans of Italy a most dismal backwater—had been in fact a hotbed of creative religious and social ideas around the beginning of what we now call the first millennium. Chafing under Roman domination, experimenting with new notions of morality and new ethical lifestyles, the Jews of Palestine gave birth to religious groups of breathtaking originality. One coalesced around Jesus. After his death, under the impetus of the Jew-turned-Christian Paul (d.c.67), a new and radical brand of monotheism under Jesus' name was actively preached to Gentiles (non-Jews), not only in Palestine, but also beyond. Its core belief was that men and women were saved—redeemed and accorded eternal life in heaven—by their faith in Jesus Christ.

At first Christianity was of nearly perfect indifference to elite Romans, who were devoted to the gods who had served them so well over years of conquest and prosperity. Nor did it attract many of the lower classes, who were still firmly rooted in old local religious traditions. The Romans had never insisted that the provincials whom they conquered give up their beliefs; they simply added official Roman gods into local pantheons. For most people, both rich and poor, the rich texture of religious life at the local level was both comfortable and satisfying. In dreams they encountered their personal gods, who served them as guardians and friends. At home they found their household gods, evoking family ancestors. Outside, on the street, they visited temples and monuments to local gods, reminders of home-town pride. Here and there could be seen monuments to the "divine emperor," put up by rich town benefactors. Everyone engaged in the festivals of the public cults, whose ceremonies gave rhythm to the year. Paganism was thus at one and the same time personal, familial, local, and imperial.

But Christianity had its attractions, too. Romans and other city-dwellers of the middle class could never hope to become part of the educated upper crust. Christianity gave them dignity by substituting "the elect" for the elite. Education, long and expensive, was the ticket into Roman high society. Christians had their own solid, less expensive knowledge. It was the key to an even "higher" society.

In the provinces, Christianity attracted men and women who had never been given the chance to feel truly Roman. (Citizenship was not granted to all provincials until 212.) The new religion was confident, hopeful, and universal. As the Empire settled into an era of peaceful complacency in the second century, its hinterlands opened up to the influence of the center, and vice versa. Men and women whose horizons in earlier times would have stretched no farther than their village now took to the roads as traders—or confronted a new cosmopolitanism right at their doorsteps. Uprooted from old traditions, they found comfort in small assemblies—churches—where they were welcomed as equals and where God was the same, no matter what region the members of the church hailed from.

The Romans persecuted Christians, but at first only locally, sporadically, and above all in times of crisis. At such moments the Romans feared that the gods were venting their wrath on the Empire because Christians would not carry out the proper sacrifices. True, the Jews also refused to honor the Roman gods, but the Romans could usually tolerate—just barely—Jewish practices as part of their particular cultural identity. Christians, however, claimed their God not only for themselves but for all. Major official government persecutions of Christians began in the 250s, with the third-century crisis.

Meanwhile the Christian community organized itself. By 304, on the eve of the promulgation of Diocletian's last great persecutory edict, when perhaps only 10 per cent of the population was Christian, numerous churches dotted the imperial landscape. (See Map 1.2.) Each church was two-tiered. At the bottom were the people (the "laity," from the Greek *laikos*, meaning "of the people"). Above them were the clergy (from *kleros*, or "Lord's portion"). In turn, the clergy were supervised by their bishop (in Greek *episkopos*, "overseer"), assisted by his "presbyters" (from the Greek *presbyteros*, "elder": the priests who served with the bishops), deacons, and lesser servitors. Some bishops—those of Alexandria, Antioch, Carthage, Jerusalem, and Rome, whose bishop was later called the "pope"—were more important than others. No religion was better prepared for official recognition.

This it received in 313, in the so-called Edict of Milan. Emperors Licinius and Constantine declared toleration for all the religions in the Empire "so that whatever divinity is enthroned in heaven may be gracious and favorable to us."[1] In fact, the Edict helped Christians above all: they had been the ones persecuted, and now, in addition to enjoying the toleration declared in the Edict, they regained their property. Constantine was the chief force behind the Edict: it was issued just after his triumphant battle at the Milvian Bridge against his rival emperor Maxentius in 312, a victory that he attributed

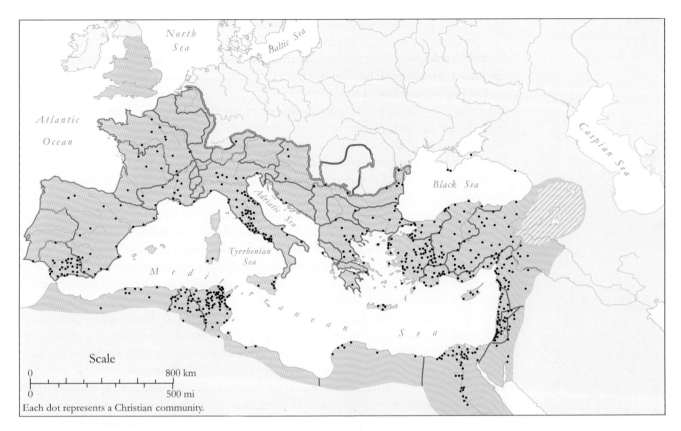

Scale

0 ——————————— 800 km

0 ——————————— 500 mi

Each dot represents a Christian community.

to the God of the Christians. Constantine seems to have converted to Christianity; he certainly favored it, building and endowing church buildings, making sure that property was restored to churches that had been stripped during the persecutions, and giving priests special privileges. Under him, the ancient Greek city of Byzantium became a new Christian city, residence of emperors, and named for the emperor himself: Constantinople. The bishop of Constantinople became a patriarch, a "superbishop," equal to the bishops of Antioch and Alexandria, although not as important as the bishop of Rome. In one of the crowning measures of his career, Constantine called and then presided over the first ecumenical (universal) church council, the Council of Nicaea, in 325. There the assembled bishops hammered out some of the canon law and doctrines of the Christian church.

After Constantine, it was simply a matter of time before most people considered it both good and expedient to convert. Though several emperors espoused "heretical"—unacceptable—forms of Christianity, and one (Julian, the "Apostate") professed paganism, the die had been cast. In a series of laws starting in 380 with the Edict of Thessalonica and continuing throughout his reign, Emperor Theodosius I (r.379–395) declared that the form of Christianity determined at the Council of Nicaea applied to all Romans, and he outlawed all the old public and private cults. Christianity was now the official religion of the Roman Empire. In some places, Christian mobs took to smashing local pagan temples.

Map 1.2: Christian Churches Founded before the Great Persecution of Diocletian (303–304)

In these ways—via law, coercion, and conviction—a fragile religion hailing from one of the most backward of the provinces triumphed everywhere in the Roman world.

But "Christianity" was not simply one thing. In North Africa, Donatists—who considered themselves purer than other Christians because they had not backpedaled during the period of persecutions—fought bitterly with Catholics all through the fourth century, willingly killing and dying so that "the lapsed" might not "hold ecclesiastical office again."[2] As paganism gave way, Christian disagreements came to the fore: what was the nature of God? where were God and the sacred to be found? how did God relate to humanity? In the fourth and fifth centuries, Christians fought with each other ever more vehemently over doctrine and over the location of the holy.

DOCTRINE

The so-called "Church Fathers" were the victors in the battles over doctrine. Already in Constantine's day, Saint Athanasius (c.295–373)—then secretary to the bishop of Alexandria, later bishop there himself—had led the challenge against the beliefs of the Christians next door. He called them "Arians," rather than Christians, after the priest Arius (250–336), another Alexandrian and a competing focus of local loyalties. Athanasius promoted his views at the Council of Nicaea (325) and won. It is because of this that he is the orthodox catholic "Father" and Arius is the "heretic." For both Athanasius and Arius, God was triune, that is, three persons in one: the Father, the Son, and the Holy Spirit. Their debate was about the nature of these persons. For the Arians, the Father was pure Godhead while the Son (Christ) was created. Christ was, therefore, flesh though not quite flesh, neither purely human nor purely divine, but mediating between the two. To Athanasius and the assembled bishops at Nicaea, this was heresy—the wrong "choice" (the root meaning of the Greek term *hairesis*)—and a damnable faith. The Council of Nicaea wrote the party line: "We believe in one God, the Father almighty … And in one Lord Jesus Christ, the Son of God, begotten from the Father, … begotten not made, of one substance [*homousios*] with the Father."[3] Arius was condemned and banished. His doctrine, however, persisted. It was the brand of Christianity that Ulfila (311–c.382), a Gothic bishop with Roman connections, preached to the Goths along the Danube, at the same time translating the Bible into the Gothic language.

Arianism was only the tip of the iceberg. Indeed, the period 350–450 might be called the "era of competing doctrines." As church councils met—especially at Ephesus (431) and at Chalcedon (451)—to chisel ever more closely the contours of right doctrine, dissent multiplied. Monophysites (a later, convenient term for those who opposed the rulings of Chalcedon) held that the "flesh" that God had assumed as Christ was nevertheless divine. Eventually this view, which tended to assimilate human flesh to Christ's and thus divinize humankind, became the doctrine of the Armenian, Coptic (Egyptian), and Ethiopian Christian churches. On the other hand, Pelagius (from Britain, d. after 418) was interested less in the nature of Christ than in that of humanity: for him conversion bleached out sins, and thereafter people could follow God by their own will. Entirely opposite to

Pelagius was Saint Augustine (354–430), bishop of Hippo and the most influential Western churchman of his day. For Augustine human beings were capable of nothing good without God's grace working through them: "Come, Lord, act upon us and rouse us up and call us back! Fire us, clutch us, let your sweet fragrance grow upon us!"[4]

Doctrinal debates were carried on everywhere, and with passion. Gregory of Nyssa (*c.*335–*c.*395) reported that at Constantinople,

> if one asks anyone for change, he will discuss with you whether the Son is begotten or unbegotten. If you ask about the quality of bread you will receive the answer, "the Father is greater, the Son is less." If you suggest a bath is desirable, you will be told "there was nothing before the Son was created."[5]

Like arguments over sports teams today, these disputes were more than small talk: they identified people's loyalties. They also brought God down to earth. God had debased himself to take on human flesh. It was critical to know how he had done so and what that meant for the rest of humanity.

For these huge questions, Saint Augustine wrote most of the definitive answers for the West, though they were certainly modified and reworked over the centuries. In the *City of God*, a huge and sprawling work, he defined two cities: the earthly one in which our feet are planted, in which we are born, learn to read, marry, get old, and die; and the heavenly one, on which our hearts and minds are fixed. The first, the "City of Man," is impermanent, subject to fire, war, famine, and sickness; the second, the "City of God," is the opposite. Only there is true, eternal happiness to be found. Yet the first, however imperfect, is where the institutions of society—local churches, schools, governments—make possible the attainment of the second. Thus "if anyone accepts the present life in such a spirit that he uses it with the end in view of [the City of God], … such a man may without absurdity be called happy, even now."[6] In Augustine's hands, the old fixtures of the ancient world were reused and reoriented for a new Christian society.

THE SOURCES OF GOD'S GRACE

The City of Man was fortunate. There God had instituted his church. Christ had said to Peter, the foremost of his apostles (his "messengers"):

> Thou art Peter [*Petros*, or "rock" in Greek]; and upon this rock I will build my church, and the gates of hell shall not prevail against it. And I will give to thee the keys of the kingdom of heaven. And whatsoever thou shalt bind upon earth, it shall be bound also in heaven; and whatsoever thou shalt loose on earth, it shall be loosed also in heaven. (Matt. 16:18–19)

Although variously interpreted (above all by the popes at Rome, who took it to mean that, as the successors of Saint Peter, the first bishop of Rome, they held the keys), no one doubted that this declaration confirmed that the all-important powers of binding (imposing penance on) and loosing (forgiving) sinners were in the hands of Christ's earthly heirs, the priests and bishops. In the Mass, the central liturgy of the earthly church, the bread and wine on the altar became the body and blood of Christ, the "Eucharist." Through the Mass the faithful were joined to one another; to the souls of the dead, who were remembered in the liturgy; and to Christ himself.

The Eucharist was one potent source of God's grace. There were others. Above all, there were certain people so beloved by God, so infused with his grace, that they were both models of virtue and powerful wonder-workers. These were the saints. In the early church, the saints had largely been the martyrs, but martyrdom ended with Constantine. The new saints of the fourth and fifth centuries had to find ways to be martyrs even while alive. Like Saint Symeon Stylites (c.390–459), they climbed tall pillars and stood there for decades; or, like Saint Antony (250–356), they entered tombs to fight, heroically and successfully, with the demons (whose reality was as little questioned as the existence of germs is today). They were the "athletes of Christ," greatly admired by the surrounding community. Purged of sin by their ascetic rigors—giving up their possessions, fasting, praying, not sleeping, not engaging in sex—holy men and women offered compelling role models. Twelve-year-old Asella, born into Roman high society, was inspired by such models to remain a virgin: she shut herself off from the world in a tiny cell where, as her admirer Saint Jerome put it, "fasting was her pleasure and hunger her refreshment."[7]

Beyond offering models of Christian virtue, the saints interceded with God on behalf of their neighbors and played social peace-keeper. Saint Athanasius told the story of Saint Antony: after years of solitude and asceticism the saint emerged

as if from some shrine, initiated into the mysteries and filled with God.… When he saw the crowd [awaiting him], he was not disturbed, nor did he rejoice to be greeted by so many people. Rather, he was wholly balanced, as if he were being navigated by the Word [of God] and existing in his natural state. Therefore, through Antony the Lord healed many of the suffering bodies of those present, and others he cleansed of demons. He gave Antony grace in speaking, and thus he comforted many who were grieved and reconciled into friendship others who were quarreling.[8]

Healer of illnesses and of disputes, Antony brought spiritual, physical, and civic peace. This was power indeed.

But who would control it? Bishop Athanasius of Alexandria laid claim to Antony's legacy by writing about it. Yet writing was only one way to appropriate and harness the power of the saints. When holy men and women died, their power lived on in their relics (whatever they left behind: their bones, hair, clothes, sometimes even the dust near their tombs). Pious people knew this very well. They wanted access to these "special dead." Rich and influential Romans got their own holy monopolies simply by moving saintly bones home with them.

Men like Saint Ambrose (339–397), bishop of Milan, tried to make clergymen, not pious laypeople, the overseers of relics. Ambrose had the newly discovered relics of Saints Gervasius and Protasius moved from their original resting place into his newly built cathedral and buried under the altar, the focus of communal worship. In this way, he allied himself, his successors, and the whole Christian community of Milan with the power of those saints. But laypeople continued to find private ways to keep precious bits of the saints near to them, as later reliquary lockets attest.[9]

Art from the Provinces to the Center

Just as Christianity came from the periphery to transform the center, so too did provincial artistic traditions. Classical Roman art, nicely exemplified by the wall paintings of Pompeii (Plates 1.1, 1.2, and 1.3), was characterized by light and shadow, a sense of atmosphere—of earth, sky, air, light—and a feeling of movement, even in the midst of calm. Figures—sometimes lithe, sometimes stocky, always "plastic," suggesting volume and real weight on the ground—interacted, touching one another or talking, and caring little or nothing about the viewer.

Plate 1.1 pictures an event well known to Romans from their myths. A handsome man lifts the veil that covers a beautiful woman, exposing her naked body to their mutual delight. A winged boy, a quiver strapped around his shoulder and an arrow in his hand, hovers nearby, while another boy, below the couple, plays with a man's helmet. Any Roman would know from the "iconography"—the symbolic meaning of the elements—that the man is the god Mars, the woman the goddess Venus, and the two boys are their sons, the winged one Cupid. Venus was married to Vulcan, but she and Mars carried on a passionate love affair until Vulcan caught them in a net as they were embracing and displayed them, to their shame, to all the other gods. The artist has chosen to depict a seductive moment before the couple embraces. Even though the story is illustrated for the pleasure of its viewers, the figures act as if no one is looking at them. They are self-absorbed, glimpsed as if through a window onto their private world.

That world was recognizably natural, the same as the one the viewers lived in. In Plate 1.2 craggy mountains are the focus. A shepherd, painted with sketchy lines, pushes a goat toward a shrine, perhaps to sacrifice the animal. On the left, another goat frolics. Shadowy shepherds and goats appear in the distance. The scene is based on observation of the natural world, here interpreted as both tranquil and grand.

Roman decorative motifs drew on nature as well. Plate 1.3, a fresco from a house at Boscoreale, just north of Pompeii, depicts a city filled with houses (one of which has a projecting balcony) mounting a terraced landscape. Marking off the scene at the right is a column wound round with golden tendrils and faux gemstones—a decorative flourish modeled on natural vegetation.

The relief on a Roman sarcophagus (stone coffin) carved in the second century (Plate 1.4) depicts the funeral procession of the mythical hero Meleager. It shows that even in

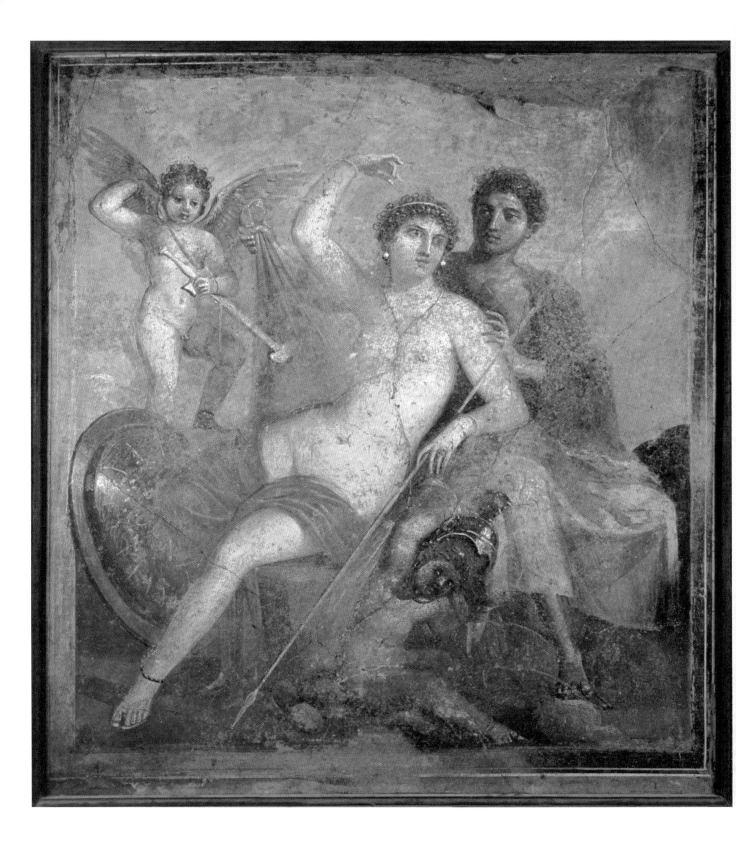

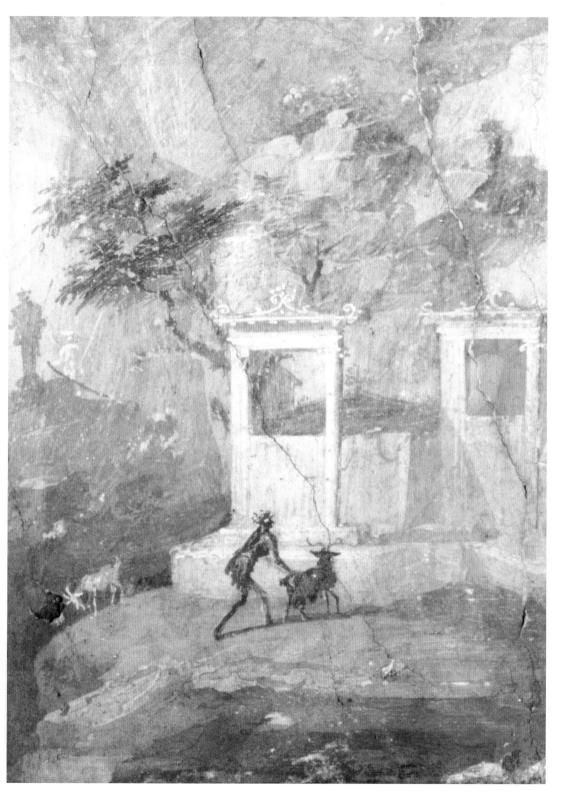

Plate 1.1 (facing page): Mars and Venus, Pompeii (1st cent.). Venus, goddess of love and beauty, and Mars, god of war, are utterly absorbed in both themselves and one another as they adorn the wall of a private house at Pompeii.

Plate 1.2: Landscape, Pompeii (1st cent.). The Roman artist of this painting created the illusion of space, air, and light directly on the flat surface of a wall (probably of a house).

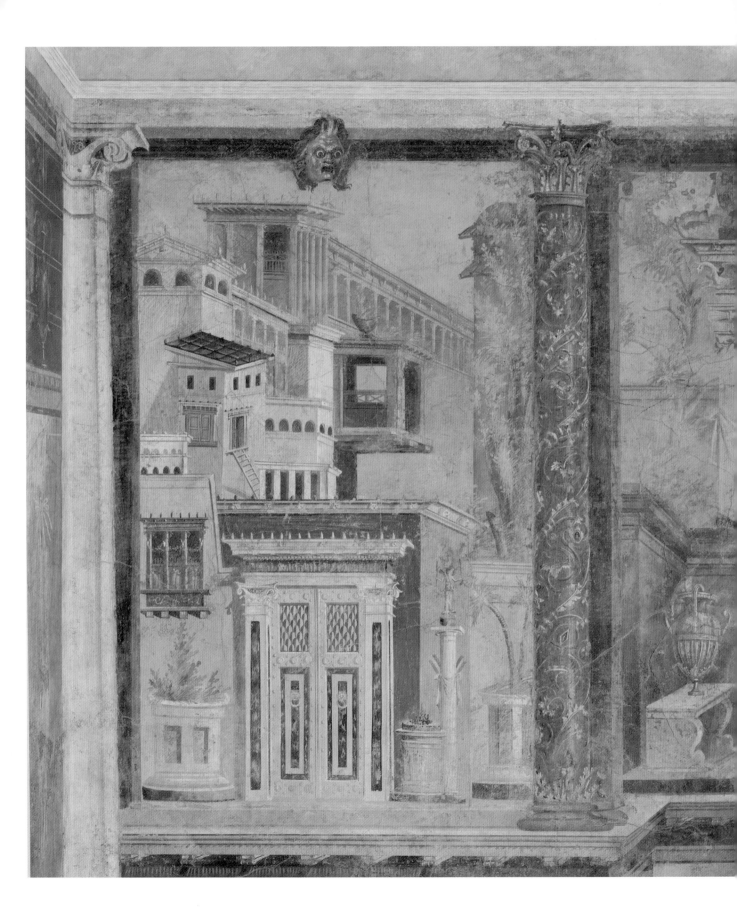

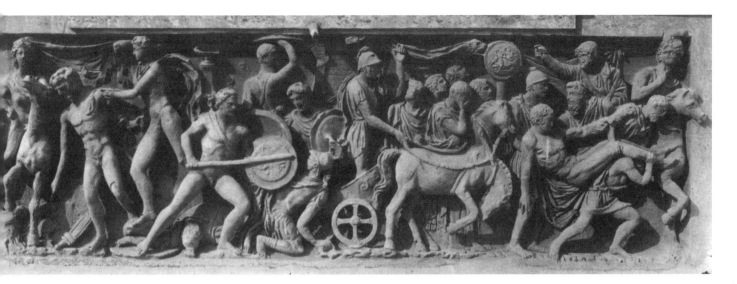

the medium of sculpture, classical artists were concerned with atmosphere and movement, figures turning and interacting with one another, and space created by "perspective," where some elements seem to recede while others come to the fore.

But even in the classical period there were other artistic conventions and traditions in the Roman Empire. For many years these provincial artistic traditions had been tamped down by the juggernaut of Roman political and cultural hegemony. But in the third century, with the new importance of the provinces, these regional traditions re-emerged. As provincial military men became the new heroes and emperors, artistic tastes changed as well. The center—Rome, Italy, Constantinople—now borrowed its artistic styles from the periphery.

To understand some of the regional traditions, consider the sculpted depiction of Venus from the north of Britain (Plate 1.5); a tombstone from the region of Carthage—Tunis, Tunisia today—(Plate 1.6); and a large stone coffer for holding the bones of the dead from Jerusalem (Plate 1.7). All of these were made under the shadow of Roman imperial rule. Yet they are little like Roman works of art. Above all, the artists who made these pieces valued decorative elements divorced from natural forms. The Jerusalem coffer plays with formal, solemn geometrical patterns of light and shadow. The tombstone flattens its figures, varying them by cutting lines for folds, hands, and eyes. Any sense of movement here comes from the incised patterns, not from the rigidly frontal figures. Even the Venus from Britain, though clearly based on a classical model, was created by an artist in love with decoration. The "landscape" consists of wavy lines; the faces are depicted with simple incisions.

There may be something to the idea that such works of art were "inferior" to Roman products—but not much. The artists who made them had their own values and were not particularly interested in classical notions of beauty. The Venus from Britain is clearly the work of a sculptor who wanted to show the opposite of human interaction. Though Venus is attended by two water nymphs, they look straight out at the viewer, not at one another. They exist in an abstract space largely devoid of any natural features. Hair and land

Plate 1.3 (facing page): A City Scene, Boscoreale (1st cent. BCE). In the bedroom of an extremely wealthy patron, an artist filled an entire wall with architectural scenes, each divided by an ornate column, one of which is on the right.

Plate 1.4 (above): Meleager on a Roman Sarcophagus (2nd cent.). This relief depicts part of the story of the hero Meleager, who awarded the hide of a ferocious boar to Atalanta, a huntress who had aided him in pursuing it. Meleager's uncles were furious that the prize had been awarded to a woman, and in the ensuing dispute Meleager killed them. The loss of her brothers so pained Meleager's mother that she impulsively brought about her son's death. Here, on the left, Meleager slays one of his uncles; on the right, mourners carry home the hero's dead body.

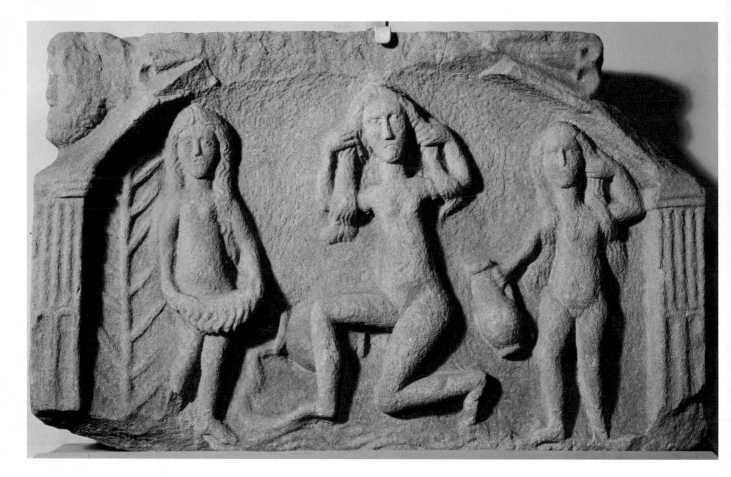

Plate 1.5: Venus and Two Nymphs, Britain (2nd or early 3rd cent.). This relief was originally made to decorate the front of a water tank that stood before the headquarters of the Roman fort at High Rochester (today in Northumberland). This was an "outpost" of the Roman army, a fort on the road to Scotland. Compare the depiction of Venus here with that of Venus in Plate 1.1 to see the very different notions of the human body and of beauty that co-existed in the Roman Empire.

Plate 1.6 (facing page): Tombstone, near Carthage (2nd cent.?). The stiff, frontal figures on this relief show a delight in order, hierarchy, and decoration.

are indicated by lines. Eyes stare out into space. All of this gives the relief an otherworldly feel, as if Venus existed in a place that transcended the here and now of the natural world.

The same emphasis on transcendence explains the horizontal zones of the limestone tombstone (Plate 1.6). It may seem absurd to compare this piece with the Pompeian painting of mountains and shepherd (Plate 1.2). Yet it is crucial to realize that the subjects are largely the same: people and animals participating in a religious sacrifice. It is the approach that is different. On the provincial tombstone, the stress is on hierarchical order. In the center of the top zone is a god. In the middle zones are people busying themselves with proper religious ceremonies. At the bottom, the lowest rung, are three people praying. The proper order of the cosmos, not the natural order, is the focus. This tombstone is no window onto a private world; rather, it teaches and preaches to those who look at it.

The decorated coffer (Plate 1.7) is entirely decorative. As we have seen, at the heart of Rome (Plate 1.3) decorative elements took their cue from the natural world. The sculptor of the stone coffer was interested, by contrast, in abstract geometrical shapes and in the patterns created by repetition. The columns that separate the roundels on the side of the coffer serve the same purpose as those on the fresco at Boscoreale, but on the coffer they are turned into abstract designs. Only the border of the coffer suggests nature: leaves forming a rectangular wreath.

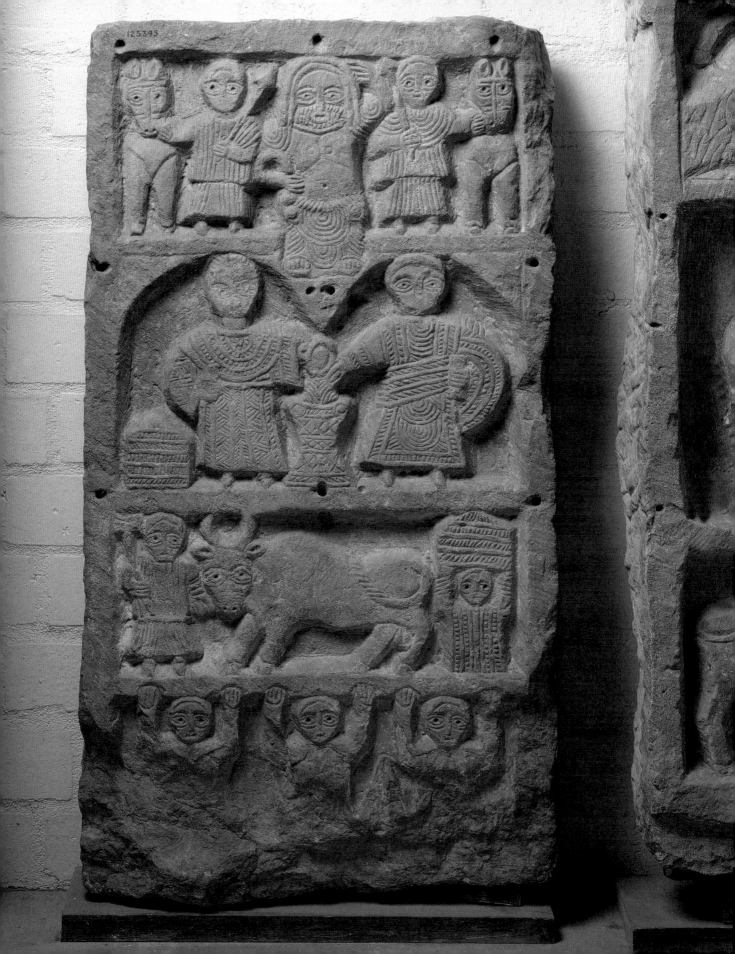

Plate 1.7: Decorated Coffer from Jerusalem (1st cent.?). The human figure was of no interest to the carver of this stone chest, for whom geometrical forms seemed more appropriate for its sober contents: the bones of the dead.

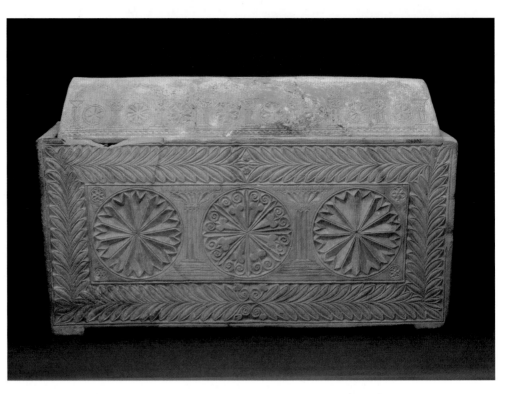

Plate 1.8: Base of the Hippodrome Obelisk (*c.*390). Nothing illustrates changing imperial artistic tastes so well as this carving, placed right in the middle of the most imperial part of Constantinople. It was inspired more by the style of Plate 1.6 than by the traditional classical style of Plate 1.4.

Plate 1.9 (facing page): Orant Fresco (2nd half of 4th cent.). In a private house located in a posh neighborhood in Rome, an imposing figure commands the lower wall of a small room serving as a *confessio*, which contained the remains of martyrs. At the time, the house functioned as a *titulus*, or community church. We see here the sorts of lay devotional initiatives—a *confessio* in a private house—that Bishop Ambrose hoped to end.

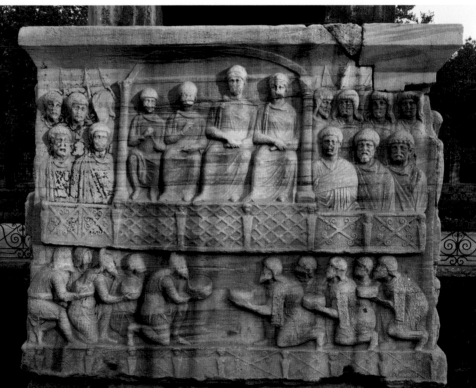

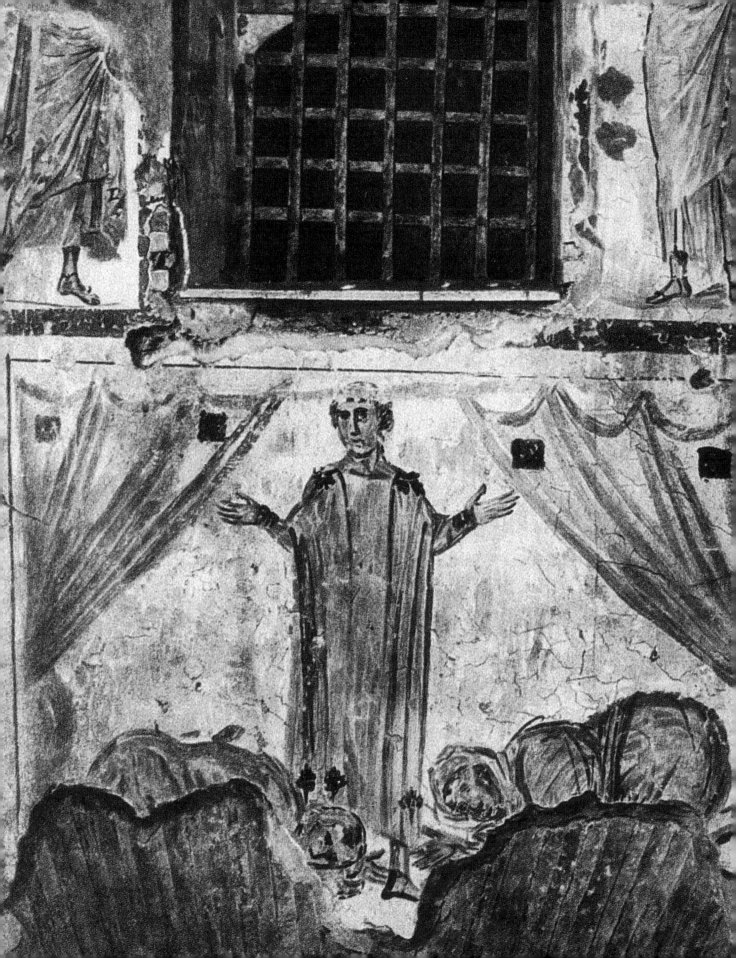

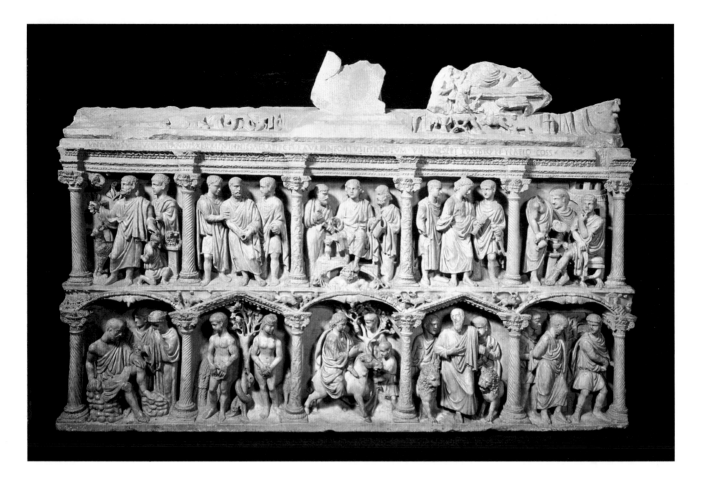

Plate 1.10: Sarcophagus of Junius Bassus (359). Like the Meleager relief (Plate 1.4), the figures on this sarcophagus, carved nearly in the round, gesture and interact. But their subject is now entirely Christian. Reading the scenes from left to right, they portray: (top) Abraham and Isaac; Peter's arrest; Christ enthroned between Saints Peter and Paul, his feet resting on the scarf of Heaven; Christ's arrest; the judgment of Pilate; (bottom) Job sitting on the dunghill, comforted by friends; Adam and Eve; Christ's triumphal entry into Jerusalem; Daniel (clothed by a later, prudish carver, but originally naked) in the lion's den; the arrest of Saint Paul.

The extraordinary development of the fourth century was the center's appropriation of these provincial artistic styles. The trend is graphically illustrated by a marble base made at Constantinople *c.*390 to support a gigantic ancient obelisk, transported at great cost from Egypt and set up with considerable difficulty at the Hippodrome, the great sports arena. (For the location of the Hippodrome, see Map 4.1 on p. 116.) The four-sided base depicts the games and races that took place in the stadium. The side shown in Plate 1.8 is decisively divided into two tiers. At the top are the imperial family and other dignitaries, all formal, frontal, staring straight ahead. Directly in the center is the imperial group, higher than all others. Beneath, in the lower tier, are bearded, hairy-coated barbarians, bringing humble offerings to those on high. The two levels are divided by a decorative frame, a rough indication of the "sky boxes" inhabited by the emperor and his retinue. The folds of the drapery are graceful but stylized. The hairstyles are caps. The ensemble is meant to preach eternal truths: the highness of imperial power and its transcendence of time and place.

Although this style of art was not initially Christian, it was quickly adopted by Christians. It was suited to a religion that saw only fleeting value in the City of Man, sought to transcend the world, and had a message to preach. A good example is a fourth-century wall painting in a small *confessio*—a place where martyrs or their relics were buried.

(See Plate 1.9.) The wall, originally in an alcove on the landing of a private house in Rome, is today beneath a church dedicated to the martyr-saints Giovanni and Paolo. The painting shows a man standing in the ancient "orant" position, much like the figures on the bottom of the tombstone in Plate 1.6. Whoever the man might represent (there are conflicting interpretations), it is clear that he dominates the scene, while at his feet are two figures in postures of humility, suggesting a spiritual hierarchy. The curtains that frame the scene may symbolize a place of eternal rest. Certainly the fresco, like the tombstone, marked a burial site, since behind the grill above the orant were the remains of a martyr or martyrs. Like the figures on the tombstone, those in the fresco have no weight, exist in no landscape, and interact with no one. We shall continue to see the influence of this transcendent style throughout the Middle Ages.

Nevertheless, around the very same time as this fresco was produced, more classical artistic styles were making a brief comeback even in a Christian context. Sometimes called the "renaissance of the late fourth and early fifth centuries," this was the first of many recurring infusions of the classical spirit in medieval art. Consider the sarcophagus of Junius Bassus, carved in 359 (Plate 1.10). Look at just the bottom central panel, which depicts a man on a horse-like donkey. Two young men greet him, one peeking out from behind an oak tree, the other laying down a cloak. The rider's garment drapes convincingly around his body, which has weight, volume, and plasticity. There is a sense of depth and lively human interaction, just as there was in the Meleager sarcophagus (Plate 1.4). But this is a Christian coffin, and the rider is Christ, entering Jerusalem.

THE BARBARIANS

The classicizing style exemplified by Junius Bassus' coffin did not long survive the sack of Rome by the Visigoths in 410. The sack was a stunning blow. Like a married couple in a bitter divorce, both Romans and Goths had once wooed one another; they then became mutually and comfortably dependent; eventually they fell into betrayal and strife. Nor was the Visigothic experience unique. The Franks, too, had been recruited into the Roman army, some of their members settling peacefully within the imperial borders. The Burgundian experience was similar.

The Romans called all these peoples "barbarians." They called some of them "Germani" —Germans—because they materialized from beyond the Rhine, in the region that the Romans called Germania. Historians today tend to differentiate these peoples linguistically: "Germanic peoples" are those who spoke Germanic languages. Whatever name we give them (they certainly had no collective name for themselves), these peoples were, by the fourth century, long used to a settled existence. Archaeologists have found evidence in northern Europe of hamlets built and continuously inhabited for centuries by Germanic groups before any entered the Empire. A settlement near Wijster, near the North Sea (today in the Netherlands), is a good example of one such community. Inhabited largely between *c.*150 and *c.*400, it consisted of well over fifty large rectangular wooden houses—these were partitioned so that they could be shared by humans and animals—and many smaller out-buildings, some of which were used as barns or workrooms, others as dwellings. Palisades—fences made of wooden stakes—enclosed each of these complexes. The people who lived at Wijster cultivated grains and raised cattle. They also raised horses, as we know from the fact that they frequently buried their horses in carefully dug rectangular pits. Some were craftsmen, like the carpenters who built the houses, the ironworkers who made the tools, and the cobbler who made a shoe found on the site. Some were craftswomen, like the spinners and weavers who used the spindle-whorls and loom-weights that were found there.

The disparate sizes of its houses suggest that the community at Wijster was hardly egalitarian. The cemetery there made the same point, since, while most of the graves contained no goods at all, a very few were richly furnished with weapons, necklaces, and jewelry. It seems that the wealthy few also had access to Roman products: archaeologists have unearthed a couple of Roman coins, bits of Roman glass, and numerous fragments of provincial Roman pottery. But even the rich at Wijster were probably not very powerful: it is very likely that here, as elsewhere in the Germanic world, kings leading military retinues lorded it over the community, commanding labor services and a percentage of its agricultural production.

How did the better-off inhabitants of Wijster get their Roman dinnerware? They probably produced surplus enough to trade for other goods. All along the empire's border, Germanic traders bartered with Roman provincials. No physical trait distinguished buyers from sellers. But barbarians and Romans had numerous *ethnic* differences—differences created by preferences and customs surrounding food, language, clothing, hairstyle, behaviors, and all the other elements that go into a sense of identity. Germanic ethnicities were often in flux as tribes came together and broke apart (and Roman ethnic identity also changed, for example as some began to sport Germanic clothing).

Consider the Goths. Their "ethnogenesis"—the ethnicities that came into being and changed over time—made them not one people but many. If it is true that a group called the "Goths" (Gutones) can be found in the first century in what is today northwestern Poland, that does not mean that they much resembled those "Goths" who, in the third century, organized and dominated a confederation of steppe peoples and forest dwellers of mixed origins north of the Black Sea (today Ukraine). The second set of Goths was a splinter of the first; by the time they got to the Black Sea, they had joined with many other groups. In short, the Goths were multiethnic.

Taking advantage—and soon becoming a part—of the crisis of the third century, the Black Sea Goths invaded and plundered the nearby provinces of the Roman Empire. The Romans responded at first with annual payments to buy peace, but soon they stopped, preferring confrontation. Around 250, Gothic and other raiders and pirates plundered parts of the Balkans and Anatolia (today Turkey). It took many years of bitter fighting for Roman armies, reinforced by Gothic and other mercenaries, to stop these raids. Afterwards, once again transformed, the Goths emerged as two different groups: eastern (later, Ostrogoths), again north of the Black Sea, and western (later, Visigoths), in what is today Romania. By the mid-330s the Visigoths were allies of the Empire and fighting in their armies. Some rose to the position of army leaders. By the end of the fourth century, many Roman army units were made up of whole tribes—Goths or Franks, for example—fighting as "federates" for the Roman government under their own chiefs.

This was the marriage.

It fell apart, however, under the pressure of the Huns, a nomadic people from the semi-arid, grass-covered plains (the "steppeland") of west-central Asia. The Huns invaded the Black Sea region in 376, attacking and destroying its settlements like lightning and moving into Romania. The Visigoths, joined by other refugees driven from their settlements by the Huns, petitioned Emperor Valens (r.364–378) to be allowed into the Empire. He agreed. Barbarians had long been settled within the borders as army recruits. But in this case the numbers were unprecedented: tens of thousands, perhaps even up to 200,000. The Romans were overwhelmed, unprepared, and resentful. About two centuries later the Gothic historian Jordanes recalled a humanitarian crisis:

> [The Goths] crossed the Danube and settled Dacia Ripensis, Moesia and Thrace by permission of the emperor. Soon famine and want came upon them, as often happens to a people not yet well settled in a country. Their princes … began to lament the plight of their army and begged Lupicinus and Maximus, the Roman commanders, to open a market. But to what will not the "cursed lust for gold" compel men to assent? The generals, swayed by avarice, sold them at a high price not only the flesh of sheep and oxen, but even the carcasses of dogs and unclean animals, so that a slave would be bartered for a loaf of bread or ten pounds of meat. When their goods and chattels failed, the greedy trader demanded their sons in return for the necessities of life. And the parents consented even to this.[10]

The parents did not consent for long. In 378 the Visigoths rebelled against the Romans, killing Emperor Valens at the battle of Adrianople. The defeat meant more than the death of an emperor; it badly weakened the Roman army. Because the emperors needed soldiers and the Visigoths needed food and a place to settle, various arrangements were tried: treaties making the Visigoths federates; promises of pay and reward. But the rewards were considered insufficient, and under their leader Alaric (d.410), the Visigoths set out both to avenge their wrongs and to find land. Their sack of Rome in 410 inspired Augustine to write the *City of God*. By 418 the Visigoths had settled in southern Gaul, and by 484 they had taken most of Spain as well. The impact of the Visigoths on the Roman Empire was so decisive that some historians have taken the date 378 to mark the end of the Roman Empire, while others have chosen the date 410. (Other historians, to be sure, have disagreed with both dates!)

Meanwhile, beginning late in 406 and perhaps also impelled by the Huns, other barbarian groups—Alans, Vandals, and Sueves—entered the Empire by crossing the Rhine River. They first moved into Gaul, then into Spain. The Vandals crossed into North Africa; the

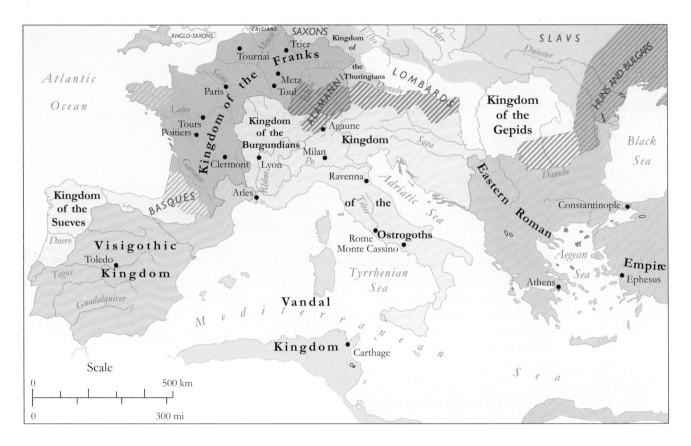

Map 1.3: The Former Western Empire, *c.*500

Sueves remained in Spain, though the Visigoths conquered most of their kingdom in the course of the sixth century. When, after the death in 453 of the powerful Hunnic leader Attila, the empire that he had created along the Danubian frontier collapsed, still other groups—Ostrogoths, Rugi, Gepids—moved into the Roman Empire. Each arrived with a "deal" from the Roman government; they hoped to work for Rome and reap its rewards. In 476 the last Roman emperor in the West, Romulus Augustulus (r.475–476), was deposed by Odoacer (433–493), a barbarian (from one of the lesser tribes, the Sciri) leading Roman troops. Odoacer promptly had himself declared king of Italy and, in a bid to "unite" the Empire, sent Augustulus' imperial insignia to Emperor Zeno (r.474–491). But Zeno in his turn authorized Theodoric, king of the Ostrogoths, to attack Odoacer in 489. Four years later, Theodoric's conquest of Italy was complete. Not much later the Franks, long used to fighting for the Romans, conquered Gaul under Clovis (r.481/482–511), a Roman official and king of the Franks, by defeating a provincial governor of Gaul and several barbarian rivals. Meanwhile other barbarian groups set up their own kingdoms.

Around the year 500 the former Roman Empire was no longer like a scarf flung around the Mediterranean; it was a mosaic. (See Map 1.3.) Northwest Africa was now the Vandal kingdom, Spain the Visigothic kingdom, Gaul the kingdom of the Franks, and Italy the kingdom of the Ostrogoths. The Anglo-Saxons occupied southeastern Britain; the Burgundians formed a kingdom centered in what is today Switzerland. Only the eastern half of the Empire—the long end of the scarf—remained intact.

THE NEW ORDER

What was new about the "new order" of the sixth century was less the rise of barbarian kingdoms than it was, in the West, the decay of the cities and corresponding liveliness of the countryside, the increased dominance of the rich, and the quiet domestication of Christianity. In the East, the Roman Empire continued, made an ill-fated bid to expand, and finally retrenched as an autonomous entity: the Byzantine Empire.

The Ruralization of the West

Where the barbarians settled, they did so with only tiny ripples of discontent from articulate Roman elites. It used to be thought that the Roman Empire granted the invaders vast estates confiscated from Roman landowners. It now seems that the new tribal rulers were often content to live in cities or border forts, collecting land taxes rather than land.

For Romans, the chief objection to the new barbarian overlords was their Arian Christian beliefs. (Recall that Ulfila had preached that brand of Christianity to the Goths.) Clovis, king of the Franks, may have been the first Germanic king to overcome this problem. (If so, Sigismund, king of the Burgundians, was a close second.) Clovis flirted with Arianism early on, but he soon converted to the Catholic Christianity of his Gallic neighbors.

In other respects as well, the new rulers took over Roman institutions; they issued laws, for example. *The Visigothic Code*—drawing on Roman imperial precedents like *The Theodosian Code* (see below, p. 34), on the regulations for rural life found in Roman provincial law codes, and possibly on tribal customary law as well—was drawn up during the course of the fifth through seventh centuries. Sigismund, king of the Burgundians (r. 516–524), issued a code of Burgundian laws in 517. A Frankish law code was compiled under King Clovis, fusing provincial Roman and Germanic procedures into a single whole.

Written in Latin, these laws revealed their Roman inspiration even in their language. Barbarian kings, some well educated themselves, depended on classically trained advisors to write up their letters and laws. In Italy, in particular, an outstanding group of Roman administrators, judges, and officers served the Ostrogothic king Theodoric the Great (r. 493–526). They included the learned Boethius (d. 524/526), who wrote the tranquil *Consolation of Philosophy* as he awaited execution for treason, and the encyclopedic Cassiodorus (490–583), who wrote letters on behalf of Theodoric in the guise of a pious lawgiver. "As it is my desire, when petitioned, to give a lawful consent, so I do not like the laws to be cheated through my favors, especially in that area where I believe reverence for God to be concerned," Cassiodorus wrote (in Theodoric's name) to Jews at Genoa, allowing them, in accordance with Roman law and reverence for God, to add a roof to their synagogue, but nothing more.[11] Since the fourth century, Romans had become used to barbarian leaders; in the sixth, there was nothing very strange in having them as kings.

Far stranger was the disappearance of the urban middle class. The new taxes of the fourth century had much to do with this. The town councilors—the *curiales*, traditional leaders and spokesmen for the cities—had been used to collecting the taxes for their communities, making up any shortfalls, and reaping the rewards of prestige for doing so. In the fourth century, new land and head taxes impoverished the *curiales*, while very rich landowners—out in the countryside, surrounded by their bodyguards and slaves—simply did not bother to pay. Now the tax burdens fell on poorer people. Families pressed to pay taxes they could not afford escaped to the great estates of the rich, giving up their free status in return for land and protection. By the seventh century, the rich had won; the barbarian kings no longer bothered to collect general taxes.

The cities, most of them walled since the time of the crisis of the third century, were no longer thriving or populous, though they remained political and religious centers. For example, the episcopal complex at Tours (in Gaul) was within the walls of a fortification built *c.*400. (See Map 1.4.) Although it still functioned as an institution of religion and government, almost no one lived in the city any longer. But outside of Tours, in a cemetery that the Romans had carefully sited away from ordinary habitation, a new church rose over the relics of the local saint, Martin. This served as a magnet for the people of the surrounding countryside and even farther away. A baptistery was constructed nearby, to baptize the infants of pilgrims and others who came to the tomb of Saint Martin hoping for a miracle. Sometimes people stayed for years. Gregory, bishop of Tours (r.573–594), our chief source for the history of Gaul in the sixth century, described Chainemund, a blind woman:

Map 1.4: Tours, *c.*600

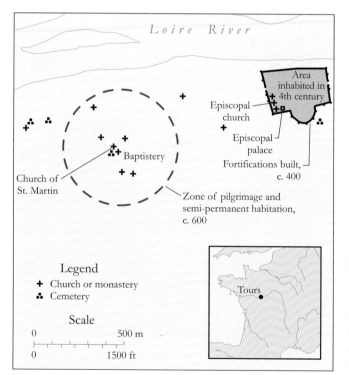

She was a very pious woman, and full of faith she went to the venerable church of the blessed bishop Martin. She was ... [blind and] covered with abrasions on her entire body. For a sickness had attacked all her limbs with sores, and her appearance was so horrible and so repulsive to look at that she was considered by the people as a leper. Every day she felt her way and went to the church of the glorious champion. After almost three years, while she was standing in front of his tomb, her eyes were opened and she saw everything clearly. All the weakness in her limbs disappeared ... and a healthy skin grew back.[12]

With people like Chainemund flocking to the tomb, it is no wonder that archaeologists have found evidence of semi-permanent habitations right at the cemetery.

The shift from urban to rural settlements brought with it a new localism. The active long-distance trade of the Mediterranean slowed down, and although it did not stop, it penetrated very little beyond the coast. Consider the fate of pottery, a cheap necessity of the ancient world. In the sixth century, fine mass-produced African red pottery adorned even the most humble tables along the Mediterranean Sea coast. Inland, however, most people had to make do with local handmade wares, as regional networks of exchange eroded long-distance connections.

For some—the rich—the new disconnection of the rural landscape from the wider world had its charms. When they were inclined, they could still take advantage of luxury goods. In some regions they could even enjoy a life of splendid isolation:

> On the summit of the high rock a magnificent palace is built.... Marble columns hold up the imposing structure; from the top you can see boats gliding by on the surface of the river in summertime.... Water is channeled off along ducts following the contours of the mountain.... On these slopes, formerly sterile, Nicetius has planted juicy vines, and green vineshoots clothe the high rock that used to bear nothing but scrub. Orchards with fruit-trees growing here and there fill the air with the perfume of their flowers.[13]

The owner of this haven was Nicetius (d.c.566), bishop of Trier in the mid-sixth century. He retreated to it when his pastoral cares gave him the chance. Bishops like Nicetius were among the rich; most rose to their episcopal status in their twilight years, after they had married and had sired children to inherit their estates. (Their wives continued to live with them but—or so it was expected—not to sleep with them.) Great lay landlords, kings, queens, warriors, and courtiers controlled and monopolized most of the rest of the wealth of the West, now based largely on land.

Monasteries, too, were beginning to become important corporate landowners. In the sixth century many monks lived in communities just far enough away from the centers of power to be holy, yet near enough to be important. Monks were not quite laity (since they devoted their entire life to religion), yet not quite clergy (since they were only rarely ordained), but something in between and increasingly admired. It is often said that Saint Antony was the "first monk," and though this may not be strictly true, it is not far off the mark. Like Antony, monks lived a life of daily martyrdom, giving up their wealth, family ties, and worldly offices. Like Antony, who toward the end of his life came out of the tombs he had once retreated to in order to be with others, monks lived in communities. Some communities were of men only, some of women, some of both (in separate quarters). Whatever the sort, monks lived in obedience to a "rule" that gave them a stable and orderly way of life.

The rule might be unwritten, as it was at Saint-Maurice d'Agaune, a monastic community set up in 515 by Sigismund on the eve of his accession to the Burgundian throne. The monks at Agaune, divided into groups that went to the church in relay, carried out a grueling regime of non-stop prayer every day. Built outside the Burgundian capital of Geneva, high on a cliff that was held to be the site of the heroic martyrdom of a Christian Roman legion, this monastery tapped into a holy landscape and linked it to Sigismund and his episcopal advisors.

Other rules were written. Caesarius, bishop of Arles (r.502–542) wrote one for his sister, the "abbess" (head) of a monastery of women. He wrote another for his nephew, the "abbot" of a male monastery. In Italy, Saint Benedict (d.*c*.550/560) wrote the most famous of the monastic rules some time between 530 and 560. With its adoption, much later, by the Carolingian kings of the ninth century, it became the monastic norm in the West. Unlike the rule of Agaune, where prayer was paramount, the Benedictine Rule divided the day into discrete periods of prayer, reading, and labor. Nevertheless, the core of its program, as at Agaune, was the "liturgy"—not just the Mass, but also an elaborate round of formal worship that took place seven times a day and once at night. At these specific times, the monks chanted—that is sang—the "Offices," most of which consisted of the psalms, a group of 150 poems in the Old Testament:

> During wintertime … first this verse is to be said three times: "Lord, you will open my lips, and my mouth will proclaim your praise." To that should be added Psalm 3 and the Gloria [a short hymn of praise]. After that, Psalm 94 with an antiphon [a sort of chorus], or at least chanted. Then an Ambrosian hymn [written by Saint Ambrose of Milan] should follow, and then six psalms with antiphons.[14]

By the end of each week the monks were to have completed all 150 psalms.

Benedict's monastery, Monte Cassino, was in the shadow of Rome, far enough to be an "escape" from society but near enough to link it to the papacy. Pope Gregory the Great (590–604), arguably responsible for making the papacy the greatest power in Italy, took the time to write a biography of Benedict and praise his Rule. Monasteries, by their ostentatious rejection of wealth and power, became partners of the powerful. The monks were seen as models of virtue, and their prayers were thought to reach God's ear. It was crucial to ally with them.

Little by little the Christian religion was domesticated to the needs of the new order, even as it shaped that order to fit its demands. Chainemund was not afraid to go to the cemetery outside of Tours. There were no demons there; they had been driven far away by the power of Saint Martin. The fame of Saint Benedict, Gregory reported, drew "pious noblemen from Rome," who "left their sons with him to be schooled in the service of God."[15] Benedict's monasteries had become perfectly acceptable alternatives to the old avenues to prestige: armies and schools. Saint Radegund, founder of a convent at Poitiers (not far from Tours), obtained a fragment of the Holy Cross and other precious relics for her nuns. As one of her hagiographers, Baudonivia, wrote, "She got what she had prayed for: that she might glory in having the blessed wood of the Lord's cross enshrined in gold and gems and many of the relics of the saints that had been kept in the [Eastern half of the Roman Empire] living in that one place [her monastery]."[16] The reliquaries that "enshrined" the relics were themselves precious objects, like the so-called reliquary of Theuderic (Plate 1.11), a small box made of cloisonné enamel (bits of enamel framed by metal), garnets, glass gems, and a cameo. Holy tombs and relics brought the sacred into the countryside, into city convents, and into the texture of everyday life.

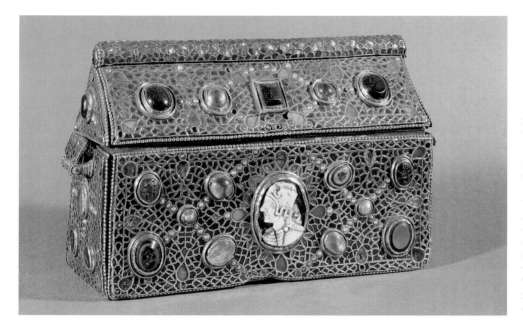

The Retrenchment of the East

After 476 there was a "new order" in the East as well, but at first it was less obvious. For one thing, there was still an emperor with considerable authority. The towns continued to thrive, and the best of the small-town educated elite went off to Constantinople, where they found good jobs as administrators, civil servants, and financial advisors. While barbarian kings in the West were giving in to the rich and eliminating general taxes altogether, the eastern emperors were collecting state revenues more efficiently than ever. Emperor Justinian (r.527–565) had the money to wage major wars—in a failed attempt to revive the Roman Empire of the first centuries—even as he rebuilt Hagia Sophia ("Holy Wisdom"), the great church of Constantinople, when it burned down. Ten thousand workers covered its domed ceiling with gold and used 40,000 pounds of silver for its decoration. When a terrible plague hit the whole Mediterranean region and beyond in the 540s, Justinian (after whom the plague is now named) paid to dispose of the rotting corpses piled up along the shore of Constantinople. He hired workers to build stretchers, carry out the bodies, and deposit the remains in burial pits. (Pope Gregory the Great had a more spiritual response to a later wave of the same plague: he called for "tears of penitence" rather than grave diggers.[17])

Nevertheless, the eastern Roman Empire was not the old Roman Empire writ small. It was becoming a "Middle Eastern state," akin to Persia. Borrowing the ceremony and pomp of the Persian "king of kings" for himself, Justinian was pleased to be represented in the mosaics of San Vitale at Ravenna (Plate 1.12) in a crown and jewels, his head surrounded by a gleaming halo, his ministers—both secular and ecclesiastic—flanking him on both sides. When the Visigoths sacked Rome, the eastern Emperor Theodosius II (r.408–450) did not send an army; he built walls around Constantinople instead. When the roads fell into disrepair, Justinian let many of them decay. When the Slavs pressed on the Roman frontier

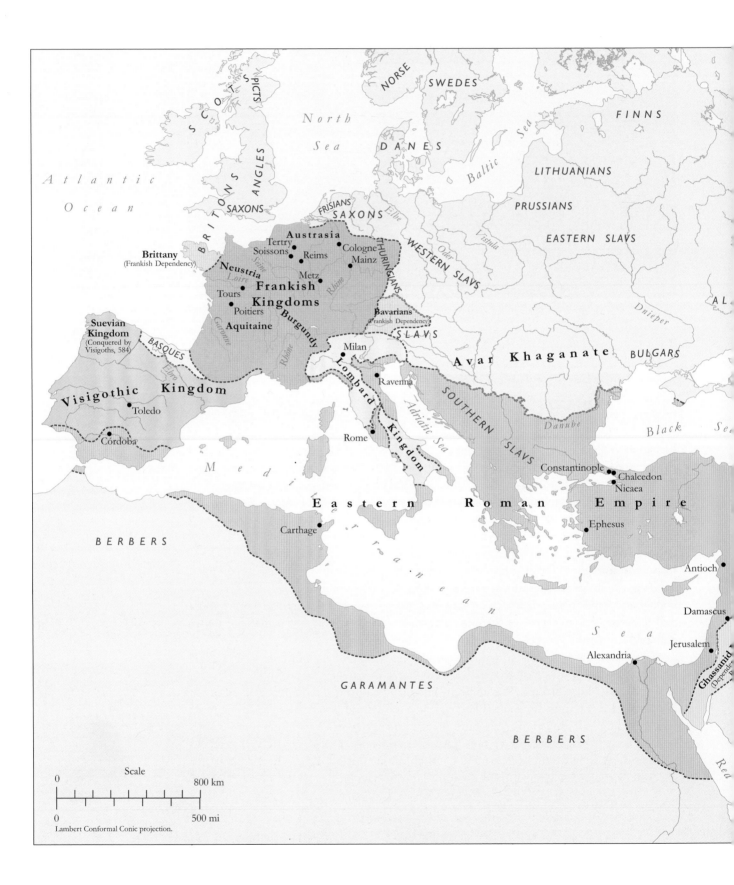

SCOTS

PICTS

NORSE

SWEDES

FINNS

North

Sea

DANES

Baltic

Sea

LITHUANIANS

BRITONS

ANGLES

SAXONS

FRISIANS

SAXONS

Elbe

Oder

Vistula

WESTERN SLAVS

PRUSSIANS

EASTERN SLAVS

Atlantic

Ocean

Austrasia

Tertry

Soissons

Reims

Cologne

Mainz

Metz

THURINGIANS

Brittany
(Frankish Dependency)

Neustria

Seine

Frankish

Loire

Kingdoms

Tours

Rhine

Poitiers

Garonne

Aquitaine

Burgundy

Bavarians
(Frankish Dependency)

SLAVS

Dnieper

AL

**Suevian
Kingdom**
(Conquered by
Visigoths, 584)

BASQUES

Ebro

Rhône

Milan

Lombard

Ravenna

A v a r   K h a g a n a t e

BULGARS

Visigothic   **Kingdom**

Toledo

Kingdom

Rome

*Adriatic
Sea*

SOUTHERN

SLAVS

Danube

Black   Sea

Córdoba

M e d i

t

Constantinople

Chalcedon

Nicaea

BERBERS

E a s t e r n

Carthage

e

r

R o m a n

E m p i r e

Ephesus

r

a

n

e

a

n

Antioch

S e a

Damascus

Jerusalem

Alexandria

Ghassanid
(Dependency)

GARAMANTES

BERBERS

Red

Scale

0

800 km

0

500 mi

Lambert Conformal Conic projection.

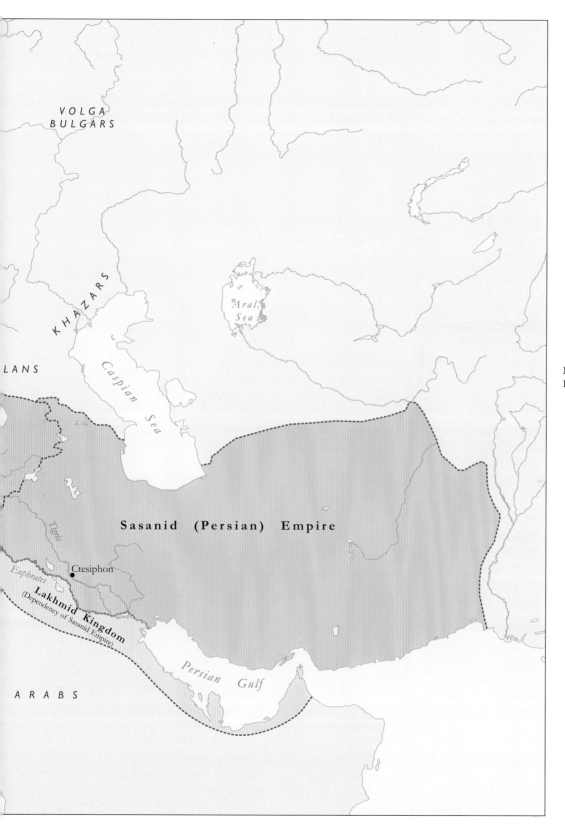

VOLGA
BULGARS

KHAZARS

ALANS

LANS

Caspian Sea

Aral
Sea

Sasanid (Persian) Empire

Tigris

Euphrates

Ctesiphon

Lakhmid Kingdom
(Dependency of Sasanid Empire)

Persian Gulf

ARABS

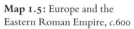

Map 1.5: Europe and the
Eastern Roman Empire, *c.*600

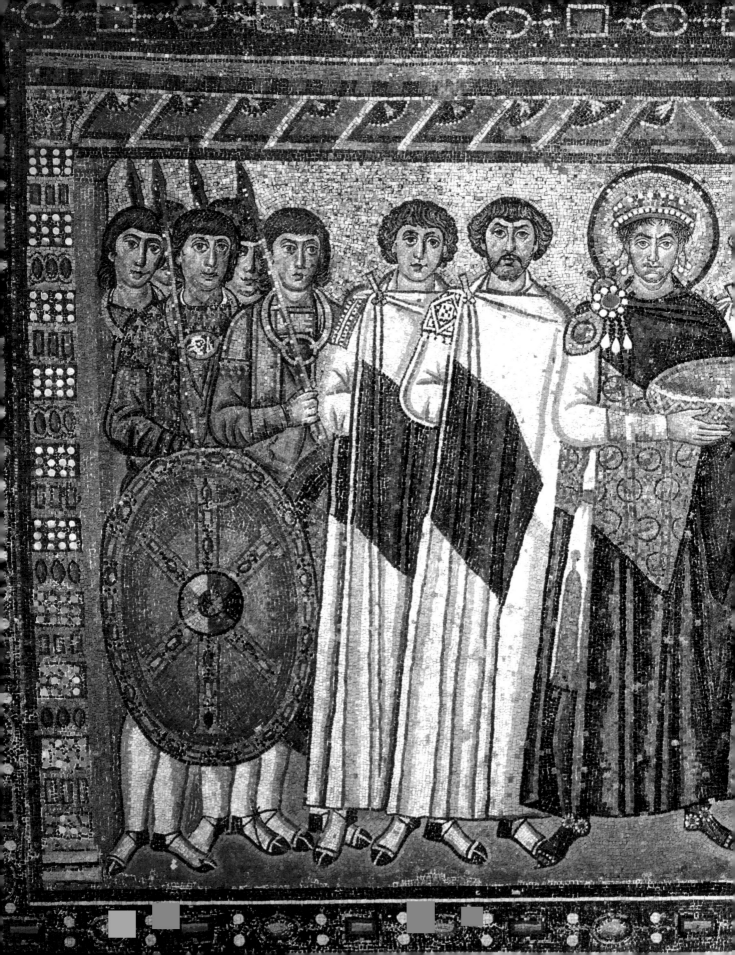

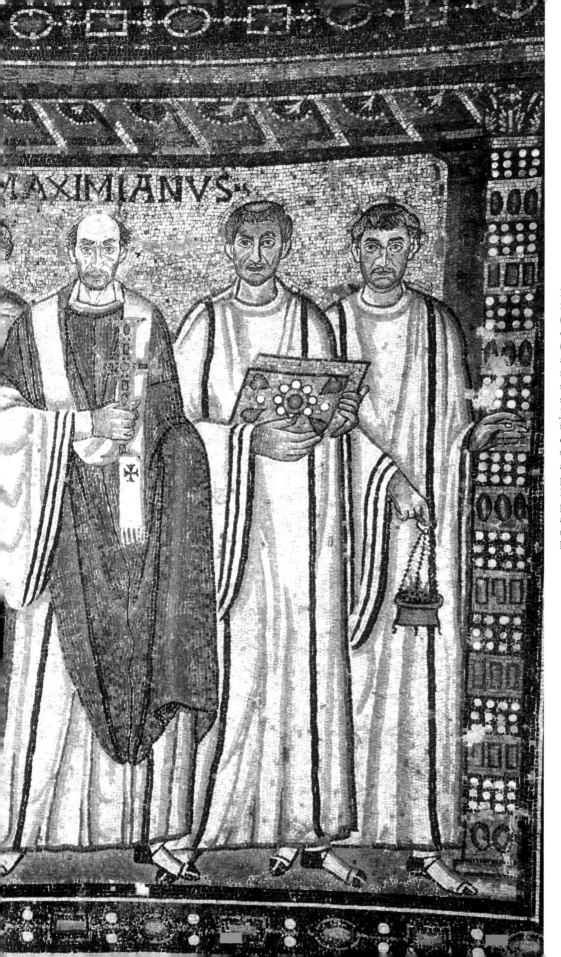

Plate 1.12: Mosaic from San Vitale, Ravenna (*c*.545–*c*.550). Flanked on one side by churchmen (holding a cross and a Bible) and on the other by military men (holding spears and a shield inscribed with the sign of Christ), Emperor Justinian is here depicted in an offertory procession, during which the items for the Mass are brought to the altar. He himself carries the paten, which contains the Eucharistic bread. By both his position in the composition and his role in the Mass, he is thus made the link between heavenly and earthly orders.

in the Balkans, Justinian let them enter. The "plague of Justinian," which continued to attack sporadically until the mid-eighth century, led to manpower and revenue shortages.

The fifth and sixth centuries saw retrenchment in the East. For the first time emperors issued compendia of Roman laws. *The Theodosian Code*, which gathered together imperial "constitutions" (general laws) alongside "rescripts" (rulings on individual cases), was published in 438. Western barbarian law codes of the sixth century attempted to match this achievement, but they were overshadowed by the great legal initiatives of Justinian, which included the *Codex Justinianus* (529, revised in 534), an imperial law code, and the *Digest* (533), an orderly compilation of Roman juridical thought. From then on the laws of the eastern Roman Empire were largely (though not wholly) fixed, though Justinian's books were soon eclipsed by short summaries in Greek, while in the West they had little impact until the twelfth century.

Under Justinian, this redefined Roman Empire sought to recapture its past glory. It quickly took North Africa from the Vandals in 534. It added a strip of southeastern Spain in 552. Meanwhile Justinian's armies pressed on to wrench—but with great difficulty—Italy from the Ostrogoths. The first two enterprises were fairly successful; eastern Roman rule lasted in North Africa for another century. The last venture, however, was a disaster. The long war in Italy, which began in 535 and ended only in 553, devastated the country. Soon the Lombards, Germanic warriors employed by Justinian to help take Italy, returned to Italy on their own behalf. By 572 they were masters of part of northern Italy and, further south, of Spoleto and Benevento. (See Map 1.5.)

For the eastern Roman Empire, the western undertaking was a sideshow. The Empire's real focus was on the Sasanid Empire of the Persians. The two "super-powers" confronted one another with wary forays throughout the sixth century. They thought that to the winner would come the spoils. Little did they imagine that the real winner would be a new and unheard of group: the Muslims.

★   ★   ★   ★   ★

The crisis of the third century demoted the old Roman elites, bringing new groups to the fore. Among these were the Christians, who insisted on one God and one way to understand and worship him. Made the official religion of the Empire under Theodosius, Christianity redefined the location of the holy: no longer was it in private households or city temples but in the precious relics of the saints and the Eucharist; in those who ministered on behalf of the church on earth (the bishops); and in those who led lives of ascetic heroism (the monks).

Politically the Empire, once a vast conglomeration of conquered provinces, was in turn largely conquered by its periphery. In spite of themselves, the Romans had tacitly to acknowledge and exploit the interdependence between the center and the hinterlands. They invited the barbarians in, but then declined to recognize the needs of their guests. The repudiation came too late. The barbarians were part of the Empire, and in the western half they took it over. In the next century they would show how much they had learned from their former hosts.

212	Roman citizenship granted to all free inhabitants of the provinces
235–284	Crisis of the Third Century
284–305	Reign of Diocletian
306–337	Reign of Constantine
313	Edict of Milan
325	Council of Nicaea
378	Battle of Adrianople; Emperor Valens killed by Visigoths
380	Edict of Thessalonica; Christian becomes the official religion of the Roman Empire
410	Visigoths sack Rome
476	Deposition of Romulus Augustulus
c.530– c.560	The Benedictine Rule written
527–565	Emperor Justinian
541–750	The "Plague of Justinian"
590–604	Pope Gregory the Great

NOTES

1 *The Edict of Milan*, in *Reading the Middle Ages: Sources from Europe, Byzantium, and the Islamic World*, ed. Barbara H. Rosenwein, 2nd. ed. (Toronto: University of Toronto Press, 2014), p. 3.

2 *A Donatist Sermon*, in *Reading the Middle Ages*, p. 11.

3 *The Nicene Creed*, in *Reading the Middle Ages*, p. 13.

4 *The Confessions of Saint Augustine* 8.4, trans. Rex Warner (New York: Mentor, 1963), p. 166.

5 Quoted in W.H.C. Frend, *The Rise of the Monophysite Movement: Chapters in the History of the Church in the Fifth and Sixth Centuries* (Cambridge: Cambridge University Press, 1972), p. xii.

6 Augustine, *The City of God*, in *Reading the Middle Ages*, p. 17.

7 Jerome, *Letter 24 (To Marcella)*, in *Reading the Middle Ages*, p. 27.

8 Athanasius, *Life of St. Antony of Egypt*, in *Reading the Middle Ages*, p. 34.

9 See, for example, the "Reliquary Locket," in *Reading the Middle Ages*, color plate 3, p. 234.

10 Charles Christopher Mierow, trans., *The Gothic History of Jordanes* (Princeton, NJ: Princeton University Press, 1915), pp. 88–89.

11 Cassiodorus, *Variae (State Papers)*, in *Reading the Middle Ages*, p. 47.

12 Gregory of Tours, *The Miracles of the Bishop Saint Martin*, trans. Raymond Van Dam, in *Saints and Their Miracles in Late Antique Gaul* (Princeton, NJ: Princeton University Press 1993), p. 210.

13 Venantius Fortunatus, quoted in Georges Duby, *The Early Growth of the European Economy: Warriors and Peasants from the Seventh to the Twelfth Century* (Ithaca, NY: Cornell University Press, 1974), p. 58, spelling and punctuation slightly modified.

14 *The Benedictine Rule*, in *Reading the Middle Ages*, p. 21.

15 Gregory the Great, "The Life and Miracles of Saint Benedict," in Mary-Ann Stouck, ed., *Medieval Saints: A Reader* (Toronto: University of Toronto Press), p. 177.

16 Baudonivia, *The Life of St. Radegund*, in *Reading the Middle Ages*, p. 45.

17 Gregory the Great, *Letter to Bishop Dominic of Carthage*, in *Reading the Middle Ages*, p. 10.

FURTHER READING

Brown, Peter. *The World of Late Antiquity, 150–750*. London: Thames and Hudson, 1971.

Burrus, Virginia, ed. *Late Ancient Christianity*. Minneapolis: Fortress Press, 2010.

Fleming, Robin. *Britain after Rome: The Fall and Rise, 400 to 1070*. London: Penguin, 2010.

Gaddis, Michael. *There Is No Crime for Those Who Have Christ: Religious Violence in the Christian Roman Empire*. Berkeley: University of California Press, 2005.

Geary, Patrick J. *The Myth of Nations: The Medieval Origins of Europe*. Princeton, NJ: Princeton University Press, 2002.

Heather, Peter. *Empires and Barbarians: The Fall of Rome and the Birth of Europe*. Oxford: Oxford University Press, 2009.

Heinzelmann, Martin. *Gregory of Tours: History and Society in the Sixth Century*. Trans. Christopher Carroll. Cambridge: Cambridge University Press, 2001.

Little, Lester K., ed. *Plague and the End of Antiquity: The Pandemic of 541–750*. Cambridge: Cambridge University Press, 2007.

Moorhead, John. *Justinian*. London: Longman, 1994.

Rapp, Claudia. *Holy Bishops in Late Antiquity: The Nature of Christian Leadership in an Age of Transition*. Berkeley: University of California Press, 2005.

Scott, Sarah, and Jane Webster, eds. *Roman Imperialism and Provincial Art*. Cambridge:Cambridge University Press, 2003.

Ward-Perkins, Bryan. *The Fall of Rome and the End of Civilization*. Oxford: Oxford University Press, 2005.

To test your knowledge of this chapter, please go to

www.utphistorymatters.com

for Study Questions.

PART I
THREE
CULTURES
FROM ONE

TWO

THE EMERGENCE OF SIBLING CULTURES
(*c*.600–*c*.750)

THE RISE OF ISLAM in the Arabic world and its triumph over territories that for centuries had been dominated by either Rome or Persia is the first astonishing fact of the seventh and eighth centuries. The second is the persistence of the Roman Empire both politically, in what historians call the "Byzantine Empire," and culturally, in the Islamic world and Europe. By 750 three distinct and nearly separate civilizations—Byzantine, European, and Islamic—crystallized in and around the territory of the old Roman Empire. They professed different values, struggled with different problems, adapted to different standards of living. Yet all three bore the marks of common parentage—or, at least, of common adoption. They were sibling heirs of Rome.

SAVING BYZANTIUM

In the seventh century, the eastern Roman Empire was so transformed that by convention historians call it something new, the "Byzantine Empire," from the old Greek name for Constantinople: Byzantium. (Often the word "Byzantium" alone is used to refer to this empire as well.) War, first with the Sasanid Persians, then with the Arabs, was the major transforming agent. Gone was the ambitious imperial reach of Justinian; by 700, Byzantium had lost all its rich territories in North Africa and its tiny Spanish outpost as well. (See Map 2.1.) True, it held on tenuously to bits and pieces of Italy and Greece. But in the main it had become a medium-sized state, in the same location but about two-thirds the size of Turkey today. Yet, if small, it was also tough.

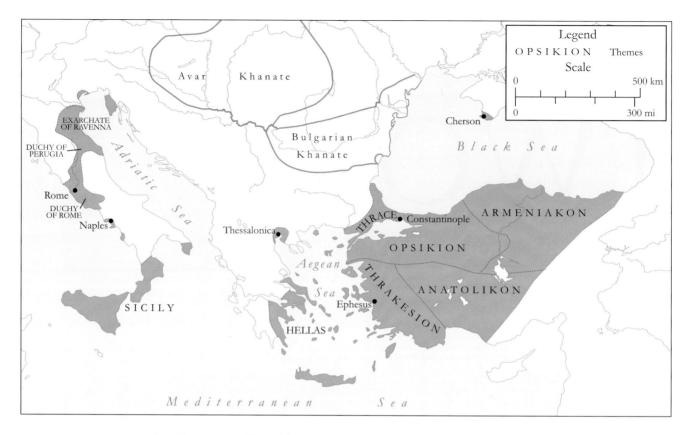

Map 2.1: The Byzantine Empire, *c.*700

Sources of Resiliency

Byzantium survived the onslaughts of outsiders by preserving its capital city, which was well protected by high, thick, and far-flung walls that embraced farmland and pasture as well as the city proper (see Map 4.1 on p. 116). Within, the emperor (still calling himself the Roman emperor) and his officials serenely continued to collect the traditional Roman land taxes from the provinces left to them. This allowed the state to pay regular salaries to its soldiers, sailors, and court officials. The navy, well supplied with ships, patrolled the Mediterranean Sea. It was proud of its prestigious weapon, Greek Fire—a mixture of crude oil and resin, heated and projected via a tube over the water, where it burned, engulfing enemy ships with its flames. The armies of the empire, formerly posted as frontier guards, were now pulled back and set up as regional units within the empire itself. These armies and their regions, both called "themes," were led by *strategoi* (sing. *strategos*), generals who were gradually given responsibility for both military and civil matters. They countered enemy raids while remaining close to sources of supplies and new recruits. Each soldier was given land in his theme to help him purchase his uniform and arms. In this way, the themes maintained the traditions of the imperial Roman army: well trained and equipped, Byzantium's troops served as reliable defenders of their newly compact state.

Invasions and Their Consequences

The Sasanid Empire of Persia, its capital at Ctesiphon, its ruler styled "king of kings," was as venerable as the Roman Empire—and as ambitious. (See Map 1.5 on pp. 30–31.) King Chosroes II (r.590–628), not unlike Justinian a half-century before him, dreamed of recreating past glories. In his case the inspiration was the ancient empire of Xerxes and Darius, which had sprawled from a lick of land just west of Libya to a great swathe of territory ending near the Indus River. Taking advantage of a dispute between two claimants to the imperial throne, Chosroes marched into Byzantine territory in 607. By 613 he had taken Damascus, by 614 Jerusalem. The whole of Egypt fell to the Persians in 619. But Emperor Heraclius (r.610–641) rallied his troops and turned triumph into defeat; all territories taken by the Persians were back in Byzantine hands by 630. (For Heraclius and his successors, see the list on p. 337: Byzantine Emperors.) On a map it would seem that nothing much had happened; in fact, the cities fought over were depopulated and ruined, and both Sasanid and Byzantine troops and revenues were exhausted.

Meanwhile, the Byzantines had to contend with Slavs and other groups north of the Danube. Map 1.5 on pp. 30–31 makes the situation clear: Slavs—farmers and stockbreeders in the main—were pushing into the Balkans, sometimes accompanied by Avars, multi-ethnic horseback warriors and pastoralists. In 626, just before Heraclius wheeled around and bested the Persians on his frontiers, he was confronted with Avars and their Sasanid allies besieging—unsuccessfully, as it turned out—the very walls of Constantinople. It took another half-century for the Bulgars, a Turkic-speaking nomadic group, to become a threat, but in the 670s they began moving into what is today Bulgaria, defeating the Byzantine army in 680 and again in 681. By 700 very little of the Balkan Peninsula was Byzantine. (See Map 2.1.) The place where once the two halves of the Roman Empire had met (see Map 1.1 on pp. 2–3) was now a wedge that separated East from West.

An even more dramatic obliteration of the old geography took place when attacks by Arab Muslims in the century after 630 ended in the conquest of Sasanid Persia and the further shrinking of Byzantium. We shall soon see how and why the Arabs poured out of Arabia. But first we need to know what the shrunken Byzantium was like.

DECLINE OF URBAN CENTERS

The city-based Greco-Roman culture on which the Byzantine Empire was originally constructed had long been gradually giving way. Invasions and raids hastened this development. Many urban centers, once bustling nodes of trade and administration, disappeared or reinvented themselves. Some became fortresses; others were abandoned; still others remained as skeletal administrative centers. The public activities of marketplaces, theaters, and town squares yielded to the pious pursuits of churchgoers or the private affairs of the family.

The story of Ephesus is unique only in its details. Ephesus had once been an opulent commercial and industrial center. Turned to rubble by an earthquake near the end of the third century, it rebuilt itself on a grand scale during the course of the fourth and especially the fifth centuries. Imagine it in about 500. (See Figure 2.1, concentrating on the labels in red.) It had two main centers, both fitting comfortably within the old walls that had been constructed in the Hellenistic period. The most important center was the Embolos, a grand avenue paved with marble. Extending the length of more than two football fields, the Embolos began at its west end on a Market Square and the Library of Celsus, while it opened out on its east end onto the so-called State Agora, only bits of which were restored after the earthquake. All along the Embolos' length were statues, monumental fountains, and arcades. Along its north side were the Baths of Varius and other public buildings. Flanking its south were poor living quarters built over the rubble of once-elegant "terrace houses." There was no question about the religious affiliation of this sector of the city: the Embolos was well Christianized by numerous crosses etched onto the marble slabs of its fountains and paving stones. Small churches were scattered about the vicinity.

The second center of Ephesus around 500 was to the northwest, nearer the harbor. Here numerous old temples and cultural centers were now being reused for homes, baths, and churches. Richly furnished houses were erected in the Harbor Baths, while a chapel was built in the Byzantine palace and a church was constructed in the Stadium. Above all, there was the new Church of St. Mary, the seat of the bishopric, which had been built into the southern flank of an old temple (the Olympieion) next to the bishop's palace and the baptistery.

In short, Ephesus around 500 suggests the comfortable integration of Christian and old Roman institutions. Baths expressed the value of cleanliness; temples were turned into churches; a chapel nestled in the shadow of the old Stadium. Grand fountains and heroic statues continued to be built along the Embolos by proud city benefactors.

But the events of the sixth and seventh centuries transformed the city. The Persian wars disrupted Ephesus' trade and threatened its prosperity. Repeated visitations of the Plague of Justinian took their grim demographic toll. The residences along the length of the Embolos were destroyed in 614, perhaps as the result of an earthquake or of Persian invasions. Arab attacks on Ephesus began in 654–655.

In the face of these disasters, the face of Ephesus changed. (Consider Figure 2.1 again, now focusing on the elements in green.) As if tightening its belt, the city put up new walls to enclose the harbor area. The Embolos lost its centrality. Its southern flank became an "industrial zone," with mills, stone-cutting and ceramic factories, while other workshops were built on the edge of where the terrace houses had once stood. No doubt this location protected the harbor from both noise and pollution. A road south of the Embolos became the workaday thoroughfare, while the "Byzantine palace," closely protected by the seventh-century walls, became the new center of administration.

Yet the new walls did not stave off disaster and decay. The Baths of Vedius were destroyed—though some families made their homes in the rubble until the roof collapsed, probably at the end of the sixth century. The Church of St. Mary itself was partially

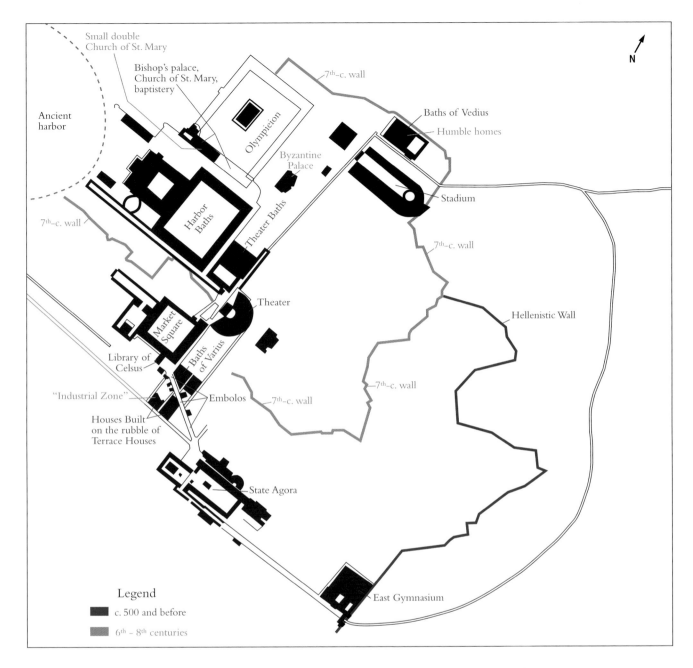

Figure 2.1: Late Antique Ephesus

destroyed—perhaps in the early seventh century—and rebuilt as two separate smaller churches within the original space. Finally, in the wake of the Arab attacks, the bishop abandoned his palace by the harbor and moved to a church about a mile and a half outside of the city.

The fate of Ephesus—much reduced in size but nevertheless still a center of production and habitation—was echoed in many cities circling the eastern Mediterranean in Syria, Palestine, and Egypt. Elsewhere, the urban centers of the Byzantine Empire became little more than fortresses in the course of the seventh and eighth centuries. Constantinople itself was spared this fate only in part. As with other cities, its population shrank, and formerly inhabited areas right within the walls were abandoned or turned into farms. As the capital of both church and state, however, Constantinople boasted an extraordinarily thriving imperial and ecclesiastical upper class. It also retained some trade and industry. Even in the darkest days of the seventh-century wars, it had taverns, brothels, merchants, and a money economy. Its factories continued to manufacture fine silk textiles. Although Byzantium's economic life became increasingly rural in the seventh and eighth centuries, institutions vital to urban growth remained at Constantinople, ensuring a revival of commercial activity once the wars ended.

RURALIZATION

With the decline of cities came the rise of the countryside. Agriculture had all along been the backbone of the Byzantine economy. Apart from large landowners—the state, the church, and a few wealthy individuals—most Byzantines were free or semi-free peasant farmers. In the interior of Anatolia, on the great plateau that extends from the Mediterranean to the Black Sea, peasants must often have had to abandon their farms when Arab raiders came. Some may have joined the other pastoralists of the region, ready to drive their flocks to safety. Elsewhere (and, in times of peace, on the Anatolian plains as well), peasants worked small plots (sometimes rented, sometimes owned outright), herding animals, cultivating grains, and tending orchards.

These peasants were subject as never before to imperial rule. With the disappearance of the traditional town councilors—the *curiales*—cities and their rural hinterlands were now controlled directly by the reigning imperial governor and the local "notables"—a new elite consisting of the bishop and big land owners favored by the emperor. Freed from the old buffers that separated it from commoners, the state adopted a thoroughgoing agenda of "family values," narrowing the grounds for divorce, setting new punishments for marital infidelity, and prohibiting abortions. Legislation gave mothers greater power over their offspring and made widows the legal guardians of their minor children. Education was still important—the young Saint Theodore of Sykeon (d.613), for example, joined the other boys at his village school, where presumably he learned some classical Greek literature—but now for many pious Christians the classical heritage took second place to the Psalter, the book of 150 psalms in the Old Testament thought to have been written by King David. Thus, at the age of twelve, Saint Theodore

> wanted to imitate David in his holy hymn-writing and accordingly began to learn the Psalter. With difficulty and much labor he learnt as far as the sixteenth psalm, but he could not manage to get the seventeenth psalm by heart. He was studying it in the chapel of the holy martyr Christopher (which was near the village) and as he could not learn it, he threw himself on his face and besought God to make him quick of learning in his study of the psalms. And the merciful God, Who said, "Ask and it shall be given you" [Matt. 7:7], granted him his request.[1]

Like many other people in the sixth century, Saint Theodore came down with the plague. Unlike many, he recovered. He was healed, according to his biographer, by drops of dew that fell from an icon of Christ. Soon it would be icons themselves, understood as images of the divine, that would be credited with doing miracles. But before about 680, images of saints, Mary, and the Godhead were less important than relics for Christian worshippers in both the East and the West. It was the dew, which had had contact with the image of Christ, that cured Theodore, not the divine power of the image itself. A diptych carved around this time (see Plate 2.1: Seeing the Middle Ages) was meant to honor, not adore, Christ and the Virgin.

However, a dramatic shift in ideas about images occurred in the Byzantine Empire around 680. A cult of images became as important there as the cult of saints. The change was bluntly summed up by a church council held in Constantinople in 692, which decreed that "in order that what is perfect, even in paintings, may be portrayed before the eyes of all, … Christ our God should be set forth in images in human form."[2] Stories circulated of saintly images that spoke; it became common for worshippers to bow down to sacred portraits. Images became more than representations of divine beings; they became—like relics, like reliquaries—containers of the holy.

These new ideas responded to the crises of the day. In the late seventh century, Byzantines were confronted by plagues, earthquakes, and (above all) wars against Slavs, Avars, and Bulgars (who were settling Byzantium's northern perimeter) and newly unleashed Islamic forces (which were raiding in Anatolia). How could this happen to God's Chosen People (as the Byzantines thought of themselves)? The answer was clear: God was angry with them for their sins. What recourse did they have but to seek new avenues to access divine favor? While still depending on relics to protect and fortify them, many Byzantines sought the aid of holy images as well. Monks were especially enthusiastic patrons of these powerful works of art.

Soon there was a backlash against these new-fangled ideas. Emperor Leo III the Isaurian (r.717–741) agreed that the crises were God's punishment for the sins of the Byzantines. But he thought that their chief sin was idolatry. In 726, after a terrifying volcanic eruption in the middle of the Aegean Sea, Leo seems to have denounced sacred portraits publicly. Historians used to report that Leo also had his soldiers tear down a great golden icon of Christ at the Chalke, the gateway to the imperial palace, and replace it with a cross. Newer research notes that no contemporary sources record this incident. Most likely it was a legend invented much later. Nevertheless, around 726, or perhaps a bit before it, Leo erected a cross in front of the imperial palace. It affirmed not only the Cross's salvific place in the lives of all Christians but also its unwavering role in imperial victories. The two events around 726 may be taken to signify the beginning of the "iconoclastic" (anti-icon or, literally, icon-breaking) period. In 730, Leo required the pope at Rome and the patriarch of Constantinople to subscribe to a new policy: to remove sacred images, or at least to marginalize them, if they inspired the wrong kind of devotion.

SEEING THE MIDDLE AGES

Originally fastened together with hinges, these two small ivory panels (each about 11½ in × 7 in) depict (on the left) Christ flanked by Saints Peter and Paul and (on the right) Mary with the Christ Child between two angels. Although they have been trimmed at the bottom, enough of the decoration there remains to show the monogram of Bishop Maximianus of Ravenna (r.546–556/557), who was appointed by Justinian.[1] The style is Byzantine, and it is likely that Maximianus commissioned the diptych from artists trained either at Constantinople or Alexandria.

Carved before images of holy people were themselves considered holy (a notion that probably took hold only around 680), the ivory diptych here is more about power in this world than in the next. Both Christ and the Virgin sit

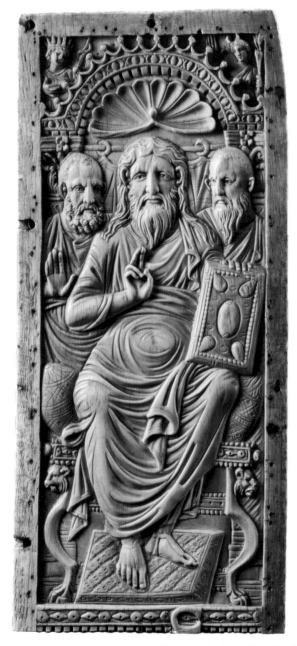
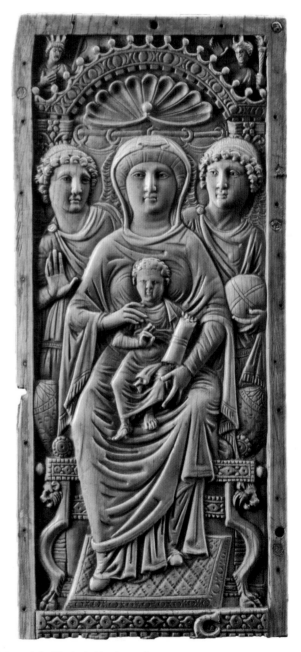

Plate 2.1: An Ivory Diptych of Christ and the Virgin (mid-6th cent.)

on backless stools held up by lion legs—this was a depiction of an "imperial" throne. Christ appears as the Ancient of Days, a powerful judge known from the dream recorded in Daniel 7:9 and 7:22. There the Ancient of Days wore a "garment white as snow, and the hair of his head [was] like clean wool." After horrible beasts prevailed over the saints, "the Ancient of Days came and gave judgment to the saints of the most High, and the time came, and the saints obtained the kingdom." In the diptych, Christ holds an ornately decorated Gospel book in his left hand while, with his right, he gives a gesture of blessing.

On the other diptych panel, Mary sits with a very adult-looking Christ Child on her lap. He is holding a scroll, rolled and tied, with his left hand and, like the Ancient of Days, gives a gesture of blessing with his right hand. Angels dressed like soldiers flank both mother and child. One is holding an orb signifying the earth (proof that medieval people did *not* believe the earth was flat!).

Both figures sit in front of arches that would have reminded contemporary viewers of palace architecture. Above them, in the corners of each diptych, are tiny busts symbolizing the sun and the moon.

Why would Maximianus want to depict Christ and the Virgin in these ways?

The answer is probably to be found in the role and significance of consular diptychs. After emperors named a man to consular rank, the lucky nominee often demonstrated his joy, largess, wealth, and prestige by distributing double images of himself to friends, relatives, and associates. Closed, the diptychs advertised their donors; open, they served as useful wax writing tablets.

A leaf from the consular diptych of Magnus, dated 518 and manufactured at Constantinople, is a typical, if exceptionally elegant, example.

Here Magnus, who was probably a relative of the reigning emperor, is depicted on the same sort of backless throne that Christ and Mary were given. He is presiding over circus games, as is made clear by the handkerchief he is grasping in his right hand: a wave of the kerchief signaled the start of the games. With his left hand he holds up an eagle-topped scepter. The diptych sponsored by Maximianus substituted the blessing for the signal and Holy Scripture for the scepter. The two attendants flanking Magnus represent Rome (right) and Constantinople (left), protecting and honoring him like the background figures that hover behind Christ and Mary in Maximianus' diptych.

Maximianus was not a consul; he was a bishop. By commissioning an ivory diptych, however, he was claiming the honor due a consul. By commissioning one that presented sacred persons instead of himself, he was claiming even more: association with the highest sources of holiness.

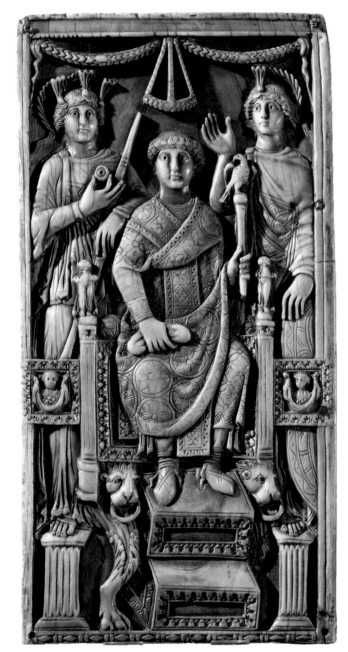

Panel from the consular diptych of Magnus

Note

1 See the mosaic of Justinian at San Vitale at Ravenna (above, Plate 1.12, pp. 32–33), where Maximianus, identified by name in large letters above his head, accompanies the emperor.

Leo was the harbinger of a new religious current. There had always been churchmen who objected to compassing the divine in the limiting form of a material image, but they had been in the minority. By the end of Leo's reign, a majority was inspired to criticize images. At the Synod of 754, a meeting of over 300 bishops and Emperor Constantine V (r.741–775) held in Constantinople, sacred images were banned outright. Its decrees made clear how material representations threatened, according to iconoclasts, to befoul the purity of the divine. Christ himself had declared he should be represented through the bread and wine—and in no other way. As for the saints, they (in the words of the Synod)

> live on eternally with God, although they have died. If anyone thinks to call them back again to life by a dead art, discovered by the heathen, he makes himself guilty of blasphemy.… It is not permitted to Christians … to insult the saints, who shine in so great glory, by common dead matter.[3]

Plate 2.2 (facing page): Cross at Hagia Sophia (orig. mosaic 6th cent.; redone 768/769). In this section of a mosaic just off the gallery at Hagia Sophia, the original mosaicist depicted a holy figure in a medallion. Beneath the image was an inscription identifying the saint. During the iconoclastic period, the figure and inscription were hacked out. The saint was replaced by a gold cross with flared arm tips; it was surrounded by a rainbow of colored tesserae (the bits of glass or stone used in mosaics) to make the cross seem to glow. Below the cross can be clearly seen the rectangular space in which the original inscription was replaced by tesserae to match the background color.

Above all, iconoclastic churchmen worried about losing control over the sacred. Unlike relics, images could be reproduced infinitely and without clerical authorization. Their cultivation at monasteries threatened to encroach on clerical authority. Banning icons had multiple purposes.

Ultimately, however, iconoclasm was an utter failure, though the ban on icons lasted until 787 and was revived, in modified form, between 815 and 843. Not only did the iconoclastic movement come to an end, but during the eighth century the position of those who supported icons—represented by men such as John of Damascus (c.675–749)—elaborated ever more ardent arguments on behalf of holy images:

> Of old [before the coming of Christ], God the incorporeal and uncircumscribed was never depicted. Now, however, when God is seen clothed in flesh and conversing with men [in the form of Jesus], I make an image of the God whom I see. I do not worship matter, I worship the God of matter, who became matter for my sake, and deigned to inhabit matter, who worked out my salvation through matter. I will not cease from honoring that matter which works my salvation.[4]

The idea that icons held the "real presence" of the divine—a notion that began around 680—marked a watershed between the early Christian and the medieval Byzantine states.

Iconophiles (literally "icon lovers") not only won the battle but also wrote the history. They vilified Constantine V and the other iconoclastic emperors, calling them "impious" and "unholy," and accusing them and their allies of destroying books and white-washing or obliterating images.[5] Modern historians can verify only some of these charges. One example remains from Hagia Sophia. A room used by the patriarch—located just off the southwest corner of the gallery—was originally covered with mosaics, including medallions with images of saints. During the iconoclastic period, the images were cut out and replaced by crosses. (See Plate 2.2.) Elsewhere, new churches were decorated with crosses from the start, while artists of the iconoclastic period were commissioned to depict

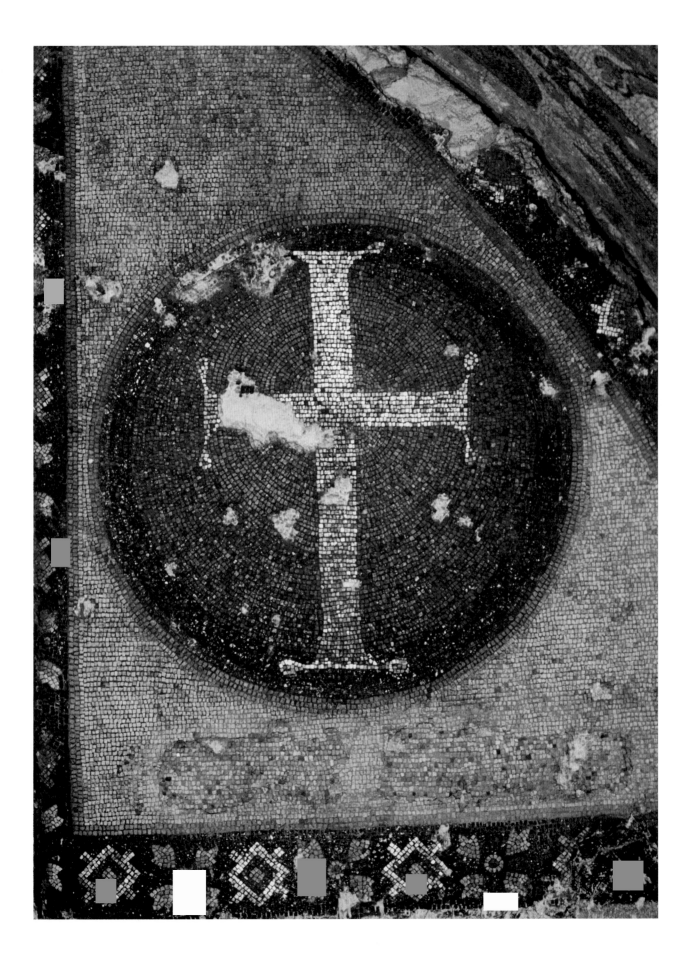

(depending on the use of the building) ornaments, trees, birds, hunting, horse races, and other non-sacred motifs. The iconoclasts thought that they thereby ensured God's favor—that, once again, the Byzantines were God's "Chosen People."

THE RISE OF THE "BEST COMMUNITY": ISLAM

Like the Byzantines, the Muslims thought of themselves as God's people. In the Qur'an, the "recitation" of God's words, Muslims are "the best community ever raised up for mankind … having faith in God" (3:110). The community's common purpose is "submission to God," the literal meaning of "Islam." The Muslim (a word that derives from "Islam") is "one who submits." Under the leadership of Muhammad (c.570–632) in Arabia, Islam created a new world power in less than a century.

The Shaping of Islam

"One community" was a revolutionary notion for the disparate peoples of Arabia (today Saudi Arabia), who converted to Islam in the course of the early seventh century. Pre-Islamic Arabia lay between the two great empires of the day—Persia and Byzantium—and felt the cross-currents as well as the magnetic pull of their economies and cultures. Its land supported Bedouins: nomads (the word "arab" is derived from the most prestigious of these, the camel-herders) and semi-nomads. But by far the majority of the population was neither; it was sedentary. To the southwest, where rain was adequate, farmers worked the soil. Elsewhere people settled at oases, where they raised date palms (a highly prized food); some of these communities were prosperous enough to support merchants and artisans. Both the nomads and the settled population were organized as tribes—communities whose members considered themselves related through a common ancestor.

Herding goats, sheep, or camels, the nomads and semi-nomads lived in small groups, largely making do with the products (leather, milk, meat) of their animals, and raiding one another for booty—including women. "Manliness" was the chief Bedouin virtue; it meant not sexual prowess (though polygyny—having more than one wife at a time—was practiced), but rather bravery, generosity, and a keen sense of honor. Lacking written literature, the nomads cultivated oral stories and poetry filled with striking images: "I passed the night in watch, / lightning kindled along its edges, / flickering, / With a dark trail behind it...."[6]

Islam began as a religion of the sedentary, but it soon found support and military strength among the nomads. The movement began at Mecca, a commercial center and the launching pad of caravans organized to sell Bedouin products—mainly leather goods and raisins—to the more urbanized areas at the Syrian border. (See Map 2.2.) Mecca was also a holy place. Its shrine, the Ka'ba, was rimmed with the images of hundreds of gods. Within its sacred precincts, where war and violence were prohibited, pilgrims bartered and traded.

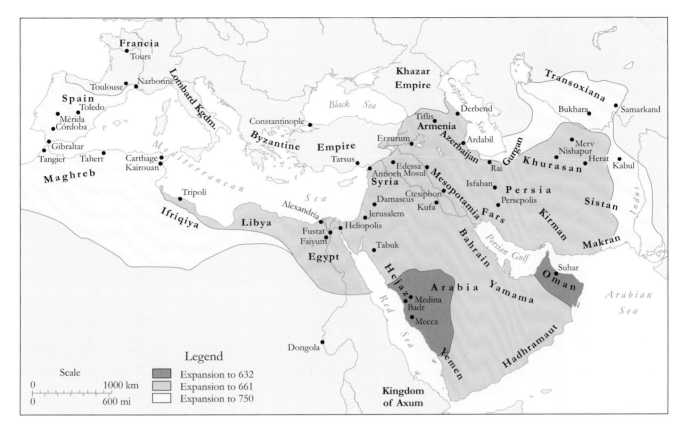

Muhammad, the prophet of Islam, was born in this commercial and religious center around 570. Orphaned as a child, he came under the guardianship of his uncle, a leader of the Quraysh tribe, which dominated Mecca and controlled access to the Ka'ba. Muhammad became a trader, married, had children, and seemed comfortable and happy. But he sought something more: he would sometimes leave home, escaping to a nearby mountain to pray.

"In the Name of God the Compassionate the Caring / Recite in the name of your lord who created – / From an embryo created the human / Recite your lord is all-giving."[7] Thus began a series of searing words and visions that, beginning around 610, came to Muhammad during his retreats. The key word was God, *one* God (the Arabic word for God is Allah). The key command was to "recite." Muhammad obeyed, and later, as these recitations were written down and arranged—a process that was completed in the early seventh century—they became the Qur'an, the holy book of Islam. The Qur'an is understood to be God's revelation as told to Muhammad by the angel Gabriel, and then recited in turn by Muhammad to others. Its first chapter—or sura—is the *fatihah*, or Opening:

In the name of God
    the Compassionate the Caring
Praise be to God
    lord sustainer of the world
the Compassionate the Caring
master of the day of reckoning

To you we turn to worship
    and to you we turn in time of need
Guide us along the road straight
the road of those to whom you are giving
    not those with anger upon them
    not those who have lost the way.[8]

The Qur'an continues with a far longer sura, followed by others (114 in all) of gradually decreasing length. For Muslims the Qur'an covers the gamut of human experience—the sum total of history, prophecy, and the legal and moral code by which men and women should live—as well as the life to come.

Banning infanticide, Islam gave girls and women new dignity. It allowed for polygyny, but this was limited to four wives at one time, all to be treated equally. It mandated dowries and offered some female inheritance rights. At first women even prayed with men, though that practice ended in the eighth century. The nuclear family (newly emphasized, as was happening around the same time at Byzantium as well; see p. 44) became more important than the tribe. In Islam there are three essential social facts: the individual, God, and the *ummah*, the community of the faithful. There are no intermediaries between the divine and human realms, no priests, Eucharist, or relics.

A community of believers coalesced around Muhammad as God's prophet. They adhered to a strict monotheism, prepared for the final Day of Judgment, and carried out the tasks that their piety demanded—daily prayers, charity, periods of fasting, and so on. Later these were institutionalized as the "five pillars" of Islam.[9] The early believers' idea of the righteous life included living in the world, marrying, and having children. For them, virtue meant mindfulness of God in all things. They could take moderate—though not excessive—pleasure in God's bounty. Their notions of righteousness did not call for the asceticism.

At Mecca, where Quraysh tribal interests were bound up with the Ka'ba and its many gods, Muhammad's message was unwelcome. But it was greeted with enthusiasm at Medina, an oasis about 200 miles to the northeast of Mecca. Feuding tribes there invited Muhammad to join them and arbitrate their disputes. He agreed, and in 622 he made the *Hijra*, or flight from Mecca to Medina. There he became not only a religious but also a secular leader. This joining of the political and religious spheres set the pattern for Islamic government thereafter. After Muhammad's death, the year of the *Hijra*, 622, became the year 1 of the Islamic calendar, marking the establishment of the Islamic era.

Muhammad consolidated his leadership by asserting hegemony over three important groups: the Jews, the Meccans, and the nomads. At Medina itself he took control by ousting and sometimes killing his main competitors, the Jewish clans of the city. Against the Meccans he fought a series of battles; the battle of Badr (624), waged against a Meccan caravan, marked the first Islamic military victory. After several other campaigns, Muhammad triumphed and took over Mecca in 630, offering leniency to most of its inhabitants, who in turn converted to Islam. Meanwhile, Muhammad allied himself with numerous nomadic groups, adding their contingents to his army. Warfare was thus integrated into the new religion as a part of the duty of Muslims to strive in the ways of God; *jihad*, often translated as "holy war," in fact means "striving." Through a combination of military might, conversion, and negotiation, Muhammad united many, though by no means all, Arabic tribes under his leadership by the time of his death in 632.

Out of Arabia

"Strive, O Prophet," says the Qur'an, "against the unbelievers and the hypocrites, and deal with them firmly. Their final abode is Hell; And what a wretched destination" (9:73). Cutting across tribal allegiances, the Islamic *ummah* was itself a formidable "supertribe" dedicated to victory over the enemies of God. After Muhammad's death, armies of Muslims led by caliphs—a title that at first seems to have derived from *khalifat Allah*, "deputy of God," but that later came to mean "deputy of the Apostle of God, Muhammad"— moved into Sasanid and Byzantine territory, toppling or crippling the once-great ancient empires. (See Map 2.2.) Islamic armies captured the Persian capital, Ctesiphon, in 637 and continued eastward to take Persepolis in 648, Nishapur in 651, and then, beyond Persia, to Kabul in 664 and Samarkand in 710. To the west, they picked off, one by one, the great Mediterranean cities of the Byzantine Empire: Antioch and Damascus in 635, Alexandria in 642, Carthage in 697. By the beginning of the eighth century, Islamic warriors held sway from Spain to India.

Following page:

Genealogy 2.1: Muhammad's Relatives and Successors to 750

What explains their astonishing triumph? Above all, they were formidable fighters, and their enemies were relatively weak. The Persian and Byzantine Empires had exhausted one another after years of fighting. Nor were their populations particularly loyal; some—Jews and Christians in Persia, Monophysite Christians in Syria—even welcomed the invaders. In large measure they were proved right: the Muslims made no attempt to convert them, imposing a tax on them instead. Then, too, the Muslims sometimes did not need to fight; they conquered through diplomacy instead. In Spain, for example, they treated with a local leader, Theodemir (or Tudmir), offering him and his men protection—"[they will not] be separated from their women and children. They will not be coerced in matters of religion"—in return for loyalty and taxes.[10]

Although Arabic culture was not strikingly city-based, Muhammad himself was attached to Mecca and Medina, and the Muslims almost immediately fostered urban life in the regions that they conquered. In Syria and Palestine, most of the soldiers settled within existing coastal cities; their leaders, however, built palaces and hunting lodges in the countryside. Everywhere else the invaders created large permanent camps of their own, remaining separate from the indigenous populations. Some of these camps were eventually abandoned, but others—such as those at Baghdad and Cairo—became centers of new and thriving urban agglomerations.

Men and women who had been living along the Mediterranean—in Syria, Palestine, North Africa, and Spain—went back to work and play much as they had done before the

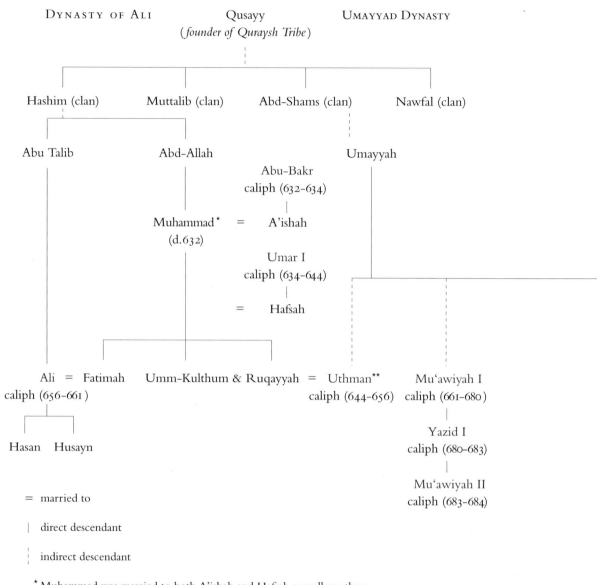

DYNASTY OF ALI   Qusayy   UMAYYAD DYNASTY
(*founder of Quraysh Tribe*)

Hashim (clan)   Muttalib (clan)   Abd-Shams (clan)   Nawfal (clan)

Abu Talib   Abd-Allah   Umayyah

Abu-Bakr
caliph (632–634)

Muhammad*   =   A'ishah
(d.632)

Umar I
caliph (634–644)

=   Hafsah

Ali   =   Fatimah   Umm-Kulthum & Ruqayyah   =   Uthman**   Mu'awiyah I
caliph (656–661)   caliph (644–656)   caliph (661–680)

Hasan   Husayn   Yazid I
caliph (680–683)

Mu'awiyah II
caliph (683–684)

=   married to

| direct descendant

⋮   indirect descendant

* Muhammad was married to both A'ishah and Hafsah as well as others
** Uthman was married to two of Muhammad's daughters, Umm-Kulthum and Ruqayyah

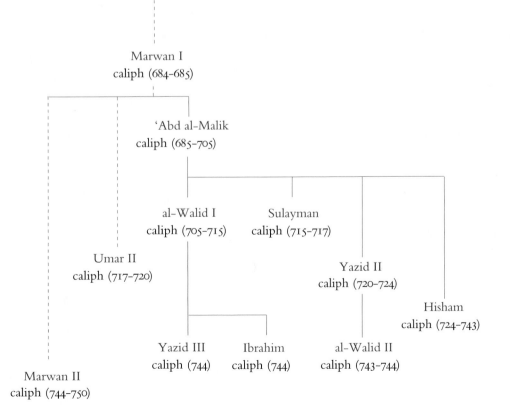

Marwan I
caliph (684–685)

'Abd al-Malik
caliph (685–705)

al-Walid I
caliph (705–715)

Sulayman
caliph (715–717)

Umar II
caliph (717–720)

Yazid II
caliph (720–724)

Hisham
caliph (724–743)

Yazid III
caliph (744)

Ibrahim
caliph (744)

al-Walid II
caliph (743–744)

Marwan II
caliph (744–750)

Plate 2.3 (facing page):
Damascus Great Mosque
Mosaic (706). It is likely
that Byzantine artisans were
hired to cover the mosque
at Damascus with mosaics
both inside and out. Even
if not from Byzantium, the
mosaicists drew on Byzantine
artistic traditions that were still
recognizably based on classical
Roman motifs. Compare this
detail of the western portico
of the Damascus mosque,
which shows two cities
separated by trees, with the
Boscoreale city scene in Plate
1.3. We see a similar jumble
of buildings, one arrayed on
top of the other as if climbing
a cliff. The way in which the
trees work to divide the scene
in the Damascus portico is also
Romano-Byzantine. But in
another way, the mosaicists
rejected that inheritance,
imposing a different—an
Islamic—ideal: they depicted
no human or animal. To be
sure, we should not expect
that Mars would seduce Venus
here (recall Plate 1.1)! But
more remarkably, no living
being whatsoever paraded on
its walls (compare with Plate
1.12, with mosaics of Emperor
Justinian and his courtly
entourage). In what ways
might this ideal have affected
Byzantium itself?

invasions. Safe in Muslim-controlled Damascus, Saint John of Damascus (d.749) thundered against iconoclasm: "I do not worship matter [i.e., the paint and wood of an icon]; I worship the God of matter, who became matter for my sake."[11] He would never have been allowed to write such words within the Byzantine Empire. Another Christian, al-Akhtal (c.640–710), found employment at the court of Caliph 'Abd al-Malik (r.685–705), where he poured forth verses of praise: "So let him in his victory long delight! / He who wades into the deep of battle, auspicious his augury, / The Caliph of God through whom men pray for rain."[12]

Maps of the Islamic conquest divide the world into Muslims and Christians. But the "Islamic world" was only slightly Islamic; Muslims constituted a minority of the population. Then, even as their religion came to predominate, they were themselves absorbed, at least to some degree, into the cultures that they had conquered.

The Culture of the Umayyads

Dissension, triumph, and disappointment accompanied the naming of Muhammad's successors. The caliphs were not chosen from the old tribal elites but rather from a new inner circle of men close to Muhammad. The first two caliphs, Abu-Bakr and Umar, ruled without serious opposition. They were the fathers of two of Muhammad's wives. But the third caliph, Uthman, husband of two of Muhammad's daughters and great-grandson of the Quraysh leader Umayyah, aroused resentment. (See Genealogy 2.1: Muhammad's Relatives and Successors to 750.) His family had come late to Islam, and some of its members had once even persecuted Muhammad. The opponents of the Umayyads supported Ali, the husband of Muhammad's daughter Fatimah. After a group of discontented soldiers murdered Uthman, civil war broke out between the Umayyads and Ali's faction. It ended when Ali was killed in 661 by one of his own erstwhile supporters. Thereafter, the caliphate remained in Umayyad hands until 750.

Yet the *Shi'ah*, the supporters of Ali, did not forget their leader. They became the "Shi'ites," faithful to Ali's dynasty, mourning his martyrdom, shunning the "mainstream" caliphs of the other Muslims ("Sunni" Muslims, as they were later called), awaiting the arrival of the true leader—the *imam*—who would spring from the house of Ali.

Meanwhile, the Umayyads made Damascus, previously a minor Byzantine city, into their capital. Here they adopted many of the institutions of the culture that they had conquered, issuing coins like those of the Byzantines (in the east they used coins based on Persian models), and employing former Byzantine officials as administrators (John of Damascus came from such a family). Caliph 'Abd al-Malik (who, as we have seen, won high praise from the poet al-Akhtal) turned Jerusalem—already sacred to Jews and Christians—into an Islamic Holy City as well. His successor, al-Walid I (r.705–715) built major mosques (places of worship for Muslims) at Damascus, Medina, and Jerusalem. The one at Damascus retains most of its original elements; Plate 2.3 demonstrates how effortlessly Byzantine motifs were absorbed—yet also transformed—in their new Islamic

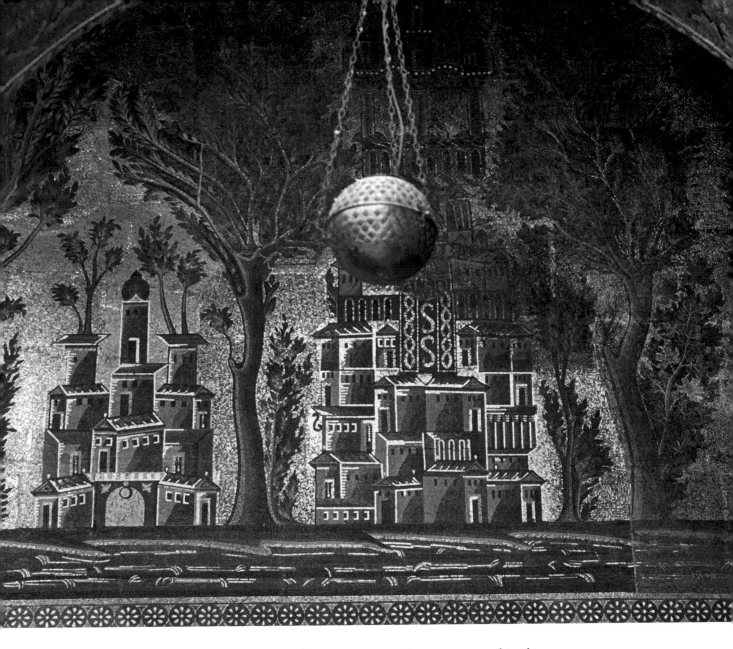

context. Cityscapes and floral motifs drawn from Byzantine traditions were combined to depict an idealized world created by the triumph of Islam.

Arabic, the language of the Qur'an, became the official tongue of the Islamic world. As translators rendered important Greek and other texts into this newly imperial language, it proved to be both flexible and capacious. Around this time, Muslim scholars determined the definitive form of the Qur'an and began to compile pious narratives about the Prophet's sayings, or *hadith*. A new literate class—composed mainly of the old Persian and Syrian elite, now converted to Islam and schooled in Arabic—created new forms of prose and poetry. A commercial revolution in China helped to vivify commerce in the Islamic world. At hand was a cultural flowering in a land of prosperity.

THE MAKING OF WESTERN EUROPE

No reasonable person in the year 750 would have predicted that, of the three heirs of the Roman Empire, Western Europe would, by 1500, be well on its way to dominating the world. While Byzantium cut back, reorganized, and forged ahead, while Islam spread its language and rule over a territory that stretched nearly twice the length of the United States today, Western Europe remained an impoverished backwater. Fragmented politically and linguistically, its cities (left over from Roman antiquity) mere shells, its tools primitive, its infrastructure—what was left of Roman roads, schools, and bridges—collapsing, Europe lacked identity and cohesion. That these and other strengths did indeed eventually develop over a long period of time is a tribute in part to the survival of some Roman traditions and institutions and in part to the inventive ways in which people adapted those institutions and made up new ones to meet their needs and desires.

Impoverishment and Its Variations

Taking in the whole of Western Europe around this time means dwelling long on its variety. Dominating the scene was Gaul, now taken over by the Franks; we may call it Francia. To its south were Spain (ruled first by the Visigoths, and then, after *c.*715, by the Muslims) and Italy (divided between the pope, the Byzantines, and the Lombards). To the north, joined to rather than separated from the Continent by the lick of water called the English Channel, the British Isles were home to a plethora of tiny kingdoms, about three quarters of which were native ("Celtic") and the last quarter Germanic ("Anglo-Saxons").

There were clear differences between the Romanized south—Spain, Italy, southern Francia—and the north. (See Map 2.3.) Travelers going from Anglo-Saxon England to Rome would have noticed them. There were many such travelers: some, like the churchman Benedict Biscop, were voluntary pilgrims; others were slaves on forced march. Making their way across England, voyagers such as these would pass fenced wooden farmsteads much like the ones at Wijster (see pp. 21–22). These farmsteads typically had a relatively large house, outbuildings, and perhaps a sunken house, its floor below the level of the soil, its damp atmosphere suitable for weaving. Even royal complexes were made of wood and looked much like humble villages: see Figure 2.2 on p. 60.

Most such farmsteads—each held by a family—were built in clusters of four to five, making up tiny hamlets. Peasants planted their fields with barley (used to make a thick and nourishing ale) as well as oats, wheat, rye, beans, and flax. Two kinds of plows were used. One was heavy: it had a coulter and moldboard, often tipped with iron, to cut through and turn over heavy soils. The other was a light "scratch plow," suitable for making narrow furrows in light soils. Because the first plow was hard to turn, the fields it produced tended to be long and rectangular in shape. The lighter plow was more agile: it was used to cut the soil in one direction and then at right angles to that, producing a square field. There were many animals on these farms: cattle, sheep, horses, pigs, and dogs. In some cases, the peasants who worked the land and tended the animals were relatively independent, owing little to anyone outside their village. In other instances, regional lords—often kings—commanded a share of the peasants' produce and, occasionally, labor services. But all was not pastoral or agricultural in England: here and there, and especially toward the south, were commercial settlements—real emporia.

Map 2.3: Western Europe, *c.750*

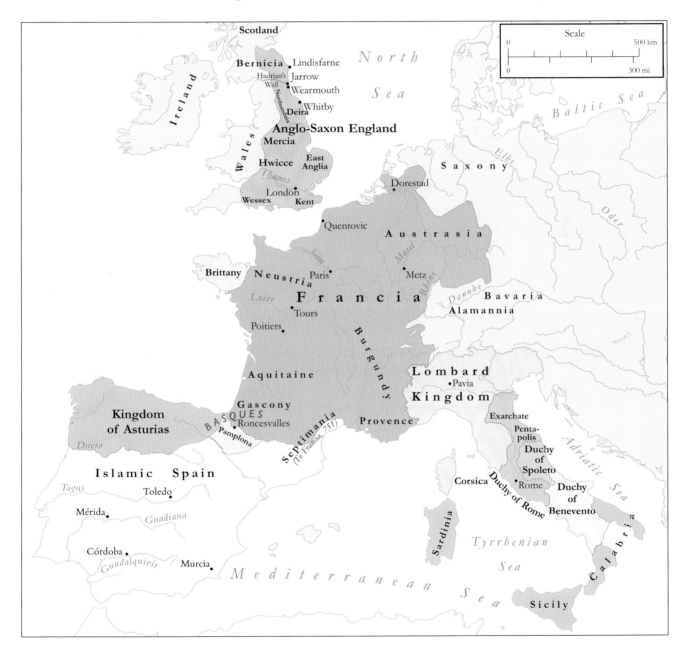

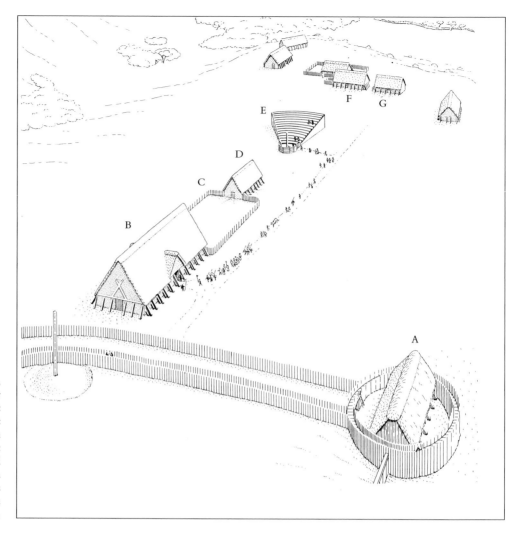

Figure 2.2: Yeavering, Northumberland. Strategically situated near the eastern coast of England, the "royal palace" at Yeavering boasted a fort (A), an amphitheater where the court assembled (E), and a great hall (B). Smaller buildings included a simple dwelling (G) and perhaps a temple (F). At (C) was a fenced-in courtyard.

Crossing the Channel, travelers would enter northern Francia, also dotted with emporia (such as Quentovic and Dorestad) but additionally boasting old Roman cities, now mainly religious centers. Paris, for example, was to a large extent an agglomeration of churches: Montmartre, Saint-Laurent, Saint-Martin-des-Champs—perhaps 35 churches were jammed into an otherwise nearly abandoned city. In the countryside around Paris, peasant families, each with its own plot, tended lands and vineyards that were largely owned by aristocrats. Moving eastward, our voyagers would pass through thick forests and land more often used as pasture for animals than for cereal cultivation. Along the Mosel River they would find villages with fields, meadows, woods, and water courses, a few supplied with mills and churches. Some of the peasants in these villages would be tenants or slaves of a lord; others would be independent farmers who owned all or part of the land that they cultivated.

Near the Mediterranean, by contrast, the terrain still had an urban feel. Here the great hulks of Roman cities, with their stone amphitheaters, baths, and walls, dominated the landscape even though, as at Byzantium, their populations were much diminished. Peasants, settled in small hamlets scattered throughout the countryside, cultivated their own plots of land. In Italy many of them were real landowners; aristocratic landlords were less important here than in Francia. The soil of this region was lighter than in the north, easily worked with scratch plows to produce the barley and rye (in northern Italy) and wheat (elsewhere) that were the staples—along with meat and fish—of the peasant diet.

By 700, there was little left of the old long-distance Mediterranean commerce of the ancient Roman world. But, although this was an impoverished society, it was not without wealth or lively patterns of exchange. In the first place, money was still minted, but increasingly in silver rather than gold. The change of metal was due in part to a shortage of gold in Europe. But it was also a nod to the importance of small-scale commercial transactions—sales of surplus wine from a vineyard, say, for which small coins were the most practical. In the second place, North Sea merchant-sailors—carrying, for example, ceramic plates and glass vessels—had begun to link northern Francia, the east coast of England, Scandinavia, and the Baltic Sea. Brisk trade gave rise to new emporia and revivified older Roman cities along the coasts. In the third place, a gift economy—that is, an economy of give and take—was flourishing. Booty was seized, tribute demanded, harvests hoarded, and coins struck, all to be redistributed to friends, followers, dependents, and the church. Kings and other rich and powerful men and women amassed gold, silver, ornaments, and jewelry in their treasuries and grain in their storehouses to give out in ceremonies that marked their power and added to their prestige. Even the rents that peasants paid to their lords, mainly in kind, were often couched as "gifts."

Politics and Culture

If variations were plentiful in even so basic a matter as material and farming conditions, the differences were magnified by political and cultural conditions. We need now to take Europe kingdom by kingdom.

FRANCIA

Francia comes first because it was the major player, a real political entity that dominated what is today France, Belgium, the Netherlands, Luxembourg, and much of Germany. In the seventh century, it was divided into three related kingdoms—Neustria, Austrasia, and Burgundy—each of which included parts of a fourth, southern region, Aquitaine. By 700, however, the political distinctions between them were melting, and Francia was becoming one kingdom.

The line of Clovis—the Merovingians—ruled these kingdoms. (See Genealogy 2.2: The Merovingians.) The dynasty owed its longevity to biological good fortune and excellent political sense: it allied itself with the major lay aristocrats and ecclesiastical authorities of Gaul—men and women of high status, enormous wealth, and marked local power. To

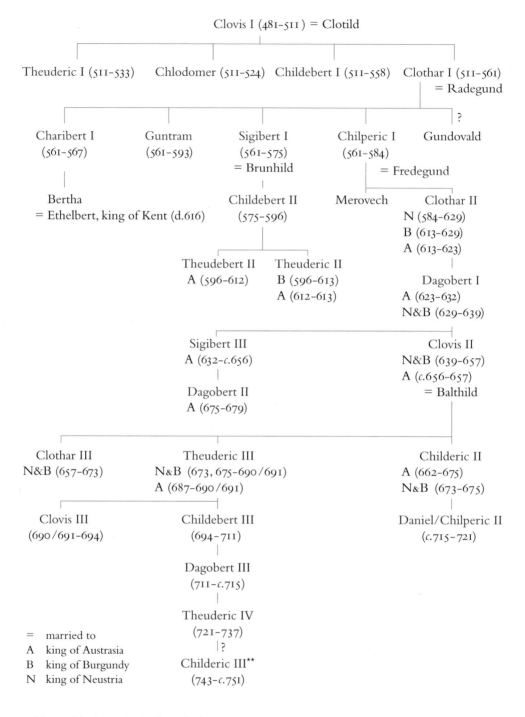

Clovis I (481–511) = Clotild

Theuderic I (511–533)   Chlodomer (511–524)   Childebert I (511–558)   Clothar I (511–561)
= Radegund
?

Charibert I   Guntram   Sigibert I   Chilperic I   Gundovald
(561–567)   (561–593)   (561–575)   (561–584)
= Brunhild   = Fredegund

Bertha   Childebert II   Merovech   Clothar II
= Ethelbert, king of Kent (d.616)   (575–596)   N (584–629)
B (613–629)
A (613–623)

Theudebert II   Theuderic II   Dagobert I
A (596–612)   B (596–613)   A (623–632)
A (612–613)   N&B (629–639)

Sigibert III   Clovis II
A (632–c.656)   N&B (639–657)
A (c.656–657)
Dagobert II   = Balthild
A (675–679)

Clothar III   Theuderic III   Childeric II
N&B (657–673)   N&B (673, 675–690/691)   A (662–675)
A (687–690/691)   N&B (673–675)

Clovis III   Childebert III   Daniel/Chilperic II
(690/691–694)   (694–711)   (c.715–721)

Dagobert III
(711–c.715)

Theuderic IV
(721–737)
= married to |?
A king of Austrasia   Childeric III**
B king of Burgundy   (743–c.751)
N king of Neustria

* Many of the Merovingian kings had more   ** The parentage of Childeric III is not clear.
than one wife. The children listed here   His father may equally well have been
(selected as only the most important of the   Daniel/Chilperic II as Theuderic IV.
fathers' progeny) are those of the king but
not necessarily of the wife named here.

that alliance, the kings brought their own sources of power: a skeletal Roman administrative apparatus, family properties, appropriated lands once belonging to the Roman state, and the profits and prestige of leadership in war.

The royal court—which moved with the kings as they traveled from one palace to another, as they had no capital city—was the focus of political life. Here gathered talented young men, clerics—all upwardly mobile aristocrats. The most important courtiers had official positions: there was, for example, the referendary and the cupbearer. Highest of all was the "mayor of the palace," who controlled access to the king and brokered deals with aristocratic factions.

Queens were an important part of the court as well. One of them, Balthild (d.680), had once been one of the unwilling travelers from England. Purchased there as a slave by the mayor of the palace of Neustria, she parlayed her beauty into marriage with the king himself. (Merovingian kings often married slaves or women captured in war. By avoiding wives with powerful kindred, they staved off challenges to their royal authority.) Balthild's biographer praised her for ministering to all the men at court. When her husband, King Clovis II, died in 657, Balthild served as regent for her minor sons, acting, in effect, as king during this time. Meanwhile, she gave generously to churches and monasteries. By the end of her life, Balthild was counted a saint.

Just as a king's power radiated outward from his court, so too did aristocrats command their own lordly centers. Like kings, they had many "homes" at one time, scattered throughout Francia. Tending to their estates, honing their skills in the hunt, aristocratic men regularly led armed retinues to war. They proved their worth in the regular taking of booty and rewarded their faithful followers afterwards at generous banquets.

And they bedded down. The bed—or rather the production of children—was the focus of marriage, the key to the survival of aristocratic families and the transmission of their property and power. Though churchmen had many ideas about the value of marriage, they had nothing to do with the ceremony; no one married in a church. Rather, marriage was a family affair, and a very expensive one. There was more than one form of marriage: in the most formal, the husband-to-be gave his future bride a handsome dowry of clothes, bedding, livestock, and land. Then, after the marriage was consummated, he gave his wife a morning gift of furniture and perhaps the keys to the house. Very rich men often had, in addition to their wife, one or more "concubines" at the same time. These enjoyed a less formal type of marriage, receiving a morning gift but no dowry.

The wife's role was above all to maintain the family. A woman passed from one family (that of her birth) to the next (that of her marriage) by parental fiat. When they married, women left the legal protection of their father for that of their husband. Did women have any freedom of action? Yes. For one thing, they had considerable control over their dowries. Some participated in family land transactions: sales, donations, exchanges, and the like. Upon the death of their husbands, widows received a portion of the household property. Although inheritances generally went from fathers to sons, many fathers left bequests to their daughters, who could then dispose of their property more or less as they liked. In 632, for example, the nun Burgundofara, who had never married, drew up a

Genealogy 2.2 (facing page):
The Merovingians*

will giving to her monastery the land, slaves, vineyards, pastures, and forests that she had received from her two brothers and her father. In the same will, she gave other property near Paris to her brothers and sister.

Burgundofara's generous piety was extraordinary only in degree. The world of kings, queens, and aristocrats intersected with that of the church. The arrival (c.590) on the Continent of the fierce Irish monastic reformer Saint Columbanus (543–615) marked a new level of association between the two. Columbanus's brand of monasticism, which stressed exile, devotion, and discipline, made a powerful impact on Merovingian aristocrats. They flocked to the monasteries that he established in both Francia and Italy, and they founded new ones on their own lands in the countryside. In Francia alone there was an explosion of monasteries: between the years 600 and 700, an astonishing 320 new houses were established, most of them outside of the cities. Some of the new monks and nuns were grown men and women; others were young children, given to a monastery by their parents. This latter practice, called oblation, was well accepted and even considered essential for the spiritual well-being of both children and their families.

Irish monasticism introduced aristocrats on the Continent to a deepened religious devotion. Those who did not actively join or patronize a monastery still read, or listened to others read, books preaching penance, and they chanted the psalms. Sometimes they claimed one of their own as a saint and martyr. Leudegar, bishop of Autun (r.c.662–c.677?), was, according to his biographer "a new martyr in Christian times…. Just as he was nobly born according to earthly descent, so … he stood out prominently ahead of others, no matter what the office … to which he was promoted."[13] The Merovingian laity, especially the aristocratic laity, developed a culture of domestic piety at about the same time as the Byzantines did.

Deepened piety did not, in this case, lead to the persecution of others—something that (as we shall see) happened in later centuries. In particular, where Jews were settled in Western Europe—along the Mediterranean coast and inland, in Burgundy, for example— they remained integrated into every aspect of secular life. They used Hebrew in worship, but otherwise they spoke the same languages as Christians and used Latin in their legal documents. Their children were often given the same names as Christians (and Christians often took biblical names, such as Solomon); they dressed as everyone else dressed; and they engaged in the same occupations. Many Jews planted and tended vineyards, in part because of the importance of wine in synagogue services, in part because the surplus could easily be sold. Some were rich landowners, with slaves and dependent peasants working for them; others were independent peasants of modest means. While some Jews lived in cities—the few that remained—most, like their Christian neighbors, lived on the land.

THE BRITISH ISLES

Celtic groups from the north and west had often attacked Roman Britain. When the last of the Roman garrisons left Britain c.410, new immigrants—Saxon and other Germanic groups—arrived piecemeal. They came as families, in small boats made of animal skins, to settle and farm along Britain's east coast. Irish immigrants gradually settled in the west. Elsewhere—in what is today the north and west of England, Scotland, and Ireland—Celtic kingdoms survived.

Where the Germanic tribes settled, their tastes, expectations, styles, and religious practices affected the indigenous British population, and vice versa. In the eighth century the monk-historian Bede portrayed this amalgamated culture as utterly pagan: Anglo-Saxon England was, in his words, "a barbarous, fierce, and unbelieving nation."[14] But the story that archaeology tells is more nuanced: holy sites of the saints remained magnets for pilgrimage, burial and settlement. Most, perhaps all, of the British Isles remained Christian. Wales was already Christian when, in the course of the fifth century, missionaries converted Ireland and Scotland. (Saint Patrick, apostle to the Irish, is only the most famous of these.) However, in contrast to Bede's vision of a highly organized church led by the pope, post-Roman Britain's Christianity was decentralized and local. The same was true in the Celtic kingdoms—Wales, Ireland, and Scotland—which supported relatively non-hierarchical church organizations. Rural monasteries often served as the seats of bishoprics as well as centers of population and settlement. Abbots and abbesses, often members of powerful families, enjoyed considerable power and prestige.

At the end of the sixth century the Roman form of Christianity arrived to compete with the diverse forms already flourishing in the British Isles. In 597 missionaries sent by Pope Gregory the Great, led by Augustine (not the fifth-century bishop of Hippo!), arrived at the court of King Ethelbert of Kent (d.616). According to Bede, Ethelbert was a pagan. Yet he was married to a Christian Frankish princess, and he welcomed the missionaries kindly: "At the king's command they sat down and preached the word of life to himself and all his officials and companions there present." While he refused to convert because "[I cannot] forsake those beliefs which I and the whole people of the Angles have held so long," the king did give the missionaries housing and material support.[15]

Above all, the king let them preach. This was key: Augustine had in mind more than the conversion of a king: he wanted to set up an English church on the Roman model, with ties to the pope and a clear hierarchy. Successful in his work of evangelization, he divided England into territorial units (dioceses) headed by an archbishop and bishops. Augustine himself became the first archbishop of Canterbury. There he set up the model English ecclesiastical complex: a cathedral, a monastery, and a school to train young clerics.

There was nothing easy or quick about the conversion of England to the Roman brand of Christianity. Christian traditions there clashed over matters as large as the organization of the church and as seemingly small as the date of Easter. Everyone agreed that they could not be saved unless they observed the day of Christ's Resurrection properly and on the right date. But what was the right date? Each side was wedded to its own view. A turning point came at the Synod of Whitby, organized in 664 by the Northumbrian King Oswy to

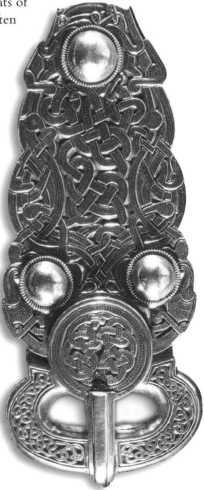

Plate 2.4: Belt Buckle from Sutton Hoo (early 7th cent.). Beginning in 1939 and continuing through the 1980s, archaeologists excavated seventeen curious mounds at Sutton Hoo, a barren stretch of land in southeast England. Their finds included numerous Anglo-Saxon cremations and burials, the bones of horses, spears, shields, helmets, large open boats, jewelry, silver bowls, and many other objects, including this heavy buckle made of gold.

decide between the Roman and Irish dates. When Oswy became convinced that Rome spoke with the very voice of Saint Peter, the heavenly doorkeeper, he opted for the Roman calculation of the date and embraced the Roman church as a whole.

The pull of Rome—the symbol, in the new view, of the Christian religion itself—was almost physical. In the wake of Whitby, Benedict Biscop, a Northumbrian aristocrat-turned-abbot and founder of two important English monasteries, Wearmouth and Jarrow, made numerous arduous trips to Rome. He brought back books, saints' relics, liturgical vestments, and even a cantor to teach his monks the proper melodies in a time before written musical notation existed. A century later, the Anglo-Saxon monk Wynfrith changed his name to the more Roman-sounding Boniface (672/675–754) after he went to Rome to get a commission from Pope Gregory II (715–731) to preach the Word to people living east of the Rhine. Though they were already Christian, their brand of Christianity was not Roman enough for Saint Boniface.

As Roman culture confronted Anglo-Saxon, the results were particularly eclectic. This is best seen in the visual arts. The Anglo-Saxons, like other barbarian (and, indeed, Celtic) tribes, had artistic traditions particularly well suited to adorning flat surfaces. Belt buckles, helmet nose-pieces, brooches, and other sorts of jewelry of the rich were embellished with semi-precious stones and enlivened with decorative patterns, often made up of intertwining snake-like animals. A particularly fine example is a buckle from Sutton Hoo (see Plate 2.4), perhaps the greatest archaeological find from the Anglo-Saxon period.

The books that Benedict Biscop (and others like him) imported from Rome contained not only new texts but also illustrations that relied, at least distantly, on ancient Roman artistic traditions (see Plates 1.1–4). English artists soon combined their native decorative impulses with that classical interest in human forms. The result was perfectly suited to flat pages. Consider the Lindisfarne Gospels, which were probably made at the monastery of Lindisfarne in the first third of the eighth century. (The Gospels are the four canonical accounts of Christ's life and death in the New Testament.) The artist of this sumptuous book was clearly uniting Anglo-Saxon, Irish, and Roman artistic traditions when he introduced each Gospel with three full-page illustrations: first, a portrait of the "author" (the evangelist); then an entirely ornamental "carpet" page; finally, the beginning words of the Gospel text. Plates 2.5 to 2.7 illustrate the sequence for the Gospel of Luke. The figure of Luke (see Plate 2.5), though clearly human, floats in space. His "throne" is a square of ribbons, his drapery a series of looping lines. The artist captures the essence of an other-worldly saint without the distraction of three-dimensionality. The carpet page (see Plate 2.6), with its interlace panels, has some of the features of the Sutton Hoo brooch as well as Irish interlace patterns. It is more than decorative, however: the design clearly evokes a cross. The next page (see Plate 2.7) begins with a great letter, Q (for the first word, "quoniam"), as richly decorated as the cross of the carpet page; gradually, in the course of the next few words, the ornamentation diminishes. In this way, after the fanfare of author and carpet pages, the reader is ushered into the Gospel text itself.

The amalgamation of traditions in England is perhaps most clearly illustrated by the so-called Franks Casket, probably made in Northumbria around the same time as—or a

Plate 2.5 (facing page): Saint Luke, Lindisfarne Gospels (1st third of 8th cent.?). Inspired by Late Roman traditions, the artist—who was also the scribe of this book—introduced the Gospel of Luke with an author's portrait. The winged calf perched on Luke's halo is his symbol.

Following pages:

Plate 2.6: Carpet Page, Lindisfarne Gospels (1st third of 8th cent.?). Anglo-Saxon and Celtic artistic ornamental traditions lie behind this elaborate cross, which follows Luke's portrait in Plate 2.5 and faces (as here) the first text page, depicted in Plate 2.7.

Plate 2.7: First Text Page, Gospel of Saint Luke, Lindisfarne Gospels (1st third of 8th cent.?). The third page in the Luke Gospel sequence begins the text itself: "Quoniam quidem multi conati sunt ordinare narrationem," "Since many have undertaken to put in narrative order...."

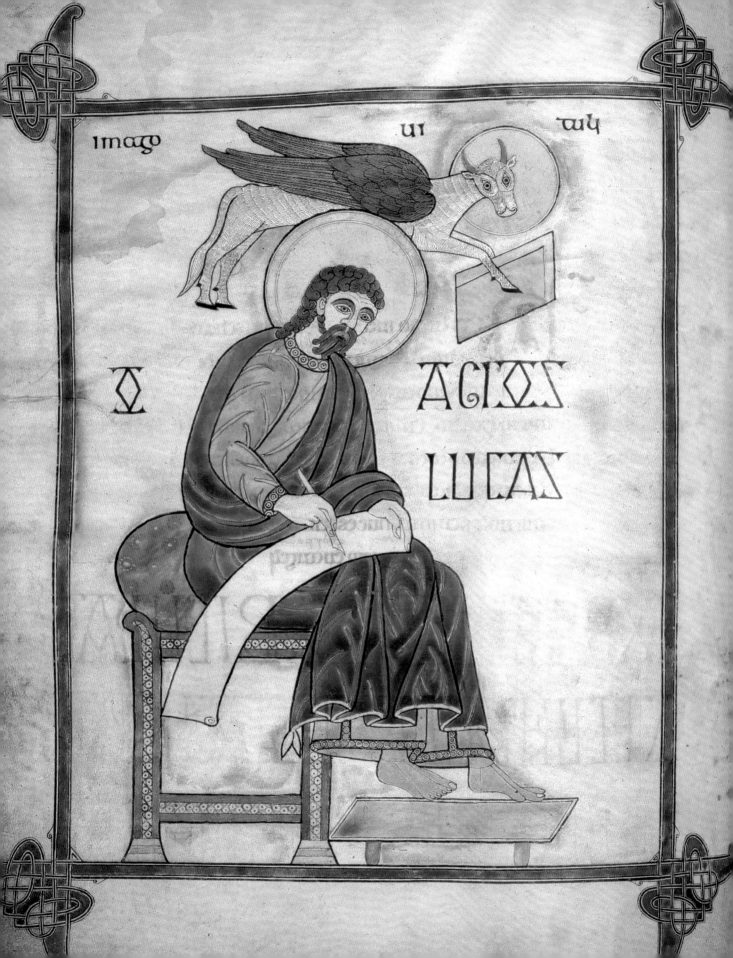

imago ui tul

ACICX

LUCAS

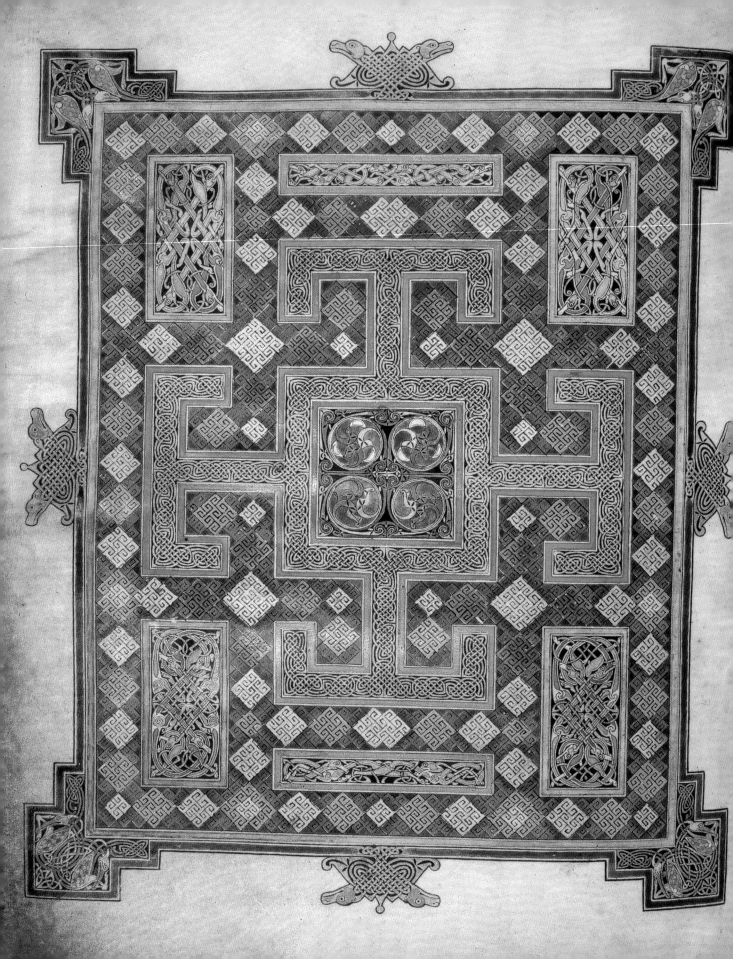

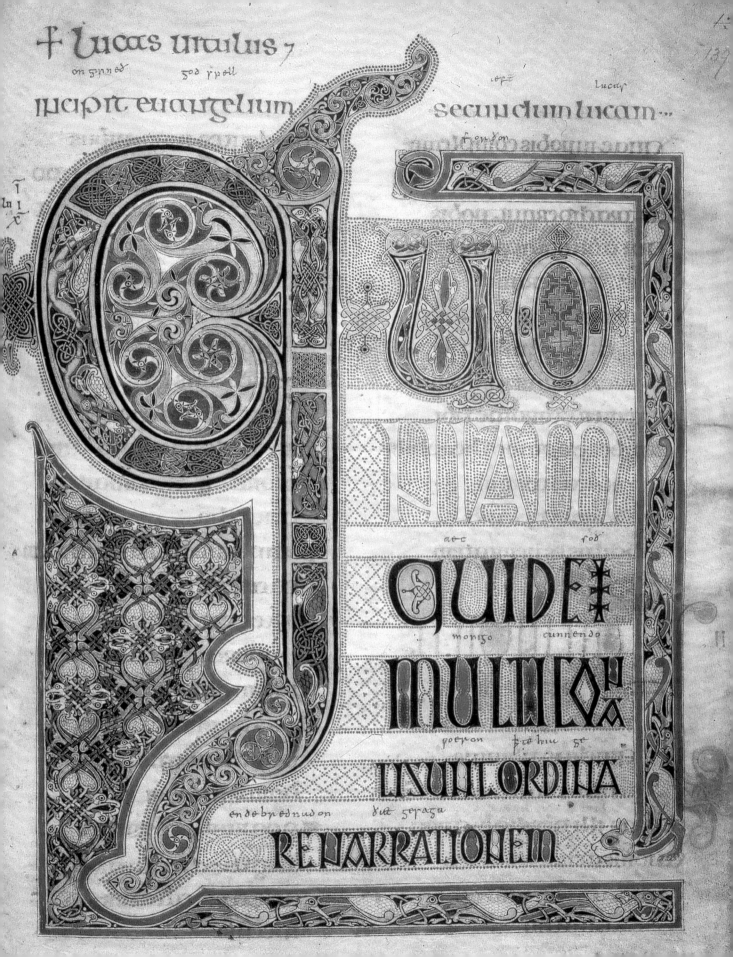

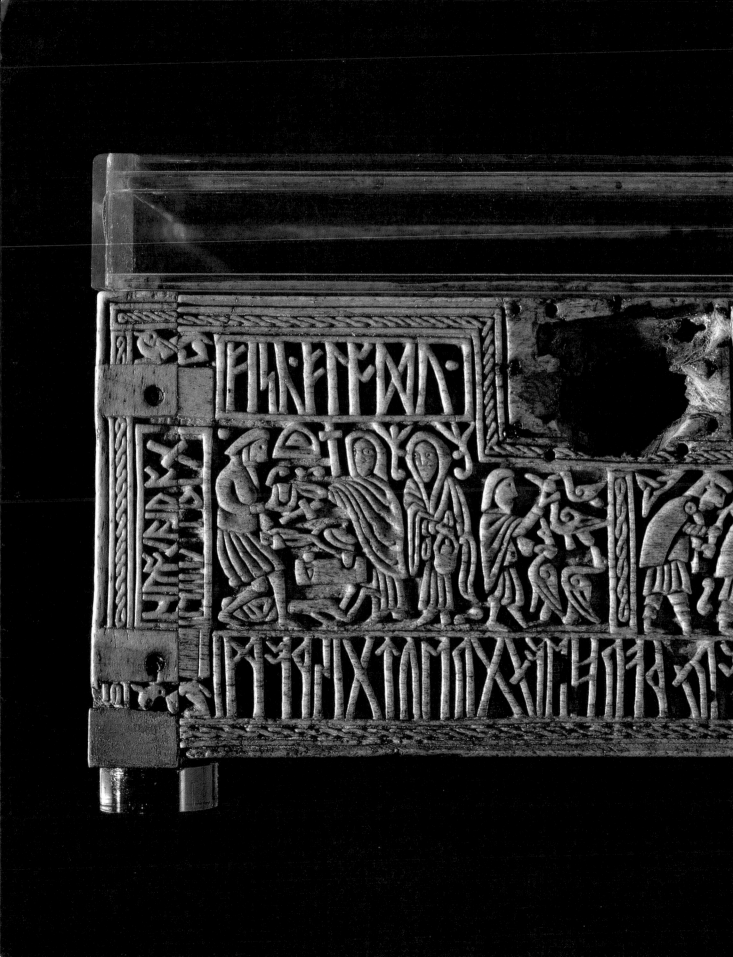

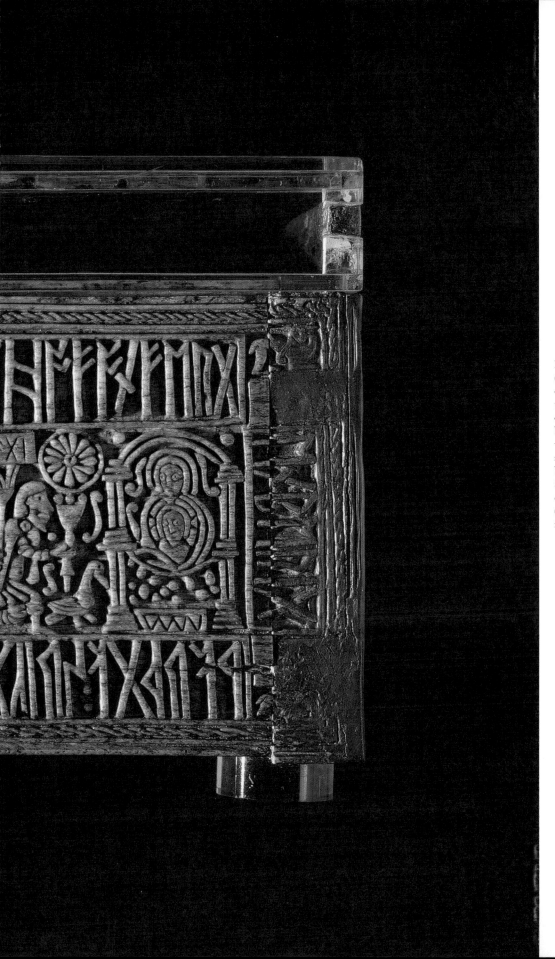

Plate 2.8: Franks Casket (1st half of 8th cent.). Made up of panels of carved whalebone, the Franks Casket combines not only various literary traditions but also some artistic ones. The whole idea of having figural scenes on a casket was classical, but the style here is Anglo-Saxon. Compare the style of cloaks and figures on the left (the Weland scene) with Luke in Plate 2.5.

bit later than—the Lindisfarne Gospels. Carved out of whale bone, this box is decorated with scenes from Roman, Jewish, Christian, and Germanic tales. The front panel (Plate 2.8), for example, melds a Christian story with one from the Anglo-Saxon tradition. On the left, the princess Beadohild is tricked by Weland the Smith into bearing his son, the hero Widia. Weland, an otherworldly figure of incredible skill at the forge, was celebrated in the Anglo-Saxon poems *Beowulf* and *Deor*. On the right side of the same panel, the Magi bring gifts to Christ, seated on Mary's lap. That, of course, was a story from the Gospels. Yet both scenes play on the same theme: a mother who bears the son of an otherworldly father.

Just as the Anglo-Saxons held on to their artistic styles and their ancient legends, so too did they retain their language. In England, the vernacular—the language of the people, as opposed to Latin—was quickly turned into a written language and used in every aspect of English life, from government to entertainment. But the same was true in Ireland; the uniqueness of Anglo-Saxon culture should not be exaggerated. The model for the Franks Casket probably came from a similar one carved earlier in Francia or Italy, and certainly comparable cultural creativity and the fusion of diverse elements were equally characteristic of early medieval Ireland and Scotland.

THE SOUTH: SPAIN AND ITALY

It is just possible that the exemplar for the Franks Casket came from Spain, which boasted an equally lively mix of cultures. Here, especially in the south and east, some Roman cities had continued to flourish after the Visigothic invasions. Merchants from Byzantium regularly visited Mérida, for example, and the sixth-century bishops there constructed lavish churches and set up a system of regular food distribution. Under King Leovigild (r.569–586), all of Spain came under Visigothic control. Under his son Reccared (r.586–601), the monarchy converted from Arian to Catholic Christianity. This event (587) cemented the ties between the king and the Hispano-Roman population, which included the great landowners and leading bishops. Two years later, at the Third Council of Toledo, most of the Arian bishops followed their king by announcing their conversion to Catholicism, and the assembled churchmen enacted decrees for a united church in Spain, starting with the provision "that the statutes of the Councils and the decrees of the Roman Pontiffs be maintained."[16] Here, as in England a few decades later, Rome and the papacy had become the linchpins of the Christian religion.

The Roman inheritance in Spain was clear not only in the dominance of the Hispano-Roman aristocracy and the adoption of its form of Christianity but also in the legal and intellectual culture that prevailed there. Nowhere else in Europe were church councils so regular or royal legislation so frequent. Nowhere else were the traditions of classical learning so highly regarded. Only in seventh-century Spain could a man like Isidore of Seville (c.560–636) draw on centuries of Latin learning to write the encyclopedic *Etymologies*, in which the essence of things was explained by their linguistic roots. "There are six stages in a lifetime: ... The third age, adolescence (*adolescentia*), is mature (*adultus* is the past participle of *adolescere*) enough for procreating,"[17] he wrote, as if the very nature of adolescence was revealed by the Latin word for it. The book was wildly popular.

The bishops and kings of Spain cooperated to a degree unprecedented in other regions. While the king gave the churchmen free rein to set up their own hierarchy (with the bishop of Toledo at the top) and to meet regularly at synods to regulate and reform the church, the bishops in turn supported the king. They even anointed him, daubing him with holy oil in a ritual that paralleled the ordination of priests and echoed the anointment of kings in the Old Testament. While the bishops in this way made the king's cause their own, their lay counterparts, the great landowners, helped supply the king with troops.

Unlike the Merovingians, however, the Visigothic kings were not able to establish a stable dynasty. The minority of a king's son almost always sparked revolts by rival families, and the child's deposition was often accompanied by wholesale slaughter of his father's followers and confiscation of their lands. This may help to explain why Visigothic courtiers painted a particularly lustrous picture of their kings, resplendent and dazzling, their throne "radiant with shining gold," and why royal laws punished treason by death or blinding.[18]

It was precisely the centralization of the Visigothic kingdom that proved its undoing. In 711, a small Islamic raiding party killed the Visigothic king and thereby dealt the whole state a decisive blow. Between 712 and 715, as we have seen, armies led by Arabs took over the peninsula through a combination of war and diplomacy.

The conquest of Spain was less Arabic or Islamic than Berber. The generals who led the invasion of Spain were Arabs, to be sure; but the rank-and-file fighters were Berbers from North Africa. While the Berbers were converts to Islam, they did not speak Arabic. The Arabs considered them crude mountainfolk, only imperfectly Muslim. Perhaps a million people settled in Spain in the wake of the invasions, the Arabs taking the better lands in the south, the Berbers getting less rich properties in the center and north. Most of the conquered population consisted of Christians, along with a sprinkling of Jews. A thin ribbon of Christian states—Asturias, Pamplona, and so on—survived in the north. There was thus a great variety of religions on the Iberian Peninsula. (See Map 2.3.) The history of Spain would for many centuries thereafter be one of both acculturation and war.

Unlike Visigothic Spain, Lombard Italy presented no united front. In the center of the peninsula was the papacy, always hostile to the Lombard king in the north. (See Map 2.3.) To Rome's east and south were the dukes of Benevento and Spoleto. Although theoretically the Lombard king's officers, in fact they were virtually independent rulers. Although many Lombards were Catholics, others, including important kings and dukes, were Arians. The "official" religion varied with the ruler in power. Rather than signal a major political event, then, the conversion of the Lombards to Catholic Christianity occurred gradually, ending only in the late seventh century. Partly as a result of this slow development, the Lombard kings, unlike the Visigoths, Franks, or even Anglo-Saxons, never enlisted the wholehearted support of any particular group of churchmen.

Yet the Lombard kings did not lack advantages. They controlled extensive estates, and they made use of the Roman institutions that survived in Italy. The kings made the cities their administrative bases, assigning dukes to rule from them and setting up one, Pavia, as their capital. Recalling emperors like Constantine and Justinian, the kings built churches and monasteries at Pavia, maintained city walls, and minted coins. Revenues from tolls, sales taxes, port duties, and court fines filled their coffers.

Emboldened by their attainments in the north, the Lombard kings tried to make some headway against the independent dukes of southern Italy. But that threatened to surround Rome with a unified Lombard kingdom. The pope, fearing for his own position, called on the Franks for help.

THE POPE: A MAN IN THE MIDDLE

By the end of the sixth century, the pope's position was ambiguous. As bishop of Rome, he wielded real secular power within the city as well as a measure of spiritual leadership farther afield. Yet in other ways he was just a subordinate of Byzantium. Pope Gregory the Great (590–604), whom we have already met a number of times, laid the foundations for the papacy's later spiritual and temporal ascendancy. (See Popes and Antipopes to 1500 on pp. 338–341.) During Gregory's tenure, the pope became the greatest landowner in Italy; he organized Rome's defense and paid for its army; he heard court cases, made treaties, and provided welfare services. The missionary expedition he sent to England was only a small part of his involvement in the rest of Europe. A prolific author of spiritual works, Gregory digested and simplified the ideas of Church Fathers such as Saint Augustine, making them accessible to a wider audience. In his *Moralia in Job*, he set forth a model of biblical exegesis that was widely imitated for centuries. His handbook for clerics, *Pastoral Care*, went hand-in-hand with his practical church reforms in Italy, where he tried to impose regular episcopal elections and enforce clerical celibacy.

At the same time, even Gregory was only one of many bishops in the former Roman Empire, now ruled from Constantinople. For a long time the emperor's views on dogma, discipline, and church administration prevailed at Rome. However, this authority began to unravel in the seventh century. In 692, Emperor Justinian II convened a council that determined 102 rules for the church. When he sent the rules to Rome for papal endorsement, Pope Sergius I (687–701) found most of them acceptable, but he was unwilling to agree to the whole because it permitted priestly marriages (which the Roman church did not want to allow), and it prohibited fasting on Saturdays in Lent (which the Roman church required). Outraged by Sergius's refusal, Justinian tried to arrest the pope, but the imperial army in Italy (theoretically under the emperor's command) came to the pontiff's aid instead. Justinian's arresting officer was reduced to cowering under the pope's bed. Clearly Constantinople's influence and authority over Rome had become tenuous. Sheer distance as well as diminishing imperial power in Italy meant that the popes had in effect become the leaders of non-Lombard Italy.

The gap between Byzantium and the papacy widened in the early eighth century, when Emperor Leo III tried to increase the taxes on papal property to pay for his wars against the Arabs. Gregory II, the pope who later commissioned Saint Boniface's evangelical work (see above, p. 66), responded by leading a general tax revolt. Meanwhile, Leo's fierce policy of iconoclasm collided with the pope's tolerance of images. For Gregory, as for Saint John of Damascus, holy images could and should be venerated, though not worshiped. Increasing friction with Byzantium meant that when the pope felt threatened by the Lombard kings, as he did in the mid-eighth century, he looked elsewhere for support. Pope Stephen II (752–757) appealed to the Franks – not to the Merovingians, who had just lost the throne, but to Pippin III, the king who had taken the royal crown. Pippin listened to the pope's entreaties and marched into Italy with an army to fight the Lombards. The new Frankish/papal alliance would change the map of Europe in the coming decades.

★   ★   ★   ★   ★

The "fall" of the Roman Empire meant the rise of its heirs. In the East the Muslims swept out of Arabia—and promptly set up a Roman-style government where they conquered. The bit in the east that they did not take—the part ruled from Constantinople—still considered itself the Roman Empire. In the West, impoverished kingdoms looked to the city of Rome for religion, culture, and inspiration. However much East and West, Christian and Muslim, would come to deviate from and hate one another, they could not change the fact of shared parentage.

CHAPTER TWO KEY EVENTS

c.570–632	Life of Muhammad
587	Reccared, Visigothic king, converts to Catholic Christianity
590	Saint Columbanus arrives on the Continent
590–604	Pope Gregory the Great
597	Augustine arrives at the court of King Ethelbert
607–630	Sasanid–Byzantine wars
622	*Hijra*; Muhammad's migration from Mecca to Medina
624	Battle of Badr
633	Beginning of Islamic conquests outside of Arabia
661	Death of Ali
661–750	Umayyad caliphate
664	Synod of Whitby
c.680	Holy images come to be valued as "icons"
681	Bulgars enter Byzantine territory
711–715	Conquest of Spain by Islamic-led armies
726–787, 815–843	Iconoclasm at Byzantium

NOTES

1 *The Life of St. Theodore of Sykeon*, in *Reading the Middle Ages: Sources from Europe, Byzantium, and the Islamic World*, ed. Barbara H. Rosenwein, 2nd ed. (Toronto: University of Toronto Press, 2014), p. 62.

2 Quoted in Leslie Brubaker and John Haldon, *Byzantium in the Iconoclast Era c. 680–850: A History* (Cambridge: Cambridge University Press, 2011), p. 61.

3 *The Synod of 754*, in *Reading the Middle Ages*, p. 67.

4 John of Damascus, *On Holy Images*, in *Reading the Middle Ages*, p. 65.

5 See *The Chronicle of Theophanes Confessor*, in *Reading the Middle Ages*, p. 69.

6 Al-A'sha, *Bid Hurayra Farewell*, in *Reading the Middle Ages*, p. 71.

7 Qur'an Sura 96, in *Reading the Middle Ages*, p. 75.

8 Qur'an Sura 1, in *Reading the Middle Ages*, p. 74.

9 The five pillars are: 1) the *zakat*, a tax to be used for charity; 2) Ramadan, a month of fasting to mark the battle of Badr (see p. 52); 3) the *hajj*, an annual pilgrimage to Mecca to be made at least once in a believer's lifetime; and 4) the *salat*, formal worship at least three times a day (later increased to five), including 5) the *shahadah*, or profession of faith: "There is no god but God, and Muhammad is His prophet."

10 *The Treaty of Tudmir*, in *Reading the Middle Ages*, p. 76.

11 John of Damascus, *On Holy Images*, in *Reading the Middle Ages*, p. 65.

12 Al-Akhtal, *The Tribe Has Departed*, in *Reading the Middle Ages*, p. 78.

13 *The Passion of Leudegar*, in *Reading the Middle Ages*, p. 83.

14 Bede, *The Ecclesiastical History of the English People*, in *Reading the Middle Ages*, p. 94.

15 Ibid., p. 96.

16 *The Third Council of Toledo*, in *Reading the Middle Ages*, p. 50.

17 Isidore of Seville, *Etymologies*, in *Reading the Middle Ages*, p. 81.

18 The image of the "radiant throne" is from Eugenius of Toledo, quoted in Geneviève Bührer-Thierry, "'Just Anger' or 'Vengeful Anger'? The Punishment of Blinding in the Early Medieval West," in *Anger's Past: The Social Uses of an Emotion in the Middle Ages*, ed. Barbara H. Rosenwein (Ithaca, NY: Cornell University Press, 1998), p. 79.

FURTHER READING

Brown, Warren, Marios Costambeys, Matthew Innes, and Adam Kosto, eds. *Documentary Culture and the Laity in the Early Middle Ages*. Cambridge: Cambridge University Press, 2012.

Brubaker, Leslie, and John Haldon. *Byzantium in the Iconoclast Era c. 680–850: A History*. Cambridge: Cambridge University Press, 2011.

Donner, Fred M. *Muhammad and the Believers: At the Origins of Islam*. Cambridge, MA: Harvard University Press, 2010.

Evans, Helen C., with Brandie Ratliff. *Byzantium and Islam: Age of Transition, 7th–9th Century*. New Haven, CT: Yale University Press, 2012.

Fleming, Robin. *Britain after Rome: The Fall and Rise, 400 to 1070*. London: Penguin, 2010.

Haldon, J.F. *Byzantium in the Seventh Century: The Transformation of a Culture*. Cambridge: Cambridge University Press, 1990.

Herrin, Judith. *Byzantium: The Surprising Life of a Medieval Empire*. Princeton, NJ: Princeton University Press, 2007.

Lassner, Jacob, and Michael Bonner. *Islam in the Middle Ages: The Origins and Shaping of Classical Islamic Civilization*. Santa Barbara, CA: Greenwood/Praeger, 2010.

Mayr-Harting, Henry. *The Coming of Christianity to Anglo-Saxon England*. University Park: Pennsylvania State University Press, 1991.

Robinson, Chase F. *'Abd al-Malik*. Oxford: Oxford University Press, 2005.

Shoemaker, Stephen J. *The Death of a Prophet: The End of Muhammad's Life and the Beginnings of Islam*. Philadelphia: University of Pennsylvania Press, 2012.

Wagner, Walter. *Opening the Qur'an: Introducing Islam's Holy Book*. South Bend, IN: University of Notre Dame Press, 2008.

Wickham, Chris. *The Inheritance of Rome: A History of Europe from 400–1000*. New York: Penguin, 2009.

Wood, Ian. *The Merovingian Kingdoms, 450–751*. London: Longman, 1994.

To test your knowledge of this chapter, please go to

www.utphistorymatters.com

for Study Questions.

THREE

CREATING NEW IDENTITIES (*c.750–c.900*)

IN THE SECOND HALF of the eighth century the periodic outbreaks of the Plague of Justinian that had devastated half of the globe for two centuries came to an end. In their wake came a gradual but undeniable upswing in population, land cultivation, and general prosperity. At Byzantium an empress took the throne, in the Islamic world the Abbasids displaced the Umayyads, while in Francia the Carolingians deposed the Merovingians. New institutions of war and peace, learning, and culture developed, giving each state— Byzantium, the Islamic caliphate, Francia—its own characteristic identity (though with some telling similarities).

BYZANTIUM: FROM TURNING WITHIN TO CAUTIOUS EXPANSION

In 750 Byzantium was a state with its back to the world: its iconoclasm isolated it from other Christians; its theme structure focused its military operations on internal defense; and its abandonment of classical learning set it apart from its past. By 900, all this had changed. Byzantium was iconophile (icon-loving), aggressive, and cultured.

New Icons, New Armies, New Territories

Within Byzantium, iconoclasm sowed dissension. In the face of persecution and humiliation, men and women continued to venerate icons, even in the very bedrooms of the imperial palace. The tide turned in 780 when Leo IV died and his widow, Irene, in effect became head of the Byzantine state as regent for her son Constantine VI. Long a secret iconophile, Irene immediately moved to replace important iconoclast bishops. Then she called a council at Nicaea in 787, the first there since the famous one of 325. The meeting went as planned, and the assembled bishops condemned iconoclasm. But iconoclastic fervor still lingered, and a partial ban on icons was put into effect between 815 and 843.

At first the end of iconoclasm displeased the old guard in the army, but soon a new generation was in charge. Already before Irene's rule Byzantium's militia had been reformed and the theme organization supplemented by an even more responsive force. In the mid-eighth century, Emperor Constantine V (r.741–775) had created new crack regiments, the *tagmata* (sing. *tagma*). These were mobile troops, not tied to any theme. Many were composed of cavalry, the elite of fighting men; others—infantry, muleteers—provided necessary backup. At first deployed largely around Constantinople itself to shore up the emperors, the *tagmata* were eventually used in cautious frontier battles. Under the ninth- and tenth-century emperors, they helped Byzantium to expand.

To the west, in the Balkans, Emperor Nicephorus I (r.802–811) remodeled the old thematic territories and added new ones. Settled by immigrant Slavs as well as native Greeks, the Balkans presented an alluring prize for both the Byzantines and the Bulgars. Moving into Slavic territory, Nicephorus tried to take Sardica (today Sofia, Bulgaria), which had long been outside Byzantine control, but his soldiers mutinied when the emperor asked them to rebuild the city. To secure at least the northern border of the area, Nicephorus uprooted thousands of families from Anatolia and sent them to settle in the Balkans.

Still keen to knock out Bulgarian power in the region, Nicephorus marshaled a huge army. Escorted by the luminaries of his court, he plundered the Bulgarian capital, Pliska, and then coolly made his way west. But the Bulgarians blockaded his army as it passed through a narrow river valley, fell on the imperial party, and killed the emperor. The toll on the fleeing soldiers and courtiers was immense. Theophanes the Confessor, who detested both Nicephorus (because of his iconoclastic policies) and the Bulgars, may well have made up the story that Khan Krum (r.803–814) covered Nicephorus's skull with silver and turned it into a ceremonial drinking cup, for it cast a bad light on both khan and emperor. But it was a good metaphor for Byzantium's difficulties. Further Byzantine defeats in the region in the late ninth century led to yet more shuffling of themes. The end result may be seen in Map 3.1, to which Map 2.1 on p. 40 (Byzantium at its smallest) should be compared.

Another glance at the two maps reveals a second area of modest expansion, this time on Byzantium's eastern front. In the course of the ninth century the Byzantines had worked out a strategy of skirmish warfare in Anatolia. When Muslim raiding parties attacked, the *strategoi* evacuated the population, burned the crops, and, while sending out a few troops to harass the invaders, largely waited out the raid within their local fortifications. But by 860, the threat of invasion was largely over (though the menace of Muslim navies—on Sicily and in southern Italy, for example—remained very real). In 900, Emperor Leo VI (r.886–912) was confident enough to go on the offensive, sending the *tagmata* in the direction of Tarsus. The raid was a success, and in its wake at least one princely family in Armenia

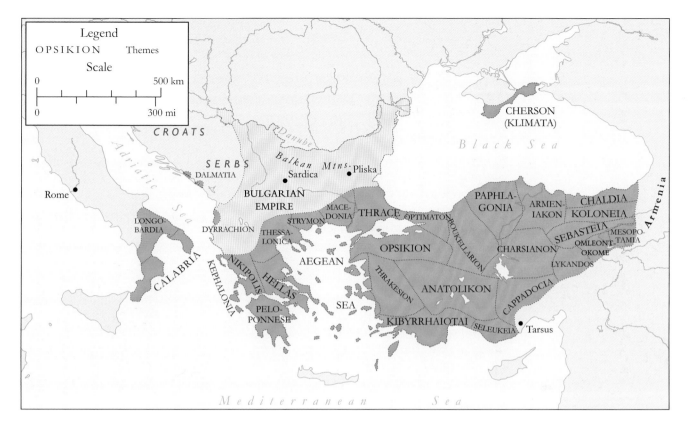

Map 3.1: The Byzantine and Bulgarian Empires, *c.*920

broke off its alliance with the Arabs, entered imperial service, and ceded its principality to Byzantium. Reorganized as the theme of Mesopotamia, it was the first of a series of new themes that Leo created in an area that had been largely a no-man's-land between the Islamic and Byzantine worlds.

The rise of the *tagmata* eventually had the unanticipated consequence of downgrading the themes. The soldiers of the themes got the "grunt work"—the inglorious job of skirmish warfare—without the honor and (probably) extra pay. The *tagmata* were the professionals, gradually taking over most of the fighting, especially as the need to defend the interior of Anatolia receded. By the same token, the troops of the themes became increasingly inactive.

Christianity and the Rise of East Central Europe

To the north of Byzantium was a huge swathe of territory stretching to the Baltic Sea. Once states coalesced there, it would become East Central Europe. But while states (in this case under the aegis of Germanic leaders) were forming in Europe's west, the east-central region remained in flux as new groups, mainly of Slavic and Turkic origins, entered, created ephemeral political entities, and then disappeared. The Slavs made up the majority of these immigrants. As farmers (on the whole), however, they were normally subject to others, such as the Avars, Turkic-speaking warrior nomads who created a great empire on the Pannonian Plain. (See Map 2.1 on p. 40.) But the Avars were wiped out by the Franks in 796 (see below, p. 98).

Thereafter, East Central Europe took shape like a carpet unrolled from south to north; Lithuania was the last to create a fairly permanent state (see p. 258), Bulgaria the first. Christianization went hand-in-hand with state formation; in the ninth century Byzantines and Franks (who preached the Roman Catholic brand of Christianity) competed to take advantage of the new political stability in the region. For these proselytizers, spreading the Gospel had not only spiritual but also political advantages: it was a way to bring border regions under their respective spheres of influence. For the fledgling East Central European states, conversion to Christianity meant new institutions to buttress the ruling classes, recognition by one or another of the prestigious heirs of Rome, and enhanced economic and military opportunities.

The process of Christianization began in Moravia and Bulgaria. In Moravia, Duke Ratislav (r.846–870) made a bid for autonomy from Frankish hegemony by calling on Byzantium for missionaries. The imperial court was ready. Two brothers, Constantine (later called Cyril) and Methodius, set out in 863 armed with translations of the Gospels and liturgical texts. Born in Thessalonica, they well knew about the Slavic languages, which had been purely oral. Constantine devised an alphabet using Greek letters to represent the sounds of one Slavic dialect (the "Glagolitic" alphabet). He then added Greek words and grammar where the Slavic lacked Christian vocabulary and suitable expressions. The resulting language, later called Old Church Slavonic, was an effective tool for conversion: "What man can tell all the parables / Denouncing nations without their own books / And who do not preach in an intelligible tongue? / ... Whoever accepts these letters, / To him Christ speaks wisdom," reads the prologue to Constantine/Cyril's translation of the Gospels.[1] However much Byzantium valued the Greek language, and however keen it was to control all matters from Constantinople, it was nevertheless willing at times to work with regional linguistic and cultural traditions. The Roman church, by contrast, was more rigid, insisting that the Gospels and liturgy be in Latin. In the end, however, Moravia opted for Rome.

But the Byzantine brand of Christianity prevailed in Bulgaria, Serbia, and later (see Chapter 4) Russia. We have seen how hostile the relations between the Bulgar khan and the Byzantine emperors were. Yet c.864, Khan Boris (r.852–889) not only converted to Christianity under Byzantine auspices but also adopted the name of the Byzantine emperor of the time, Michael III (r.842–867), becoming Boris-Michael. How did Bulgaria end up in the Byzantine camp? To answer this question, consider the position of the Bulgar khan. Leader of warrior nomads, he claimed heaven's mandate; but as ruler of a state that embraced a large Christian population of Greek-speaking former Byzantines, he was obliged to take on the trappings of a Byzantine ruler as well. He employed Greeks to administer his state, used Greek officials in his writing-office, authenticated his documents with Byzantine-style seals, and adopted Byzantine court ceremonies.[2] In addition, in the course of the ninth century, Bulgar contact with Byzantines increased as a result of refugees fleeing—and war-prisoners being forced—into the Bulgar state. The religion of these newcomers began to "rub off" on the ruling classes. Finally, as questions Boris-Michael put to the pope in 866 suggest, the pagan religion of the Bulgars involved practices rather than dogma. It was therefore possible (though hardly easy) to convert by exchanging one sort of act with another: "When you used to go into battle," the pope wrote, "you indicated that you carried the tail of a horse as your military emblem, and you ask what you should carry now in its place. What else, of course, but the sign of the cross?"[3]

At the same time, it seems clear that when Boris accepted baptism, he had no intention of becoming subservient to Byzantium. Just before his conversion he had flirted with the Roman Christianity of the Franks, and two years later he was writing to the pope (as above) about what insignia to take into battle, along with many other detailed questions. By 870 he had arranged for an archbishop independent of Constantinople to live near him at Pliska, his capital city.

Cultural Flowering at Byzantium

The creation of the Glagolitic alphabet in the mid-ninth century was one of many scholarly and educational initiatives taking place in the Byzantine Empire in the ninth century. Constantinople had always had schools, books, and teachers dedicated above all to training civil servants. But in the eighth century the number of bureaucrats was dwindling, schools were decaying, and books, painstakingly written out on papyrus, were disintegrating. Ninth-century confidence reversed this trend, while fiscal stability and surplus wealth in the treasury greased the wheels. Emperor Theophilus (r.829–842) opened a public school in the palace headed by Leo the Mathematician, a master of geometry, mechanics, medicine, and philosophy. Controversies over iconoclasm sent churchmen scurrying to the writings of the Church Fathers to find passages that supported their cause. With the end of iconoclasm, the monasteries, staunch defenders of icons, garnered renewed prestige and gained new recruits. Because their abbots insisted that they read Christian texts, the monks had to get new manuscripts in a hurry. Practical need gave impetus to the creation of a new kind of script: minuscule. This was made up of lower-case letters, written in cursive, the letters strung together. It was faster and easier to write than the formal capital uncial letters that had previously been used. Words were newly separated by spaces, making them easier to read. Papyrus was no longer easily available from Egypt, so the new manuscripts were made out of parchment—animal skins scraped and treated to create a good writing surface. Far more expensive than papyrus, parchment was nevertheless much more durable, making possible their preservation over the long haul.

A general cultural revival was clearly under way by the middle of the century. As a young man, Photius, later patriarch of Constantinople (r.858–867, 877–886), had already read hundreds of books, including works of history, literature, and philosophy. As patriarch, he gathered a circle of scholars around him; wrote sermons, homilies, and theological treatises; and tutored Emperor Leo VI. For his own part, Constantine-Cyril, the future missionary to the Slavs, was reportedly such a brilliant student in Thessalonica that an imperial official invited him to the capital, where he met Photius:

> When he arrived at Constantinople, he was placed in the charge of masters to teach him. In three months he learned all the grammar and applied himself to other studies. He studied Homer and geometry and with Leo [the Mathematician] and Photius dialectic and all the teachings of philosophy, and in addition [he learned] rhetoric, arithmetic, astronomy, music, and all the other "Hellenic" [i.e., pagan Greek] teachings.[4]

The resurrection of "Hellenic" books helped inspire an artistic revival. Even during the somber years of iconoclasm, artistic activity did not entirely end at Byzantium. But the new exuberance and sheer numbers of mosaics, manuscript illuminations, ivories, and enamels after 870 suggest a new era. Sometimes called the Macedonian Renaissance, after the ninth- and tenth-century imperial dynasty that fostered it, the new movement found its models in both the hierarchical style that was so important during the pre-iconoclastic period (see Plate 1.12 on pp. 32–33) and the natural, plastic style of classical art and its revivals (see Plate 1.1 on p. 12 and Plate 1.10 on p. 20).

In the hands of Byzantine artists, these different styles worked together. Consider a lavish manuscript of the *Homilies* of Gregory of Nazianzus, made *c.*880 at Constantinople. It begins with several pages that represent the imperial family of Basil I (r.867–886), the original recipient of the manuscript. Plate 3.1 shows one of these opening pages: the emperor's wife, Eudocia, is flanked by two of her sons, potential heirs to the throne. All of the figures are flat and weightless. They stare out at the viewer, isolated from one another. In the center is the empress, towering above her sons not because she was physically taller than they but in order to telegraph her higher status. The artist is far more interested in the patterns of the richly ornamented clothing than in delineating any body underneath. The entire miniature celebrates hierarchy, transcendence, and imperial power. Yet in the very same manuscript are pages that draw eagerly upon the classical heritage. In Plate 3.2, on the left, the prophet Ezekiel stands in a landscape of bones, the hand of God reaching toward him to tell him that the bones will rise and live again (Ezek. 37:1–11). On the right the prophet stands next to an archangel. All the figures have roundness and weight; they turn and interact. It is true that their drapery flutters and loops unnaturally, giving the scene a non-classical excitement; and it is true that the angel "floats," one foot in front of the prophet, one arm a bit behind him. But it is in just this way that the Byzantines adapted classical traditions to their overriding need to represent transcendence.

Not surprisingly, the same period saw the revival of monumental architecture. Already Emperor Theophilus was known for the splendid palace that he had built on the outskirts of Constantinople, and Basil I was famous as a builder of churches. Rich men from the court and church imitated imperial tastes, constructing palaces, churches, and monasteries of their own.

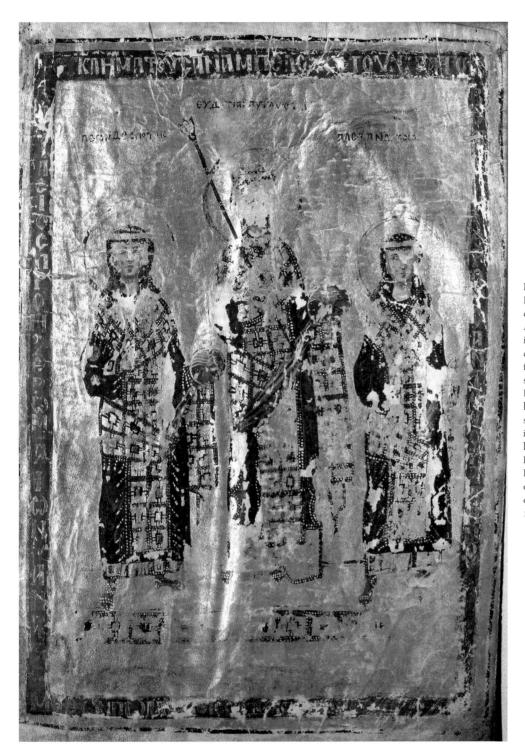

Plate 3.1: The Empress Eudocia and Her Sons, *Homilies* of Gregory Nazianzus (*c.*880). After the end of iconoclasm in 843, two distinct, but complementary, artistic styles flourished at Byzantium, easily seen by comparing this plate to Plate 3.2. The frontal, formal, hierarchical, and decorative style represented by this illumination harks back to late imperial work, such as the Hippodrome obelisk base in Plate 1.8 on p. 18 and the image of Justinian flanked by officials of church and state in Plate 1.12 on pp. 32–33.

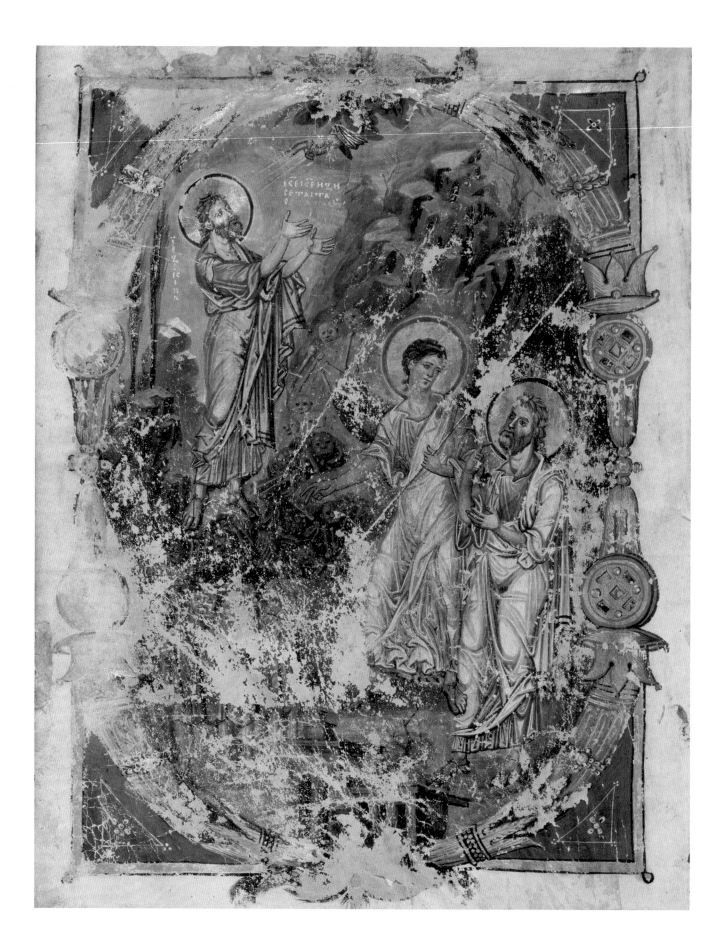

THE SHIFT TO THE EAST IN THE ISLAMIC WORLD

Just as at Byzantium the imperial court determined both culture and policies, so too in the Islamic world of the ninth century were the caliph and his court the center of power. The Abbasids, who ousted the Umayyad caliphs in 750, moved their capital city to Iraq (part of the former Persia) and stepped into the shoes of the Sasanid king of kings, the "shadow of God on earth." Yet much of their time was spent less in imposing their will than in conciliating different interest groups.

The Abbasid Reconfiguration

Years of Roman rule had made Byzantium relatively homogeneous. Nothing was less true of the Islamic world, made up of regions wildly diverse in geography, language, and political, religious, and social traditions. Each tribe, family, and region had its own expectations and desires for a place in the sun. The Umayyads paid little heed. Their power base was Syria, formerly a part of Byzantium. There they rewarded their hard-core followers and took the lion's share of conquered land for themselves. They expected every other region to send its taxes to their coffers at Damascus. This annoyed regional leaders, even though they probably managed to keep most of the taxes that they raised. Moreover, with no claims to the religious functions of an *imam*, the Umayyads could never gain the adherence of the followers of Ali. Soon still other groups began to complain. Where was the equality of believers preached in the Qur'an? The Umayyads privileged an elite; Arabs who had expected a fair division of the spoils were disappointed. So too were non-Arabs who converted to Islam: they discovered that they had still to pay the old taxes of their non-believing days.

The discontents festered, and two main centers of resistance emerged: Khurasan (today eastern Iran) and Iraq. (See Map 3.2.) Both had been part of the Persian Empire; the rebellion was largely a coming together of old Persian and newly "Persianized" Arab factions. In the 740s this defiant coalition at Khurasan decided to support the Abbasid family. This was an extended kin group with deep-rooted claims to the caliphate, tracing its lineage back to the very uncle who had cared for the orphaned Muhammad. With militant supporters, considerable money, and the backing of a powerful propaganda organization, the Abbasids organized an army in Khurasan and, marching it undefeated into Iraq, picked up more support there. In 749 they defeated the Umayyad governor at Kufa. Less than a year later the last Umayyad caliph, abandoned by almost everyone and on the run in Egypt, was killed in a short battle. In 750 al-Saffah was solemnly named the first Abbasid caliph.

The new dynasty seemed to signal a revolution. (See list of Caliphs: The Abbasids on p. 342.) Most importantly, the Abbasids recognized the crucial centrality of Iraq and built their capital cities there: Baghdad became the capital in 762, Samarra in the 830s in the aftermath of a bitter civil war. The Abbasids took the title of *imam* and even, at one point, wore the green color of the Shi'ites.

Plate 3.2 (facing page): Ezekiel in the Valley of Dry Bones, *Homilies* of Gregory Nazianzus (*c*.880). Although painted in the same manuscript as Plate 3.1, this miniature's style is inspired by a different—classical—tradition. Compare the drapery and modeling of the figure of Ezekiel on the right-hand side of this miniature (where he stands next to an archangel) with the figure of Saint Paul at the bottom, extreme right-hand corner, of the sarcophagus of Junius Bassus in Plate 1.10 on p. 20.

Yet as they became entrenched, the Abbasids in turn created their own elite, under whom other groups chafed. In the eighth century most of their provincial governors, for example, came from the Abbasid family itself. When building Baghdad, Caliph al-Mansur (r.754–775) allotted important tracts of real estate to his Khurasan military leaders. In the course of time, as Baghdad prospered and land prices rose, the Khurasani came to constitute a new, exclusive, and jealous elite. At the same time as they favored these groups, the Abbasids succeeded in centralizing their control even more fully than the Umayyads had done. This is clearest in the area of taxation. The Umayyads had demanded in vain that all taxes come to them. But the Abbasid caliph al-Mu'tasim (r.833–842) was able to control and direct provincial revenues to his court in Iraq.

Control, however, was uneven. Until the beginning of the tenth century, the Abbasid caliphs generally could count on ruling Iraq (their "headquarters"), Syria, Khurasan, and Egypt. But they never had the Iberian Peninsula; they lost Ifriqiya (today Tunisia) by about 800; and they never controlled the Berbers in the soft underbelly of North Africa. In the course of the tenth century, they would lose effective control even in their heartlands. That, however, was in the future (see Chapter 4).

Map 3.2: The Islamic World, *c.*800

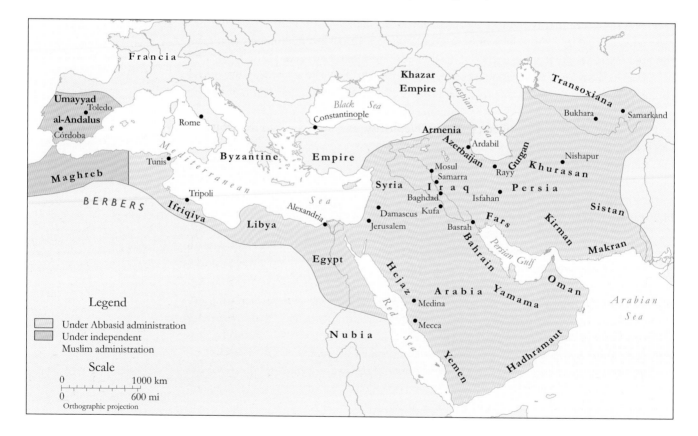

Whatever control the Abbasids had depended largely on their armies. Unlike the Byzantines, the Abbasids did not need soldiers to stave off external enemies or to expand outwards. (The Byzantine strategy of skirmish warfare worked largely because the caliphs led raids to display their prowess, not to take territory. The serious naval wars that took Sicily from Byzantium were launched from Ifriqiya, independent of the caliphs.) Rather, the Abbasids needed troops to collect taxes in areas already conquered but weakly controlled.

Well into the ninth century the caliphs' troops were paid, but not mustered, by them. Generals recruited their own troops from their home districts, tribes, families, and clients. When the generals were loyal to the caliphs, this military system worked well. In the dark days of civil war, however, when two brothers fought over the caliphate (811–819), no one controlled the armies. After al-Ma'mun (r.813–833) won this civil war, he had no reliable army to back him up. His brother and successor, al-Mu'tasim, found the solution in a new-style, private army. He bought and trained his own slaves, many of them Turks and thus unrelated to other tribal groups. These men were given governorships as well as military posts. They were the reason that al-Mu'tasim was able to collect provincial taxes so effectively. He could not foresee that in time the Turks would come to constitute a new elite, one that would eventually help to overpower the caliphate itself.

Under the Abbasids, the Islamic world became wealthy. The Mediterranean region had always been a great trade corridor; in the ninth century, Baghdad, at the crossroads of East and West, drew that trade into a wider network. All of Iraq participated in the commercial buoyancy. A treatise on trade, probably from this period, listed Iraqi imports:

> From India are imported tigers, panthers, elephants, panther skins, rubies, white sandal, ebony, and coconuts. From China are imported silk [textiles], [raw] silk, chinaware, paper, ink, peacocks, racing horses, saddles, felts, cinnamon, Greek unblended rhubarb … racing horses, female slaves, knickknacks with human figures … hydraulic engineers, expert agronomists, marble workers, and eunuchs. From Arabia: Arab horses, ostriches, pedigreed she-camels … From Egypt: trotting donkeys, suits of fine cloth, papyrus, balsam, and—from its mines—topazes of superior quality. From the land of the Khazars [on the lower Volga River]: slaves of both sexes, coats of mail, [and] helmets.[5]

Brilliant porcelains from China inspired Islamic artisans to add tin to their own glazes to achieve a bright white color, over which they added decorative motifs. Dining off ornate plates and bowls, pouring their water from richly decorated pitchers, the Islamic upper and middle classes could boast splendid tableware. (See Plate 3.3.) Their clothes, made of richly woven fabrics, were luxurious as well. Wall-hangings and rugs adorned their homes, and elaborately carved censers spread their perfume.

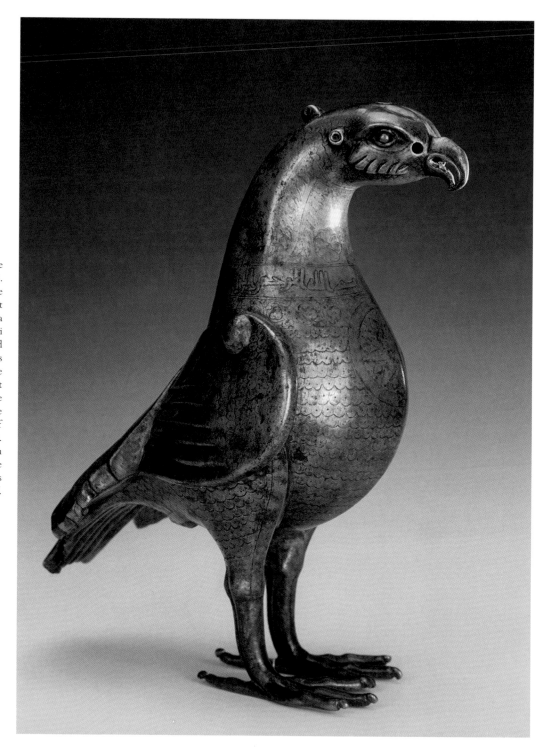

Plate 3.3: Water Pitcher in the Shape of an Eagle (796–797). At one time this brass eagle had a handle and was no doubt used as a water pitcher by a well-to-do Syrian or Iraqi family. Inlaid with silver and copper, most of which has disappeared, it includes the name of the craftsman who made it (Suleiman), inscribed on the eagle's neck along with the date and a blessing ("In the name of Allah merciful, compassionate. Blessing from Allah."). Suleiman also named the city where he made the pitcher, but that has rubbed off.

New Cultural Forms

With revenues from commerce and (above all) taxes from agriculture in their coffers, the Abbasid caliphs paid their armies, salaried their officials (drawn from the many talented men—but, in this relentlessly male-dominated society, not women—in the Persian, Arab, Christian, and Jewish population), and presided over a cultural revival even more impressive than the one at Constantinople.

In the ninth century, most spectacularly under caliphs Harun al-Rashid and al-Ma'mun, literature, science, law, and other forms of scholarship flourished. Books of all sorts were relatively cheap (and therefore accessible) in the Islamic world because they were written on paper. The caliphs launched scientific studies via a massive translation effort that brought the philosophical, medical, mathematical, and astrological treatises of the Indian and Greek worlds into Islamic culture. They encouraged new literary forms, including the experimental, irreverent "New Poetry" of men like Abu Nuwas (d.813/815):

> So I advanced in their [some young men's] company
>> And was told to climb with them [to the spot we were
>>> making for];
> There vessels were unveiled for them (like wives exposed for
>> the first time)
>> While a bird warbled in a melancholy strain.
> I skipped up to the glasses, and polished them,
>> Leaving them like dazzling snow;
> My dexterity impressed the beardless young men
>> (Though with my skill I intended no good for them);
> I served them without respite wine mixed with water
>> —It was as warming and bright as kindled fire—
> Until I noticed their heads incline,
>> Bent and crooked with drunkenness
> And their tongues tied and heavy,
>> They now either slept or reclined;
> I got up trembling to have sex with them
>> (All those who creep stealthily tremble [at the thought]!);
> Their trouser-bands stymied my pleasure [at first]
>> But then, with subtle art, I untied them
> To reveal each man's quivering backside ...[6]

Although scurrilous, such poetry, beautifully and cleverly written, was appreciated as *adab*, a literature (both in verse and prose) of refinement. (*Adab* means "good manners.")

Shoring up the regime with astrological predictions; winning theological debates with the pointed weapons of Aristotle's logical and scientific works; understanding the theories of bridge-building, irrigation, and land-surveying with Euclid's geometry—these were just some of the reasons why scholars in the Islamic world labored over translations and created original scientific works. Their intellectual pyrotechnics won general support. Patrons of scientific writing included the caliphs, their wives, courtiers, generals, and ordinary people with practical interests. Al-Khwarizmi (d.c.850), author of a book on algebra (the word itself is from the Arabic *al-jabr*), explained that his subject was useful for "inheritances, bequests, tax assessments, legal verdicts, commercial transactions, land surveying, water rights, [the construction of buildings, and the digging of canals]."[7] The same scholar also wrote the first Arabic treatise on the Indian method of calculation—Indian numerals are what *we* call Arabic numerals—and the use of the zero, essential (to give one example) for distinguishing 100 from 1.

How should one live to be pleasing to God? This was the major question that inspired the treatises on *hadith* (traditions about the Prophet) that began to appear in the Abbasid period. Each *hadith* began with the chain of oral transmitters (the most recent listed first) that told a story about Muhammad; there then followed the story itself. Thus, for example, in the compilation of *hadith* by al-Bukhari (810–870) on the issue of fasting during Ramadan (the yearly period of fasting from sunrise to sunset), he took up the question of the distracted "faster who eats and drinks from forgetfulness":

> 'Abdan related to us [saying], Yazid b. Zurai' informed us, saying, Hisham related to us, saying: Ibn Sirin related to us from Abu Huraira, from the Prophet—upon whom be blessing and peace—that he said: "If anyone forgets and eats or drinks, let him complete his fast, for it was Allah who caused him thus to eat or drink."[8]

Here 'Abdan was the most recent witness to a saying of the Prophet, with Abu Huraira the closest to the source. A well-known "Companion" of the Prophet Muhammad, Abu Huraira was named as the ultimate authority for thousands of *hadith*.

Even the Qur'an did not escape scholarly scrutiny. While some interpreters read it literally as the word of God and thus part of God, others viewed it as something (like humankind) created by God and therefore separate from Him. For Caliph al-Ma'mun, taking the Qur'an literally undermined the caliph's religious authority. Somewhat like the Byzantine Emperor Leo III (see p. 45), whose iconoclastic policies were designed to separate divinity from its representations, al-Ma'mun determined to make God greater than the Qur'an. In 833 he instituted the Mihna, or Inquisition, demanding that the literalists profess the Qur'an's createdness. But al-Ma'mun died before he could punish those who refused, and his immediate successors were relatively ineffective in pursing the project. The scholars on the other side—the literalists and those who looked to the *hadith*—carried the day, and in 848 Caliph al-Mutawakkil (r.847–861) ended the Mihna, emphatically reversing the caliphate's position on the matter. Sunni Islam thus defined itself against the views of a caliph who, by asserting great power, lost much. The caliphs ceased to be the source of religious doctrine; that role went to the scholars, the *ulama*. It was around this time that the title "caliph" came to be associated with the phrase "deputy of the Prophet of God" rather than the "deputy of God." The designation reflected the caliphate's decreasing political as well as religious authority (see Chap. 4).

Al-Andalus: A Society in the Middle

Taking advantage of the caliphs' waning prestige was the ruler of al-Andalus (Islamic Spain). In the mid-eighth century Abd al-Rahman I, an Umayyad prince on the run from the Abbasids, managed to gather an army, make his way to Iberia, and defeat the provincial governor at Córdoba. In 756 he proclaimed himself "emir" (commander) of al-Andalus. His dynasty governed al-Andalus for two and a half centuries. In 929, emboldened by his growing power and the depletion of caliphal power at Baghdad, Abd al-Rahman III (r.912–961) took the title caliph. Nevertheless, like the Abbasid caliphs, the Umayyad rulers of Spain headed a state poised to break into its regional constituents.

Al-Andalus under the emirs was hardly Muslim and even less Arab. As the caliphs came to rely on Turks, so the emirs relied on a professional standing army of non-Arabs, the *al-khurs*, the "silent ones"—men who could not speak Arabic. They lived among a largely Christian—and partly Jewish—population; even by 900, only about 25 per cent of the people in al-Andalus were Muslim. This had its benefits for the regime, which taxed Christians and Jews heavily. Although, like Western European rulers, they did not have the land tax that the Byzantine emperors and caliphs could impose, the emirs did draw some of their revenue from Muslims, especially around their capital at Córdoba. (See Map 3.3.)

Money allowed the emirs to pay salaries to their civil servants and to preside over a cultural efflorescence that reflected the region's unique ethnic and religious mix. The Great Mosque in Córdoba is a good example. Begun under Abd al-Rahman I and expanded by his successors, it drew on the design of the Roman aqueduct at Mérida for its rows of columns connected by double arches. (See Plate 3.4.) For the shape of the arches, however, it borrowed a form—the "Visigothic" horseshoe arch—from the Christians. For the decorative motif of alternating light and dark stones, it looked to the Great Mosque of Damascus.

The cultural "mix" went beyond architectural forms. Some Muslim men took Christian wives, and religious practices seem to have melded a bit. In fact, the Christians who lived in al-Andalus were called "Mozarabs"—"would-be Arabs"—by Christians elsewhere. It used to be thought that an account of the martyrdom of 48 Christians at Córdoba between 850 and 859 was proof of implacable hostility between Christians and Muslims there. But recent research suggests that the account's idiosyncratic author, Eulogius, exaggerated for effect. It is likely that Christians and Muslims on the whole got along fairly well. Christians dressed like Muslims, worked side-by-side with them in government posts, and used Arabic in many aspects of their life. At the time of the supposed martyrdoms, there were in the region of Córdoba alone at least four churches and nine monasteries.

Still, some Andalusian Christians were discontented—Eulogius was one—and they were glad to have contact with the north. For to the north of al-Andalus, beyond the Duero River, were tiny Christian principalities. Partaking in the general demographic and economic growth of the period, they had begun to prosper a little. One, Asturias, became a kingdom. A local chronicler lauded King Alfonso III (r.866–910) for defeating the Muslims and imposing Christian rule: "He depopulated Coimbra, which was held by

Following pages:

Map 3.3: Europe, *c*.814

Plate 3.4: Great Mosque, Córdoba (785–787). The Great Mosque of Córdoba gave monumental identity to the new Umayyad rulers in al-Andalus. Note the two tiers of arches, the first set on pre-Islamic columns despoiled from Roman and Visigothic buildings, the second springing from high piers. With their alternating red and white stones and repeated pattern, the arches suggest lively arcades leading from west to east.

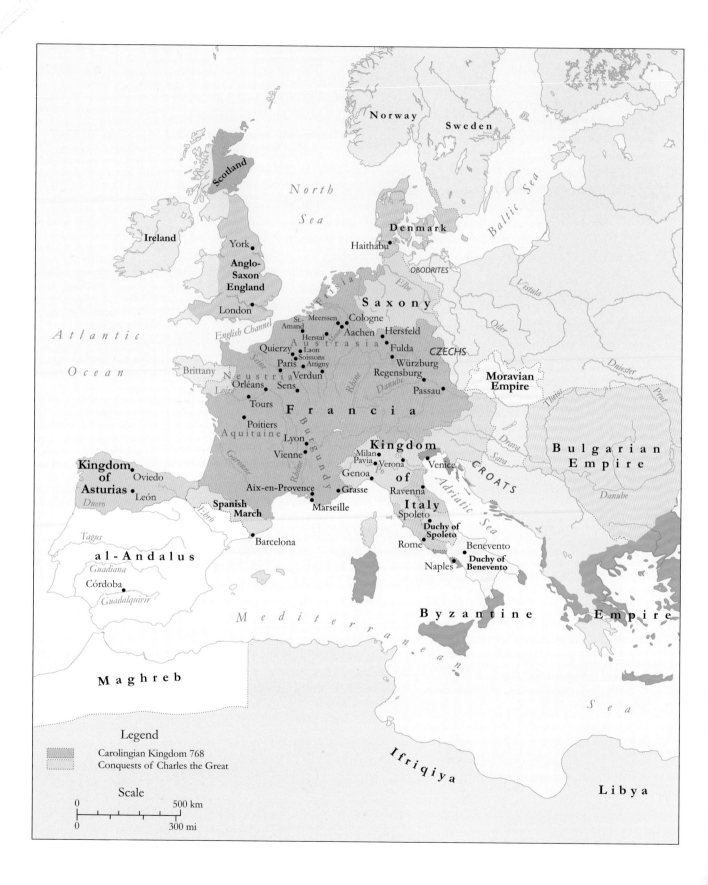

Scotland

Ireland

York

Anglo-
Saxon
England

London

NORWAY

Sweden

North

Sea

Denmark

Haithabu

OBODRITES

S a x o n y

Baltic Sea

Vistula

Elbe

Cologne
Aachen   Hersfeld
Meerssen
St.-
Amand   Herstal   Fulda   **CZECHS**
Quierzy   Laon   Würzburg
Soissons
Paris   Attigny   Regensburg
Verdun   Passau

English Channel

Atlantic

Ocean

Brittany

N e u s t r i a

Orléans   Sens

Tours

Poitiers

Aquitaine

A u s t r a s i a

Seine

Loire

Rhine

Danube

F r a n c i a

B u r g u n d y

Lyon
Vienne

**Moravian
Empire**

Dniester

Theiss

Prut

**B u l g a r i a n
E m p i r e**

**Kingdom
of
Asturias**

Oviedo

León

Duero

Rhône

Garonne

Aix-en-Provence

Spanish
March

Barcelona

Tagus

a l - A n d a l u s

Guadiana

Córdoba

Guadalquivir

Ebro

Marseille

Milan
Pavia   Verona   Venice
Genoa   *Po*

Kingdom

of

Grasse   Ravenna

Italy
Spoleto

Rome   **Duchy of
Spoleto**

Naples

Benevento
**Duchy of
Benevento**

CROATS

*Adriatic
Sea*

Drava

Sava

Danube

B y z a n t i n e   **E m p i r e**

M e d i t e r r a n e a n

S e a

M a g h r e b

I f r i q i y a

L i b y a

Legend

Carolingian Kingdom 768
Conquests of Charles the Great

Scale

0 ———————— 500 km

0 ———————— 300 mi

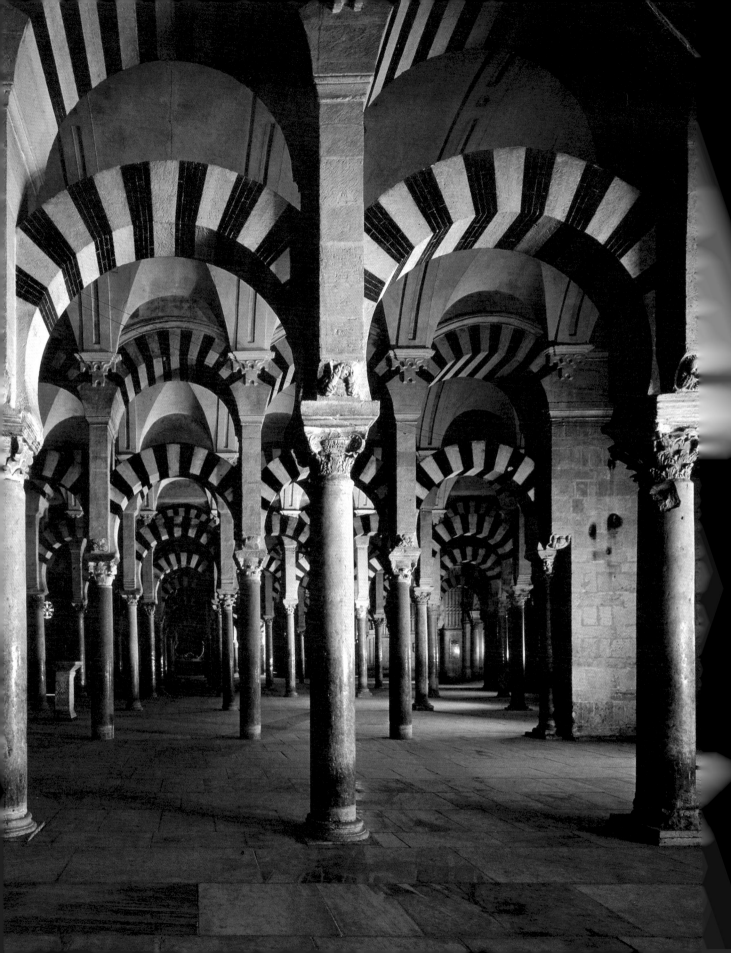

the enemy, and afterward peopled it with Galicians. He subjected many more fortresses to his rule. In his time the church grew and his kingdom increased in size. The cities of Braga, Oporto, Orense, Eminio, Viseo, and Lamego were populated with Christians."[9]

Alfonso and his successors built churches, encouraged monastic foundations, collected relics, patronized literary efforts, and welcomed Mozarabs from the south. As they did so, they looked to Christian models still farther north—to Francia, where Charlemagne and his heirs ruled as kings "by grace of God."

AN EMPIRE IN SPITE OF ITSELF

Between Byzantium and the Islamic world was Francia. While the other two were politically centralized, subject to sophisticated tax systems, and served by salaried armies and officials, Francia inherited the centralizing traditions of the Roman Empire without its order and efficiency. Francia's kings could not collect a land tax, the backbone of the old Roman and the more recent Byzantine and Islamic fiscal systems. There were no salaried officials or soldiers in Francia. Yet the new dynasty of kings there, the Carolingians, managed to muster armies, expand their kingdom, encourage a revival of scholarship and learning, command the respect of emperors and caliphs, and forge an identity for themselves as leaders of the Christian people. Their successes bore striking resemblance to contemporary achievements at Constantinople and Baghdad. How was this possible? The answer is at least threefold: the Carolingians took advantage of the same gentle economic upturn that seems to have taken place generally; they exploited to the full the institutions of Roman culture and political life that remained to them; and at the same time, they were willing to experiment with new institutions and take advantage of unexpected opportunities.

The Making of the Carolingians

The Carolingian take-over was a "palace coup." After a battle (at Tertry, in 687) between Neustrian and Austrasian noble factions, one powerful family with vast estates in Austrasia came to monopolize the high office of mayor for the Merovingian kings in both places. In the first half of the eighth century these mayors took over much of the power and most of the responsibilities of the kings.

Charles Martel (mayor 714–741) gave the name Carolingian (from *Carolus*, Latin for Charles) to the dynasty. In 732 he won a battle near Poitiers against an army led by the Muslim governor of al-Andalus, ending raids from al-Andalus. But Charles had other enemies: he spent most of his time fighting vigorously against regional Frankish aristocrats intent on carving out independent lordships for themselves. Playing powerful factions against one another, rewarding supporters, defeating enemies, and dominating whole regions by controlling monasteries and bishoprics that served as focal points for both religious piety and land donations, the Carolingians created a tight network of supporters.

Moreover, they chose their allies well, reaching beyond Francia to the popes and to Anglo-Saxon churchmen, who (as we have seen) were closely tied to Rome. When the Anglo-Saxon missionary Boniface (d.754) wanted to preach in Frisia (today the Netherlands) and Germany, the Carolingians readily supported him as a prelude to their own conquests. Although many of the areas where Boniface missionized had long been Christian, their practices were local rather than tied to Rome. By contrast, Boniface's newly appointed bishops were loyal to Rome and the Carolingians, not to regional aristocracies. They knew that their power came from papal and royal fiat rather than from local power centers.

Men like Boniface opened the way to a more direct alliance between the Carolingians and the pope. Historians used to think that Pippin III (d.768), the son of Charles Martel, obtained approval from Pope Zacharias (741–752) to depose the reigning Merovingian king. Recent research suggests that such an early liaison between the pope and the Carolingians was manufactured by later writers. But it is certain that after Pippin took the throne in 751, Pope Stephen II (752–757) traveled to Francia. He anointed Pippin, blessed him, and begged him to send an army against the encircling Lombards: "Hasten, hasten, I urge and protest by the living and true God, hasten and assist! ... Do not suffer this Roman city to perish in which the Lord laid my body [i.e., the body of Saint Peter] and which he commended to me and established as the foundation of the faith. Free it and its Roman people, your brothers, and in no way permit it to be invaded by the people of the Lombards."[10]

In the so-called Donation of Pippin (756), the new king forced the Lombards to give some cities back to the pope. The arrangement recognized that the papacy was now ruler in central Italy of a territory that had once belonged to Byzantium. Before the 750s, the papacy had been part of the Byzantine Empire; by the middle of that decade, it had become part of the West. It was probably soon thereafter that members of the papal chancery (writing office) forged a document, the *Donation of Constantine*, which had the fourth-century Emperor Constantine declare that he was handing the western half of the Roman Empire to Pope Sylvester.

The chronicler of Charles Martel had already tied his hero's victories to Christ. The Carolingian partnership with Rome and Romanizing churchmen added to the dynasty's Christian aura. Anointment—daubing the kings with holy oil—provided the finishing touch. It reminded contemporaries of David, king of the Israelites: "Then Samuel took the horn of oil and anointed him in the midst of his brethren; and the spirit of the Lord came upon David from that day forward" (1 Sam. [or Vulgate 1 Kings] 16:13).

Charlemagne

The most famous Carolingian king was Charles (r.768–814), called "the Great" ("le Magne" in Old French). Large, tough, wily, and devout, he was everyone's model king. Einhard (d.840), his courtier and scholar, saw him as a Roman emperor: he patterned his *Life of Charlemagne* on the *Lives of the Caesars*, written in the second century by the Roman biographer Suetonius. Alcuin (d.804), also the king's courtier and an even more famous scholar, emphasized Charlemagne's religious side, nicknaming him "David," the putative author of the psalms, victor over the giant Goliath, and king of Israel. Empress Irene at Constantinople saw Charlemagne as a suitable husband for herself (though the arrangement eventually fell through).

Charlemagne's fame was largely achieved through warfare. While the Byzantine and Islamic rulers clung tightly to what they had, Charlemagne waged wars of plunder and conquest. He invaded Italy, seizing the Lombard crown and annexing northern Italy in 774. He moved his armies northward, fighting the Saxons for more than thirty years, forcibly converting them to Christianity, and annexing their territory. To the southeast, he sent his forces against the Avars, capturing their strongholds, forcing them to submit to his overlordship, and making off with cartloads of plunder. His expedition to al-Andalus gained Charlemagne a band of territory north of the Ebro River, a buffer between Francia and the Islamic world called the "Spanish March." Even his failures were the stuff of myth: a Basque attack on Charlemagne's army as it returned from Spain became the core of the epic poem *The Song of Roland*.

Ventures like these depended on a good army. Charlemagne's was led by his *fideles*, faithful aristocrats, and manned by free men, many the "vassals" (clients) of the aristocrats. The king had the *bannum*, the right to call his subjects to arms (and, more generally, to command, prohibit, punish, and collect fines when his ban was not obeyed). Soldiers provided their own equipment; the richest went to war on horseback, the poorest had to have at least a lance, shield, and bow. There was no standing army; men had to be mobilized for each expedition. No *tagmata*, themes, or Turkish slaves were to be found here! Yet, while the empire was expanding, it was a very successful system; men were glad to go off to war when they could expect to return enriched with booty.

By 800, Charlemagne's kingdom stretched 800 miles from east to west, even more from north to south when Italy is counted. (See Map 3.3.) On its eastern edge was a strip of "buffer regions" extending from the Baltic to the Adriatic; they were under Carolingian overlordship. Such hegemony was reminiscent of an empire, and Charlemagne began to act according to the model of Roman emperors, sponsoring building programs to symbolize his authority, standardizing weights and measures, and acting as a patron of intellectual and artistic enterprises. He built a capital "city"—a palace complex, in fact—at Aachen, complete with a chapel patterned on San Vitale, the church built by Justinian at Ravenna (see p. 29). So keen was Charlemagne on Byzantine models that he had columns, mosaics, and marbles from Rome and Ravenna carted up north to use in his own buildings.

Further drawing on imperial traditions, Charlemagne issued laws in the form of "capitularies," summaries of decisions made at assemblies held with the chief men of the realm. He appointed regional governors, called "counts," to carry out his laws, muster his armies, and collect his taxes. Chosen from Charlemagne's aristocratic supporters, they were compensated for their work by temporary grants of land rather than with salaries. This was not Roman; but Charlemagne lacked the fiscal apparatus of the Roman emperors (and of his contemporary Byzantine emperors and Islamic caliphs), so he made land substitute for money. To discourage corruption, he appointed officials called *missi dominici* ("those sent out by the lord king") to oversee the counts on the king's behalf. The *missi*, chosen from the same aristocratic class as bishops and counts, traveled in pairs across Francia. They were to look into the affairs—large and small—of the church and laity.

In this way, Charlemagne set up institutions meant to echo those of the Roman Empire. It was a brilliant move on the part of Pope Leo III (795–816) to harness the king's imperial pretensions to papal ambitions. In 799, accused of adultery and perjury by a hostile faction at Rome, Leo narrowly escaped blinding and having his tongue cut out. Fleeing northward to seek Charlemagne's protection, he returned home under escort, the king close behind. Charlemagne arrived in late November 800 to an imperial welcome orchestrated by Leo. On Christmas Day of that year, Leo put an imperial crown on Charlemagne's head, and the clergy and nobles who were present acclaimed the king "Augustus," the title of the first Roman emperor. In one stroke the pope managed to exalt the king of the Franks, downgrade Irene at Byzantium, and enjoy the role of "emperor maker" himself.

About twenty years later, when Einhard wrote about this coronation, he said that the imperial titles at first so displeased Charlemagne "that he stated that, if he had known in advance of the pope's plan, he would not have entered the church that day, even though it was a great feast day."[11] In fact, Charlemagne continued to use the title "king" for about a year; then he adopted a new one that was both long and revealing: "Charles, the most serene Augustus, crowned by God, great and peaceful emperor who governs the Roman Empire and who is, by the mercy of God, king of the Franks and the Lombards." According to this title, Charlemagne was not the Roman emperor crowned by the pope but rather God's emperor, who governed the Roman Empire along with his many other duties.

Charlemagne's Heirs

When Charlemagne died, only one of his sons remained alive: Louis, nicknamed "the Pious." (See Genealogy 3.1: The Carolingians.) Emperor he was (from 814 to 840), but over an empire that was a conglomeration of territories with little unity. He had to contend with the revolts of his sons, the depredations of outside invaders, the regional interests of counts and bishops, and above all an enormous variety of languages, laws, customs, and traditions, all of which tended to pull his empire apart. He contended with gusto, his chief unifying tool being Christianity. Calling on the help of the monastic reformer Benedict of Aniane (d.821), Louis imposed the Benedictine Rule on all the monasteries in Francia. Monks and abbots served as his chief advisors. Louis's imperial model was Theodosius I, who had made Christianity the official religion of the Roman Empire (see p. 7). Organizing inquests by the *missi*, Louis looked into allegations of exploitation of the poor, standardized the procedures of his chancery, and put all Frankish bishops and monasteries under his control.

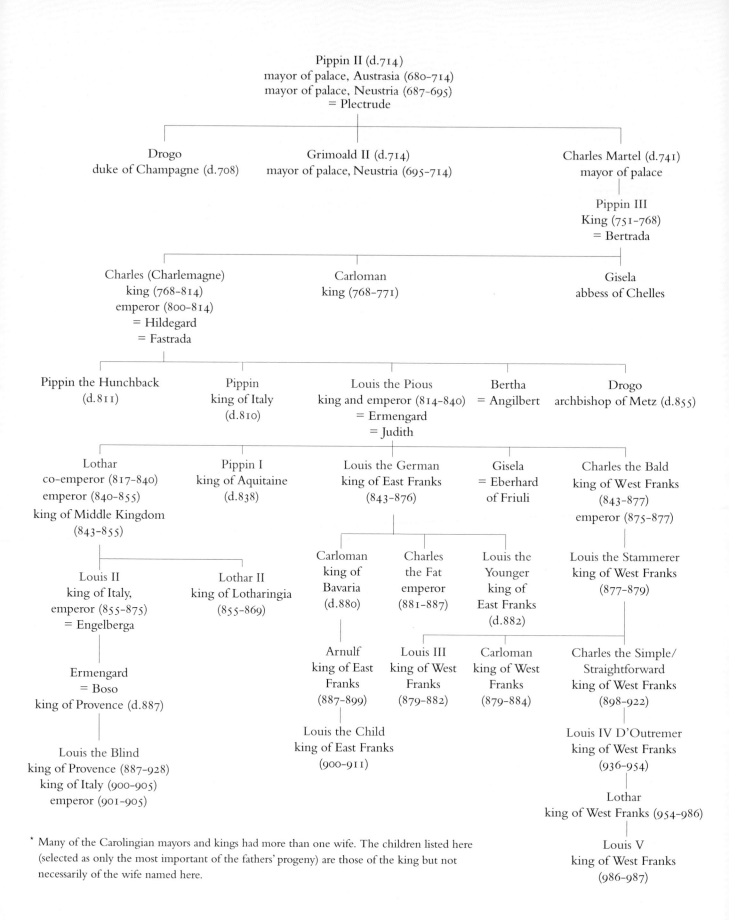

Pippin II (d.714)
mayor of palace, Austrasia (680–714)
mayor of palace, Neustria (687–695)
= Plectrude

Drogo
duke of Champagne (d.708)

Grimoald II (d.714)
mayor of palace, Neustria (695–714)

Charles Martel (d.741)
mayor of palace

Pippin III
King (751–768)
= Bertrada

Charles (Charlemagne)
king (768–814)
emperor (800–814)
= Hildegard
= Fastrada

Carloman
king (768–771)

Gisela
abbess of Chelles

Pippin the Hunchback
(d.811)

Pippin
king of Italy
(d.810)

Louis the Pious
king and emperor (814–840)
= Ermengard
= Judith

Bertha
= Angilbert

Drogo
archbishop of Metz (d.855)

Lothar
co-emperor (817–840)
emperor (840–855)
king of Middle Kingdom
(843–855)

Pippin I
king of Aquitaine
(d.838)

Louis the German
king of East Franks
(843–876)

Gisela
= Eberhard
of Friuli

Charles the Bald
king of West Franks
(843–877)
emperor (875–877)

Louis II
king of Italy,
emperor (855–875)
= Engelberga

Lothar II
king of Lotharingia
(855–869)

Carloman
king of
Bavaria
(d.880)

Charles
the Fat
emperor
(881–887)

Louis the
Younger
king of
East Franks
(d.882)

Louis the Stammerer
king of West Franks
(877–879)

Ermengard
= Boso
king of Provence (d.887)

Arnulf
king of East
Franks
(887–899)

Louis III
king of West
Franks
(879–882)

Carloman
king of West
Franks
(879–884)

Charles the Simple/
Straightforward
king of West Franks
(898–922)

Louis the Blind
king of Provence (887–928)
king of Italy (900–905)
emperor (901–905)

Louis the Child
king of East Franks
(900–911)

Louis IV D'Outremer
king of West Franks
(936–954)

Lothar
king of West Franks (954–986)

Louis V
king of West Franks
(986–987)

* Many of the Carolingian mayors and kings had more than one wife. The children listed here
(selected as only the most important of the fathers' progeny) are those of the king but not
necessarily of the wife named here.

Charlemagne had employed his sons as "sub-kings," but Louis politicized his family still more. Early in his reign he had his wife crowned empress; named his first-born son, Lothar, emperor and co-ruler; and had his other sons, Pippin and Louis (later called "the German"), agree to be sub-kings under their older brother. It was neatly planned. But when Louis's first wife died he married Judith, daughter of a relatively obscure kindred (the Welfs) that would later become enormously powerful in Saxony and Bavaria. In 823 she and Louis had a son, Charles (later "the Bald"), and this upset the earlier division of the empire. A family feud turned into bitter civil war as brothers fought one another and their father for titles and kingdoms. In 833 matters came to a head when Louis, effectively taken prisoner by Lothar, was forced to do public penance. Lothar expected the ritual to get his father off the throne for life. But Louis played one son against the other and made a swift comeback. The episode showed how Carolingian rulers could portray themselves as accountable to God and yet, in that very act of subservience, make themselves even more sacred and authoritative in the eyes of their subjects.

After Louis's death a period of war and uncertainty (840–843) among the three remaining brothers (Pippin had died in 838) ended with the Treaty of Verdun (843). (See Map 3.4a.) The empire was divided into three parts, an arrangement that would roughly define the future political contours of Western Europe. The western third, bequeathed to Charles

Genealogy 3.1 (facing page):
The Carolingians*

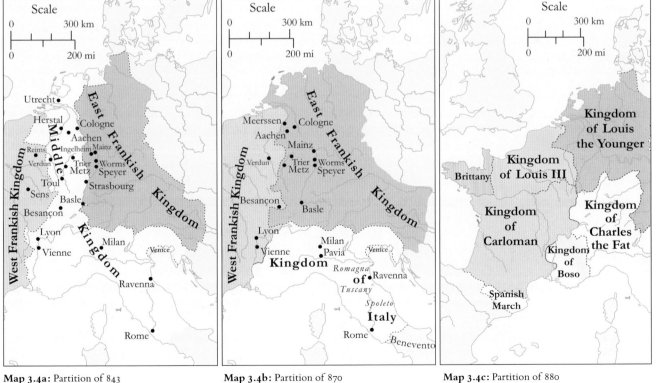

Map 3.4a: Partition of 843 (Treaty of Verdun)

Map 3.4b: Partition of 870 (Treaty of Meerssen)

Map 3.4c: Partition of 880

the Bald (r.843–877), would eventually become France, and the eastern third, given to Louis the German (r.843–876), would become Germany. The "Middle Kingdom," which became Lothar's portion (r. as co-emperor 817; as emperor 840–855), had a different fate: parts of it were absorbed by France and Germany, while the rest eventually coalesced into the modern states of Belgium, the Netherlands, and Luxembourg—the so-called Benelux countries—as well as Switzerland and Italy. All this was far in the future. As the brothers had their own children, new divisions were tried: one in 870 (the Treaty of Meerssen), for example, and another in 880. (See Maps 3.4b and 3.4c.) After the death of Emperor Charles the Fat (888), various kings and lesser rulers, many of them non-Carolingians, came to the fore in the irrevocably splintered empire.

Dynastic problems were not the primary cause of the breakup of the Carolingian Empire, however. Nor were the invasions by outsiders—Vikings, Muslims, and, starting in 899, Magyars (Hungarians)—which harassed the Frankish Kingdom throughout the ninth century. These certainly weakened the kings: without a standing army, they were unable to respond to lightning raids, and what regional defense there was fell into the hands of local leaders, such as counts. The Carolingians lost prestige and money as they paid out tribute to stave off further attacks. But the invasions were not all bad; to some degree they even helped fortify the king. The Carolingian Empire atomized because linguistic and other differences between regions—and familial and other ties within regions—were simply too strong to be overcome by directives from a central court. Even today a unified Europe is only a distant ideal. Anyway, as we shall see, fragmentation had its own strengths and possibilities.

The Wealth of a Local Economy

The Carolingian economy was based on plunder, trade, and agriculture. After the Carolingians could push no further and the raids of Charlemagne's day came to an end, trade and land became the chief resources of the kingdom. To the north, in Viking trading stations such as Haithabu (see Map 3.3), archaeologists have found Carolingian glass and pots alongside Islamic coins and cloth, showing that the Carolingian economy meshed with that of the Abbasid caliphate. Silver from the Islamic world probably came north from the Caspian Sea, up the Volga River to the Baltic Sea. (You can figure out the likely route from the map at the front of this book.) There the coins were melted down and the silver traded to the Carolingians in return for wine, jugs, glasses, and other manufactured goods. The Carolingians turned the silver into coins of their own, to be used throughout the empire for small-scale local trade. Baltic Sea emporia such as Haithabu supplemented those—Quentovic and Dorestad, for example (see Map 2.3 on p. 59)—that served the North Sea trade.

Nevertheless, the backbone of the Carolingian economy was land. A few written records, called *polyptyques*, document the output of the Carolingian great estates—"villae," as they were called in Latin, "manors," as we term them. On the far-flung and widely scattered manors of rich landowners—churches, monasteries, kings, and aristocrats—a major reorganization and rationalization was taking place. The most enterprising landlords instituted a three-field rather than a two-field cultivation system. It meant that two-thirds of the land rather than one-half was sown with crops each year, yielding a tidy surplus.

Consider Lambesc, near Aix-en Provence, one of the many manors belonging to the cathedral of Saint Mary of Marseille. It was not a compact farm but rather a conglomeration of essential parts, with its lands, woods, meadows, and vineyards scattered about the countryside. All were worked by peasant families, some legally free, some unfree, each settled on its own holding—here called a *colonica*; elsewhere often called a *mansus*, or "manse"— usually including a house, a garden, small bits of several fields, and so on. The peasants farmed the land that belonged to them and paid yearly dues to their lord—in this case the Church of Saint Mary, which, in its *polyptyque*, kept careful track of what was owed:

> [There is a] holding [*colonica*] in Siverianis [a place-name within the manor of Lambesc]. Valerius, colonus [tenant]. Wife [is named] Dominica. Ducsana, a daughter 5 years old. An infant at the breast. It pays in tax: 1 pig; 1 suckling [pig]; 2 fattened hens; 10 chickens; 20 eggs.[12]

Valerius and his wife apparently did not work the *demesne*—the land, woods, meadows, and vineyards directly held by Saint Mary—but other tenants had that duty. At Nidis, in the region of Grasse, Bernarius owed daily service, probably farming the *demesne*, and also paid a penny (1 denarius) in yearly dues. On many manors women were required to feed the lord's chickens or busy themselves in the *gynecaeum*, the women's workshop, where they made and dyed cloth and sewed garments.

Clearly the labor was onerous and the accounting system complex and unwieldy; but manors organized on the model of Saint Mary made a profit. Like the Church of Saint Mary and other lords, the Carolingian kings benefited from their own extensive manors. Nevertheless, farming did not return great surpluses, and as the lands belonging to the king were divided up in the wake of the partitioning of the empire, Carolingian dependence on manors scattered throughout their kingdom proved to be a source of weakness.

The Carolingian Renaissance

With the profits from their manors, some monasteries and churches invested in books. These were not made of paper—a product that, although used in the Islamic world, did not reach the West until the eleventh century—but rather of parchment: animal skins soaked, scraped, and cut into sheets. Nor were Carolingian books printed, since the printing press was not invented until around 1450. Rather, they were manuscripts, written by hand in scribal workshops (*scriptoria*; sing. *scriptorium*). Consider the monastery of Saint-Amand (today in northern France), which made books both for its own use and for the needs of many other institutions: its *scriptorium* produced Gospels, works of the Church Fathers, grammars, and above all liturgical books for the Mass and other church services.

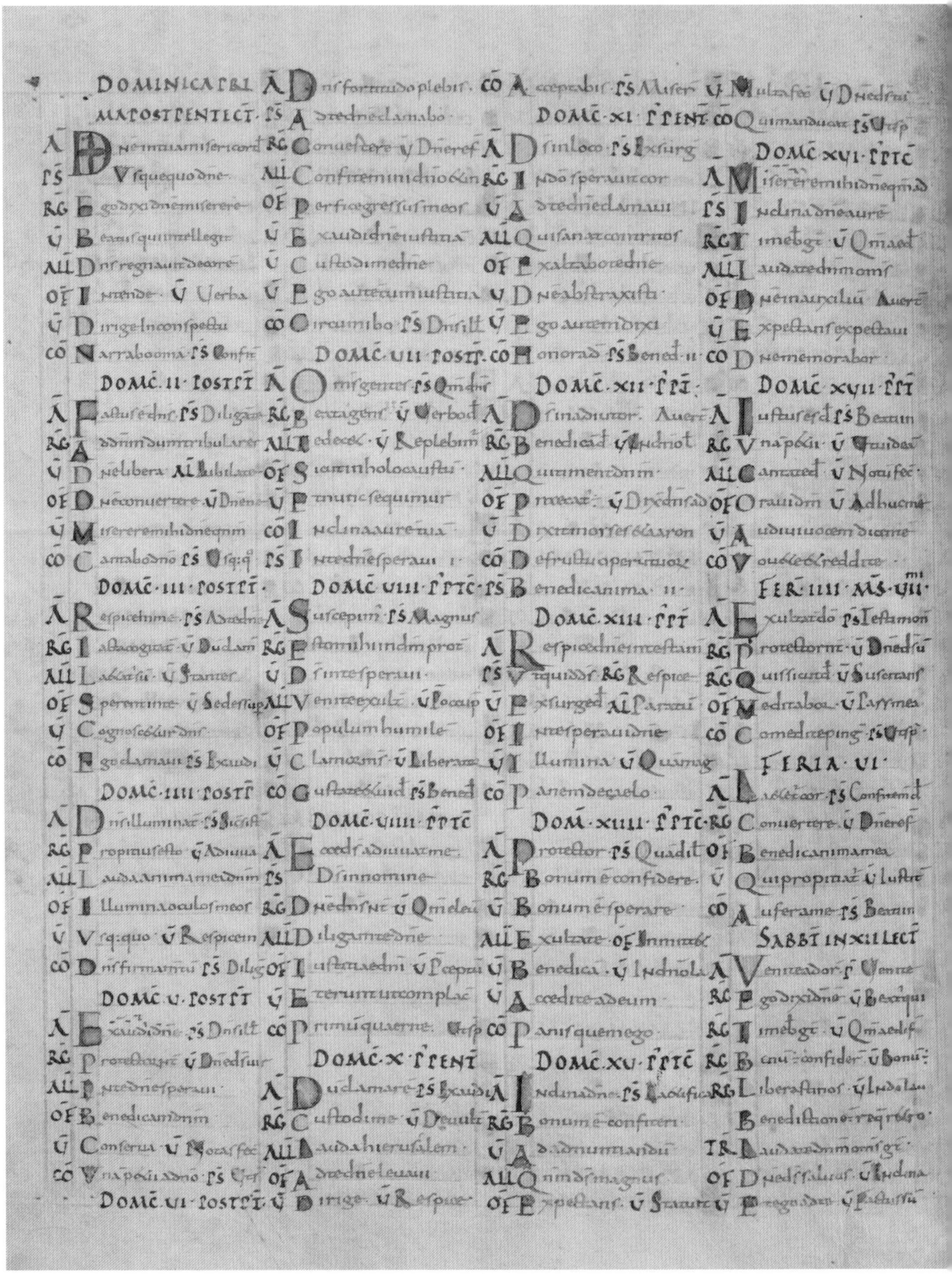

Plate 3.5: Sacramentary of Saint-Germain-des-Prés (early 9th cent.). The scribe of this list of incipits (the "first words") of mass chants provided a musical reminder of one (seven lines from the bottom, on the left) by adding neumes above the first words, "Exaudi Domine," "Hear, O Lord."

Plate 3.5 shows a page from a Sacramentary (a liturgical book) that was produced at Saint-Amand for the Parisian monastery of Saint-Germain-des-Prés. For the most part, it provided only the texts of mass chants. But in one instance the scribe added some "dots and dashes" above a word. They illustrate one early form of musical notation. These "notes" did not indicate pitches to the monks who sang the melodies. Nor did they suggest rhythms. But they did remind the monks of the melody associated with one chant beginning with the word *Exaudi*.

The development of written music was a response to royal policy. Before the Carolingians came to power, the music at churches and monasteries had been determined by local oral traditions. But the special relationship that the Carolingians had with Rome included importing Roman chant melodies to Francia. This reform—the imposition of the so-called "Gregorian chant"—posed great practical difficulties. It meant that every monk and priest had to learn a year's worth of Roman music; but how? A few cantors were imported from Rome; but without a system of notation, it was easy to forget new tunes. The monks of Saint-Amand were part of a revolution in musical technology.

The same Sacramentary reveals another key development of the era: the use of minuscule writing. As at Byzantium, and at about the same time, the Carolingians experimented with letterforms that were quick to write and easy to read. "Caroline minuscule" lasted into the eleventh century, when it gave way to a more angular script, today called "Gothic." But the Carolingian letter forms were rediscovered in the fifteenth century—by scholars who thought that they represented ancient Roman writing!—and they became the model for modern lower-case printed fonts.

The Carolingian court was behind much of this activity. Most of the centers of learning, scholarship, and book production began under men and women who at one time or another were part of the royal court. Alcuin, perhaps the most famous of the Carolingian intellectuals, was "imported" by Charlemagne from England—where, as we have seen (p. 66), monastic scholarship flourished—to head up the king's palace school. Chief advisor to Charlemagne and tutor to the entire royal family, Alcuin eventually became abbot of Saint-Martin of Tours, grooming a new generation of teachers. More unusual but equally telling was the experience of Gisela, Charlemagne's sister. She too was a key royal advisor, the one who alerted the others at home about Charlemagne's imperial coronation at Rome in 800. She was also abbess of Chelles, a center of manuscript production in its own right. Chelles had a library, and its nuns were well educated. They wrote learned letters and composed a history (the "Prior Metz Annals") that treated the rise of the Carolingians as a tale of struggle between brothers, sons, and fathers eased by the wise counsel of mothers, aunts, and sisters.

Women and the poor make up the largely invisible half of the Carolingian Renaissance. But without doubt some were part of it. One of Charlemagne's capitularies ordered that the cathedrals and monasteries of his kingdom should teach reading and writing to all who could learn. There were enough complaints (by rich people) about upstart peasants who found a place at court that we may be sure that some talented sons of the poor were getting an education. A few churchmen expressed the hope that schools for "children" would be established even in small villages and hamlets. Were they thinking of girls as well as boys? Certainly one woman—admittedly noble—in the mid-ninth century in the south of France proves that education was available even to laywomen. We would never know about Dhuoda had she not worried enough about her absent son to write a *Handbook for Her Son* full of advice. Only incidentally does it become clear in the course of her deeply felt moral text that Dhuoda was drawing on an excellent education: she clearly knew the Bible, writings of the Church Fathers, Gregory the Great, and "moderns," like Alcuin. Her Latin was fluent and sophisticated. And she understood the value of the written word:

> My great concern, my son William, is to offer you helpful words. My burning, watchful heart especially desires that you may have in this little volume what I have longed to be written down for you, about how you were born through God's grace.[13]

Plate 3.6 (facing page): The Pleiades (2nd quarter, 9th cent.). In this Carolingian manuscript from the region between France and Germany (today), an artist painted nearly forty miniatures of the constellations named in a poem by Aratos.

The original manuscript of Dhuoda's text is not extant. Had it survived, it would no doubt have looked like other "practical texts" of the time: the "folios" (pages) would have been written in Caroline minuscule, each carefully designed to set off the poetry—Dhuoda's own and quotes from others—from the prose; the titles of each chapter (there are nearly a hundred, each very short) would have been enlivened with delicately colored capital letters. The manuscript would probably not have been illuminated; fancy books were generally made for royalty, for prestigious ceremonial occasions, or for books that were especially esteemed, such as the Gospels.

There were, however, many such lavish productions. In fact, Carolingian art and architecture mark a turning point. For all its richness, Merovingian culture had not stressed artistic expression, though some of the monasteries inspired by Saint Columbanus produced a few illuminated manuscripts. By contrast, the Carolingians, admirers and imitators of Christian Rome, vigorously promoted a vast, eclectic, and ideologically motivated program of artistic work. They were reviving the Roman Empire. We have already seen how Charlemagne brought the very marble of Rome and Ravenna home to Aachen to build his new palace complex. A similar impulse inspired Carolingian art.

As with texts, so with pictures: the Carolingians revered and imitated the past while building on and changing it. Their manuscript illuminations were inspired by a vast repertory of models: from the British Isles (where, as we have seen, a rich synthesis of decorative and representational styles had a long tradition), from late-antique Italy (which yielded its models in old manuscripts), and from Byzantium (which may have inadvertently provided some artists, fleeing iconoclasm, as well as manuscripts).

In Plate 3.6, the heads of seven beautiful women emerge from cloud-banks in a ninth-century manuscript on the heavenly constellations. The book was a copy of the *Phainomena* by the classical Greek poet Aratos (*fl.* 3rd cent. BCE) in the later Latin version by Germanicus Caesar (*fl.* 1st cent. CE). The women represent the Pleiades, the seven daughters of Atlas who were turned into stars. Their hair styles and even the modeling of their heads were inspired by art that harks back to the classical style of the Venus in Plate 1.1. The woman

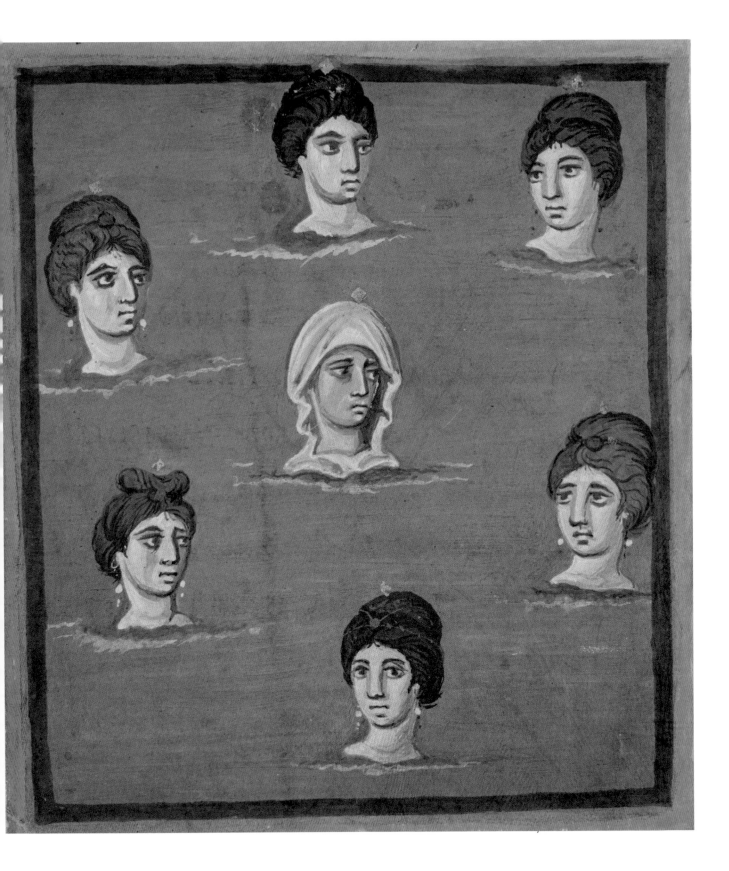

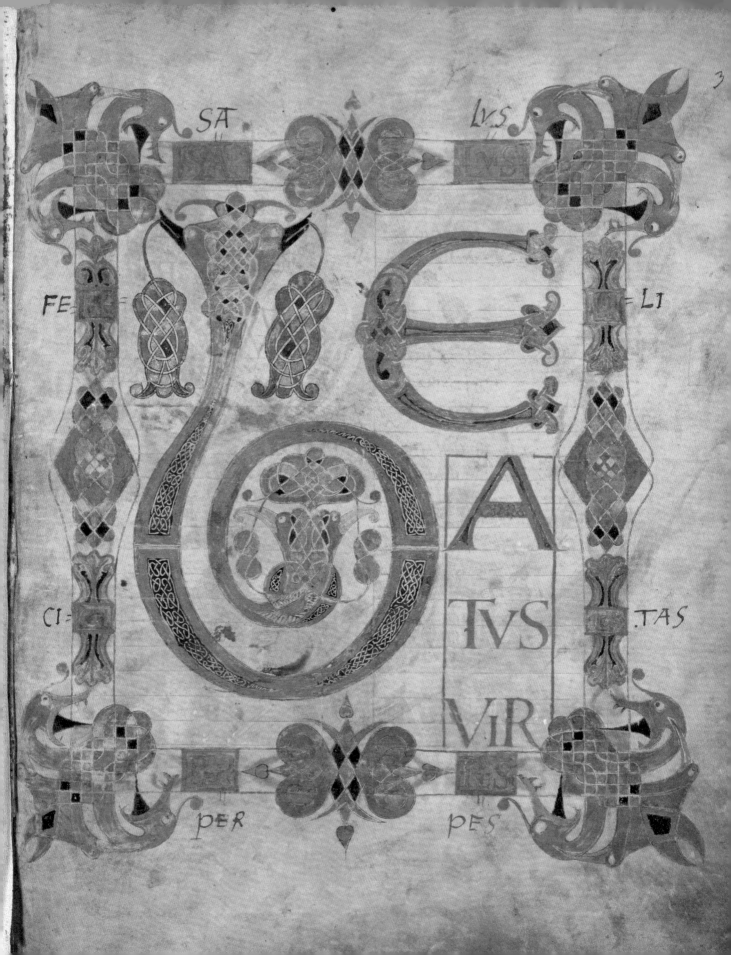

in the center wears a veil; she was Merope, who hid herself out of shame for loving a mortal. In this manuscript ancient models inspired both text and illustration.

An entirely different tradition lies behind the grand letters on the opening page of a Psalter (Plate 3.7). Painted at the same time as Plate 3.6, the only "classical" element here is the Latin language. Rather, the page owes much to the decorative style of the British Isles, as illustrated (for example) by Plate 2.7 (on p. 69). "Beatus vir," ("Blessed is the man"), the first words of the first psalm, are here given luminous treatment with the use of gold leaf and a restrained palette. The page is then framed with designs of the same colors, with interlaced birds and dragon heads at the corners.

Combining the two traditions in a startlingly original manner, an artist at Saint-Amand (where Plate 3.5 was also produced) created a classically inspired scene framed by columns sporting the stylized birds and interlace designs of the Insular style. (See Plate 3.8.) Much as in a Pompeian wall painting, the figure—the evangelist John—has volume and weight. As at Pompeii, he seems to live in a world of his own, separate from the viewer. But unlike at Pompeii (see, for example, Plate 1.2), the atmosphere of that world has become three well-defined zones: at the bottom, earth of brushy brown; in the middle, a huge swathe of blue broken by ornamental trees; above, clouds of bright yellow and orange. The figure, too, has an unclassical twist, its pleated drapery giving it a somewhat frenetic urgency. By mixing various styles, the artist found a new mode of expressing the transcendent.

In this portrait, Saint John seems to be caught in the act of listening to a voice, ready to write down the words. The artist is almost telling us a story about John. But the narrative impulse is given its fullest expression in the Utrecht Psalter, a manuscript containing all 150 psalms and 16 other songs known as canticles. Here each poem is accompanied by drawings that depict its important elements in unified composition. In Plate 3.9, the illustration for Psalm 8, the artist sketched sheep and oxen on the bottom left, birds flying and fish swimming on the bottom right, to render literally verses 8 and 9:

> Thou hast subjected all things under his feet, all sheep and oxen: moreover the beasts also of the fields. / The birds of the air, and the fishes of the sea, that pass through the paths of the sea.

It may plausibly be said that the various artistic styles elaborated during the Carolingian Renaissance—fed by classical, decorative, abstract traditions but combined in new and original ways—formed the basis of all subsequent Western art.

★　　★　　★　　★　　★

In the course of the eighth and ninth centuries, the three heirs of Rome established clearly separate identities, each largely bound up with its religious affiliation. Byzantium saw itself as the radiating center of Orthodox faith; the caliphate asserted itself as the guarantor of Islam; and Francia and the papacy cooperated and vied for the leadership of Christian Europe. From this perspective, there were few commonalities. Yet today we are struck

Plate 3.7 (facing page): Psalter Page (2nd quarter, 9th cent.). In this sumptuous manuscript dedicated to King Louis the German (r.843–876) the artist (a monk at the monastery of Saint Omer, today in northern France) drew on the decorative, abstract traditions of the British Isles. Nevertheless, following the principle of "less is more," he pared down the colors and the "busyness" of his model, as a quick comparison with Plate 2.7, p. 69, illustrates.

Following pages:

Plate 3.8: Saint John (2nd half, 9th cent.). Neither classically naturalistic nor entirely decorative in inspiration, this painting of the evangelist Saint John evokes a heavenly reality that is only vaguely anchored in earthly things. The book that John is writing (note the ink horn in his left hand) gives the opening line of his Gospel: "In principio erat verbum" ("In the beginning was the Word").

Plate 3.9: Utrecht Psalter (c.820–835). Never completed, the Utrecht Psalter was commissioned by Archbishop Ebbo of Reims and executed at a nearby monastery. Providing a visual "running commentary" on every psalm, it may have been meant for Emperor Louis the Pious and his wife Queen Judith.

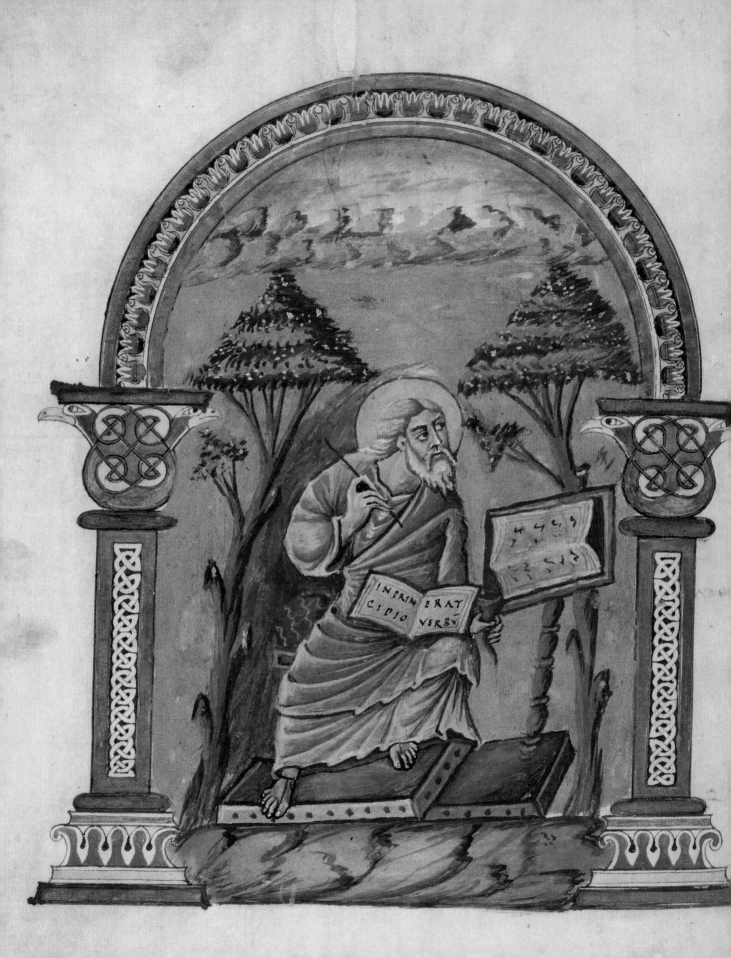

CIRCUMDABITTE
ETPROPTERHANCINALTU
INREGREDERE · DNSIUDI
CATPOPULOS
IUDICAMEDNESECUN
DUIUSTITIAMMEA · ET
SECUNDUMINNOCEN
TIAMMEAMSUPERME
CONSUMMETURNEQUITI
APECCATORUETDIRI
GESIUSTUM · ETSCRUTANS
CORDAETRENESDS
IUSTUMADIUTORIUM
MEUMADNO · QUISAL
VIII INFINEM

UOSFACITRECTOSCORDE
DSIUDEXIUSTUSETFORTIS
ETPATIENS · NUMQUIDI
RASCETURPERSINGU
LOSDIES
NISICONUERSIFUERITIS
GLADIUMSUUMUIBRA
BITARCUMSUUMTE
TENDITETPARAUITILLU
ETINEOPARAUITUASA
MORTIS · SAGITTASSU
ASARDENTIBUSEFFECIT
ECCEPARTURITINIUS
TITIAM · CONCEPITDO
PROTORCOLARIBUS

LOREMETPEPERITINIQUI
TATEM
LACUMAPERUITETEFFODIT
EUM · ETINCIDITINFOUE
AMQUAMFECIT
CONUERTETURDOLOR
EIUSINCAPUTEIUS · ET
INUERTICEMIPSIUSINI
QUITASEIUSDESCENDET
CONFITEBORDNOSECUN
DUMIUSTITIAMEIUS ·
ETPSALLAMNOMINI
DNIALTISSIMI ;

PSALMUSDAUID

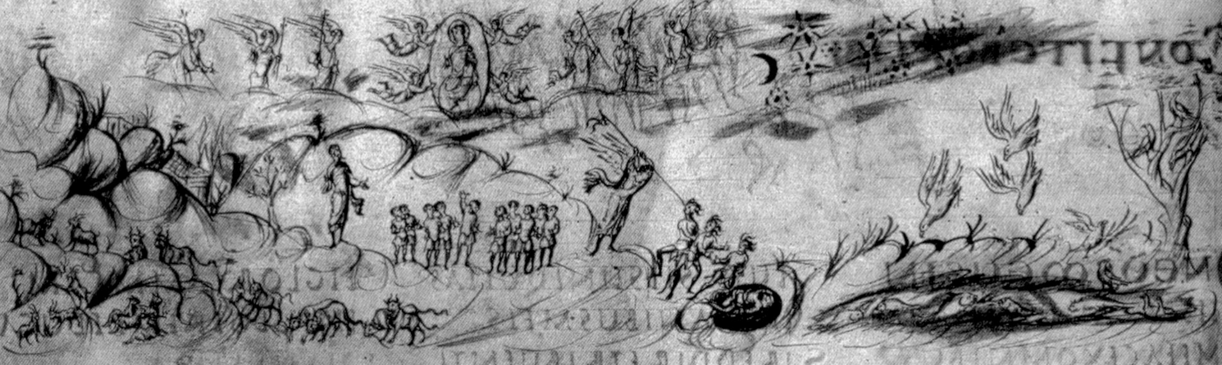

QUAMADMIRABILE
ESTNOMENTUUM
INUNIUERSATERRA
QNMELEUATAESTMAG
NIFICENTIATUA · SU
PERCAELOS
EXOREINFANTIUMETLAC

TANTIUM · PERFECISTI
LAUDEMPROPTERINI
MICOSTUOS · UTDESTRU
ASINIMICUMETULTORE
QNMUIDEBOCAELOSTU
OSOPERADIGITORU
TUORUM · LUNAMETS
TELLASQUAETUFUNDASTI

QUIDESTHOMOQUOD
MEMORESEIUS · AUT
FILIUSHOMINISQUO
NIAMUISITASEUM
MINUISTIEUMPAULOMI
NUSABANGELIS · GLO
RIAETHONORECORO
NASTIEUM · ETCONS

more by the similarities than by the differences. All were centralizing monarchies shored up by military might. All had a bit of wealth, though the eastern half certainly had more than the western. All had pretensions to God-given power. And all used culture and scholarship to give luster and expression to their political regimes. All may also have known, without explicitly admitting it, how strong the forces of dissolution were.

CHAPTER THREE KEY EVENTS

732	Charles Martel's victory over Muslim-led army near Poitiers
750	Abbasid caliphate begins
751	Deposition of last Merovingian king; Pippin III (the first Carolingian king) elevated to kingship
756	"Donation of Pippin"
756	Emirate of Córdoba established
762	Baghdad founded as the Abbasid capital city
768–814	Reign of Charlemagne (Charles the Great)
800	Charlemagne crowned emperor
814–840	Reign of Louis the Pious
843	End of iconoclasm in Byzantine Empire
843	Treaty of Verdun
c.860	Arab invasions of Byzantium end
863	Missionary expedition of Constantine (Cyril) and Methodius begins
c.864	Bulgarian Khan Boris-Michael converts to Christianity

NOTES

1 Constantine/Cyril, *Prologue to the Gospel*, in *Reading the Middle Ages: Sources from Europe, Byzantium, and the Islamic World*, ed. Barbara H. Rosenwein, 2nd ed. (Toronto: University of Toronto Press, 2014), p. 159.

2 For one such seal, see *Reading the Middle Ages*, Plate 11, p. 247.

3 Pope Nicholas I, *Letter to Answer the Bulgarians' Questions*, in *Reading the Middle Ages*, p. 163.

4 *The Life of Constantine-Cyril*, quoted in *Byzantium: Church, Society, and Civilization Seen through Contemporary Eyes*, ed. Deno John Geanakoplos (Chicago: University of Chicago Press, 1984), p. 409.

5 "Imports of Iraq," in *Medieval Trade in the Mediterranean World: Illustrative Documents*, trans. Robert S. Lopez and Irving W. Raymond (New York: Columbia University Press, 1997), p. 28.

6　Abu Nuwas, *Turning the Tables*, in *Reading the Middle Ages*, p. 123.

7　Quoted in Michael Cooperson, *Al-Ma'mun* (Oxford: Oneworld, 2005), p. 99.

8　Al-Bukhari, *On Fasting*, in *Reading the Middle Ages*, p. 122.

9　The *Chronicle of Albelda*, in *Reading the Middle Ages*, p. 124–25.

10　Pope Stephen II, *Letter to King Pippin III*, in *Reading the Middle Ages*, p. 134.

11　Einhard, *Life of Charlemagne*, in *Reading the Middle Ages*, p. 145.

12　*Polyptyque of the Church of Saint Mary of Marseille*, in *Carolingian Civilization: A Reader*, ed. Paul Edward Dutton, 2nd ed. (Toronto: University of Toronto Press, 2004), p. 215.

13　Dhuoda, *Handbook for her Son*, in *Reading the Middle Ages*, p. 151.

FURTHER READING

Bennison, Amira K. *The Great Caliphs: The Golden Age of the 'Abbasid Empire*. New Haven, CT, and London: Yale University Press, 2009.

Benson, Bobrick. *The Caliph's Splendor: Islam and the West in the Gold Age of Baghdad*. New York: Simon and Schuster, 2012.

Berend, Nora, ed. *Christianization and the Rise of Christian Monarchy: Scandinavia, Central Europe and Rus' c.900–1200*. Cambridge: Cambridge University Press, 2007.

Collins, Samuel W. *The Carolingian Debate over Sacred Space*. New York: Palgrave Macmillan, 2012.

Cooperson, Michael. *Al-Ma'mun*. Oxford: Oneworld, 2005.

Costambeys, Marios, Matthew Innes, and Simon MacLean. *The Carolingian World*. Cambridge: Cambridge University Press, 2011.

DeJong, Mayke. *The Penitential State: Authority and Atonement in the Ages of Louis the Pious, 814–840*. Cambridge: Cambridge University Press, 2009.

Fouracre, Paul. *The Age of Charles Martel*. Harlow, Essex: Longman, 2000.

Goldberg, Eric J. *Struggle for Empire: Kingship and Conflict under Louis the German, 817–876*. Ithaca, NY: Cornell University Press, 2006.

Hallaq, Wael B. *The Origins and Evolution of Islamic Law*. Cambridge: Cambridge University Press, 2005.

Herrin, Judith. *Women in Purple: Rulers of Medieval Byzantium*. Princeton, NJ: Princeton University Press, 2002.

Kennedy, Philip F. *Abu Nuwas: A Genius of Poetry*. Oxford: Oneworld, 2005.

Levy, Kenneth. *Gregorian Chant and the Carolingians*. Princeton, NJ: Princeton University Press, 1998.

McCormick, Michael. *Origins of the European Economy: Communications and Commerce, AD 300–900*. Cambridge: Cambridge University Press, 2001.

McKitterick, Rosamond. *Charlemagne: The Formation of a European Identity*. Cambridge: Cambridge University Press, 2008.

Nelson, Janet L. *Charles the Bald*. London: Longman, 1992.

———. *The Frankish World, 750–900*. London: Hambledon Press, 1996.

Sophoulis, Panos. *Byzantium and Bulgaria, 775–831*. Leiden: Brill, 2012.

Treadgold, Warren. *The Byzantine Revival, 780–842*. Stanford, CA: Stanford University Press, 1988.

Verhulst, Adriaan. *The Carolingian Economy*. Cambridge: Cambridge University Press, 2002.

Whittow, Mark. *The Making of Byzantium, 600–1025*. Berkeley: University of California Press, 1996.

Wormald, Patrick, and Janet L. Nelson, eds. *Lay Intellectuals in the Carolingian World*. Cambridge: Cambridge University Press, 2011.

To test your knowledge of this chapter, please go to
www.utphistorymatters.com
for Study Questions.

FOUR

POLITICAL COMMUNITIES REORDERED
(c.900–c.1050)

THE LARGE-SCALE centralized governments of the ninth century dissolved in the tenth. The fission was least noticeable at Byzantium, where, although important landowning families emerged as brokers of patronage and power, the primacy of the emperor was never effectively challenged. In the Islamic world, however, new dynastic groups established themselves as regional rulers. In Western Europe, Carolingian kings ceased to control land and men, while new political entities—some extremely local and weak, others quite strong and unified—emerged in their wake.

BYZANTIUM: THE STRENGTHS AND LIMITS OF CENTRALIZATION

By 1025 the Byzantine Empire once again touched the Danube and Euphrates Rivers. Its emperors maintained the traditional cultural importance of Constantinople by carefully orchestrating the radiating power of the imperial court. Yet at the same time, powerful men in the countryside gobbled up land and dominated the peasantry, challenging the dominance of the center.

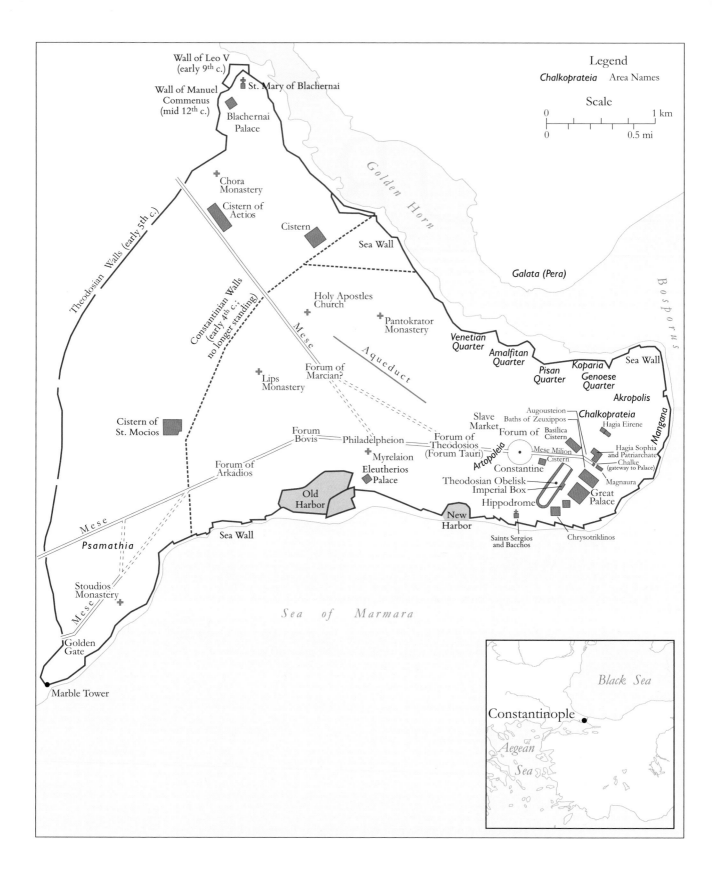

Wall of Leo V
(early 9th c.)

Wall of Manuel
Commenus
(mid 12th c.)

St. Mary of Blachernai

Blachernai
Palace

Golden Horn

Legend

Chalkoprateia Area Names

Scale

0   1 km
0   0.5 mi

Chora
Monastery

Cistern of
Aetios

Cistern

Theodosian Walls (early 5th c.)

Sea Wall

Galata (Pera)

Bosporus

Constantinian Walls
(early 4th c.;
no longer standing)

Holy Apostles
Church

Mese

Pantokrator
Monastery

Aqueduct

*Venetian
Quarter*

*Amalfitan
Quarter*

*Pisan
Quarter*

Koparia

Sea Wall

*Genoese
Quarter*

Forum of
Marcian?

Lips
Monastery

Akropolis

Cistern of
St. Mocios

Slave
Market

Augousteion
Baths of Zeuxippos

Chalkoprateia

Hagia Eirene

Forum
Bovis

Philadelpheion

Forum of
Theodosios
(Forum Tauri)

Forum of
Constantine

Basilica
Cistern

Mangana

Mese Milion

Hagia Sophia
and Patriarchate

Forum of
Arkadios

Myrelaion

Eleutherios
Palace

Artopoleia

Cistern

Chalke
(gateway to Palace)

Constantine

Magnaura

Mese

Theodosian Obelisk
Imperial Box

Old
Harbor

New
Harbor

Hippodrome

Great
Palace

Psamathia

Sea Wall

Saints Sergios
and Bacchos

Chrysotriklinos

Stoudios
Monastery

Mese

Sea of Marmara

Golden
Gate

Marble Tower

Black Sea

Constantinople

*Aegean
Sea*

The Imperial Court

The Great Palace of Constantinople, a sprawling building complex begun under Constantine, was expanded and beautified under his successors. (See Map 4.1.) Far more than the symbolic emplacement of imperial power, it was the central command post of the empire. Servants, slaves, and grooms; top courtiers and learned clergymen; cousins, siblings, and hangers-on of the emperor and empress lived within its walls. Other courtiers—civil servants, officials, scholars, military men, advisers, and other dependents—lived as near to the palace as they could manage. They were "on call" at every hour. The emperor had only to give short notice and all assembled for impromptu but nevertheless highly choreographed ceremonies. These were in themselves instruments of power; the emperors manipulated courtly formalities to indicate new favorites or to signal displeasure.

The court was mainly a male preserve, but there were powerful women at the Great Palace as well. Consider Zoe (d.1050), the daughter of Constantine VIII. Contemporaries acknowledged her right to rule through her imperial blood. But they were happier when she was married, her blood-right legitimizing the rule of her husband. In most cases, though, the emperors themselves boasted the hereditary bloodline, and their wives were the ones to marry into the imperial family. In that case the empress normally could exercise power only as a widow acting on behalf of her children.

There was also a "third gender" at the Great Palace: eunuchs—men who had been castrated, normally as children, and raised to be teachers, doctors, or guardians of the women at court. Their status began to rise in the tenth century. Originally foreigners, they were increasingly recruited from the educated upper classes in the Byzantine Empire itself. In addition to their duties in the women's quarter of the palace, some of them accompanied the emperor during his most sacred and vulnerable moments—when he removed his crown; when he participated in religious ceremonies; even when he dreamed, at night. They hovered by his throne, like the angels flanking Mary in the diptych panel in Plate 2.1 on p. 46. No one, it was thought, was as faithful, trustworthy, or spiritually pure as a eunuch.

One tenth-century courtier complained that the imperial palace was rife with "suspicion, jealousy, fear, flattery, servility, ignorance, deceit, softness, languor, insolence, senselessness, peevishness, slander, and other impurities and filth."[1] Perhaps so; but it also assiduously cultivated the opposite image—of perfect, stable, eternal order. The emperor wore the finest silks, decorated with gold. In artistic representations, he was the largest figure. Sometimes he was shown seated on a high throne with admiring officials beneath him. At other times he stood, as in Plate 4.1, which depicts Emperor Basil II (r.976–1025), broad of shoulder and well-armed, as cowering figures grovel beneath his feet, and Christ, helped by an archangel, places a crown on his head.

Map 4.1 (facing page): Constantinople, *c.*1100

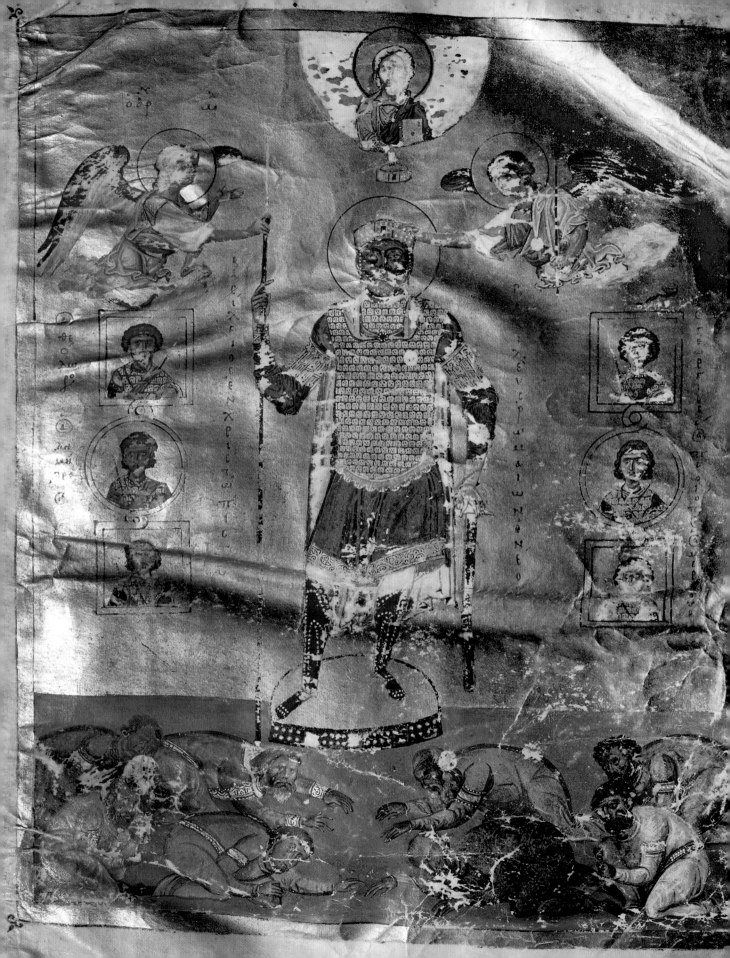

A Wide Embrace and Its Tensions

The artist who painted this image of Basil at the start of a Psalter had reason to substitute him for the usual portrait of King David, the presumed author of the psalms. Like the biblical slayer of Goliath, Basil also was a giant-slayer—in this case via wars of expansion. To be sure, he was following in the footsteps of earlier tenth-century soldier-emperors. Crete, lost to the Muslims in the ninth century, was retaken by Romanus II in 961; Nicephorus II reconquered Cyprus in 965 and Antioch in 969. But Basil conquered Bulgaria (in 1018), which, as we have seen (above pp. 82–83), had created a rival empire right on Byzantium's northern flank. Basil put the whole of the Balkans under Byzantine rule and divided its territory into themes. No wonder he was nicknamed the "Bulgar Slayer."

At the same time, moreover, Basil was busy setting up protectorates against the Muslims on his eastern front; at the end of his life he was preparing an expedition to Sicily. By 1025 the Byzantine army was rarely used to protect the empire's interior; it was mobilized to move outward, both east- and westward.

No longer was the Byzantine Empire the tight fist centered on Anatolia that it had been in the dark days of the eighth century. On the contrary, it was an open hand: sprawling, multi-ethnic, and multilingual. To the east it embraced Armenians, Syrians, and Arabs; to the north it included Slavs and Bulgarians (by now themselves Slavic speaking) as well as Pechenegs, a Turkic group that had served as allies of Bulgaria; to the west, in the Byzantine toe of Italy, it included Lombards, Italians, and Greeks. There must have been Muslims right in the middle of Constantinople: a mosque there, built in the eighth century, was restored and reopened in the eleventh century. Soldiers from the region of Kiev formed the backbone of Basil's "Varangian Guard," his elite troops. By the mid-eleventh century, Byzantine mercenaries included "Franks" (mainly from Normandy), Arabs, and Bulgarians as well. In spite of ingrained prejudices, Byzantine princesses had occasionally been married to foreigners before the tenth century, but in Basil's reign this happened to a sister of the emperor himself.

All this openness went only so far, however. Toward the middle of the eleventh century, the Jews of Constantinople were expelled and resettled in a walled quarter in Pera, on the other side of the Golden Horn (see Map 4.1). Even if they did not expel Jews so dramatically, many Byzantine cities forbade Jews from mixing with Christians. Around the same time, the rights of Jews as "Roman citizens" were denied; henceforth, in law at least, they had only servile status. The Jewish religion was condemned as a heresy.

Ethnic diversity was in part responsible for new regional political movements that threatened centralized imperial control. More generally, however, regional revolts were the result of the rise of a new class of wealthy provincial landowners, the *dynatoi* (sing. *dynatos*), "powerful men." Benefiting from a general quickening in the economy and the rise of new urban centers, they took advantage of the unaccustomed wealth, buying land from still impoverished peasants as yet untouched by the economic upswing. In his *Novel* (New Law) of 934, Emperor Romanus I Lecapenus (r.920–944) bewailed the "intrusion" of the rich

Plate 4.1 (facing page): Emperor Basil II (r.976–1025). Painted on shiny gold leaf, this depiction of Emperor Basil II shows him triumphant over his enemies. Beneath his armor he is wearing a long-sleeved purple tunic trimmed with gold. Two archangels hover above him. Gabriel, on the left, gives him a lance, while Michael, on the right, transmits to him the crown offered by Christ. The emperor grasps a sword in one hand, while in his other hand he holds a staff that touches the neck of one of the semi-prone figures beneath his feet. On either side of the emperor are busts of saints.

into a village or hamlet for the sake of a sale, gift, or inheritance.... For the domination of these persons has increased the great hardship of the poor ... [and] will cause no little harm to the commonwealth unless the present legislation puts an end to it first.[2]

The *dynatoi* made military men their clients (even if they were not themselves military men) and often held positions in government. The Dalasseni family was fairly typical of this group. The founder of the family was an army leader and governor of Antioch at the end of the tenth century. One of his sons, Theophylact, became governor of "Iberia"—not Spain but rather a theme on the very eastern edge of the empire. Another, Constantine, inherited his father's position at Antioch. With estates scattered throughout Anatolia and a network of connections to other powerful families, the Dalasseni at times could defy the emperor and even coordinate rebellions against him. From the end of the tenth century, imperial control had to contend with the decentralizing forces of provincial *dynatoi* such as these. But the emperors were not dethroned, and a man like Basil II could triumph over the families that challenged his reign to emerge even stronger than before.

Map 4.2: The Byzantine Empire, *c.*1025

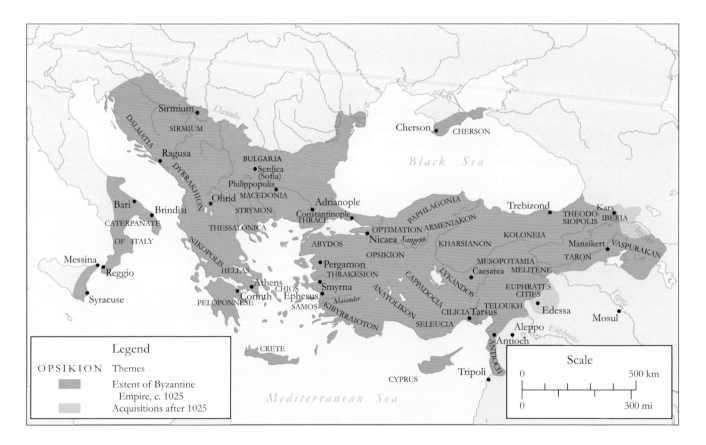

The Formation of Rus'

Basil made a different type of conquest when the leader of the Rus, a people settled in the region between the Gulf of Finland and the Black Sea, converted to the Byzantine form of Christianity. Well before the ninth century, Scandinavians—known as Rus in the East but as Vikings in the West—had traveled eastward, to the regions of Lake Ladoga and Lake Ilmen (see Maps 4.3 and 4.5). Mainly interested in trapping animals for furs and capturing people as slaves, they took advantage of river networks and other trade routes that led as far south as Iraq and as far west as Austria, exchanging their human and animal cargos for silks and silver. Other peoples in the region were also engaged in long-distance trade, above all the Khazars, whose powerful state, straddling the Black and Caspian Seas, dominated part of the silk road. (See Map 3.2 on p. 88 for the location of the Khazar Empire.) A Turkic-speaking group whose elites converted to Judaism in the ninth century, the Khazars were ruled by a khagan, much like the Avars and the Bulgars. Scandinavians had no khagans, but they were influenced enough by Khazar culture to adopt the title for the ruler of their own fledgling ninth-century state at Novgorod, the first Rus polity.

Soon northern Rus' (the apostrophe is used to indicate the state formed by the Rus people) had an affiliate in the south—in the region of Kiev. This was very close to the Khazars, to whom it is likely that the Kievan Rus at first paid tribute. While on occasion attacking both Khazars and Byzantines, Rus rulers saw their greatest advantage in good relations with the Byzantines, who wanted their fine furs, wax, honey, and—especially—slaves. In the course of the tenth century, with the blessing of the Byzantines, the Rus brought the Khazar Empire to its knees.

Nurtured through trade and military agreements, good relations between Rus' and Byzantium were sealed through religious conversion. In the mid-tenth century quite a few Christians lived in Rus'. But the official conversion of the Rus to Christianity came under Vladimir (r.980–1015). Ruler of Rus' by force of conquest (though from a princely family), Vladimir was anxious to court the elites of both Novgorod and Kiev. He did so through wars with surrounding peoples that brought him and his troops plunder and tribute. Strengthening his position still further, in 988 he adopted the Byzantine form of Christianity, took the name "Basil" in honor of Emperor Basil II, and married Anna, the emperor's sister. Christianization of the general population seems to have followed quickly. In any event, the *Russian Primary Chronicle*, a twelfth-century text based in part on earlier materials, reported that under Vladimir's son Yaroslav the Wise (r.1019–1054), "the Christian faith was fruitful and multiplied, while the number of monks increased, and new monasteries came into being."[3]

Vladimir's conversion was part of a larger process of state formation and Christianization taking place around the year 1000. In Scandinavia and the new states of East Central Europe, as we shall see, the process resulted in Catholic kingships rather than the Orthodox principality that Rus' became. Given its geographic location, it was anyone's guess how Rus' would go: it might have converted to the Roman form of Christianity of its western neighbors. Or it might have turned to Judaism under the influence of the Khazars. Or,

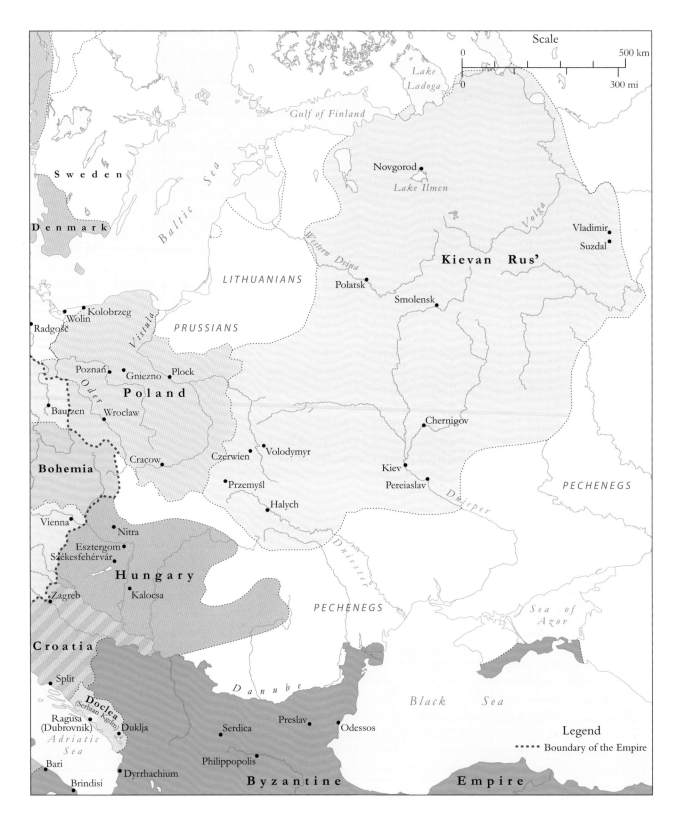

Scale

0   500 km

0   300 mi

Lake Ladoga

Gulf of Finland

S w e d e n

Baltic Sea

Novgorod

Lake Ilmen

Volga

Vladimir

Suzdal

D e n m a r k

LITHUANIANS

Western Dvina

Polatsk

Kievan Rus'

Kolobrzeg

Wolin

Radgošč

Vistula

PRUSSIANS

Smolensk

Poznań

Gniezno

Plock

Oder

Poland

Bautzen

Wrocław

Chernigov

Cracow

Czerwien

Volodymyr

Bohemia

Przemyśl

Kiev

Vienna

Nitra

Halych

Pereiaslav

PECHENEGS

Esztergom

Székesfehérvár

H u n g a r y

Kalocsa

Dnieper

Zagreb

Dniester

PECHENEGS

Sea of Azov

C r o a t i a

Split

Danube

Black Sea

Doclea
(Serbian K'gdm)

Ragusa
(Dubrovnik)

Duklja

Preslav

Odessos

Serdica

Adriatic Sea

Bari

Philippopolis

Legend

Brindisi

Dyrrhachium

B y z a n t i n e

E m p i r e

••••• Boundary of the Empire

indeed, it might have adopted Islam, given that the Volga Bulgars had converted to Islam in the early tenth century. It is likely that Vladimir chose the Byzantine form of Christianity because of the prestige of the empire under Basil.

That momentary decision left lasting consequences. Rus', ancestor of Russia, became the heir of the Byzantium. Choosing Christianity linked Russia to the West, but choosing the Byzantine form guaranteed that Russia would always stand apart from Europe.

DIVISION AND DEVELOPMENT IN THE ISLAMIC WORLD

While at Byzantium the forces of decentralization were feeble, they carried the day in the Islamic world. Where once the caliph at Baghdad or Samarra could boast collecting taxes from Kabul (today in Afghanistan) to Benghazi (today in Libya), in the eleventh century a bewildering profusion of regional groups and dynasties divided the Islamic world. Yet this was in general a period of prosperity and intellectual blossoming.

Map 4.3 (facing page): Kievan Rus', *c.*1050

The Emergence of Regional Powers

The Muslim conquest had not eliminated, but rather papered over, local powers and regional affiliations. While the Umayyad and Abbasid caliphates remained strong, they imposed their rule through their governors and army. But when the caliphate became weak, as it did in the tenth and eleventh centuries, old and new regional interests came to the fore.

A glance at a map of the Islamic world *c.*1000 (Map 4.4) shows, from east to west, the main new groups that emerged: the Samanids, Buyids, Hamdanids, Fatimids, and Zirids. But the map hides the many territories dominated by smaller independent rulers. North of the Fatimid Caliphate, al-Andalus had a parallel history. Its Umayyad ruler took the title of caliph in 929, but in the eleventh century he too was unable to stave off political fragmentation.

The key cause of the weakness of the Abbasid caliphate was lack of revenue. When landowners, governors, or recalcitrant military leaders in the various regions of the Islamic world refused to pay taxes into the treasury, the caliphs had to rely on the rich farmland of Iraq, long a stable source of income. But a deadly revolt lasting from 869 to 883 by the Zanj—black slaves from sub-Saharan Africa who had been put to work to turn marshes into farmland—devastated the Iraqi economy. Although the revolt was put down and the head of its leader was "displayed on a spear mounted in front of [the winning general] on a barge," there was no chance for the caliphate to recover.[4] In the tenth century the Qaramita (sometimes called the "Carmathians"), a sect of Shi'ites based in Arabia, found Iraq easy prey. The result was decisive: the caliphs could not pay their troops. New men— military leaders with their own armies and titles like "commander of commanders"—took the reins of power. They preserved the Abbasid line, but they reduced the caliph's political authority to nothing.

The new rulers represented groups that had long awaited power. The Buyids, for example, belonged to ancient warrior tribes from the mountains of Iran. Even in the tenth century, most were relatively new converts to Islam. Bolstered by long-festering local discontent, one of them became "commander of commanders" in 945. Thereafter, the Buyids, with help from their own Turkish mercenaries, dominated the region south of the Caspian Sea, including Baghdad (once again the home of the caliphs) itself. Yet already by the end of the tenth century, other local men were challenging Buyid rule in a political process—the progressive regionalization and fragmentation of power—echoed elsewhere in the Islamic world and in parts of Western Europe as well.

The most important of the new regional rulers were the Fatimids. They, like the Qaramita (and, increasingly in the course of time, the Buyids), were Shi'ites, taking their name from Muhammad's daughter Fatimah, wife of Ali. The Fatimid leader claimed not only to be the true *imam*, descendant of Ali, but also the *mahdi*, the "divinely guided" messiah, come to bring justice on earth. Because of this, the Fatimids were proclaimed "caliphs" by their followers—the true "successors" of the Prophet. (See the list of Fatimid caliphs on p. 342.) Allying with the Berbers in North Africa, by 909 the Fatimids had

Map 4.4: Fragmentation of the Islamic World, *c.*1000

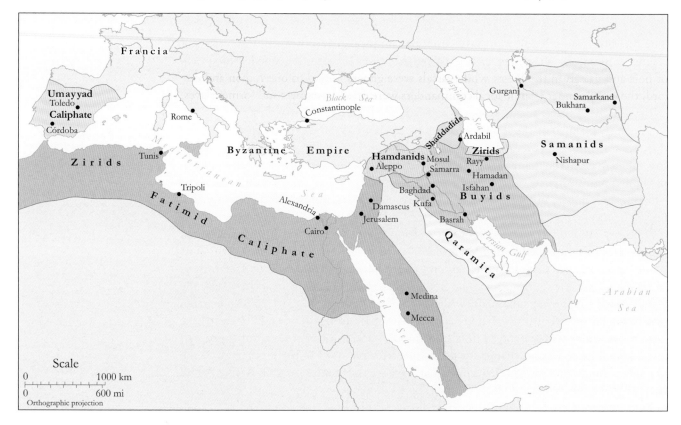

established themselves as rulers in what is today Tunisia and Libya. Within a half-century they had moved eastward (largely abandoning the Maghreb to the Zirids), to rule Egypt, southern Syria, and the western edge of the Arabian Peninsula.

The Fatimids looked east rather than west because the east was rich and because Sunnis, hostile to Shi'ite rule, dominated the western regions. The most important of these Sunni rulers were the Umayyads at Córdoba. Abd al-Rahman III (r.912–961) took the title caliph in 929 as a counterweight to the Fatimids, although he claimed to rule only all of al-Andalus, not the whole Islamic world. An active military man backed by an army made up mainly of Slavic slaves, al-Rahman defeated his rivals and imposed his rule not only on southern Iberia (as his predecessors had done) but also in northern regions (near the Christian kingdoms) and in the Maghreb. Under al-Rahman and his immediate successors, al-Andalus became a powerful centralized state. But regional Islamic rulers there worked to undermine the authority of the Umayyads, so that between 1009 and 1031 bitter civil war undid the dynasty's power. After 1031, al-Andalus was split into small emirates called *taifas*, ruled by local strongmen.

Thus in the Islamic world, far more decisively than at Byzantium, newly powerful regional rulers came to the fore. Nor did the fragmentation of power end at the regional level. To pay their armies, rulers often resorted to granting their commanders *iqta*—lands and villages—from which the *iqta*-holder was expected to gather revenues and pay their troops. As we shall see, this was a bit like the Western European institution of the fief. It meant that even minor commanders could act as local governors, tax-collectors, and military leaders. But there was a major difference between this institution and the system of fiefs and vassals in the West: while vassals were generally tied to one region and one lord, the troops under Islamic local commanders were often foreigners and former slaves, unconnected to any particular place and easily wooed by rival commanders.

Cultural Unity, Religious Polarization

The emergence of local strongmen meant not the end of Arab court culture but a multiplicity of courts, each attempting to out-do one another in brilliant artistic, scientific, theological, and literary productions. Cairo, for example, founded by the Fatimids, was already a huge urban complex by 1000. Imitating the Abbasids, the Fatimid caliphs built mosques and palaces, fostered court ceremonials, and turned Cairo into a center of intellectual life. One of the Fatimid caliphs, al-Hakim (r.996–1021), founded the *dar al-ilm*, a sort of theological college plus public library.

Even more impressive was the Umayyad court at Córdoba, the wealthiest and showiest city of the West. It boasted 70 public libraries in addition to the caliph's private library of perhaps 400,000 books. The Córdoban Great Mosque was a center for scholars from the rest of the Islamic world (the caliphs paid their salaries), while nearly 30 free schools were set up throughout the city.

Córdoba was noteworthy, not only because of the brilliance of its intellectual life, but also because of the role women played in it. Elsewhere in the Islamic world there were certainly a few unusual women associated with cultural and scholarly life. But at Córdoba this was a general phenomenon: women were not only doctors, teachers, and librarians but also worked as copyists for the many books so widely in demand.

Male scholars were, however, everywhere the norm. They moved easily from court to court. Ibn Sina (980–1037), known to the West as Avicenna, began his career serving the ruler at Bukhara in Central Asia, and then moved westward to Gurganj, Rayy, and Hamadan before ending up for thirteen years at the court of Isfahan in Iran. Sometimes in favor and sometimes decidedly not so (he was even briefly imprisoned), he nevertheless managed to study and practice medicine and write numerous books on the natural sciences and philosophy. His pioneering systematization of Aristotle laid the foundations of future philosophical thought in the field of logic: "There is a method by which one can discover the unknown from what is known. It is the science of logic.... [It is also] concerned with the different kinds of valid, invalid, and near valid inferences."[5]

Despite its political disunity, then, the Islamic world of the tenth and eleventh centuries remained in many ways an integrated culture. This was partly due to the model of intellectual life fostered by the Abbasids, which even in decline was copied by the new rulers, as we have just seen. It was also due to the common Arabic language, the glue that bound the astronomer at Córdoba to the philosopher at Cairo.

Writing in Arabic, Islamic authors could count on a large reading public. Manuscripts were churned out quickly via a well-honed division of labor: scribes, illustrators, page cutters, and book-binders specialized in each task. Children were sent to school to learn the Qur'an; listening, reciting, reading, and writing were taught in elementary schools along with good manners and religious obligations. Although a conservative like al-Qabisi (d. 1012) warned that "[a girl] being taught letter-writing or poetry is a cause for fear," he also insisted that parents send their children to school to learn "vocalization, spelling, good handwriting, [and] good reading." He even admitted that learning about "famous men and chivalrous knights" might be acceptable.[6]

Educated in the same texts across the whole Islamic world, Muslims could easily communicate, and this facilitated open networks of trade. With no national barriers to commerce and few regulations, merchants regularly dealt in far-flung, various, and sometimes exotic goods. From England came tin, while salt and gold were imported from Timbuktu in west-central Africa; from Russia came amber, gold, and copper; slaves were wrested from sub-Saharan Africa, the Eurasian steppes, and Slavic regions.

Although Muslims dominated these trade networks, other groups were involved in commerce as well. We happen to know a good deal about one Jewish community living at Fustat, about two miles south of Cairo. It observed the then-common custom of depositing for eventual ritual burial all worn-out papers containing the name of God. For good measure, the Jews in this community included everything written in Hebrew letters: legal documents, fragments of sacred works, marriage contracts, doctors' prescriptions, and so on. By chance, the materials that they left in their *geniza* (depository) at Fustat were preserved rather than buried. They reveal a cosmopolitan, middle-class society. Many were traders, for Fustat was the center of a vast and predominately Jewish trade network that stretched from al-Andalus to India.

Consider the Tustari brothers, Jewish merchants from southern Iran. By the early eleventh century, the brothers had established a flourishing business in Egypt. Informal family networks offered them many of the same advantages as branch offices: friends and family in Iran shipped the Tustaris fine textiles to sell in Egypt, while they exported Egyptian fabrics back to Iran.

Only Islam itself, ironically, pulled Islamic culture apart. In the tenth century the split between the Sunnis and Shi'ites widened to a chasm. At Baghdad, al-Mufid (d. 1022) and others turned Shi'ism into a partisan ideology that insisted on publicly cursing the first two caliphs, turning the tombs of Ali and his family into objects of veneration, and creating an Alid caliph by force. Small wonder that the Abbasid caliphs soon became ardent spokesmen for Sunni Islam, which developed in turn its own public symbols. Many of the new dynasties—the Fatimids and the Qaramita especially—took advantage of the newly polarized faith to bolster their power.

THE WEST: FRAGMENTATION AND RESILIENCE

Fragmentation was the watchword in Western Europe in many parts of the shattered Carolingian Empire. Historians speak of "France," "Germany," and "Italy" in this period as a shorthand for designating broad geographical areas (as will be the case in this book). But there were no national states, only regions with more or less clear borders and rulers with more or less authority. In some places—in parts of "France," for example—regions as small as a few square miles were under the control of different lords who acted, in effect, as independent rulers. Yet this same period saw unified European kingdoms emerge, or begin to emerge. To the north coalesced England, Scotland, and two relatively unified Scandinavian states—Denmark and Norway. In the center-east appeared Bohemia, Poland, and Hungary. In the center of Europe, a powerful royal dynasty from Saxony, the Ottonians, came to rule an empire stretching from the North Sea to Rome.

The Last Invaders of the West

Three groups invaded Western Europe during the ninth and tenth centuries: the Vikings, the Muslims, and the Magyars (called Hungarians by the rest of Europe). (See Map 4.5.) In the short run, they wreaked havoc on land and people. In the long run, they were absorbed into the European population and became constituents of a newly prosperous and aggressive European civilization.

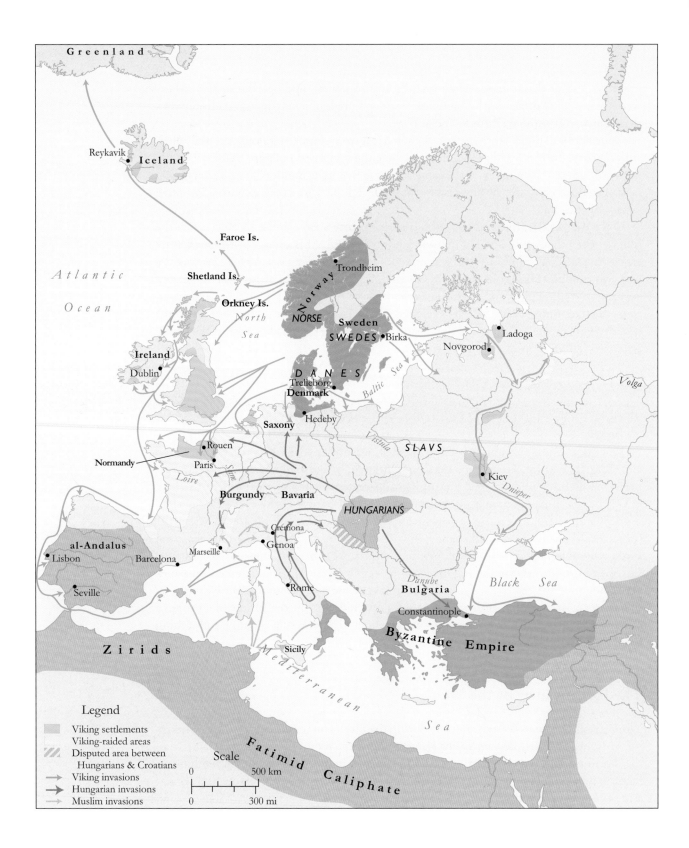

Greenland

Reykavik • **Iceland**

Atlantic

Ocean

Faroe Is.

Shetland Is.

North

Orkney Is.

Sea

NORSE

Trondheim

Ireland

Dublin

Norway

Sweden

SWEDES

• Birka

Ladoga

Novgorod •

Volga

Baltic Sea

DANES

Trelleborg •

Denmark

Vistula

SLAVS

• Hedeby

Saxony

Rouen •

Kiev

Normandy

Paris •

Seine

Dnieper

Loire

Burgundy   **Bavaria**

HUNGARIANS

Cremona

al-Andalus

• Genoa

Danube

Black Sea

• Lisbon

Barcelona •

Marseille •

Bulgaria

• Seville

• Rome

Constantinople •

Z i r i d s

Sicily

Mediterranean

Byzantine Empire

Sea

F a t i m i d

Legend

Viking settlements

Viking-raided areas

Disputed area between
Hungarians & Croatians

Viking invasions

Hungarian invasions

Muslim invasions

Scale

0   500 km

0   300 mi

C a l i p h a t e

VIKINGS

Around the same time as they made forays eastward toward Novgorod, some Scandinavians were traveling to western shores. Their kings and chieftains were competing mightily for power in a society that valued gift-giving above all to cement relationships. (See the discussion of the "gift economy" on p. 61.) The most precious and sought-after gifts were beautifully crafted and decorated jewelry made of gold and silver; weapons, too, well forged and ornamented, were highly prized. Chieftains fed their warrior followers' hunger for gifts by controlling nearby agricultural production, indigenous crafts, and long-distance trade. Some found that raids for plunder served them even better. This was the background to the "Viking invasions of Europe." Traveling in long, narrow, and shallow ships powered by wind and sails, the Vikings sailed down the coasts and rivers of France, England, Scotland, and Ireland. Some crossed the Atlantic, making themselves at home in Iceland and Greenland and, in about 1000, touching on the North American mainland. While the elites came largely for booty, lesser men, eager for land, traveled with their wives and children to settle after conquest in Ireland, Scotland, England, and Normandy (giving their name to the region: Norman = Northman, or Viking).

Map 4.5 (facing page): Viking, Muslim, and Hungarian Invasions, Ninth and Tenth Centuries

In Ireland, where their settlements were in the east and south, the newcomers added their own claims to rule an island already fragmented among four or five competing dynasties. In Scotland, however, in the face of Norse settlements in the north and west, the natives drew together under kings who—in a process we have seen elsewhere—allied themselves with churchmen and other powerful local leaders. Cináed mac Ailpín (Kenneth I MacAlpin) (d.858) established a hereditary dynasty of kings that ruled over two hitherto separate native peoples. By c.900, the separate identities were gone, and most people in *Alba*, the nucleus of the future Scotland, shared a common sense of being Scottish.

England underwent a similar process of unification. Initially divided into small competing kingdoms, it was weak prey in the face of invasion. By the end of the ninth century, the Vikings were plowing fields in eastern England and living in accordance with their own laws. (Later the region was called the Danelaw.) In Wessex, the southernmost English kingdom, King Alfred the Great (r.871–899) bought time and peace by paying a tribute with the income from a new tax, later called the Danegeld. (It eventually became the basis of a relatively lucrative taxation system in England.) In 878 he led a series of raids against the Vikings settled in his kingdom, inspired the previously cowed Anglo-Saxons to follow him, and camped outside the Viking stronghold until their leaders surrendered and accepted baptism. Soon the Vikings left Wessex.

Thereafter the pressure of invasion eased as Alfred reorganized his army, set up strongholds of his own (called *burhs*), and created a fleet of ships—a real navy. An uneasy stability was achieved, with the Vikings dominating the east of England and Alfred and his successors gaining control over most of the rest.

On the Continent, too, the invaders came to stay, above all in Normandy. The new inhabitants of the region were integrated into the political system when, in 911, their leader

Rollo converted to Christianity and received Normandy as a duchy from the Frankish king Charles the Simple (or Straightforward). Although many of the Normans adopted sedentary ways, some of their descendants in the early eleventh century ventured to the Mediterranean, where they established themselves as rulers of petty principalities in southern Italy. In 1061 the Normans began the conquest of Sicily.

MUSLIMS

Sicily, once Byzantine, was the rich and fertile plum of the conquests achieved by the Muslim invaders of the ninth and tenth centuries. That they took the island attests to the power of a new Muslim navy developed by the dynasty that preceded the Fatimids in Ifriqiya. After 909, Sicily came under Fatimid rule, but by mid-century it was controlled by independent Islamic princes, and Muslim immigrants were swelling the population.

Elsewhere the Muslim presence in Western Europe was more ephemeral. In the first half of the tenth century, Muslim raiders pillaged southern France, northern Italy, and the Alpine passes. But these were quick expeditions, largely attacks on churches and monasteries. Some of these Muslims did establish themselves at La Garde-Freinet, in Provence, becoming landowners in the region and lords of Christian serfs. They even hired themselves out as occasional fighters for the wars that local Christian aristocrats were waging against one another. But they made the mistake of capturing for ransom the holiest man of his era, Abbot Majolus of Cluny (c.906–994). Outraged, the local aristocracy finally came together and ousted the Muslims from their midst.

MAGYARS (HUNGARIANS)

By contrast, the Magyars stayed on. "Magyar" was and remains their name for themselves, though the rest of Europe called them "Hungarians," from the Slavonic for "Onogurs," a people already settled in the Danube basin in the eighth and ninth centuries. Originally nomads who raised (and rode) horses, the Magyars spoke a language unrelated to any other in Europe (except Finnish). Known as effective warriors, they were employed by Arnulf, king of the East Franks (r.887–899), when he fought the Moravians and by the Byzantine emperor Leo VI (r.886–912) during his struggle against the Bulgars. In 894, taking advantage of their position, the Hungarians, as we may now call them, conquered much of the Danube basin for themselves.

From there, for over fifty years, they raided into Germany, Italy, and even southern France. At the same time, however, the Hungarians worked for various western rulers. Until 937 they spared Bavaria, for example, because they were allies of its duke. Gradually they made the transition from nomads to farmers, and their polity coalesced into the Kingdom of Hungary. This is no doubt a major reason for the end of their attacks. At the time, however, the cessation of their raids was widely credited to the German king Otto I (r.936–973), who won a major victory over a Hungarian marauding party at the battle of Lechfeld in 955.

Public Power and Private Relationships

The invasions left new political arrangements in their wake. Unlike the Byzantines and Muslims, European rulers had no mercenaries and no salaried officials. They commanded others by ensuring personal loyalty. The Carolingian kings had had their *fideles*—their faithful men. Tenth-century rulers were even more dependent on ties of dependency: they needed their "men" (*homines*), their "vassals" (*vassalli*). Whatever the term, all were armed retainers who fought for a lord. Sometimes these subordinates held land from their lord, either as a reward for their military service or as an inheritance for which services were due. The term for such an estate, fief (*feodum*), gave historians the word "feudalism" to describe the social and economic system created by the relationships among lords, vassals, and fiefs. Some recent historians argue that the word "feudalism" has been used in too many different and contradictory ways to mean anything at all. Was it a mode of exploiting the land that involved lords and serfs? A condition of anarchy and lawlessness? Or a political system of ordered gradations of power, from the king on down? All of these definitions are possible. Ordinarily we may dispense with the word feudalism, though it can be very useful as a "fuzzy category" when contrasting, for example, the political, social, and economic organization of Antiquity with that of the Middle Ages.

LORDS AND VASSALS

The key to tenth- and eleventh-century society was personal dependency. This took many forms. Of the three traditional "orders" recognized by writers in the ninth through eleventh centuries—those who pray (the *oratores*), those who fight (the *bellatores*), and those who work (the *laboratores*)—the top two were free. The pray-ers (the monks) and the fighters (the nobles and their lower-class counterparts, the knights) participated in prestigious kinds of subordination, whether as vassals, lords, or both. Indeed, they were usually both: a typical warrior was lord of several vassals and the vassal of another lord. Monasteries normally had vassals to fight for them, while their abbots in turn were vassals of a king or other lord. At the low end of the social scale, poor vassals looked to their lords to feed, clothe, house, and arm them. At the upper end, vassals looked to their lords to enrich them with still more fiefs.

Some women were vassals, and some were lords (or, rather, "ladies," the female version). Many upper-class laywomen participated in the society of warriors and monks as wives and mothers of vassals and lords and as landowners in their own right. Others entered convents and became *oratores* themselves. Through its abbess or a man standing in for her, a convent was itself often the "lord" of vassals.

Vassalage was voluntary and public. In some areas, it was marked by a ceremony: the vassal-to-be knelt and, placing his hands between the hands of his lord, said, "I promise to be your man." This act, known as "homage," was followed by the promise of "fealty"—fidelity, trust, and service—which the vassal swore with his hand on relics or a Bible.

Then the vassal and the lord kissed. In an age when many people could not read, a public moment such as this represented a visual and verbal contract, binding the vassal and lord together with mutual obligations to help each other. On the other hand, these obligations were rarely spelled out, and a lord with many vassals, or a vassal with many lords, needed to satisfy numerous conflicting claims. "I am a loser only because of my loyalty to you," Hugh of Lusignan told his lord, William of Aquitaine, after his expectations for reward were continually disappointed.[7]

LORDS AND PEASANTS

At the lowest end of the social scale were those who worked: the peasants. In many regions of Europe, as power fell into the hands of local rulers, the distinction between "free" and "unfree" peasants began to blur; many peasants simply became "serfs," dependents of lords. This was a heavy dependency, without prestige or honor. It was hereditary rather than voluntary: no serf did homage or fealty to his lord; no serf and lord kissed each other.

Indeed, the upper classes barely noticed the peasants—except as sources of labor and revenue. In the tenth century, the three-field system became more prevalent, and the heavy moldboard plows that could turn wet, clayey northern soils came into wider use. Such plows could not work around fences, and they were hard to turn: thus was produced the characteristic "look" of medieval agriculture—long, furrowed strips in broad, open fields. (Peasants knew very well which strips were "theirs" and which belonged to their neighbors. See the late medieval lands of Toury in Map 7.8 on p. 277.) A team of oxen was normally used to pull the plow, but horses (more efficient than oxen) were sometimes substituted. The result was surplus food and a better standard of living for nearly everyone.

In search of still greater profits, some lords lightened the dues and services of peasants temporarily to allow them to open up new lands by draining marshes and cutting down forests. Other lords converted dues and labor services into money payments, providing themselves with ready cash. Peasants, too, benefited from these rents because their payments were fixed despite inflation. As the prices of agricultural products went up, peasants became small-scale entrepreneurs, selling their chickens and eggs at local markets and reaping a profit.

In the eleventh century, and increasingly so in the twelfth, peasant settlements gained boundaries and focus: they became real villages. (For the example of Toury, see Map 7.7 on p. 276.) The parish church often formed the center, next to which was the cemetery. Then, normally crowded right onto the cemetery itself, were the houses, barns, animals, and tools of the living peasants. Boundary markers—sometimes simple stones, at other times real fortifications—announced not only the physical limit of the village but also its sense of community. This derived from very practical concerns: peasants needed to share oxen or horses to pull their plows; they were all dependent on the village craftsmen to fix their wheels or shoe their horses.

Variety was the hallmark of peasant society. In Saxony and other parts of Germany free peasants prevailed. In France and England most were serfs. In Italy peasants ranged from small independent landowners to leaseholders; most were both, owning a parcel in one place and leasing another nearby.

Where the power of kings was weak, peasant obligations became part of a larger system of local rule. As landlords consolidated their power over their manors, they collected not only dues and services but also fees for the use of their flour mills, bake houses, and breweries. In some regions—parts of France and in Catalonia, for example—some lords built castles and exercised the power of the "ban": the right to collect taxes, hear court cases, levy fines, and muster men for defense. These lords were "castellans." Guillem Guifred, a castellan in Catalonia (and a bishop, too, for good measure), for example, received "half of the revenue of the courts [at Sanahuja], without deceit. From the market, half.... Of the oven, half. Of rights on minting, half."[8]

WARRIORS AND BISHOPS

Although the developments described here did not occur everywhere simultaneously (and in some places hardly at all), in the end the social, political, and cultural life of the West came to be dominated by landowners who saw themselves as both military men and regional leaders. These men and their armed retainers shared a common lifestyle, living together, eating in the lord's great hall, listening to bards sing of military exploits, hunting for recreation, competing with one another in military games. They fought in groups as well—as cavalry. In the month of May, when the grasses were high enough for their horses to forage, the war season began. To be sure, there were powerful vassals who lived on their own fiefs and hardly ever saw their lord—except for perhaps forty days out of the year, when they owed him military service. But they themselves were lords of knightly vassals who were not married and who lived and ate and hunted with them.

The marriage bed, so important to the medieval aristocracy from the start, now took on new meaning. In the seventh and eighth centuries, aristocratic families had thought of themselves as large and loosely organized kin groups. They were not tied to any particular estate, for they had numerous estates, scattered all about. With wealth enough to go around, the rich practiced partible inheritance, giving land (though not in equal amounts) to all of their sons and daughters. The Carolingians "politicized" these family relations. As some men were elevated to positions of dazzling power, they took the opportunity to pick and choose their "family members," narrowing the family circle. They also became more conscious of their male line, favoring sons over daughters. In the eleventh century, family definitions tightened even further. The claims of one son, often the eldest, overrode all else; to him went the family inheritance. (This is called "primogeniture"; but there were regions in which the youngest son was privileged, and there were also areas in which more equitable inheritance practices continued in place.) The heir in the new system traced his lineage only through the male line, backward through his father and forward through his own eldest son.

What happened to the other sons? Some of them became knights, others monks. Nor should we forget that some became bishops. In many ways the interests of bishops and lay nobles were similar: bishops were men of property, lords of vassals, and faithful to patrons, such as kings, who appointed them to their posts. In some places, bishops wielded the powers of a count or duke. Bishop Guillem Guifred (see p. 133) is a good example. Some bishops ruled cities. Nevertheless, bishops were also "pastors," spiritual leaders charged with shepherding their flock, which included the laity, priests, and monks in their diocese (a district that gained clear definition in the eleventh century).

As episcopal power expanded and was clarified in the course of the tenth and eleventh centuries, some bishops in southern France, joined by the upper crust of the aristocracy, sought to control the behavior of the lesser knights through a movement called the "Peace of God." They were not satisfied with the current practices of peace-making, in which enemies, pressured by their peers, negotiated an end to—or at least a cessation of—hostilities. (Behind the negotiation was the threat of an ordeal—for instance a trial by battle whose outcome was in the hands of God—if the two sides did not come to terms.) This system of arbitration was not always satisfactory. Hugh of Lusignan, the discontented vassal (see above, p. 132), complained that his lord "[did not] broker a good agreement." Beginning in 989, the Peace developed apace. Its forum was the regional church council, where bishops galvanized popular opinion, attracting both grand aristocrats and peasants to their gatherings. There, drawing upon bits and pieces of defunct Carolingian legislation, the bishops declared the Peace, and knights took oaths to observe it. At Bourges a particularly enthusiastic archbishop took the oath himself: "I Aimon ... will wholeheartedly attack those who steal ecclesiastical property, those who provoke pillage, those who oppress monks, nuns, and clerics."⁹ In the Truce of God, which by the 1040s was declared alongside the Peace, warfare between armed men was prohibited from Lent to Easter, while at other times of the year it was forbidden on Sunday (because that was the Lord's Day), on Saturday (because that was a reminder of Holy Saturday), on Friday (because it symbolized Good Friday), and on Thursday (because it stood for Holy Thursday).

To the bishops who promulgated the Peace, warriors fell conceptually into two groups: the sinful ones who broke the Peace, and the righteous ones who upheld church law. Although the Peace and Truce were taken up by powerful lay rulers, eager to sanctify their own warfare and control that of others, the major initiative for the movement came from churchmen eager to draw clear boundaries between the realms of the sacred and the profane.

CITIES AND MERCHANTS

These clerics were, in part, reacting to new developments in the secular realm: the growing importance of urban institutions and professions. Though much of Europe was rural, there were important exceptions. Italy was one place where urban life, though dramatically reduced in size and population, persisted. In Italy, the power structure still reflected, if feebly, the political organization of ancient Rome. Whereas in northern France great lords built their castles in the countryside, in Italy they often constructed their family seats within the walls of cities. From these perches the nobles, both lay and religious, dominated the *contado*, the rural area around the city.

In Italy, most peasants were renters, paying cash to urban landowners. Peasants depended on city markets to sell their surplus goods; their customers included bishops, nobles, and middle-class shopkeepers, artisans, and merchants. At Milan, for example, the merchants were prosperous enough to own houses in both the city center and the *contado*.

Rome, although exceptional in size, was in some ways a typical Italian city. Large and powerful families built their castles within its walls and controlled the churches and monasteries in the vicinity. The population depended on local producers for their food, and merchants brought their wares to sell within its walls. Yet Rome was special apart from its size: it was the "see"—the seat—of the pope, the most important bishop in the West. The papacy did not control the church, but it had great prestige, and powerful families at Rome fought to place one of their sons at its head.

Outside Italy cities were less prevalent. Yet even so we can see the rise of a new mercantile class. This was true less in the heartland of the old Carolingian Empire than on its fringes. In the north, England, northern Germany, Denmark, and the Low Countries bathed in a sea of silver coins; commercial centers such as Haithabu (see above, p. 102) reached their grandest extent in the mid-tenth century. Here merchants bought and sold slaves, honey, furs, wax, and pirates' plunder. Haithabu was a city of wood, but a very rich one indeed.

In the south of Europe, beyond the Pyrenees, Catalonia was equally commercialized, but in a different way. It imitated the Islamic world of al-Andalus (which was, in effect, in its backyard). The counts of Barcelona minted gold coins just like those at Córdoba. The villagers around Barcelona soon got used to selling their wares for money, and some of them became prosperous. They married into the aristocracy, moved to Barcelona to become city leaders, and lent money to ransom prisoners of the many wars waged to their south.

Kingships in an Age of Fragmentation

In such a world, what did kings do? At the least, they stood for tradition, serving as symbols of legitimacy. At the most, they united kingdoms and maintained a measure of law and order. (See Map 4.6.)

NORTHERN KINGDOMS

King Alfred of England was a king of the second sort. In the face of the Viking invasions, he developed new mechanisms of royal government, creating institutions that became the foundation of strong English kingship. We have already seen his military reforms: the system of *burhs* and the creation of a navy. Alfred was interested in religious and intellectual reforms as well. These were closely linked in his mind: the causes of England's troubles

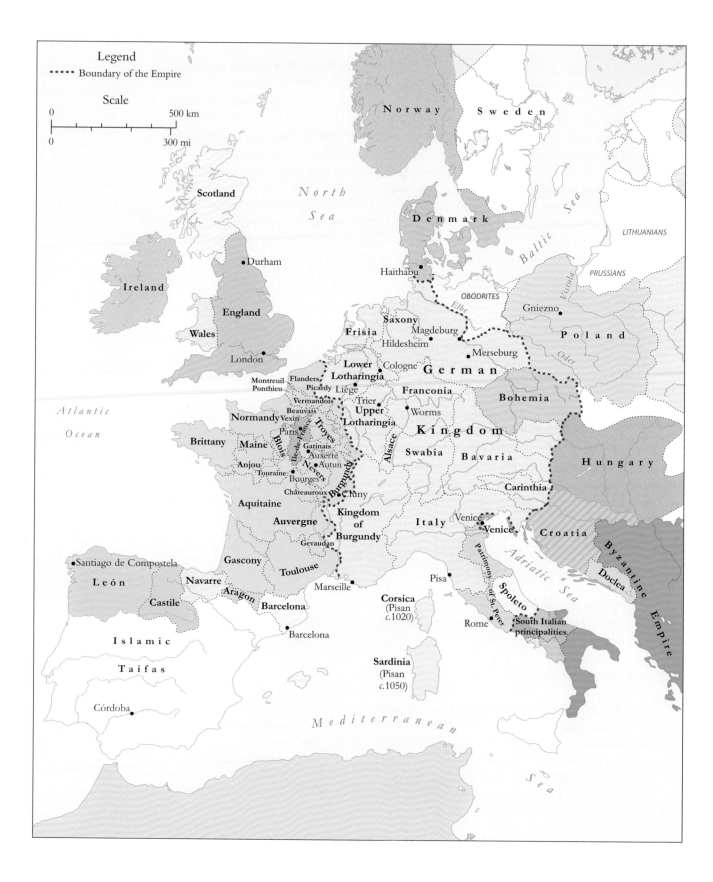

Scotland

North Sea

• Durham

Ireland

England

Wales

London •

Atlantic Ocean

N O R W A Y   **S w e d e n**

Baltic Sea

D e n m a r k

Haithabu •

LITHUANIANS

PRUSSIANS

OBODRITES

Frisia

Saxony   Magdeburg •

Hildesheim •

Lower Lotharingia   Cologne •

Flanders   Picardy   Liège •

Vermandois

Montreuil   Beauvais   **Upper**
Ponthieu   **Normandy** Vexin   **Lotharingia**

Paris •   **Troyes**

Brittany   **Maine**   **Blois**   Gatinais

Anjou   **Ile-de-France**   Auxerre •

Touraine   **Nevers**   Autun •

Châteauroux •   **Burgundy**   Cluny •
Bourges •

Aquitaine

Auvergne   **Kingdom of Burgundy**

Gevaudan •

Santiago de Compostela •   **Gascony**

León   **Navarre**   **Toulouse**   Marseille •

Aragon   **Barcelona**

Córdoba •

Castile

I s l a m i c

T a i f a s

G E R M A N

Franconia

Trier •   Worms •

K I N G D O M

Bohemia

Swabia   **Bavaria**

Hungary

Carinthia

Italy   Venice •   **Venice**

Croatia

Pisa •   **Patrimony of St. Peter**   *Adriatic Sea*

Corsica
(Pisan
c.1020)

Rome •   **Spoleto**

South Italian principalities

Byzantine Empire

Doclea

Sardinia
(Pisan
c.1050)

M e d i t e r r a n e a n

Sea

Barcelona •

(in his view) were the sins of its people, brought on by their ignorance. Alfred intended to educate "all free-born men." He brought scholars to his court and embarked on an ambitious program to translate key religious works from Latin into Anglo-Saxon (or Old English). This was the vernacular, the spoken language of the people. As Alfred wrote in his prose preface to the Anglo-Saxon translation of *The Pastoral Care* of Gregory the Great,

> I would have it known that very often it has come to my mind what men of learning there were formerly throughout England, both in religious and secular orders; and how there were happy times then throughout England; and how the kings, who had authority over this people, obeyed God and his messengers; and how they not only maintained their peace, morality and authority at home but also extended their territory outside; and how they succeeded both in warfare and in wisdom.... I recalled how the Law was first composed in the Hebrew language, and thereafter, when the Greeks learned it, they translated it all into their own language, and all other books as well. And so too the Romans, after they had mastered them, translated them all through learned interpreters into their own language.... Therefore it seems better to me ... that we too should turn into the language that we can all understand certain books which are the most necessary for all men to know.[10]

Those "certain books" included the Psalter and writings by the Church Fathers. Soon Anglo-Saxon was being used in England not only for literature but for official administrative purposes as well, in royal "writs" that kings and queens directed to their officials. England was not alone in its esteem for the vernacular: in Ireland, too, the vernacular language was a written one. But the British Isles *were* unusual by the standards of Continental Europe, where Latin alone was the language of scholarship and writing.

As Alfred harried the Danes who were pushing south and westward, he gained recognition as king of all the English not under Viking rule. His law code, issued in the late 880s or early 890s, was the first by an English king since 695. Unlike earlier codes, which had been drawn up for each separate kingdom, Alfred's contained laws from and for all the English kingdoms in common. The king's inspiration was the Mosaic law of the Bible. Alfred believed that God had made a new covenant with the victors over the Vikings; as leader of his people, Alfred, like the Old Testament patriarch Moses, issued a law for all.

His successors, beneficiaries of that covenant, rolled back the Viking rule in England. (See Genealogy 4.1: Alfred and His Progeny.) "Then the Norsemen made off in their nailed boats, / Saddened survivors shamed in battle," wrote one poet about a battle lost by the Vikings in 937.[11] But, as we have seen, many Vikings remained. Converted to Christianity, their great men joined Anglo-Saxons to attend the English king at court. The whole kingdom was divided into districts called "shires" and "hundreds," and in each shire, the king's reeve—the sheriff—oversaw royal administration.

Alfred's grandson Æthelstan (r.924–939) commanded all the possibilities early medieval kingship offered. The first king of all the Anglo-Saxon kingdoms, he was crowned in a new ritual created by the archbishop of Canterbury to emphasize harmony and unity.

Map 4.6 (facing page): Europe, *c.*1050

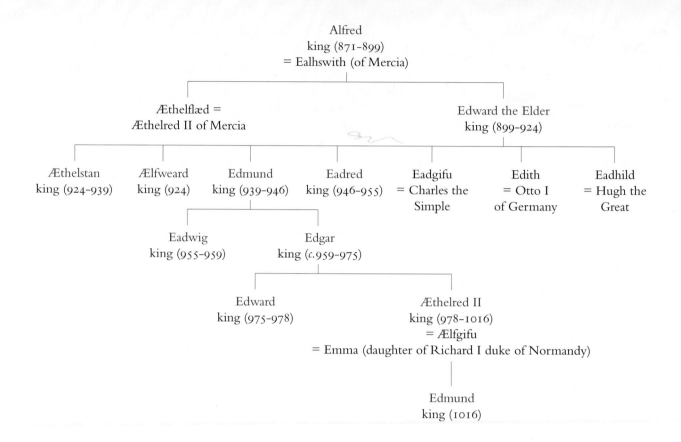

Genealogy 4.1: Alfred and His Progeny

When Æthelstan toured his realm (as he did constantly), he was accompanied by a varied and impressive retinue: bishops, nobles, thegns (the English equivalent of high-status vassals), scholars, foreign dignitaries, and servants. Well known as an effective military leader who extended his realm northwards, he received oaths of loyalty from the rulers of other parts of Britain. Churchmen attended him at court, and he in turn chose bishops and other churchmen, often drawing on the priests in his household. Like Alfred, he issued laws and expected local authorities—the ealdormen and sheriffs—to carry them out. Above all he was concerned about theft.

From the point of view of control, however, Æthelstan had nowhere near the power over England that, say, Basil II had over Byzantium at about the same time. The *dynatoi* might sometimes chafe at the emperor's directives and rebel, but the emperor had his Varangian guard to put them down and an experienced, professional civil service to do his bidding. The king of England depended less on force and bureaucracy than on consensus. The great landowners adhered to the king because they found it in their interest to do so. When they did not, the kingdom easily fragmented, becoming prey to civil war. Disunity was exacerbated by new attacks from the Vikings. One Danish king, Cnut (or Canute), even became king of England for a time (r.1016–1035). Yet under Cnut, English kingship did not change much. He kept intact much of the administrative, ecclesiastical, and military apparatus already established. By Cnut's time, Scandinavia had been Christianized, and its traditions had largely merged with those of the rest of Europe.

In fact, two European-style kingdoms—Denmark and Norway—developed in Scandinavia around the year 1000, and Sweden followed thereafter. In effect, the Vikings took home with them not only Europe's plundered wealth but also its prestigious religion, with all its implications for royal power and state-building. (Consider how closely King Alfred linked God to royal authority, morality, and territorial expansion.) The impetus for conversion in Scandinavia came from two directions. From the south, missionaries such as the Frankish monk Ansgar (d.865) came to preach Christianity, while bishops in the north of Germany imposed what claims they could over the Scandinavian church. From within Scandinavia itself, kings found it worth their while to ally with the Christian world to enhance their own position.

The Danish King Harald Bluetooth (r.*c.*958–*c.*986), much like Khan Boris-Michael of Bulgaria a century before (see p. 82), proclaimed his conversion through an artifact. Boris-Michael had used seals—items prestigious for their association with Byzantine imperial government. Harald built a mound—prestigious precisely for its non-Christian, pagan connotations—and then, about a decade later, added a giant runestone to the burial place of his father, whose body he moved from the mound into a new church he built for the occasion. The runestone, which included an image of Christ, announced that Harald had "won for himself all of Denmark and Norway and made the Danes Christian."[12] Thus graphically turning a pagan site into a Christian one, Harald announced himself the ruler of a state that extended into what is today southern Sweden and parts of Norway. His successors turned their sights further outward, culminating in the conquest of England and Norway, but this extended empire largely ended with the death of Cnut in 1035.

The processes of conversion and the development of kingship in Norway are less easily traceable because there are few sources from the time. It is clear, however, that at the beginning of the eleventh century the baptism of Olav Haraldsson allowed him to ally with the English king ousted by the Danes. It also let Olav tie himself to his own men through the bonds of godparenthood. Building on the successes of Olav in opposing Danish King Cnut's hegemony in Norway, Magnus the Good (r.1035–1047) harnessed the Christian institutions already in place.

The story of Sweden was similar to that of Denmark and Norway, but not until the twelfth century. Before then, Sweden was divided among many competing rulers, most of them professing Christianity.

KINGDOMS IN EUROPE'S WEST

Germany

Just below Denmark was Germany. There the king was as effective and powerful as the English king—and additionally worked with a much wider palette of territories, institutions, and possibilities. It is true that at first Germany seemed ready to disintegrate into duchies: five emerged in the late Carolingian period, each held by a military leader who exercised quasi-royal powers. But, in the face of their own quarrels and the threats of outside invaders, the dukes needed and wanted a strong king. With the death in 911

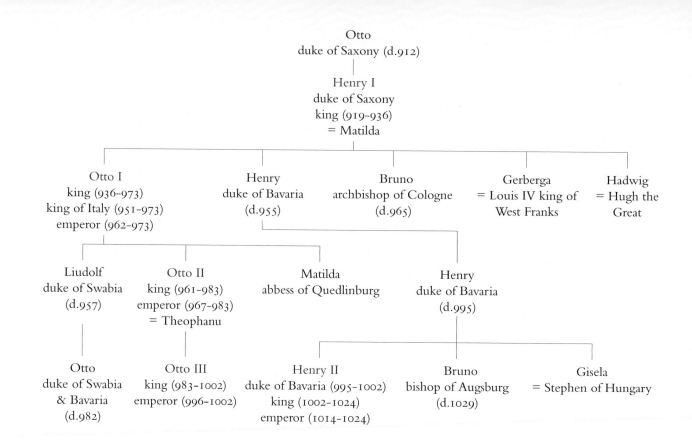

Otto
duke of Saxony (d.912)

Henry I
duke of Saxony
king (919-936)
= Matilda

Otto I	Henry	Bruno	Gerberga	Hadwig
king (936-973)	duke of Bavaria	archbishop of Cologne	= Louis IV king of	= Hugh the
king of Italy (951-973)	(d.955)	(d.965)	West Franks	Great
emperor (962-973)				

Liudolf	Otto II	Matilda	Henry
duke of Swabia	king (961-983)	abbess of Quedlinburg	duke of Bavaria
(d.957)	emperor (967-983)		(d.995)
	= Theophanu		

Otto	Otto III	Henry II	Bruno	Gisela
duke of Swabia	king (983-1002)	duke of Bavaria (995-1002)	bishop of Augsburg	= Stephen of Hungary
& Bavaria	emperor (996-1002)	king (1002-1024)	(d.1029)	
(d.982)		emperor (1014-1024)		

Genealogy 4.2: The Ottonians

of the last Carolingian king in Germany, Louis the Child, they crowned one of them-selves. Then, as attacks by the Hungarians increased, the dukes gave the royal title to their most powerful member, the duke of Saxony, Henry I (r.919–936), who proceeded to set up fortifications and reorganize his army, crowning his efforts with a major defeat of the Hungarians in 933.

Henry's son Otto I (r.936–973) defeated rival family members, rebellious dukes, and Slavic and Hungarian armies soon after coming to the throne. Through astute marriage alliances and appointments he was eventually able to get his family members to head up all of the duchies. In 951, Otto marched into Italy and took the Lombard crown. That gave him control, at least theoretically, of much of northern Italy (see Map 4.6). Soon (in 962) he received the imperial crown that recognized his far-flung power. Both to himself and to contemporaries he recalled the greatness of Charlemagne. Meanwhile, Otto's victory at Lechfeld in 955 (see p. 130) ended the Hungarian threat. In the same year, Otto defeated a Slavic group, the Obodrites, just east of the Elbe River and set up fortifications and bish-oprics in the no-man's-land between the Elbe and the Oder Rivers.

Victories such as these brought tribute, plum positions to disburse, and lands to give away, ensuring Otto a following among the great men of the realm. His successors, Otto II, Otto III—hence the dynastic name "Ottonians"—and Henry II, built on his achievements. (See Genealogy 4.2: The Ottonians.) Granted power by the magnates, they gave back in turn: they distributed land and appointed their aristocratic supporters to duchies, counties, and bishoprics. Royal power was tempered by hereditary claims and plenty of lobbying by influential men at court and at the great assemblies that met with the king to hammer out policies. The role of kings in filling bishoprics and archbishoprics was particularly important to them because, unlike counties and duchies, these positions could not be inherited. Otto I created a ribbon of new bishoprics along his eastern border, endowing them with extensive lands and subjecting the local peasantry to episcopal overlordship. Throughout Germany bishops had the right to collect revenues and call men to arms.

Bishops and archbishops constituted the backbone of Ottonian rule. Once he had chosen the bishop (usually with the consent of the clergy of the cathedral over which the bishop was to preside), the king usually received a gift—a token of episcopal support—in return. Then the king "invested" the new prelate in his post by participating in the ceremony that installed him into office. Archbishop Bruno of Cologne is a good—if extreme—example of the symbiotic relations between church and state in the German realm. An ally of the king (as were almost all the bishops), he was also Otto I's brother. Right after he was invested as archbishop in 953, he was appointed by Otto to be duke of Lotharingia. (On Map 4.6, this is the region that encompassed both Lower and Upper Lotharingia.) His job was to put down a local rebellion. Later Bruno's biographer, Ruotger, strove mightily to justify Bruno's role as a warrior-bishop:

> Some people ignorant of divine will may object: why did a bishop assume public office and the dangers of war when he had undertaken only the care of souls? If they understand any sane matter, the result itself will easily satisfy them, when they see a great and very unaccustomed (especially in their homelands) gift of peace spread far and wide through this guardian and teacher of a faithful people. ... Nor was governing this world new or unusual for rectors of the holy Church, previous examples of which, if someone needs them, are at hand.[13]

Ruotger was right: there *were* other examples near at hand, for the German kings found their most loyal administrators among their bishops. Consider, for example, the bishop of Liège; he held the rights and exercised the duties of several counts, had his own mints, and hunted and fished in a grand private forest granted to him in 1006.

Bruno was not only duke of Lotharingia, pastor of his flock at Cologne, and head (as archbishop of Cologne) of the bishops of his duchy. He was also a serious scholar. "There was nearly no type of liberal study in Greek or Latin," wrote the admiring Ruotger, "that escaped the vitality of his genius."[14] Bruno's interest in learning was part of a larger movement. With wealth coming in from their eastern tributaries, Italy, and the silver mines of Saxony (discovered in the time of Otto I), the Ottonians presided over a brilliant intellectual and artistic efflorescence. As in the Islamic world, much of this was dispersed; in Germany the centers of culture included the royal court, the great cathedral schools, and women's convents.

The most talented young men crowded the schools at episcopal courts at Trier, Cologne, Magdeburg, Worms, and Hildesheim. Honing their Latin, they studied classical authors

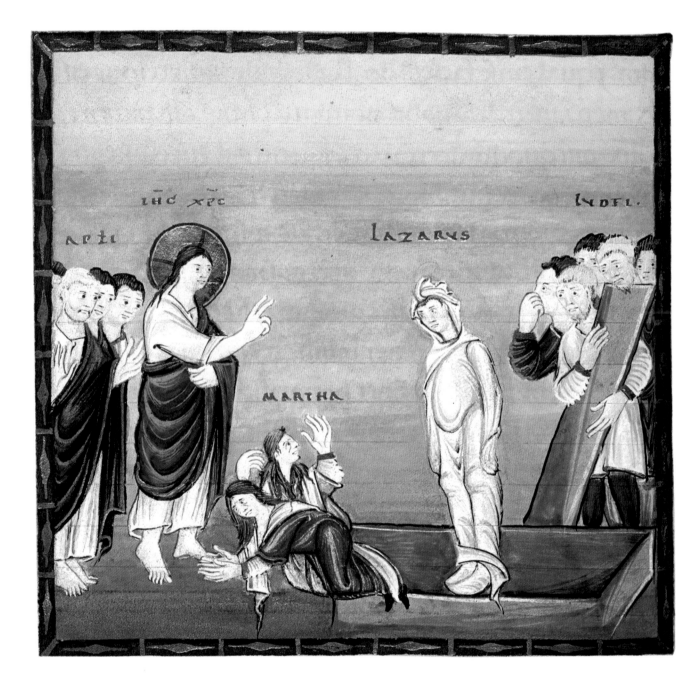

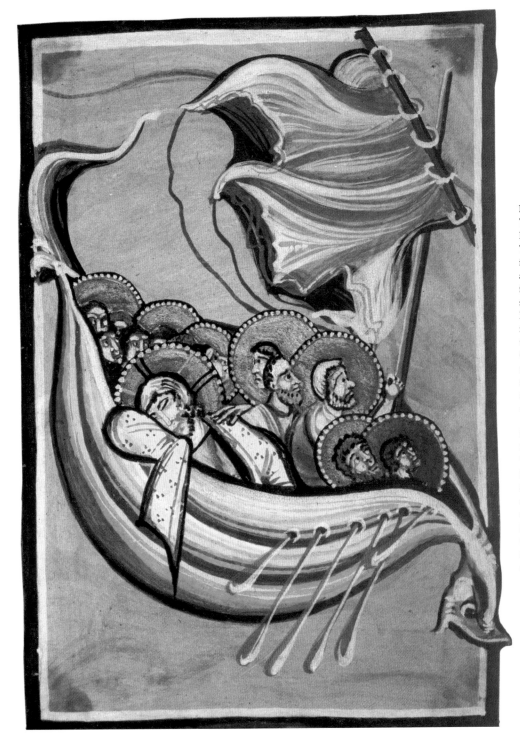

Plate 4.2 (facing page): The Raising of Lazarus, Egbert Codex (985–990). This miniature is one of 51 illustrations in a Pericopes, a book of readings arranged for the liturgical year. The story of the Raising of Lazarus, which is recounted in John 11:1–45, is read during the week before Easter. Of the many elements of this story, the artist chose a few important moments, arranging them into a unified scene.

Plate 4.3: Christ Asleep, Hitda Gospels (*c.*1000–*c.*1020). The moral of the story (which is told in Matt. 8:23–26) is right in the picture: as the apostles look anxiously toward the mast to save them from the stormy sea, one (in the exact center) turns to rouse the sleeping Christ, the real Savior.

such as Cicero and Horace as well as Scripture, while their episcopal teachers wrote histories, saints' lives, and works on canon law. One such was the *Decretum* (1008/1012) by Burchard, bishop of Worms. This widely influential collection—much like the compilations of *hadith* produced about a century before in the Islamic world—winnowed out the least authoritative canons and systematized the contradictory ones. The men at the cathedral schools were largely in training to become courtiers, administrators, and bishops themselves.

Bishops such as Egbert, archbishop of Trier (r.977–993), appreciated art as well as scholarship. Plate 4.2, an illustration of the Raising of Lazarus, from the Egbert Codex (named for its patron), is a good example of what is called the "Ottonian style." Drawing above all on the art of the late antique "renaissance" (see p. 21 and Plate 1.10), the Egbert Codex artists nevertheless achieved an effect all their own. Utterly unafraid of open space, which was rendered in otherworldly pastel colors, they focused on the figures, who gestured like actors on a stage. In Plate 4.2 the apostles are on the left-hand side, their arms raised and hands wide open with wonder at Christ. He has just raised the dead Lazarus from the tomb, and one of the Jews, on the right, holds his nose. Two women—Mary and Martha, the sisters of Lazarus—fall at Christ's feet, completing the dramatic tableau.

At around the same time, in convents that provided them with comfortable private apartments, noblewomen were writing books and supporting other artists and scholars. Plate 4.3 is from a manuscript made at Cologne between *c.*1000 and *c.*1020 for Abbess Hitda of Meschede. It draws on Byzantine and Carolingian models as well as the palette of the Egbert Codex to produce a calm Christ, asleep during a wild storm on the Sea of Galilee that ruffles the sails of the ship and seems to toss it into sheer air. The marriage of Otto II to a Byzantine princess, Theophanu, helps account for the Byzantine influence.

Among the most active patrons of the arts were the Ottonian kings themselves. In a Gospel book made for Otto III—a work fit for royal consumption—the full achievement of Ottonian culture is made clear. Plate 4.4 shows one of 29 full-page miniatures in this manuscript, whose binding alone—set with countless gems around a Byzantine carved ivory—was worth a fortune. The figure of the evangelist Luke emerges from a pure gold-leaf background, while the purple of his dress and the columns that frame him recall imperial majesty. At the same time, Luke is clearly of another world, and his Gospels have here become a theological vision.

France

By contrast with the English and German kings, those in France had a hard time coping with invasions. Unlike Alfred's dynasty, which started small and built slowly, the French kings had half an empire to defend. Unlike the Ottonians, who asserted their military prowess in decisive battles such as the one at Lechfeld, the French kings generally had to let local men both take the brunt of the attacks and reap the prestige and authority that came with military leadership. Nor did the French kings have the advantage of Germany's tributaries, silver mines, or Italian connections. Much like the Abbasid caliphs at Baghdad, the kings of France saw their power wane. During most of the tenth century, Carolingian kings alternated on the throne with kings from a family that would later be called the "Capetians." At the end of that century the most powerful men of the realm, seeking to stave off civil war, elected Hugh Capet (r.987–996) as their king. The Carolingians were displaced, and the Capetians continued on the throne until the fourteenth century. (See Genealogy 5.4: The Capetian Kings of France, on p. 177.)

The Capetians' scattered but substantial estates lay in the north of France, in the region around Paris. Here the kings had their vassals and their castles. This "Ile-de-France" (which was all there was to "France" in the period; see Map 4.6) was indeed an "island,"—an île—surrounded by independent castellans. In the sense that he, too, had little more military power than other castellans, Hugh Capet and his eleventh-century successors were similar to local strongmen. But the Capetian kings had the prestige of their office. Anointed with holy oil, they represented the idea of unity and God-given rule inherited from Charlemagne. Most of the counts and dukes—at least those in the north of France—swore homage and fealty to the king, a gesture, however weak, of personal support. Unlike the German kings, the French could rely on vassalage to bind the great men of the realm to them.

New States in East Central Europe

Around the same time as Moravia and Bulgaria lost their independence to the Magyars and the Byzantines (respectively), three new polities—Bohemia, Poland, and Hungary—emerged in East Central Europe. In many ways they formed an interconnected bloc, as their ruling houses intermarried with one another and with the great families of the Empire—the looming power to the west. Bohemia and Poland both were largely Slavic-speaking; linguistically Hungary was odd man out, but in almost every other way it was typical of the fledgling states in the region.

BOHEMIA AND POLAND

While the five German duchies were subsumed by the Ottonian state (see p. 139), Bohemia in effect became a separate duchy of the Ottonian Empire. (See Map 4.6.) Already Christianized, largely under the aegis of German bishops, Bohemia was unified in the course of the tenth century. (One of its early rulers was Wenceslas—the carol's "Good King Wenceslas"—who was to become a national saint after his assassination.) Its princes were supposed to be vassals of the emperor in Germany. Thus when Bretislav I (d.1055) tried in 1038 to expand into what was by then Poland, laying waste the land all the way to Gniezno and kidnapping the body of the revered Saint Adalbert, Emperor Henry III (d.1056) declared war, forcing Bretislav to give up the captured territory and hostages. Although left to its own affairs internally, Bohemia was thereafter semi-dependent on the Empire.

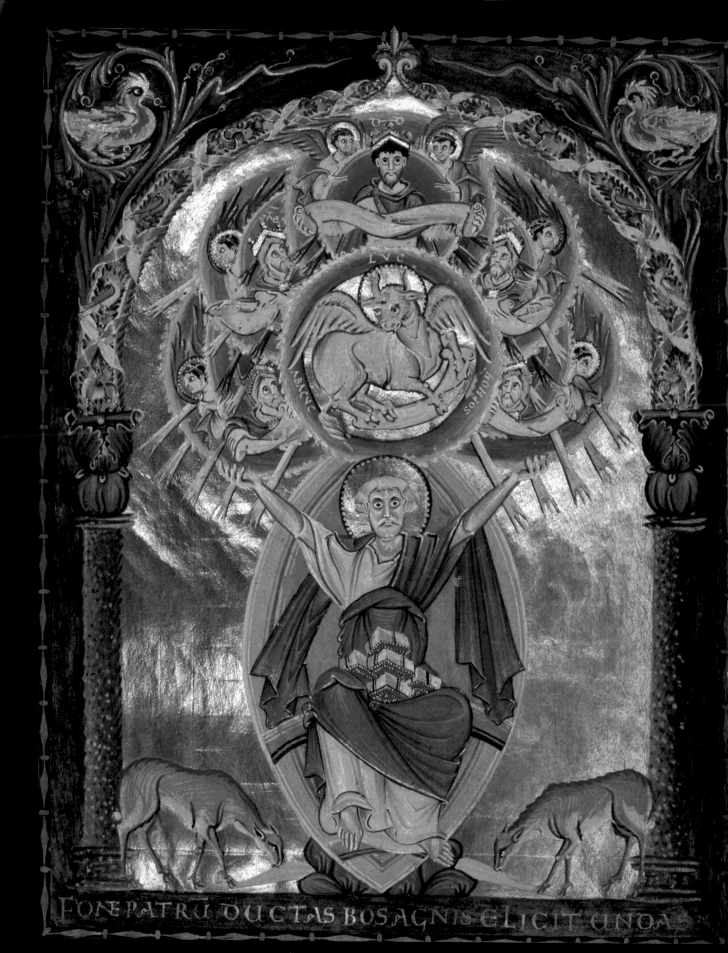

FONS PATRU DUCTAS BOS AGNIS ELIGIT UNDAS

SEEING THE MIDDLE AGES

Plate 4.4 (facing page):
Saint Luke, Gospel Book of Otto III (998–1001)

This is a complicated picture. How can we tease out its meaning? We know that the main subject is the evangelist Saint Luke, first because this illustration precedes the text of the Gospel of Saint Luke in the manuscript, and second because of the presence of the ox (who is labeled "Luc"). Compare Plate 2.5 on p. 67, which shows the same symbol and also includes the label "Agios Lucas"—Saint Luke. In that plate, Luke is writing his gospel. Here Luke is doing something different. But what?

An important hint is at the bottom of the page: the Latin inscription there says, "From the fountain of the Fathers, the ox draws water for the lambs." So Luke (the ox) draws water, or nourishment, from the Fathers for the "lambs," who are in fact shown drinking from the stream. Who are the lambs? In the same manuscript, the page depicting the evangelist Saint Matthew, which precedes his own Gospel, shows men, rather than lambs, drinking from the streams: clearly the lambs signify the Christian people.

Above Luke's head are the "Fathers." They are five of the Old Testament prophets, each provided with a label; the one to Luke's right, for example, is "Abacuc"—Habakkuk. Behind each prophet is an angel (David, at the very top, is accompanied by two), and each is surrounded by a cloud of glory, giving off rays of light that appear like forks jutting into the sky. The artist was no doubt thinking of Paul's Epistle to the Hebrews (12:1) where, after naming the great Old Testament prophets and their trials and tribulations, Paul calls them a "cloud of witnesses over our head" who help us to overcome our sins. But the artist must also have had in mind Christ's Second Coming, when, according to Apoc. 4:2–3, Christ will be seated on a "throne set in heaven" with "a rainbow round about the throne." In our plate, Luke sits in the place of Christ.

Thus this picture shows the unity of the Gospel of Luke with both the Old Testament and the final book of the Bible, the Apocalypse. Luke is the continuator and the guardian of the prophets, whose books are piled on his lap.

There is more. The figure of Luke forms the bottom half of a cross, with the ox in the center. The lamb and the ox were both sacrificial animals, signifying Christ himself, whose death on the cross redeemed mankind. Thus Luke not only "draws water for the lambs" from the Fathers, but he prefigures the Second Coming of Christ himself, the moment of salvation. The mandorla—the oval "halo" that surrounds him—was frequently used to portray Christ in glory.

Why would Emperor Otto III want to own a Gospel book of such theological sophistication? It is very likely because he saw himself as part of the divine order. He called himself the "servant of Jesus Christ," and he appears in one manuscript within a mandorla, just like Luke. (See the illustration below.) In this depiction, the symbols of the evangelists hold up the scarf of heaven that bisects the emperor: his feet touch the ground (note the cringing figure of Earth holding him up), while his head touches the cross of Christ, whose hand places a crown on his head. Otto III saw himself—much like Christ (and Luke)—as mediating between the people and God.

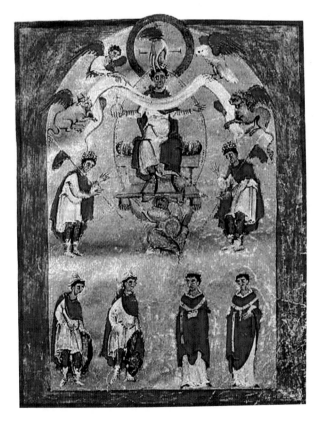

Otto III Enthroned, Aachen Gospels, (c.996)

Further Reading

Mayr-Hartung, Henry. *Ottonian Book Illumination: An Historical Study.* 2nd rev. ed. London: Harvey Miller, 1999.

Nees, Lawrence. *Early Medieval Art.* Oxford: Oxford University Press, 2002.

What was this "Poland" of such interest to Bretislav and Henry? Like the Dane Harald Bluetooth, and around the same time, the ruler of the region that would become Poland, Mieszko I (r.c.960–992), became Christian. In 990/991 he put his realm under the protection of the pope, tying it closely to the power of Saint Peter. Mieszko built a network of defensive structures manned by knights, subjected the surrounding countryside to his rule, and expanded his realm in all directions. Mieszko's son Boleslaw the Brave (or, in Polish, Chrobry) (r.992–1025), "with fox-like cunning" (as a hostile German observer put it), continued his father's expansion, for a short time even becoming duke of Bohemia.[15] Above all, Boleslaw made the Christian religion a centerpiece of his rule when Gniezno was declared an archbishopric. It was probably around that time that Boleslaw declared his alliance with Christ on a coin: on one side he portrayed himself as a sort of Roman emperor, while on the other he displayed a cross.[16] Soon the Polish rulers could count on a string of bishoprics—and the bishops who presided in them. A dynastic crisis in the 1030s gave Bretislav his opening, but, as we have seen, that was quickly ended by the German emperor. Poland persisted, although somewhat reduced in size.

HUNGARY

Polytheists at the time of their entry into the West, most Magyars were peasants, initially specializing in herding but soon busy cultivating vineyards, orchards, and grains. Above them was a warrior class, and above the warriors were the elites, whose richly furnished graves reveal the importance of weapons, jewelry, and horses to this society. Originally organized into tribes led by dukes, by the mid-tenth century the Hungarians recognized one ruling house—that of prince Géza (r.972–997).

Like the ambitious kings of Scandinavia, Géza was determined to give his power new ballast via baptism. His son, Stephen I (r.997–1038), consolidated the change to Christianity: he built churches and monasteries, and required everyone to attend church on Sundays. Establishing his authority as sole ruler, Stephen had himself crowned king in the year 1000 (or possibly 1001). Around the same time, "governing our monarchy by the will of God and emulating both ancient and modern caesars [emperors]," he issued a code of law that put his kingdom in step with other European powers.[17]

★   ★   ★   ★   ★

Political fragmentation did not mean chaos. It simply betokened a new order. At Byzantium, in any event, even the most centrifugal forces were focused on the center; the real trouble for Basil II, for example, came from *dynatoi* who wanted to be emperors, not from people who wanted to be independent regional rulers. In the Islamic world fragmentation largely meant replication, as courts patterned on or competitive with the Abbasid model were set up by Fatimid caliphs and other rulers. In Europe, the rise of local rulers was accompanied by the widespread adoption of forms of personal dependency—vassalage, serfdom—that could be (and were) manipulated even by kings, such as the Capetians, who seemed to have lost the most from the dispersal of power. Another institution that they could count on was the church. No wonder that in Rus', Scandinavia, and East Central Europe, state formation and Christianization went hand in hand.

The *real* fragmentation was among the former heirs of the Roman Empire. They did not speak the same language, they were increasingly estranged by their religions, and they knew almost nothing about one another. In the next century the West, newly prosperous and self-confident, would go on the offensive. Henceforth, without forgetting about the Byzantine and Islamic worlds, we shall focus on this aggressive and dynamic new society.

CHAPTER FOUR KEY EVENTS

*c.*790–*c.*950	Invasions into Europe by Vikings, Muslims, and Hungarians
869–883	Zanj revolt in Iraq
871–899	Reign of King Alfred the Great of England
*c.*909	Fatimids (in North Africa) establish themselves as caliphs
929	Abd al-Rahman III (at Córdoba in al-Andalus) takes title of caliph
955	Victory of Otto I over Hungarians at Lechfeld
962	Otto I crowned emperor
980–1037	Ibn Sina (Avicenna)
988	Conversion of Vladimir, ruler of Rus', to Byzantine Christianity
989	"Peace of God" movement begins
990/991	Mieszko I puts Poland under papal protection
1000 (or 1001)	Stephen I crowned king of Hungary
1025	Death of Basil II the Bulgar Slayer
*c.*1031	Al-Andalus splits into *taifas*

NOTES

1 Quoted in Henry Maguire, "Images of the Court," in *The Glory of Byzantium: Art and Culture of the Middle Byzantine Era,* A.D. *843–1261*, ed. Helen C. Evans and William D. Wixom (New York: Metropolitan Museum of Art, 1997), p.183.

2 Romanus I Lecapenus, *Novel*, in *Reading the Middle Ages: Sources from Europe, Byzantium, and the Islamic World*, ed. Barbara H. Rosenwein, 2nd ed. (Toronto: University of Toronto Press, 2014), p. 174.

3 *The Russian Primary Chronicle*, in *Reading the Middle Ages*, p. 215.

4 Al-Tabari, *The Defeat of the Zanj Revolt*, in *Reading the Middle Ages*, p. 172.

5 Ibn Sina (Avicenna), *Treatise on Logic*, in *Reading the Middle Ages*, p. 204.

6 Al-Qabisi, *A Treatise Detailing the Circumstances of Students and the Rules Governing Teachers and Students*, in *Reading the Middle Ages*, p. 199.

7 *Agreements between Count William of the Aquitanians and Hugh IV of Lusignan*, in *Reading the Middle Ages*, p. 183.

8 *Charter of Guillem Guifred*, in *Reading the Middle Ages*, p. 189.

9 Andrew of Fleury, *The Miracles of St. Benedict*, in *Reading the Middle Ages*, p. 187.

10 King Alfred, *Prefaces to Gregory the Great's Pastoral Care*, in *Reading the Middle Ages*, p. 221.

11 *The Battle of Brunanburh*, in *The Battle of Maldon and Other Old English Poems*, trans. Kevin Crossley-Holland, ed. Bruce Mitchell (London: McMillan, 1966), p. 42.

12 For an image of this runestone see *The Jelling Monument*, in *Reading the Middle Ages*, Plate 13, p. 249. For the quote, ibid., p. 226.

13 Ruotger, *Life of Bruno, Archbishop of Cologne*, in *Reading the Middle Ages*, p. 218.

14 Ibid., p. 217.

15 See Thietmar of Merseburg, *Chronicle*, in *Reading the Middle Ages*, p. 212.

16 For an image of this coin, see *Reading the Middle Ages*, Plate 12, p. 248.

17 King Stephen, *Laws*, in *Reading the Middle Ages*, p. 206.

FURTHER READING

Bachrach, David S. *Warfare in Tenth-Century Germany*. Woodbridge: Boydell, 2012.

Bagge, Sverre, Michael H. Gelting, and Thomas Lindkvist, eds. *Feudalism: New Landscapes of Debate*. Turnhout: Brepols, 2011.

Berend, Nora, ed. *Christianization and the Rise of Christian Monarchy: Scandinavia, Central Europe, and Rus' c. 900–1200*. Cambridge: Cambridge University Press, 2007.

Bonfil, Robert, Oded Irshai, Guy G. Stoumsa, et al., eds. *Jews in Byzantium: Dialetics of Minority and Majority Cultures*. Leiden: Brill, 2012.

Brink, Stefan, with Neil Price, eds. *The Viking World*. London: Routledge, 2008.

Chiarelli, Leonard C. *A History of Muslim Sicily*. Malta: Santa Venera, 2010.

Engel, Pál. *The Realm of St. Stephen: A History of Medieval Hungary, 895–1526*. Trans. Tamás Pálosfalvi. London: I.B. Tauris, 2001.

Evans, Helen C., and William D. Wixom. *The Glory of Byzantium: Art and Culture of the Middle Byzantine Era, a.d. 843–1261*. New York: Metropolitan Museum of Art, 1997.

Foot, Sarah. *Æthelstan: The First King of England*. New Haven, CT: Yale University Press, 2011.

Franklin, Simon, and Jonathan Shepard. *The Emergence of Rus, 750–1200*. London: Longman, 1996.

Jones, Anna Trumbore. *Noble Lord, Good Shepherd: Episcopal Power and Piety in Aquitaine, 877–1050*. Leiden: Brill, 2009.

Moore, R.I. *The First European Revolution, c. 970–1215*. Oxford: Wiley-Blackwell, 2000.

Neville, Leonora. *Authority in Byzantine Provincial Society, 950–1100*. Cambridge: Cambridge University Press, 2004.

Raffensperger, Christian. *Reimagining Europe: Kievan Rus' in the Medieval World*. Cambridge, MA: Harvard University Press, 2012).

Reuter, Timothy. *Germany in the Early Middle Ages, c.800–1056*. London: Longman, 1991.

Winroth, Anders. *The Conversion of Scandinavia: Vikings, Merchants, and Missionaries in the Remaking of Northern Europe*. New Haven, CT: Yale University Press, 2012.

To test your knowledge of this chapter, please go to

www.utphistorymatters.com

for Study Questions.

PART II
THE
EUROPEAN
TAKE-OFF

FIVE

THE EXPANSION OF EUROPE

(c. 1050–c. 1150)

EUROPEANS FLEXED THEIR MUSCLES in the second half of the eleventh century. They built cities, reorganized the church, created new varieties of religious life, expanded their intellectual horizons, pushed aggressively at their frontiers, and even waged war over 1,400 miles away, in what they called the Holy Land. Expanding population and a vigorous new commercial economy lay behind all this. So, too, did the weakness, disunity, and beckoning wealth of their neighbors, the Byzantines and Muslims.

THE SELJUKS

In the eleventh century the Seljuk Turks, a new group from outside the Islamic world, entered and took over its eastern half. Eventually penetrating deep into Anatolia, they took a great bite out of Byzantium. Soon, however, the Seljuks themselves split apart, and the Islamic world fragmented anew under the rule of dozens of emirs.

From the Sultans to the Emirs

Pastoralists on horseback, a Turkic people called the "Seljuks" (after the name of their most enterprising leader) crossed from the region east of the Caspian Sea into Iran in about the year 1000. Within a little over fifty years, the Seljuks had allied themselves with the caliphs as upholders of Sunni orthodoxy, defeated the Buyids, taken over the cities of Iran and Iraq, and started collecting taxes. Between 1055 and 1092, a succession of formidable

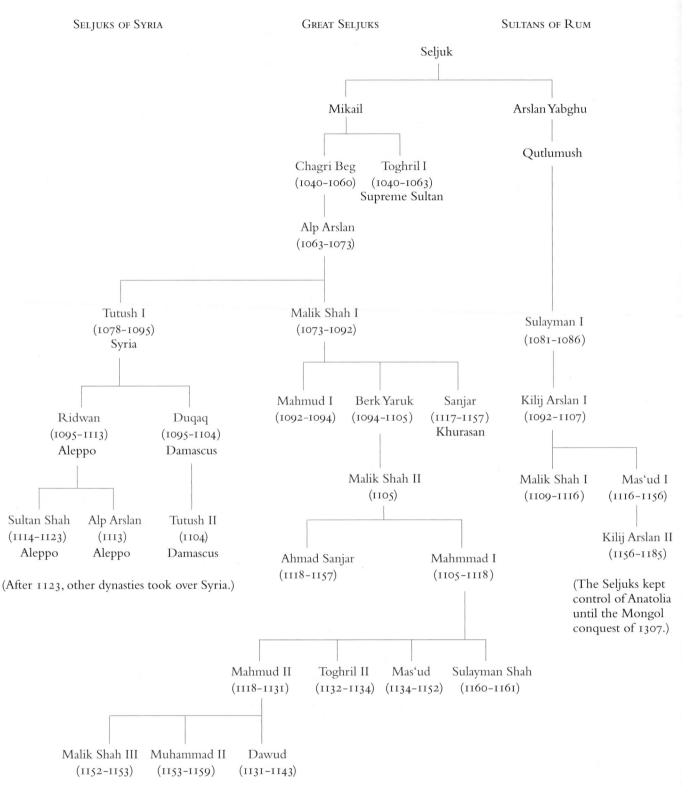

SELJUKS OF SYRIA   GREAT SELJUKS   SULTANS OF RUM

Seljuk

Mikail   Arslan Yabghu

                                     Qutlumush

Chagri Beg   Toghril I
(1040-1060)   (1040-1063)
                  Supreme Sultan

Alp Arslan
(1063-1073)

Tutush I   Malik Shah I   Sulayman I
(1078-1095)   (1073-1092)   (1081-1086)
Syria

Ridwan   Duqaq   Mahmud I   Berk Yaruk   Sanjar   Kilij Arslan I
(1095-1113)   (1095-1104)   (1092-1094) (1094-1105)   (1117-1157)   (1092-1107)
Aleppo   Damascus   Khurasan

                                            Malik Shah II   Malik Shah I   Mas'ud I
                                            (1105)   (1109-1116)   (1116-1156)

Sultan Shah   Alp Arslan   Tutush II
(1114-1123)   (1113)   (1104)
Aleppo   Aleppo   Damascus   Ahmad Sanjar   Mahmmad I   Kilij Arslan II
                                           (1118-1157)   (1105-1118)   (1156-1185)

(After 1123, other dynasties took over Syria.)   (The Seljuks kept
                                                                                         control of Anatolia
                                                                                         until the Mongol
                                                                                         conquest of 1307.)

                          Mahmud II   Toghril II   Mas'ud   Sulayman Shah
                          (1118-1131)   (1132-1134)   (1134-1152) (1160-1161)

Malik Shah III   Muhammad II   Dawud
(1152-1153)   (1153-1159)   (1131-1143)

(In 1194 the Great Seljuks were conqured by a dynasty from Iran.)

Seljuk leaders—Toghril I, Alp Arslan, and Malik Shah I (see Genealogy 5.1: The Early Seljuks)—proclaimed themselves rulers, "sultans," of a new state. Bands of herdsmen followed in their wake, moving their sheep into the very farmland of Iran (disrupting agriculture there), then continuing westward, into Armenia, which had been recently annexed by Byzantium. Meanwhile, under Alp Arslan (r.1063–1073), the Seljuk army (composed precisely of such herdsmen but also, increasingly, of other Turkic tribesmen recruited as slaves or freemen) harried Syria. This was Muslim territory, but it was equally the back door to Byzantium. Thus the Byzantines got involved, and throughout the 1050s and 1060s they fought numerous indecisive battles with the Seljuks. Then in 1071 a huge Byzantine force met an equally large Seljuk army at Manzikert (today Malazgirt, in Turkey). The battle ended with the Byzantines defeated and Anatolia open to a flood of militant nomads. (See Map 5.1.)

The Seljuks of Anatolia set up their own sultanate and were effectively independent of the Great Seljuks who ruled (and disputed among themselves) in Iran and Iraq. For the Anatolian Seljuks, this once-central Byzantine province was Rum, "Rome." Meanwhile, other Turks in the Seljuk entourage took off on their own, hiring themselves out as military leaders. Atsiz ibn Uwaq is a good example. For a while he worked for Alp Arslan, but around 1070 he was called on by the Fatimid governor of Syria to help fight off rebellious

Genealogy 5.1 (facing page): The Early Seljuks

Map 5.1: The Byzantine Empire and the Seljuk World, *c.*1090

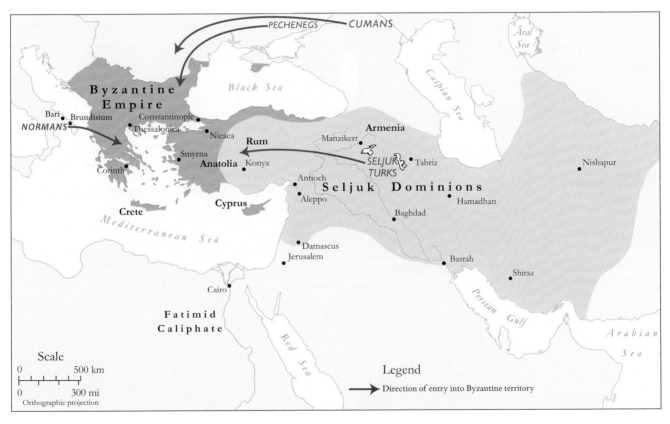

Arab tribes there. Dissatisfied with his pay and plunder, Atsiz decided to work for himself, briefly carving out his own regional principality centered on Damascus. He was, however, ousted by a son of Alp Arslan, Tutush I, in 1078.

Atsiz was born a generation too soon; later, men like him were more successful. After the death of Malik Shah I in 1092, the Seljuks could no longer maintain centralized rule over the Islamic world, even though they still were valued, if only to confer titles like "emir" on local rulers who craved legitimacy. Nor could the Fatimids prevent their own territories from splintering into tiny emirates, each centered on one or a few cities. Some emirs were from the Seljuk family; others were military men who originally served under them. We shall see that the tiny states set up by the crusaders who conquered the Levant in 1099 were, in size, not so very different from their neighboring Islamic emirates.

In the western part of North Africa, the Maghreb, Berber tribesmen forged a state similar to that of the Seljuks. Fired (as the Seljuks had been) with religious fervor on behalf of Sunni orthodoxy, the Berber Almoravids took over northwest Africa in the 1070s and 1080s. In 1086, invited by the ruler of Seville to help fight Christian armies from the north, they sent troops into al-Andalus. This military "aid" soon turned into conquest. By 1094 all of al-Andalus not yet conquered by the Christians was under Almoravid control. Almoravid hegemony over the western Islamic world ended only in 1147, with the triumph of the Almohads, a rival Berber group.

Together, the Seljuks and Almoravids rolled back the Shi'ite wave. They kept it back through a new system of higher education, the *madrasas*. As we have seen (see Chapter 4), the Islamic world had always supported elementary schools. The *madrasas*, normally attached to mosques, went beyond this by serving as centers of advanced scholarship. There young men attended lessons in religion, law, and literature. Sometimes visiting scholars arrived to debate at lively public displays of intellectual brilliance. More regularly, teachers and students carried on a quiet regimen of classes on the Qur'an and other texts. In the face of Sunni retrenchment, some Shi'ite scholars modified their teachings to be more palatable to the mainstream. The conflicts between the two sects receded as Muslims drew together to counter the crusaders.

Byzantium: Bloodied but Unbowed

There would have been no crusaders if Byzantium had remained strong. But the once triumphant empire of Basil II was unable to sustain its successes in the face of Turks and Normans. We have already discussed the triumph of the Turks in Anatolia; meanwhile, in the Balkans, the Turkic Pechenegs raided with ease. The Normans, some of whom (as we saw on p. 130) had established themselves in southern Italy, began attacks on Byzantine territory there and conquered its last stronghold, Bari, in 1071. Ten years later, Norman knights were attacking Byzantine territory in the Balkans. In 1130 the Norman Roger II (r. 1130–1154) became king of a territory that ran from southern Italy to Palermo—the Kingdom of Sicily. It was a persistent thorn in Byzantium's side.

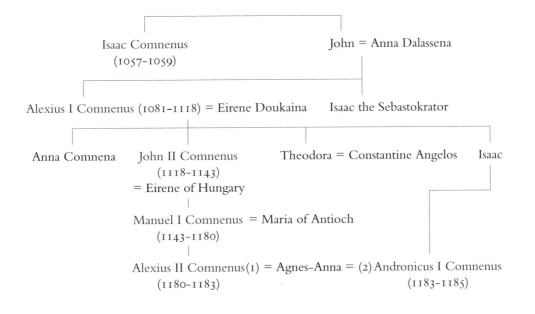

Isaac Comnenus (1057-1059)

John = Anna Dalassena

Alexius I Comnenus (1081-1118) = Eirene Doukaina   Isaac the Sebastokrator

Anna Comnena   John II Comnenus (1118-1143) = Eirene of Hungary   Theodora = Constantine Angelos   Isaac

Manuel I Comnenus = Maria of Antioch (1143-1180)

Alexius II Comnenus (1) = Agnes-Anna = (2) Andronicus I Comnenus (1180-1183)   (1183-1185)

Genealogy 5.2: The Comnenian Dynasty

Clearly the Byzantine army was no longer very effective. Few themes were still manned with citizen-soldiers, and the emperor's army was also largely made up of mercenaries— Turks and Russians, as had long been the case, and increasingly Normans and Franks as well. But the Byzantines were not entirely dependent on armed force; in many instances they turned to diplomacy to confront the new invaders. When Emperor Constantine IX (r.1042–1055) was unable to prevent the Pechenegs from entering the Balkans, he shifted policy, welcoming them, administering baptism, conferring titles, and settling them in depopulated regions. Much the same process took place in Anatolia, where the emperors at times welcomed the Turks to help them fight rival *dynatoi*. Here the invaders were sometimes also welcomed by Christians who did not adhere to Byzantine orthodoxy; the Monophysites of Armenia were glad to have new Turkic overlords. The Byzantine grip on its territories loosened and its frontiers became nebulous, but Byzantium still stood.

There were changes at the imperial court as well. The model of the "public" emperor ruling alone with the aid of a civil service gave way to a less costly, more "familial" model of government. To be sure, for a time competing *dynatoi* families swapped the imperial throne. But Alexius I Comnenus (r.1081–1118), a Dalassenus on his mother's side, managed to bring most of the major families together through a series of marriage alliances. (The Comneni remained on the throne for about a century; see Genealogy 5.2: The Comnenian Dynasty.) Until her death in *c*.1102, Anna Dalassena, Alexius's mother, held the reins of government while Alexius occupied himself with military matters. At his revamped court, which he moved to the Blachernai palace area, at the northwestern tip of the city (see Map 4.1 on p. 116), his relatives held the highest positions. Many of them received *pronoiai* (sing. *pronoia*), temporary grants of imperial lands that they administered and profited from.

Altogether, Byzantine rulers were becoming more like European ones, holding a relatively small amount of territory, handing some of it out in grants that worked a bit like fiefs, spending most of their time in battle to secure a stronghold here, a city there. Meanwhile, Western rulers were becoming less regional in focus, encroaching on Byzantine territory and (as we shall see) attacking the Islamic world as well.

THE QUICKENING OF THE EUROPEAN ECONOMY

Behind the new European expansion was a new economy. Draining marshes, felling trees, building dikes: this was the backbreaking work that brought new land into cultivation. With their heavy, horse-drawn plows, peasants were able to reap greater harvests; using the three-field system, they raised more varieties of crops. Great landowners, the same "oppressors" against whom the Peace of God fulminated (see p. 134), could also be efficient economic organizers. They set up mills to grind grain, forced their tenants to use them, and then charged a fee for the service. It was in their interest that the peasants produce as much grain as possible. Some landlords gave peasants special privileges to settle on especially inhospitable land: the bishop of Hamburg was generous to those who came from Holland to work soil that was "uncultivated, marshy, and useless."[1]

As the countryside became more productive, people became healthier, their fertility increased, and there were more mouths to feed. Even so, surprising surpluses made possible the growth of old and the development of new urban centers. Within a generation or two, city dwellers, intensely conscious of their common goals, elaborated new instruments of commerce, self-regulating organizations, and forms of self-government.

Towns and Cities

Around castles and monasteries in the countryside or at the walls of crumbling ancient towns, merchants came with their wares and artisans set up shop. At Bruges (today in Belgium; for all the places mentioned in this section, see Map 5.3), it was the local lord's castle that served as a magnet. As one late medieval chronicler put it,

> To satisfy the needs of the people in the castle at Bruges, first merchants with luxury articles began to surge around the gate; then the wine-sellers came; finally the inn-keepers arrived to feed and lodge the people who had business with the prince.... So many houses were built that soon a great city was created.[2]

Churches and monasteries were the other centers of town growth. Recall Tours as it had been in the early seventh century (Map 1.4 on p. 26), with its semi-permanent settlements around the church of Saint-Martin, out in the cemetery, and its lonely cathedral

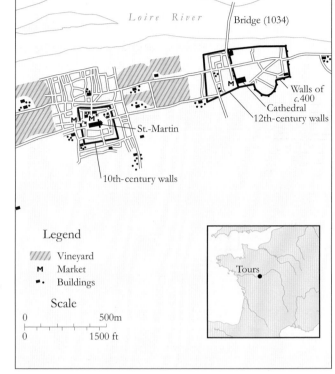

Map 5.2: Tours in the Eleventh and Twelfth Centuries

nestling against one of the ancient walls. By the twelfth century (see Map 5.2), Saint-Martin was a monastery, the hub of a small town dense enough to boast eleven parish churches, merchant and artisan shops, private houses, and two markets. To the east, the episcopal complex was no longer alone: a market had sprung up outside the old western wall, and private houses lined the street leading to the bridge. Smaller than the town around Saint-Martin, the one at the foot of the old city had only two parish churches, but it was big and rich enough to warrant the construction of a new set of walls to protect it.

Early cities developed without prior planning, but some later ones were "chartered," that is, declared, surveyed, and plotted out. A marketplace and merchant settlement were already in place at Freiburg im Breisgau when the duke of Zähringen chartered it, promising each new settler there a house lot of 5,000 square feet for a very small yearly rent. The duke had fair hopes that commerce would flourish right at his back door and yield him rich revenues.

The look and feel of medieval cities varied immensely from place to place. Nearly all included a marketplace, a castle, and several churches. Most were ringed by walls. (See Map 7.4, p. 249, for the successive walls of Piacenza, evidence of the growth of population there.) Within the walls lay a network of streets—narrow, dirty, dark, smelly, and winding—made of packed clay or gravel. Most cities were situated near waterways and had bridges; the one at Tours was built in the 1030s. Many had to adapt to increasingly crowded conditions. At the end of the eleventh century in Winchester, England, city plots were still large enough to accommodate houses parallel to the street; but soon those houses had to be torn down to make way for narrow ones, built at right angles to the roadway. The houses at Winchester were made of wattle and daub—twigs woven together and covered with clay. If they were like the stone houses built in the late twelfth century (about which we know a good deal), they had two stories: a shop or warehouse on the lower floor and living quarters above. Behind this main building were the kitchen, enclosures for livestock, and a garden. Even city dwellers clung to rural pursuits, raising much of their food themselves.

Although commercial centers developed throughout Western Europe, they grew fastest and most densely in regions along key waterways: the Mediterranean coasts of Italy, France, and Spain; northern Italy along the Po River; the river system of Rhône-Saône-Meuse; the Rhineland; the English Channel; the shores of the Baltic Sea. During the eleventh and twelfth centuries, these waterways became part of a single, interdependent economy. At the same time, new roads through the countryside linked urban centers to rural districts and stimulated the growth of fairs (regular, short-term, often lively markets). (See Map 7.3 on p. 246 for a depiction of the trade routes and urban centers of a somewhat later period.)

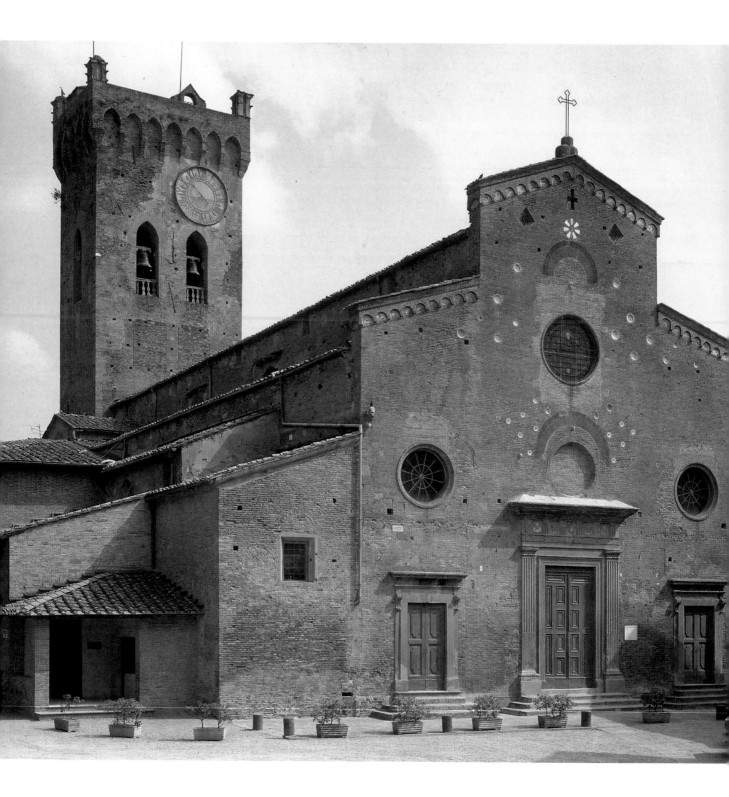

Business Arrangements

The revival of urban life and the expansion of trade, together dubbed the "commercial revolution" by historians, was sustained and invigorated by merchants. They were a varied lot. Some were local traders, like one monk who supervised a manor twenty miles south of his monastery and sold its surplus horses and grain at a local market. Others—mainly Jews and Italians—were long-distance traders, much in demand because they supplied fine wines, spices, and fabrics to the aristocracy. Some Jews had long been involved at least part time in long-distance trade as vintners. In the eleventh century, more Jews swelled their ranks when lords reorganized the countryside and drove out the Jewish landowners, forcing them into commerce and urban trades full time. Other long-distance traders came from Italy. The key players were from Genoa, Pisa, Amalfi, and Venice. Regular merchants at Constantinople, their settlements were strung like pearls along the Golden Horn (see Map 4.1 on p. 116).

Italian traders found the Islamic world nearly as lucrative as the Byzantine. Establishing bases at ports such as Tunis, they imported Islamic wares—ceramics, textiles, metalwork—into Europe. Near Pisa, for example, the façade of the cathedral of San Miniato (Plate 5.1) was decorated with shiny bowls (Plate 5.2) imported by Pisan traders from North African artisans. In turn, merchants from the West exported wood, iron, and woolen cloth to the East.

Merchants invented new forms of collective enterprises to pool their resources and finance large undertakings. The Italian *commenda*, for example, was a partnership established for ventures by sea. The *compagnia* was created by investing family property in trade. Contracts for sales, exchanges, and loans became common, with the interest on loans hidden in the fiction of a penalty for "late payment" in order to avoid the church's ban on usury.

Pooled resources made large-scale productive enterprises possible. A cloth industry began, powered by water mills. New deep-mining technologies provided Europeans with hitherto untapped sources of metals. Forging techniques improved, and iron was for the first time regularly used for agricultural tools and plows, enhancing food production. Beer, a major source of nutrition in the north of Europe, moved from the domestic hearth and monastic estates to urban centers, where brewers gained special privileges to ply their trade.

Brewers, like other urban artisans, had their own guild. Whether driven by machines or handwork, the new economy was sustained by such guilds, which regulated and protected professionals ranging from merchants and financiers to shoemakers. In these social, religious, and economic associations, members prayed for and buried one another. Craft guilds agreed on quality standards for their products and defined work hours, materials, and

Plate 5.1 (facing page): San Miniato Cathedral (late 12th cent.). The façade of the cathedral of the town of San Miniato was once decorated with *bacini*, bowls that sparkled in the Italian sun. In this picture you can see the small round cavities where they once belonged. The *bacino* in Plate 5.2 was slightly above and just to the left (from the viewer's point of view) of the oculus (the round window). The *bacini* were, in effect, cheap and attractive substitutes for marble or mosaics.

Plate 5.2 (above): Bowl, North Africa (late 12th cent.). This earthenware bowl (*bacino*), imported from North Africa and decorated with pseudo-Arabic writing, once adorned the façade of the cathedral of San Miniato. Such bowls, evidence of lively trade between the Islamic world and the West, were in great demand by Italians, not only for the façades of their churches but also for their kitchens.

prices. Merchant guilds regulated business arrangements, common weights and measures, and (like the craft guilds) prices. Guilds guaranteed their members—mostly male, except for a few professions—a place in the market. They represented the social and economic counterpart to urban walls, giving their members protection, shared identity, and recognized status.

The political counterpart to the walls was the "commune"—town self-government. City dwellers—keenly aware of their special identity in a world dominated by knights and peasants—recognized their mutual interest in reliable coinage, laws to facilitate commerce, freedom from servile dues and services, and independence to buy and sell as the market dictated. They petitioned the political powers that ruled them—bishops, kings, counts, castellans, dukes—for the right to govern themselves.

Collective movements for urban self-government were especially prevalent in Italy, France, and Germany. Already Italy's political life was city-centered; communes there were attempts to substitute the power of one group (the citizens) for another (the nobles and bishops). At Milan in the second half of the eleventh century, for example, popular discontent with the archbishop, who effectively ruled the city, led to numerous armed clashes that ended, in 1097, with the transfer of power from the archbishop to a government of leading men of the city. Outside Italy movements for urban independence—sometimes violent, as at Milan, while at other times peaceful—often took place within a larger political framework. For example, King Henry I of England (r. 1100–1135) freed the citizens of London from numerous customary taxes while granting them the right to "appoint as sheriff from themselves whomsoever they may choose, and [they] shall appoint from among themselves as justice whomsoever they choose to look after the pleas of my crown."[3] The king's law still stood, but it was to be carried out by the Londoners' officials.

CHURCH REFORM AND ITS AFTERMATH

Disillusioned citizens at Milan denounced their archbishop not only for his tyranny but also for his impurity; they wanted their pastors to be untainted by sex and by money. In this they were supported by a new-style papacy, keen on reform in the church and society. The "Gregorian Reform," as this movement came to be called, broke up clerical marriages, unleashed civil war in Germany, changed the procedure for episcopal elections, and transformed the papacy into a monarchy. It began as a way to free the church from the world; but in the end the church was deeply involved in the new world it had helped to create.

The Coming of Reform

Free the church from the world: what could it mean? In 910 the duke and duchess of Aquitaine founded the monastery of Cluny with some unusual stipulations. They endowed the monastery with property (normal and essential if it were to survive), but then they gave it and its worldly possessions to Saints Peter and Paul. In this way they put control of the monastery into the hands of the two most powerful heavenly saints. They designated the pope, as the successor of Saint Peter, to be the monastery's worldly protector if anyone should bother or threaten it. But even the pope had no right to infringe on its freedom: "From this day," the duke wrote,

> those same monks there congregated shall be subject neither to our yoke, nor to that of our relatives, nor to the sway of any earthly power. And, through God and all his saints, and by the awful day of judgment, I warn and abjure that no one of the secular princes, no count, no bishop whatever, not the pontiff of the aforesaid Roman see, shall invade the property of these servants of God, or alienate it, or diminish it, or exchange it, or give it as a benefice to any one, or constitute any prelate over them against their will.[4]

Cluny's prestige was great because of the influence of its founders, the status of Saint Peter, and the fame of the monastery's elaborate round of prayers. The Cluniac monks fulfilled the role of "those who pray" in dazzling manner. Through their prayers, they seemed to guarantee the salvation of all Christians. Rulers, bishops, rich landowners, and even serfs (if they could) gave Cluny donations of land, joining their contributions to the land of Saint Peter. Powerful men and women called on the Cluniac abbots to reform new monasteries along the Cluniac model.

The abbots of Cluny came to see themselves as reformers of the world as well as the cloister. They believed in clerical celibacy, preaching against the prevailing norm in which parish priests and even bishops were married. They also thought that the laity could be reformed, become more virtuous, and cease its oppression of the poor. In the eleventh century, the Cluniacs began to link their program to the papacy. When they disputed with bishops or laypeople about lands and rights, they called on the popes to help them out.

The popes were ready to do so. A parallel movement for reform had entered papal circles via a small group of influential monks and clerics. Mining canon (church) law for their ammunition, these churchmen emphasized two abuses: nicolaitism (clerical marriage) and simony (buying church offices). Why were these two singled out? Married clerics were considered less "pure" than those who were celibate; furthermore, their heirs might claim church property. As for simony: the new profit economy sensitized reformers to the crass commercial meanings of gifts; in their eyes, gifts given or received by churchmen for their offices or clerical duties were attempts to purchase the Holy Spirit.

Initially, the reformers got imperial backing. In the view of German king and emperor Henry III (r. 1039–1056), as the anointed of God he was responsible for the well-being of the church in the empire. (For Henry and his dynasty, see Genealogy 5.3: The Salian Kings and Emperors.) Henry denounced simony and personally refused to accept money or gifts when he appointed bishops to their posts. He presided over the Synod of Sutri (1046),

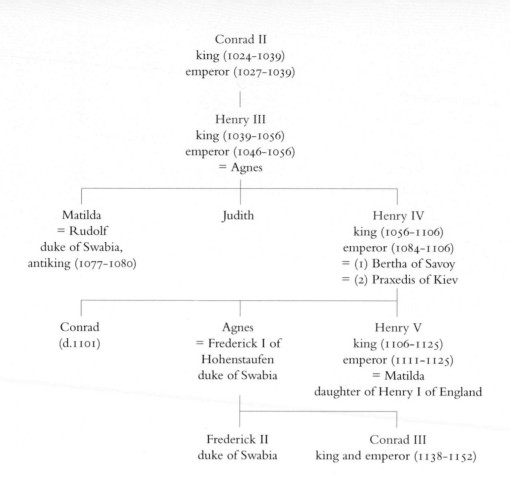

Conrad II
king (1024-1039)
emperor (1027-1039)

Henry III
king (1039-1056)
emperor (1046-1056)
= Agnes

Matilda
= Rudolf
duke of Swabia,
antiking (1077-1080)

Judith

Henry IV
king (1056-1106)
emperor (1084-1106)
= (1) Bertha of Savoy
= (2) Praxedis of Kiev

Conrad
(d.1101)

Agnes
= Frederick I of
Hohenstaufen
duke of Swabia

Henry V
king (1106-1125)
emperor (1111-1125)
= Matilda
daughter of Henry I of England

Frederick II
duke of Swabia

Conrad III
king and emperor (1138-1152)

Genealogy 5.3: The Salian Kings and Emperors

which deposed three papal rivals and elected another. When that pope and his successor died, Henry appointed Bruno of Toul, a member of the royal family, seasoned courtier, and reforming bishop. Taking the name Leo IX (1049–1054), the new pope surprised his patron: he set out to reform the church under papal, not imperial, control.

Leo revolutionized the papacy. He had himself elected by the "clergy and people" to satisfy the demands of canon law. Unlike earlier popes, Leo often left Rome to preside over church councils and make the pope's influence felt outside Italy, especially in France and Germany. To the papal curia Leo brought the most zealous church reformers of his day: Peter Damian, Hildebrand of Soana (later Pope Gregory VII), and Humbert of Silva Candida. They put new stress on the passage in Matthew's gospel (Matt. 16:19) in which Christ tells Peter that he is the "rock" of the church, with the keys to heaven and the power to bind (impose penance) and loose (absolve from sins). As the successor to the special privileges of Saint Peter, the Roman church, headed by the pope, was "head and mother of all churches." What historians call the doctrine of "papal supremacy" was thus announced.

Its impact was soon felt at Byzantium. On a mission at Constantinople in 1054 to forge an alliance with the emperor against the Normans and, at the same time, to "remind" the patriarch of his place in the church hierarchy, Humbert ended by excommunicating the patriarch and his followers. In retaliation, the patriarch excommunicated Humbert and his fellow legates. Clashes between the Roman and Byzantine churches had occurred before and had been patched up, but this one, though not recognized as such at the time, marked a permanent schism. After 1054, the Roman Catholic and Greek Orthodox churches largely went their separate ways.

More generally, the papacy began to wield new forms of power. It waged unsuccessful war against the Normans in southern Italy and then made the best of the situation by granting them parts of the region—and Sicily as well—as a fief, turning former enemies into vassals. It supported the Christian push into the *taifas* of al-Andalus, transforming the "*reconquista*"—the conquest of Islamic Spain—into a holy war: Pope Alexander II (1061–1073) forgave the sins of the Christians on their way to the battle of Barbastro.

The Investiture Conflict and Its Effects

The papal reform movement is associated particularly with Pope Gregory VII (1073–1085), hence the term "Gregorian reform." A passionate advocate of papal primacy (the theory that the pope is the head of the church), Gregory was not afraid to clash directly with the king of Germany, Henry IV (r.1056–1106), over church leadership. In Gregory's view—an astonishing one at the time, given the religious and spiritual roles associated with rulers—kings and emperors were simple laymen who had no right to meddle in church affairs. Henry, on the other hand, brought up in the traditions of his father, Henry III, considered it part of his duty to appoint bishops and even popes to ensure the well-being of church and empire together.

The pope and the king first collided over the appointment of the archbishop of Milan. Gregory disputed Henry's right to "invest" the archbishop (i.e., put him into his office). In the investiture ritual, the emperor or his representative symbolically gave the church and the land that went with it to the bishop or archbishop chosen for the job. In the case of Milan, two rival candidates for archiepiscopal office (one supported by the pope, the other by the emperor) had been at loggerheads for several years when, in 1075, Henry invested his own candidate. Gregory immediately called on Henry to "give more respectful attention to the master of the Church," namely Peter and his living representative—Gregory himself.[5] In reply, Henry and the German bishops called on Gregory, that "false monk," to resign. This was the beginning of what historians delicately call the "Investiture Conflict" or "Investiture Controversy." In fact it was war. In February 1076, Gregory called a synod that both excommunicated Henry and suspended him from office:

> I deprive King Henry [IV], son of the emperor Henry [III], who has rebelled against [God's] Church with unheard-of audacity, of the government over the whole kingdom of Germany and Italy, and I release all Christian men from the allegiance which they have sworn or may swear to him, and I forbid anyone to serve him as king.[6]

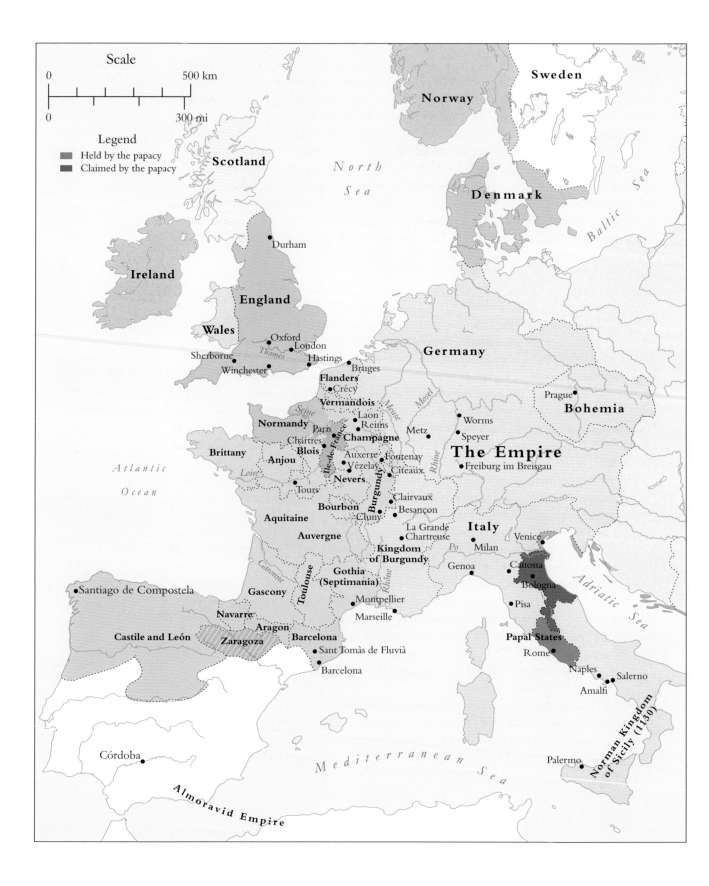

Scale

0   500 km

0   300 mi

Legend

Held by the papacy
Claimed by the papacy

Norway

Sweden

North Sea

Baltic Sea

Scotland

Ireland

Denmark

• Durham

England

Wales

Oxford •
• London
Sherborne • Hastings •
Winchester • • Bruges

Thames

Germany

Flanders
• Crécy
Vermandois
• Laon
Paris Reims
Chartres • • Worms
Normandy • **Champagne** Metz • • Speyer

Seine

Meuse

Mosel

Bohemia
Prague •

Brittany **Blois** Auxerre • **The Empire**
Anjou Île-de-France Fontenay •
Vézelay • • Cîteaux • Freiburg im Breisgau

Atlantic Ocean

Nevers Rhine
• Tours **Burgundy**
Clairvaux •
Bourbon Besançon •
Cluny •

Loire

Aquitaine
La Grande • **Italy**
Auvergne Chartreuse • Milan **Venice**
Kingdom Po
Santiago de Compostela • **of Burgundy** Genoa • Canossa •
Bologna
Gothia Pisa •
Gascony **(Septimania)**
Toulouse Montpellier •
Navarre Marseille • **Papal States**
Aragon Rome •
Castile and León **Zaragoza** **Barcelona** Naples •
Sant Tomàs de Fluvià • Salerno •
Barcelona • Amalfi •

Garonne

Rhône

Adriatic Sea

Córdoba •

Norman Kingdom of Sicily (1130)

Palermo •

Mediterranean Sea

Almoravid Empire

The last part of this decree gave it real punch: anyone in Henry's kingdom could rebel against him. The German "princes"—the aristocrats—seized the moment and threatened to elect another king. They were motivated partly by religious sentiments—many had established links with the papacy through their support of reformed monasteries—and partly by political opportunism, as they had chafed under strong German kings who had tried to keep their power in check. Some bishops, too, joined with Gregory's supporters, a major blow to Henry, who needed the troops that they supplied.

Attacked from all sides, Henry traveled in the winter of 1077 to intercept Gregory, barricaded in a fortress at Canossa, high in the Apennine Mountains (see Map 5.3). It was a refuge provided by the staunchest of papal supporters, Countess Matilda of Tuscany. In an astute and dramatic gesture, the king stood outside the castle (in cold and snow) for three days, barefoot, as a penitent. Gregory was forced, as a pastor, to lift his excommunication and to receive Henry back into the church, precisely as Henry intended. For his part, the pope had the satisfaction of seeing the king humiliate himself before the papal majesty. Although it made a great impression on contemporaries, the whole episode solved nothing. The princes elected an antiking, and bloody civil war continued intermittently until 1122.

The Investiture Conflict ended with a compromise. The Concordat of Worms (1122) relied on a conceptual distinction between two parts of investiture—the spiritual (in which the bishop-to-be received the symbols of his office) and the secular (in which he received the symbols of the material goods that would allow him to function). Under the terms of the Concordat, the ring and staff, symbols of church office, would be given by a churchman in the first part of the ceremony. Then the emperor or his representative would touch the bishop with a scepter, signifying the land and other possessions that went with his office. Elections of bishops in Germany would take place "in the presence" of the emperor—that is, under his influence. In Italy, the pope would have a comparable role.

Map 5.3 (facing page): Western Europe, *c.* 1100

In the end, then, secular rulers continued to matter in the appointment of churchmen. But just as the new investiture ceremony broke the ritual into spiritual and secular halves, so too did it imply a new notion of kingship separate from the priesthood. The Investiture Conflict did not produce the modern distinction between church and state—that would develop only very slowly—but it set the wheels in motion. At the time, its most important consequence was to shatter the delicate balance among political and ecclesiastical powers in Germany and Italy. In Germany, the princes consolidated their lands and powers at the expense of the king. In Italy, the communes came closer to their goals: it was no accident that Milan gained its independence in 1097. And everywhere the papacy gained new authority: it had become a "papal monarchy."

Papal influence was felt at every level. At the general level of canon law, papal primacy was enhanced by the publication *c.*1140 of the *Decretum*, written by a teacher of canon law named Gratian. Collecting nearly two thousand passages from the decrees of popes and councils as well as the writings of the Church Fathers, Gratian set out to demonstrate their essential agreement. In fact, the book's original title was *Harmony of Discordant Canons*. If he found any "discord" in his sources, Gratian usually imposed the harmony himself by arguing that the conflicting passages dealt with different situations. A bit later another legal scholar revised and expanded the *Decretum*, adding Roman law to the mix. At a more local level, papal denunciations of married clergy made inroads on family life. At Verona, for example, "sons of priests" disappeared from the historical record in the twelfth century. At the mundane level of administration, the papal claim to head the church helped turn the curia at Rome into a kind of government, complete with its own bureaucracy, collection agencies, and law courts. It was the teeming port of call for litigious churchmen disputing appointments and for petitioners of every sort.

The First Crusade

On the military level, the papacy's proclamations of holy wars led to bloody slaughter, tragic loss, and tidy profit. We have already seen how Alexander II encouraged the *reconquista* in Spain; it was in the wake of his call that the *taifa* rulers implored the Almoravids for help. An oddly similar chain of events took place at the other end of the Islamic world. Ostensibly responding to a request from the Byzantine Emperor Alexius for mercenaries to help retake Anatolia from the Seljuks, Pope Urban II (1088–1099) turned the enterprise into something new: a pious pilgrimage to the Holy Land to be undertaken by an armed militia—one commissioned like those of the Peace of God, but thousands of times larger—under the leadership of the papacy.

The event that historians call the First Crusade (1096–1099) mobilized a force of some 100,000 people, including warriors, old men, bishops, priests, women, children, and hangers-on. The armies were organized not as one military force but rather as separate militias, each authorized by the pope and commanded by a different individual.

Several motley bands were not authorized by the pope. Though called collectively the "Peasants' (or People's) Crusade," these irregular armies included nobles. They were inspired by popular preachers, especially the eloquent Peter the Hermit, who was described by chroniclers as small, ugly, barefoot, and—partly because of those very characteristics— utterly captivating. Starting out before the other armies, the Peasants' Crusade took a route to the Holy Land through the Rhineland in Germany.

This indirect route was no mistake. The crusaders were looking for "wicked races" closer to home: the Jews. Under Henry IV many Jews had gained a stable place within the cities of Germany, particularly along the Rhine River. The Jews received protection from the local bishops (who were imperial appointees) in return for paying a tax. Living in their own neighborhoods, the Jews valued their tightly-knit communities focused on the synagogue, which was a school and community center as well as a place of worship. Nevertheless, Jews also participated in the life of the larger Christian community. For example, Archbishop Anno of Cologne made use of the services of the Jewish money-lenders in his city, and other Jews in Cologne were allowed to trade their wares at the fairs there.

Although officials pronounced against the Jews from time to time, and although Jews were occasionally (temporarily) expelled from some Rhineland cities, they were not persecuted systematically until the First Crusade. Then the Peasants' Crusade, joined by some local nobles and militias from the region, threatened the Jews with forced conversion or death. Some relented when the Jews paid them money; others, however, attacked. Beleaguered Jews occasionally found refuge with bishops or in the houses of Christian friends, but in many cities—Metz, Speyer, Worms, Mainz, and Cologne—they were massacred:

> Oh God, insolent men have risen against me
> They have sorely afflicted us from our youth
> They have devoured and destroyed us in their wrath against us
> Saying, let us take their inheritance for ourselves.[7]

So wrote Rabbi Eliezer ben Nathan, mourning and celebrating the Jewish martyrs who perished at the hands of the crusaders.

Leaving the Rhineland, some of the irregular militias disbanded, while others sought to gain the Holy Land via Hungary, at least one stopping off at Prague to massacre more Jews there. Only a handful of these armies continued on to Anatolia, where most of them were quickly slaughtered.

From the point of view of Emperor Alexius at Constantinople, even the "official" crusaders were potentially dangerous. One of the crusade's leaders, the Norman warrior Bohemond, had, a few years before, tried to conquer Byzantium itself. Hastily forcing oaths from Bohemond and the other lords that any previously Byzantine lands conquered would be restored to Byzantium, Alexius shipped the armies across the Bosporus.

The main objective of the First Crusade—to conquer the Holy Land—was accomplished largely because of the disunity of the Islamic world and its failure to consider the crusade a serious military threat. Spared by the Turks when they first arrived in Anatolia, the crusaders first made their way to the Seljuk capital, Nicaea. Their armies were initially uncoordinated and their food supplies uncertain, but soon they organized themselves, setting up a "council of princes" that included all the great crusade leaders, while the Byzantines supplied food at a nearby port. Surrounding Nicaea and besieging it with catapults and other war machines, the crusaders took the city on June 18, 1097, dutifully handing it over to Alexius in accordance with their oath.

Gradually, however, the crusaders forgot their oath to the Byzantines. While most went toward Antioch, which stood in the way of their conquest of Jerusalem, one leader went off to Edessa, where he took over the city and its outlying area, creating the first of the Crusader States: the County of Edessa. Meanwhile the other crusaders remained stymied before the thick and heavily fortified walls of Antioch for many months. Then, in a surprise turn-around, they entered the town but found themselves besieged by Muslim armies from the outside. Their mood grim, they rallied when a peasant named Peter Bartholomew reported that he had seen in many visions the Holy Lance that had pierced Christ's body—it was, he said, buried right in the main church in Antioch. (Antioch had a flourishing Christian population even under Muslim rule.) After a night of feverish digging, the crusaders believed that they had discovered the Holy Lance, and, fortified by this miracle, they defeated the besiegers.

From Antioch, it was only a short march to Jerusalem, though disputes among the leaders delayed that next step for over a year. One leader claimed Antioch. Another eventually took charge—provisionally—of the expedition to Jerusalem. His way was eased by quarrels among Muslim rulers, and an alliance with one of them allowed free passage through what would have been enemy territory. In early June 1099, a large crusading force amassed before the walls of Jerusalem and set to work to build siege engines. In mid-July they attacked, breaching the walls and entering the city. "The Franks slaughtered more than 70,000 people.... [they] stripped the Dome of the Rock of more than forty silver candelabra," dryly noted a later Islamic historian looking back on the event.[8]

RULERS WITH CLOUT

While the papacy was turning into a monarchy, other rulers were beginning to turn their territories into states. They discovered ideologies to justify their hegemony, hired officials to work for them, found vassals and churchmen to support them. Some of these rulers were women.

The Crusader States

In the Holy Land, the leaders of the crusade set up four tiny states, European colonies in the Levant. Two (Tripoli and Edessa) were counties, Antioch was a principality, Jerusalem a kingdom. (See Map 5.4.) The region was habituated (as we have seen) to multi-ethnic and multi-religious territories ruled by a military elite; apart from the religion of that elite, the Crusader States were no exception. Yet, however much they engaged with their neighbors, the Europeans in the Levant saw themselves as a world apart, holding on to their western identity through their political institutions and the old vocabulary of homage, fealty, and Christianity.

The states won during the First Crusade lasted—tenuously—until 1291, though many new crusades had to be called in the interval to shore them up. Created by conquest, these states were treated as lordships. The new rulers carved out estates to give as fiefs to their vassals, who, in turn, gave portions of their holdings in fief to their own men. The peasants continued to work the land as before, and commerce boomed as the new rulers encouraged lively trade at their coastal ports. Italian merchants—the Genoese, Pisans, and Venetians—were the most active, but others—Byzantines and Muslim traders—participated as well. Enlightened lordship dictated that the mixed population of the states—Muslims, to be sure, but also Jews, Greek Orthodox Christians, Monophysite Christians, and others—be tolerated for the sake of production and trade. Most Europeans had gone home after the First Crusade; those left behind were obliged to coexist with the inhabitants that remained. Eastern and Western Christians learned to share shrines, priests, and favorite monastic charities—and to remain silent, or to become violent only locally and sporadically, over their many differences.

The main concerns of the crusader states' rulers were military, and these could be guaranteed as well by a woman as by a man. Thus Melisende (r.1131–1152), oldest daughter of King Baldwin II of Jerusalem, was declared ruler along with her husband, Fulk, formerly count of Anjou, and their infant son. Taking the reins of government into her own hands after Fulk's death, she named a constable to lead her army and made sure that the greatest men in the kingdom sent her their vassals to do military service. Vigorously asserting her position as queen, she found supporters in the church, appointed at least one bishop to his see, and created her own chancery, where her royal acts were drawn up.

But vassals alone, however well commanded, were not sufficient to defend the fragile Crusader States, nor were the stone castles and towers that bristled in the countryside. Knights had to be recruited from Europe from time to time, and a new and militant kind of monasticism developed in the Levant: the Knights Templar. Vowed to poverty and chastity, the Templars devoted themselves to war at the same time. They defended the town garrisons of the Crusader States and ferried money from Europe to the Holy Land. Even so, they could not prevent a new Turkic leader, Zangi, from taking Edessa in 1144. The slow but steady shrinking of the Crusader States began at that moment. The Second Crusade (1147–1149), called in the wake of Zangi's victory, came to a disastrous end. After only four days of besieging the walls of Damascus, the crusaders, whose leaders could not keep the peace among themselves, gave up and went home.

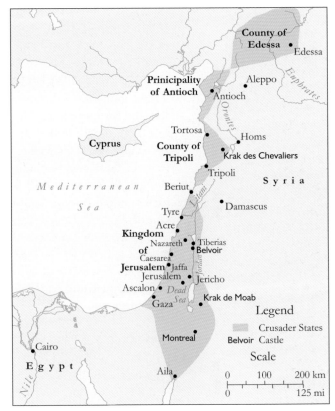

Map 5.4: The Crusader States, c.1140

England under Norman Rule

A more long-lasting conquest took place in England. England had been linked to the Continent by the Vikings, who settled in its eastern half, and in the eleventh century it had been further tied to Scandinavia under the rule of Cnut (see above, p. 138). Nevertheless, the country was drawn inextricably into the Continental orbit only with the conquest of Duke William of Normandy. (See Map 5.3.)

When William left his duchy with a large army in 1066 to dispute the crown of the childless King Edward the Confessor (r.1042–1066), he carried a papal banner, symbol of the pope's support. The one-day battle of Hastings was decisive, and William was crowned the first Norman king of England. (See Genealogy 6.1: The Norman and Angevin Kings of England, on p. 202.) Treating his conquest like booty (as the crusader leaders would do a few decades later in the Levant), William kept about 20 per cent of the land for himself and divided the rest, distributing it in large but scattered fiefs to a relatively small number of his barons—his elite followers—and family members, lay and ecclesiastical, as well as to some lesser men, such as personal servants and soldiers. In turn, these men maintained their own vassals. They owed the king military service along with the service of a fixed number of their vassals; and they paid him certain dues, such as reliefs (money paid upon inheriting a fief) and aids (payments made on important occasions).

The king also collected land taxes. To know what was owed him, in 1086 William ordered a survey of the land and landholders of England. His officials consulted Anglo-Saxon tax lists and took testimony from local jurors, who were sworn to answer a series of formal questions truthfully. Compilers standardized the materials and organized them by county. Consider, by way of example, the entry for the manor of Diddington:

> the Bishop of Lincoln had 2½ hides to the geld. [There is] land for 2 ploughs. There are now 2 ploughs in demesne; and 5 villans having 2 ploughs. There is a church, and 18 acres of meadow, [and] woodland pasture half a league long and a half broad. TRE worth 60s; now 70s. William holds it of the bishop.[9]

The hides were units of tax assessment; the ploughs and acres were units of area, while the leagues were units of length; the villans were one type of peasant (there were many kinds); and the abbreviation TRE meant "in the time of King Edward." Thus anyone consulting the survey would know that the manor of Diddington was now worth more than it had been TRE. As for the William mentioned here: he was not William the Conqueror but rather a vassal of the bishop of Lincoln. No wonder the survey was soon dubbed "Domesday Book": like the records of people judged at doomsday, it provided facts that could not be appealed. Domesday was the most extensive inventory of land, livestock, taxes, and people that had as yet been compiled anywhere in medieval Europe.

Communication with the Continent was constant. The Norman barons spoke a brand of French; they talked more easily with the peasants of Normandy (if they bothered) than with those tilling the land in England. They maintained their estates on the Continent and their ties with its politics, institutions, and culture. English wool was sent to Flanders to be turned into cloth. The most brilliant intellect of his day, Saint Anselm of Bec (or Canterbury; 1033–1109), was born in Italy, became abbot of a Norman monastery, and was then appointed archbishop in England. English adolescent boys were sent to Paris and

Chartres for schooling. The kings of England often spent more time on the Continent than they did on the island. When, on the death of William's son, King Henry I (r. 1100–1135), no male descendent survived to take the throne, two counts from the Continent—Geoffrey of Anjou and Stephen of Blois—disputed it as their right through two rival females of the royal line. (See Genealogy 6.1 again.)

Christian Spain

While initially the product of defeat, Christian Spain in the eleventh and twelfth centuries turned the tables and became, in effect, the successful western counterpart of the Crusader States. The disintegration of al-Andalus into *taifas* opened up immense opportunities for the Spanish princes to the north. Wealth flowed into their coffers not only from plundering raids and the confiscation of lands and cities but also (until the Almoravids put an end to it) from tribute, paid in gold by *taifa* rulers to stave off attacks.

But it was not just the rulers who were enriched. When Rodrigo Díaz de Vivar, the Cid (from the Arabic *sidi*, lord), fell out of favor with his lord, Alfonso VI (r. 1065–1109), king of Castile and León, he and a band of followers found employment with al-Mutamin, ruler of Zaragoza. There he defended the city against Christian and Muslim invaders alike. In 1090, he struck out on his own, taking his chances in Valencia, conquering it in 1094 and ruling there until his death in 1099. He was a Spaniard, but other opportunistic armies sometimes came from elsewhere. The one that Pope Alexander II authorized to besiege Barbastro in 1064 was made up of warriors from France.

The French connection was symptomatic of a wider process: the Europeanization of Spain. Initially the Christian kingdoms had been isolated islands of Visigothic culture. But already in the tenth century, pilgrims from France, England, Germany, and Italy were clogging the roads to the shrine of Saint James (Santiago de Compostela); in the eleventh century, monks from Cluny and other reformed monasteries arrived to colonize Spanish cloisters. Alfonso VI actively reached out beyond the Pyrenees, to Cluny—where he doubled the annual gift of 1000 gold pieces that his father, Fernando I, had given in exchange for prayers for his soul—and to the papacy. He sought recognition from Pope Gregory VII as "king of Spain," and in return he imposed the Roman liturgy throughout his kingdom, stamping out the traditional Visigothic music and texts.

In 1085 Alfonso made good his claim to be more than the king of Castile and León by conquering Toledo. (See Map 5.5.) After his death, his daughter Queen Urraca (r. 1109–1126) ruled in her own right a realm larger than England. Her strength came from many of the usual sources: control over land, which, though granted out to counts and others, was at least in theory revocable; church appointments; an army—everyone was liable to be called up once a year, even arms-bearing slaves; and a court of great men to offer advice and give their consent.

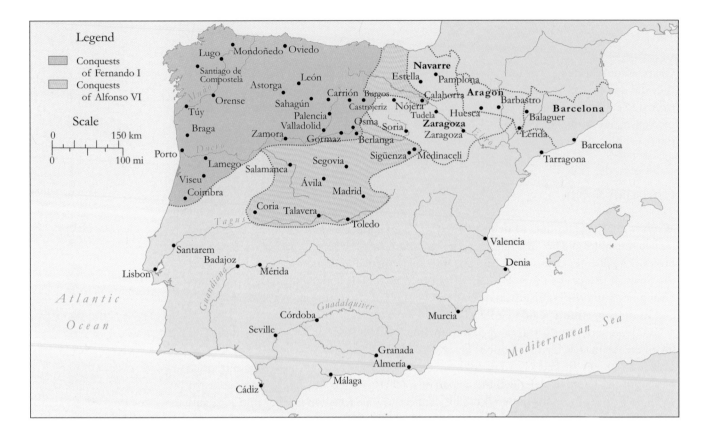

Map 5.5: Spain at the Death of Alfonso VI (1109)

Genealogy 5.4 (facing page): The Capetian Kings of France

Praising the King of France

Not all rulers had opportunities for grand conquest. How did they maintain themselves? The example of the kings of France reveals the possibilities. Reduced to battling a few castles in the vicinity of the Ile-de-France, the Capetian kings nevertheless wielded many of the same instruments of power as their conquering contemporaries: vassals, taxes, commercial revenues, military and religious reputations. Louis VI the Fat (r. 1108–1137), so heavy that he had to be hoisted onto his horse by a crane, was nevertheless a tireless defender of royal power. (See Genealogy 5.4: The Capetian Kings of France.)

Louis's virtues were amplified and broadcast by his biographer, Suger (1081–1151), the abbot of Saint-Denis, a monastery just outside Paris. A close associate of the king, Suger was his chronicler and propagandist. When Louis set himself the task of consolidating his rule in the Ile-de-France, Suger portrayed the king as a righteous hero. He was more than a lord with rights over the French nobles as his vassals; he was a peacekeeper with the God-given duty to fight unruly strongmen. Careful not to claim that Louis was head of the church, which would have scandalized the papacy and its supporters, Suger nevertheless emphasized Louis's role as vigorous protector of the faith and insisted on the sacred importance of the royal dignity. When Louis died in 1137, Suger's notion of the might and right of the king of France reflected reality in an extremely small area. Nevertheless, Louis laid the groundwork for the gradual extension of royal power. As the lord of vassals,

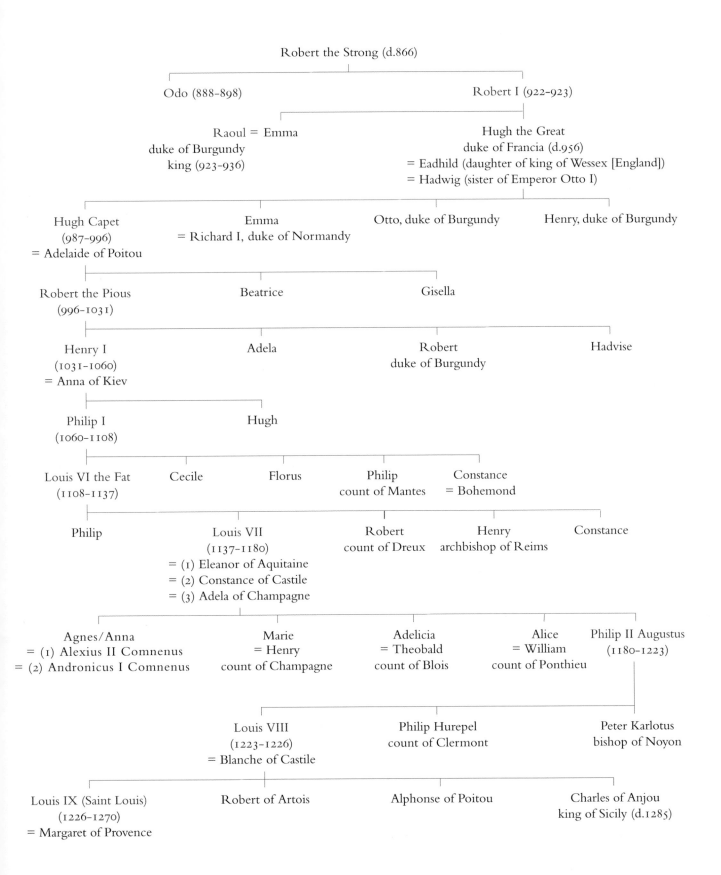

Robert the Strong (d.866)

Odo (888–898)   Robert I (922–923)

Raoul = Emma
duke of Burgundy
king (923–936)

Hugh the Great
duke of Francia (d.956)
= Eadhild (daughter of king of Wessex [England])
= Hadwig (sister of Emperor Otto I)

Hugh Capet
(987–996)
= Adelaide of Poitou

Emma
= Richard I, duke of Normandy

Otto, duke of Burgundy

Henry, duke of Burgundy

Robert the Pious
(996–1031)

Beatrice

Gisella

Henry I
(1031–1060)
= Anna of Kiev

Adela

Robert
duke of Burgundy

Hadvise

Philip I
(1060–1108)

Hugh

Louis VI the Fat
(1108–1137)

Cecile

Florus

Philip
count of Mantes

Constance
= Bohemond

Philip

Louis VII
(1137–1180)
= (1) Eleanor of Aquitaine
= (2) Constance of Castile
= (3) Adela of Champagne

Robert
count of Dreux

Henry
archbishop of Reims

Constance

Agnes/Anna
= (1) Alexius II Comnenus
= (2) Andronicus I Comnenus

Marie
= Henry
count of Champagne

Adelicia
= Theobald
count of Blois

Alice
= William
count of Ponthieu

Philip II Augustus
(1180–1223)

Louis VIII
(1223–1226)
= Blanche of Castile

Philip Hurepel
count of Clermont

Peter Karlotus
bishop of Noyon

Louis IX (Saint Louis)
(1226–1270)
= Margaret of Provence

Robert of Artois

Alphonse of Poitou

Charles of Anjou
king of Sicily (d.1285)

the king could call upon his men to aid him in times of war (though the great ones could defy him). As king and landlord, he collected dues and taxes with the help of his officials, called *prévôts*. Revenues came from Paris as well, a thriving commercial and cultural center. With money and land, Louis could employ civil servants while dispensing the favors and giving the gifts that added to his prestige and power.

NEW FORMS OF LEARNING AND RELIGIOUS EXPRESSION

The commercial revolution and rise of urban centers, the newly reorganized church, close contact with the Islamic world, and the revived polities of the early twelfth century paved the way for the growth of urban schools and new forms of religious expression. Money, learning, and career opportunities attracted many to city schools. At the same time, some people rejected urbanism and the new-fangled scholarship it supported. They retreated from the world to seek poverty and solitude. Yet the new learning and the new money had a way of seeping into the cracks and crannies of even the most resolutely separate institutions.

The New Schools and What They Taught

Connected to monasteries and cathedrals since the Carolingian period, traditional schools had trained young men to become monks or priests. Some were better endowed than others with books and teachers; a few developed reputations for particular expertise. By the end of the eleventh century, the best schools were generally connected to cathedrals in the larger cities: Reims, Paris, Bologna, Montpellier. But some teachers (or "masters," as they were called), such as the charismatic and brilliant Peter Abelard (1079–1142), simply set up shop by renting a room. Students flocked to his lectures.

What the students sought, in the first place, was knowledge of the seven liberal arts. Grammar, rhetoric, and logic (or dialectic) belonged to the "beginning" arts, the so-called trivium. Grammar and rhetoric focused on literature and writing. Logic, involving the technical analysis of texts as well as the application and manipulation of arguments, was a transitional subject leading to the second, higher part of the liberal arts, the quadrivium. This comprised four areas of study that might today be called theoretical math and science: arithmetic (number theory), geometry, music (theory rather than practice), and astronomy. Of these arts, logic had pride of place in the new schools, while masters and students who studied the quadrivium generally did so outside of the classroom.

Scholars looked to logic to clarify what they knew and lead them to further knowledge. That God existed, nearly everyone believed. But a scholar like Anselm of Bec (whom we met above, p. 174, as the archbishop of Canterbury) was not satisfied by belief alone. Anselm's faith, as he put it, "sought understanding." He emptied his mind of all concepts except that of God; then, using the tools of logic, he proved God's very existence in his *Monologion*. In Paris a bit later, Peter Abelard declared that "nothing can be believed unless it is first understood." He drew together conflicting authoritative texts on 158 key subjects in his *Sic et non* (*Yes and No*), including "That God is one and the contrary" and "That it is permitted to kill men and the contrary." Leaving the propositions unresolved, Abelard urged his students to discover the reasons behind the disagreements and find ways to reconcile them. Soon Peter Lombard (*c.*1100–1160) adopted Abelard's method of juxtaposing opposing positions, but he supplied his own reasoned resolutions as well. His *Sententiae* was perhaps the most successful theology textbook of the entire Middle Ages.

One key logical issue for twelfth-century scholars involved the question of "universals": whether a universal—something that can be said of many—is real or simply a linguistic or mental entity. Abelard argued that "things either individually or collectively cannot be called universal, i.e., said to be predicated of many." He was maintaining a position later called "nominalist."[10] The other view was the "realist" position, which claimed that things "predicated of many" were universal and real. For example, when we look at diverse individuals of one kind, say Luna and Sole, we say of each of them that they are members of the same species: cat. Realists argued that "cat" was real. Nominalists thought it a mere word.

Later in the twelfth century, scholars found precise tools in the works of Aristotle to resolve this and other logical questions. During Abelard's lifetime, very little of Aristotle's work was available in Europe because it had not been translated from Greek into Latin. By the end of the century, however, that lack had been filled by translators who traveled to Islamic or formerly Islamic cities—Toledo in Spain, Palermo in Sicily—where Aristotle had already been translated into Arabic and carefully commented on by Islamic scholars such as Ibn Sina (Avicenna; see p. 126 above) (980–1037) and Ibn Rushd (Averroes) (1126–1198). By the thirteenth century, Aristotle had become the primary philosopher for the scholastics (the scholars of medieval European universities).

The lofty subjects of the schools had down-to-earth, practical consequences in books for preachers, advice for rulers, manuals for priests, textbooks for students, and guides for living addressed to laypeople. Nor was mastery of the liberal arts the end of everyone's education. Many students went on to study theology (for which Paris was the center). Others studied law; at Bologna, for example, where Gratian worked on canon law, other jurists—such as the so-called Four Doctors—achieved fame by teaching and writing about Roman law. By the mid-twelfth century, scholars had made real progress toward a systematic understanding of Justinian's law codes (see above, p. 34). The lawyers who emerged from the school at Bologna went on to serve popes, bishops, kings, princes, or communes. Thus the learning of the schools was put to work by the newly powerful twelfth-century states, preached in the churches, and consulted in the courts.

It found a place in the treatment of the ill as well. The greatest schools of medicine were at Salerno (in Italy) and at Montpellier (in France). In the course of the late eleventh and twelfth centuries, these schools' curricula began to draw on classical Greek medical texts, which had been translated into Arabic during the ninth century. Now the Arabic texts were turned into Latin. For example, Constantine the African, who was at Salerno

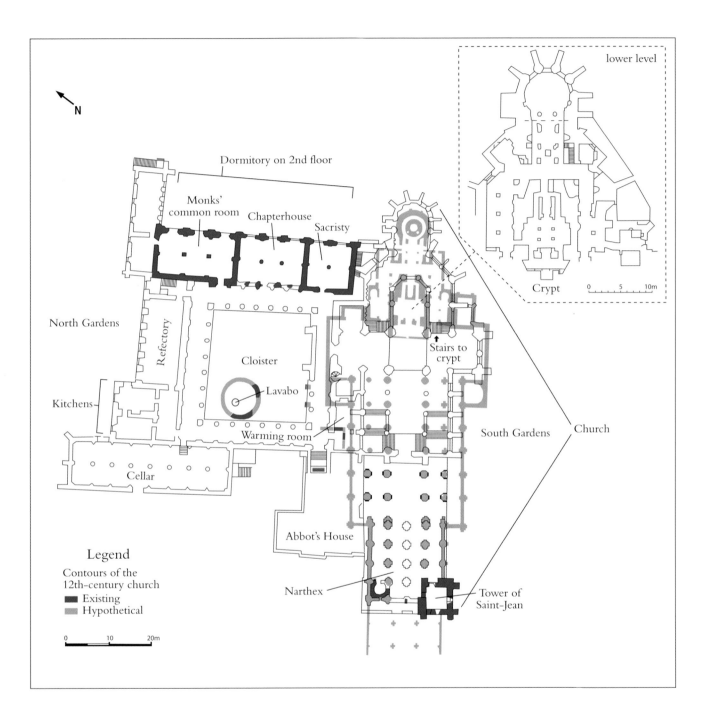

lower level

Crypt

0   5   10m

North Gardens

Dormitory on 2nd floor

Monks'
common room

Chapterhouse

Sacristy

Refectory

Cloister

Lavabo

Stairs to
crypt

Kitchens

Warming room

South Gardens

Church

Cellar

Abbot's House

Legend

Contours of the
12th-century church

■ Existing
■ Hypothetical

0   10   20m

Narthex

Tower of
Saint-Jean

before 1077, translated a key Arabic text based on Galen's *Art of Medicine*. He called it the *Isagoge* ("Introduction"), which indeed it was:

> [The principal members of the body are] the brain, the heart, the liver, and the testicles. Other members serve the aforesaid principal members, such as the nerves, which minister to the brain, and the arteries which minister to the heart, and the veins, which minister to the liver, and the spermatic vessels, which convey sperm to the testicles. Some members have their own inherent power ... for example bones, all the cartilages or the membranes that are between the skin and the flesh, the muscles, fat, and flesh ... [Other members] originate from their own innate power and derive vigor from the fundamental [members], for example, the stomach, kidneys, intestines, and all the muscles. By their own proper power, these members seek out food and transform it.[11]

Soon the *Isagoge* was gathered together with other texts into the *Articella*, a major training manual for doctors throughout the Middle Ages.

Monastic Splendor and Poverty

To care for ill monks, monasteries had infirmaries—proto-hospitals that were generally built at a short distance from the church and communal buildings (see Figure 5.3 on p. 191). The Benedictine Rule imagined that each monastic community would carry out most of its tasks within an enclosed building complex. One Benedictine monastery that has been excavated particularly fully is Saint-Germain at Auxerre. In the twelfth century (see Figure 5.1), it boasted a very large church with an elaborate narthex that served as a grand entranceway for liturgical processions. Toward the east of the church, where the altar stood and the monks sang the Offices, stairs led down to a crypt housing saintly relics constructed during the Carolingian period. To the north and south were the conventual buildings—the sacristy (which stored liturgical vessels and vestments), the "chapter house" (where the Benedictine Rule was read), the common room, dormitory (where the monks slept), refectory (dining hall), kitchens, and cellar. At the center of all was the cloister, entirely enclosed by graceful arcades. Beyond these buildings were undoubtedly others—not yet excavated—for the craftsmen and servants of the monastery, for the ill, for pilgrims and other guests. The whole purpose of this complex was to allow the monks to carry out a life of arduous and nearly continuous prayer. Every detail of their lives was ordered, every object splendid, every space adorned to render due honor to the Lord of heaven.

The architecture and sculpture of twelfth-century churches like Saint-Germain were suited to showcase both the solemn intoning of the chant and the honor due to God. The style, called Romanesque, represents the first wave of European monumental architecture. Built of stone, Romanesque churches are echo chambers for the sounds of the chant. Massive, weighty, and dignified, they are often enlivened by sculpture, wall paintings, or

Figure 5.1 (facing page): Saint-Germain of Auxerre (12th cent.)

Following page:

Plate 5.3: Durham Cathedral, Interior (1093–1133). Huge and imposing, Durham Cathedral is also inviting and welcoming, with its lively piers, warm colors, and harmonious spaces. Built by Norman bishops, it housed the relics of the Anglo-Saxon Saint Cuthbert; in just such ways did the Normans appropriate the power and prestige of English saints' cults.

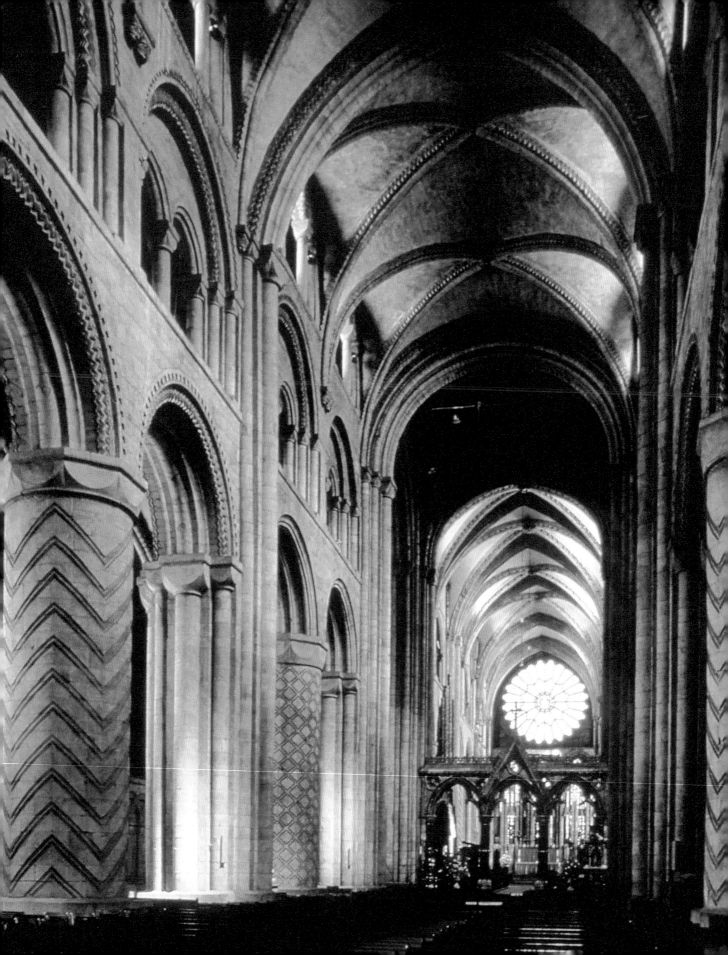

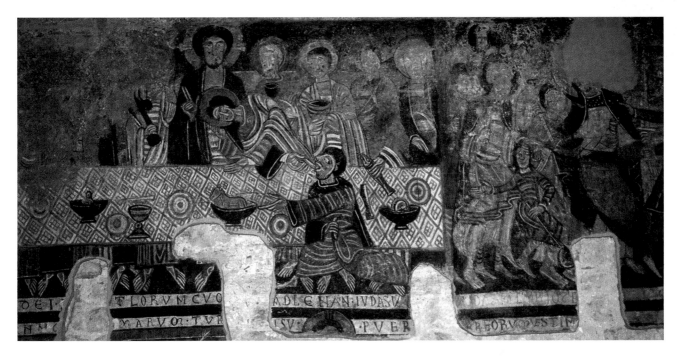

patterned textures. At Durham Cathedral (built between 1093 and 1133 in the north of England), the stone itself is a warm yellow/pink color, given added zest by piers incised with diamond or zig-zag patterns. (See Plate 5.3.) By contrast, the entire length of the vault of Sant Tomàs de Fluvià, a tiny monastic church in the County of Barcelona, was covered with paintings, a few of which remain today; Plate 5.4 shows the Last Supper. Pisa's famous leaning tower is in fact a Romanesque bell tower; here (Plate 5.5) the decoration is on the exterior, where the bright Italian sun heightens the play of light and shadow.

The church of Saint-Lazare of Autun (1120–1146) may serve as an example of a "typical" Romanesque church, though in fact the most typical aspect of that style is its extreme variety. Striking is the "barrel" or "tunnel" vault whose ribs, springing from the top of the piers, mark the long church into sections called bays. There are three levels. The first is created by the arches that open onto the side aisles of the church. The second is the gallery (or triforium), which consists of a decorative band of columns and arches. The third is the clerestory, where small windows puncture the walls. (See Plate 5.6 on p. 185.)

As at many Romanesque churches, the portals and the capitals (the "top hats" on the columns) at Autun were carved with complex scenes representing sacred stories. The story of the "Raising of Lazarus," patron saint of the church (Saint-Lazare = Lazarus), was once depicted on a tympanum (a half-circle) over the north transept door, the main entrance to the church. (For an Ottonian depiction of the scene, see Plate 4.2 on p. 142.) Although the Autun Lazarus was destroyed in the eighteenth century, a figure of Eve that remains today (see Plate 5.7 on p. 186) was once on the lintel (a horizontal beam just under the tympanum), probably right beneath Christ's feet as he performed his miracle.

The plan of Autun shown in Figure 5.2 on p. 187 indicates the placement of many of the church's carvings. It also shows that the church was in the form of a basilica (a long straight building) intersected, near the choir, by a transept. The chevet (or apse), the far

Plate 5.4: Sant Tomàs de Fluvià, The Last Supper, Painted Vault (early 12th cent.). Sant Tomàs was one of many monastic and parish churches in the county of Barcelona richly decorated with paintings in the twelfth century. Here Christ is at the Last Supper with his apostles. The depiction closely follows John 13:23 when Jesus announces that one of his disciples will betray him: "Now there was leaning on Jesus's bosom one of his disciples [John].... [John asked], 'Lord, who is it?' Jesus answered, 'He it is to whom I shall reach bread dipped.' And when he had dipped the bread, he gave it to Judas." To the right of the table a new scene begins: Jesus' disciple Peter cuts off the ear of the servant of the high priest who has come with Judas to betray him. Christ then utters the famous words from Matt. 26:52, "Put your sword back into its place; for all who take the sword will perish by the sword." Then, according to Luke 22:51, Jesus touched the servant's ear and healed him.

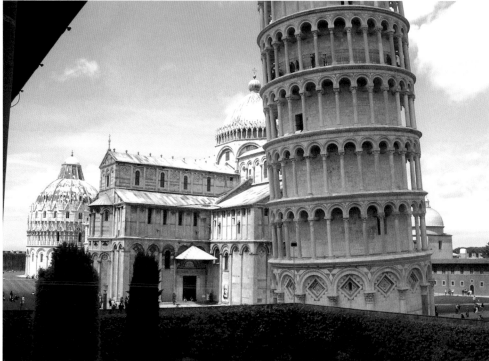

Plate 5.5: Cathedral Complex, Pisa (11th–12th cent.). The tower is part of a large complex that was meant to celebrate Pisa's emergence as a great political, economic, and military power. In this photograph, taken from the upper porch of the hospital (13th cent.), the cathedral (begun in 1064) is just behind and to the left of the tower (which started to lean in 1174, during construction). Behind that, and further to the left, is the baptistery (begun in 1152).

Plate 5.6 (facing page): Saint-Lazare of Autun, Nave (1120–1146). In this view down the nave, reminiscent of what medieval worshippers would have seen as they entered from the north and looked down the nave to the west, a great organ obscures the windows that once allowed in the light of the setting sun.

eastern part of the church, had space for pilgrims to visit the tomb of Lazarus, which held the precious bones of the saint.

Not all medieval people agreed that such opulent decoration pleased or praised God, however. At the end of the eleventh century, the new commercial economy and the profit motive that fueled it led many to reject wealth and to embrace poverty as a key element of the religious life. The Carthusian order, founded by Bruno (d. 1101), one-time bishop of Cologne, represented one such movement. La Grande Chartreuse, the chief house of the order, was built in an Alpine valley, lonely and inaccessible. Each monk took a vow of silence and lived as a hermit in his own small hut. Only occasionally would the monks join the others for prayer in a common oratory. When not engaged in prayer or meditation, the Carthusians copied manuscripts: for them, scribal work was a way to preach God's word with the hands rather than the mouth. Slowly the Carthusian order grew, but each monastery was limited to only twelve monks, the number of Christ's Apostles.

And yet even the Carthusians dedicated their lives above all to prayer. By now new forms of musical notation had been elaborated to allow monks—and other musicians—to see graphically the melody of their chants. In Plate 5.8 on p. 188, a manuscript from a Carthusian monastery in Lyon, France, the scribe used a red line to show the pitch of F (you can see the letter F at the left of each red line) and a yellow line for the C above that. The notes, square-headed and precisely placed, can easily be transcribed (by a musicologist who knows their conventions) onto a modern five-line staff.

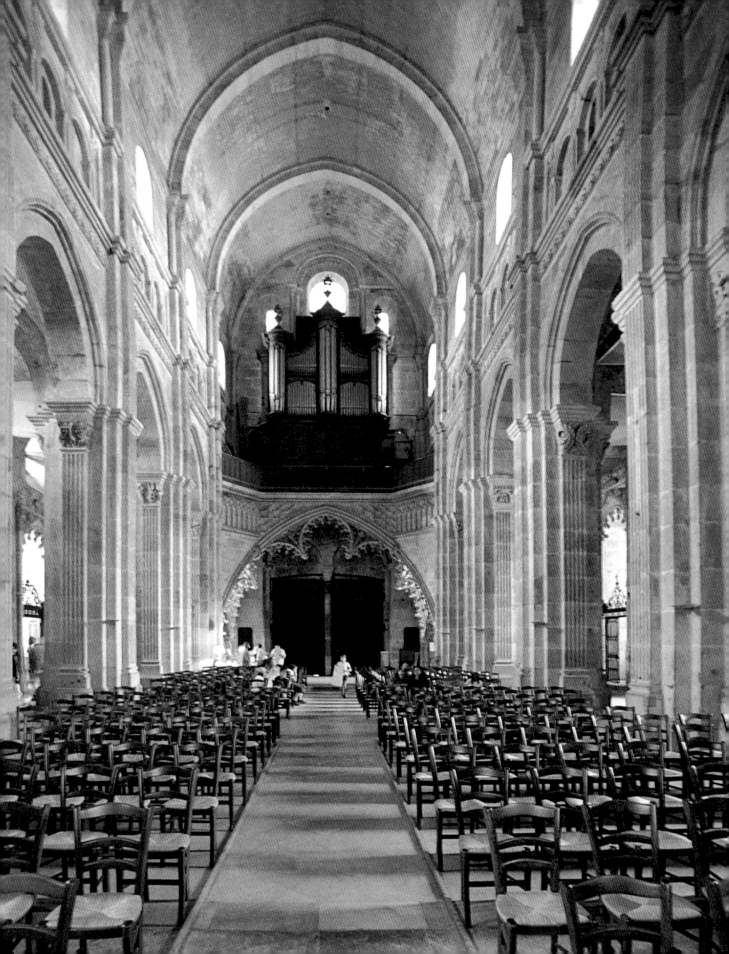

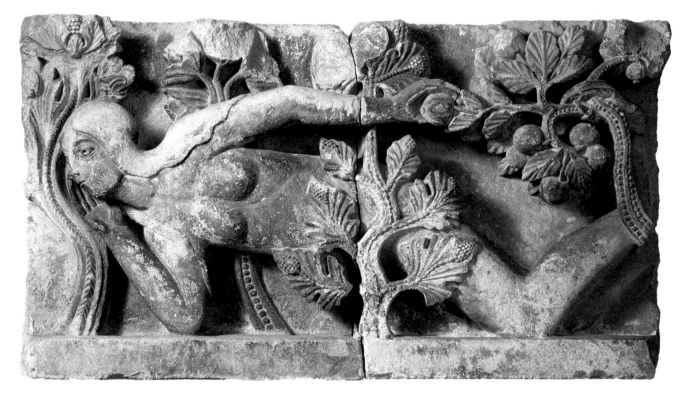

Plate 5.7: Autun, Eve (12th cent.). This relief, one of many carvings at Autun, shows a naked, snakelike Eve reaching for the forbidden apple. No doubt she faced an equally sensuous Adam. While she typifies the temptress, Eve's placement beneath the feet of the miracle-working Christ nevertheless suggests that she also represented Mary Magdalene, who, after the raising of Lazarus, anointed the feet of Jesus with oil and wiped them with her long hair. (See John 12:1–3.) Note how the sculptor made Eve's posture conform to the shape of the lintel.

Figure 5.2 (facing page): A Model Romanesque Church: Saint-Lazare of Autun

Another new monastic order, the Cistercian, expanded rapidly. The first Cistercian house was Cîteaux (in Latin, *Cistercium*), founded in 1098 by Robert of Molesme (*c*.1027/1028–1111) and a few other monks seeking a more austere way of life. Austerity they found—and also success. With the arrival of Saint Bernard (*c*.1090–1153), who came to Cîteaux in 1112 along with about thirty friends and relatives, the original center sprouted a small congregation of houses in Burgundy. (Bernard became abbot of one of them, Clairvaux.) The order grew, often by reforming and incorporating existing monasteries. By the mid-twelfth century there were more than 300 monasteries—many in France, but some as well in Italy, Germany, England, Austria, and Spain—following what they took to be the customs of Cîteaux. By the end of the twelfth century, the Cistercians were an order: their member houses adhered to the decisions of a General Chapter; their liturgical practices and internal organization were standardized. Many nuns, too, as eager as monks to live the life of simplicity and poverty that the Apostles had endured and enjoyed, adopted Cîteaux's customs; some convents later became members of the order.

Although the Cistercians claimed the Benedictine Rule as the foundation of their customs, they elaborated a style of life and an aesthetic all their own, largely governed by the goal of simplicity. They even rejected the conceit of dyeing their robes—hence their nickname, the "white monks." White, too, were their houses. Despite regional variations and considerable latitude in interpreting the meaning of "simplicity," Cistercian buildings had a different feel than the great Romanesque churches and Benedictine monasteries of black monks. Foursquare and regular, Cistercian churches and other buildings conformed to a fairly standard plan, typified by a monastery like Fountains (see Figure 5.3 on p. 191). The churches tended to be small, made of smooth-cut, undecorated stone.

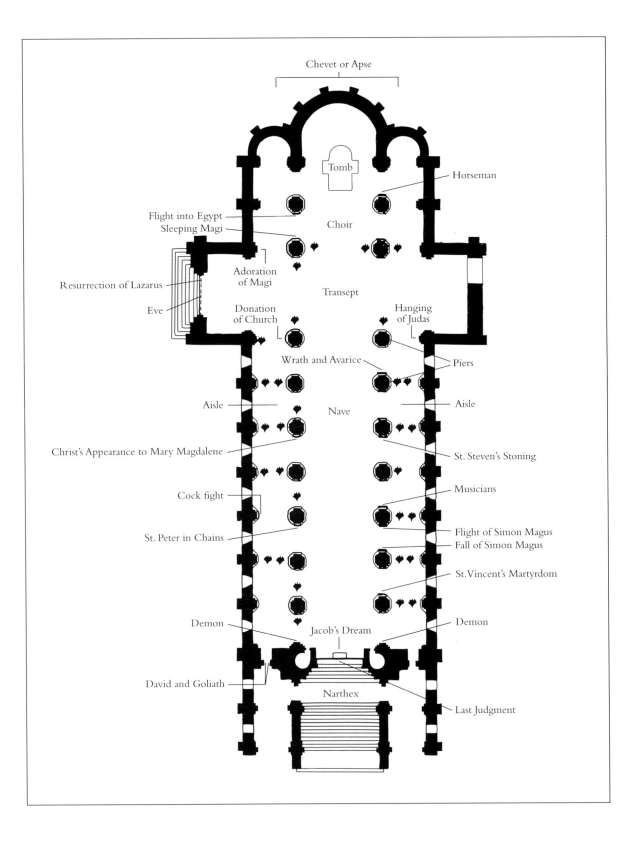

Chevet or Apse

Tomb

Horseman

Flight into Egypt

Sleeping Magi

Choir

Adoration
of Magi

Resurrection of Lazarus

Transept

Eve

Donation
of Church

Hanging
of Judas

Wrath and Avarice

Piers

Aisle

Aisle

Nave

Christ's Appearance to Mary Magdalene

St. Steven's Stoning

Cock fight

Musicians

St. Peter in Chains

Flight of Simon Magus
Fall of Simon Magus

St. Vincent's Martyrdom

Demon

Demon

Jacob's Dream

David and Goliath

Last Judgment

Narthex

⁊ inuenit illos dignos se ideo accipient regnū deco

ris de manu dñi Exaudi depcasy amā T amq̄

aurū in fornace ꝓbauit electos dñs ⁊ quasi holocau

sti hostiam accepit illos Exaudi d or cā iusti aut

in perpetuū uiuent ⁊ apud dnm est merces eoꝝ

P̄buenersy amā S cā q̄ spant in dño mutabū

fortitudine assument pennas ut aquilę uolabū

⁊n deficient cā Vos sci sy Letaminū d rex tc;

br glamini ōr re ꝙ Exultent i te dñ; br dlectent i l

Mirabil ds i s ius; ꝙ ist ipse d u i f p sue

Absterget deus omēin lacrimam ab oculi

Wall and vault paintings were eschewed, and any sculpture was modest at best. Indeed, Saint Bernard wrote a scathing attack on Romanesque sculpture in which, ironically, he admitted its sensuous allure:

> But what can justify that array of grotesques in the cloister where the brothers do their reading?… What place have obscene monkeys, savage lions, unnatural centaurs, manticores, striped tigers, battling knights or hunters sounding their horns? You can see a head with many bodies and a multi-bodied head…. With such a bewildering array of shapes and forms on show, one would sooner read the sculptures than the books.[12]

The Cistercians had few such diversions, but the simplicity of their buildings and of their clothing also had its beauty. Illuminated by the pure white light that came through clear glass windows, Cistercian churches were luminous, cool, and serene. Plate 5.9 shows the nave of Fontenay Abbey, begun in 1139. There are no wall paintings, no sculpture, no incised pillars. Yet the subtle play of thick piers and thin columns along with the alternation of curved and linear capitals lends the church a sober charm.

True to their emphasis on purity, the Cistercians simplified their communal liturgy, pruning the many additions that had been tacked on in the houses of the black monks. Only the liturgy as prescribed in the Benedictine Rule and one daily Mass were allowed. Even the music for the chant was modified: the Cistercians rigorously suppressed the B flat, even though doing so made the melody discordant, because of their insistence on strict simplicity.

On the other hand, the Benedictine Rule did not prevent the Cistercians from creating a new class of monks—the lay brothers—who were illiterate and unable to participate in the liturgy. These men did the necessary labor—field work, stock raising—to support the community at large. Compare Figure 5.3 on p. 191 with Figure 5.1 on p. 180: the Cistercian monastery was in fact a house divided. The eastern half was for the "choir" monks, the western half for the lay brethren. Each half had its own dining room, latrines, dormitories, and infirmaries. The monks were strictly segregated, even in the church, where a rood screen kept them apart.

The choir monks dedicated themselves to private prayer and contemplation and to monastic administration. The Cistercian *Charter of Charity*, in effect a constitution of the order, provided for a closely monitored network of houses, and each year the Cistercian abbots met to hammer out legislation for all of them. Cistercian monasteries held large and highly organized farms and grazing lands called "granges," and the monks spent much of their time managing their estates and flocks of sheep, both of which yielded handsome profits by the end of the twelfth century. Clearly part of the agricultural and commercial revolutions of the Middle Ages, the Cistercian order made managerial expertise a part of the monastic life.

Yet the Cistercians also elaborated a spirituality of intense personal emotion. Their writings were filled with talk of love. When we pray, wrote Saint Bernard, "our breast expands…. our interior is filled with an overflowing love."[13] The Cistercians were devoted

Plate 5.8 (facing page): Carthusian Diurnal from Lyon (12th cent.). A Diurnal contains daytime monastic chants. On this page, the scribe has indicated (just beneath each yellow line) the placement of the B natural. Although (or perhaps because) Carthusian monks rarely came together to pray, they, like other sorts of monks, wanted clear guidance for their chants.

Following pages:

Plate 5.9: Fontenay Abbey Church, Interior (1139–1147). Compare the bare walls of this Cistercian church with the frescoes of Sant Tomàs de Fluvià (Plate 5.4). How do these different artistic choices reflect different religious sensibilities?

Figure 5.3: Plan of Fountains Abbey (founded 1132)

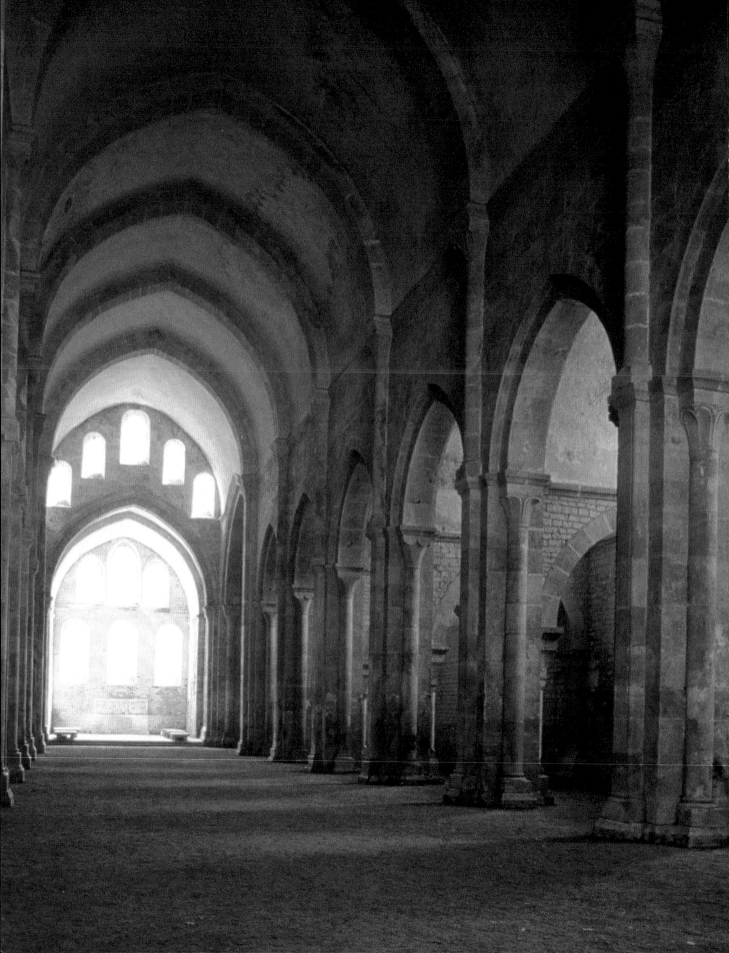

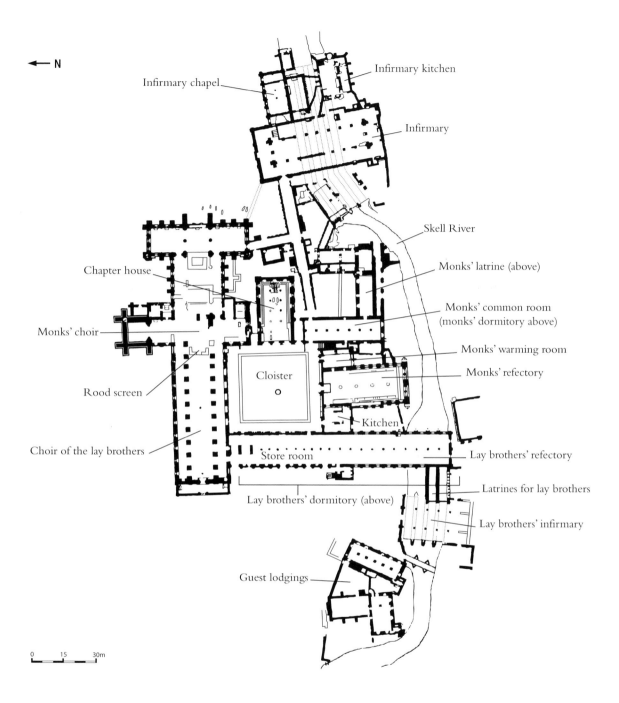

← N

Infirmary chapel

Infirmary kitchen

Infirmary

Skell River

Chapter house

Monks' latrine (above)

Monks' common room
(monks' dormitory above)

Monks' choir

Monks' warming room

Monks' refectory

Rood screen

Cloister

Kitchen

Choir of the lay brothers

Store room

Lay brothers' refectory

Latrines for lay brothers

Lay brothers' dormitory (above)

Lay brothers' infirmary

Guest lodgings

0   15   30m

to the humanity of Christ and to his mother, Mary. While pilgrims continued to stream to the tombs and reliquaries of saints, the Cistercians dedicated all their churches to the Virgin Mary (for whom they had no relics) because for them she signified the model of a loving mother. Indeed, the Cistercians regularly used maternal imagery to describe the nurturing care provided to humans by Jesus himself. The Cistercian God was approachable, human, protective, even mothering.

Were women simply metaphors for pious male monks? Or did they too partake in the new religious fervor of the twelfth century? The answer is that women's reformed monasteries proliferated at the same time as men's. Furthermore, monks and priests undertook to teach and guide women religious far more fully than they had done before. In the *Speculum Virginum (Mirror of Virgins)*, written in the form of a dialogue between a male religious advisor (Peregrinus) and a "virgin of Christ" (Theodora), exhortations to virtue were complemented by images. Some presented, as if in a "mirror," vices that should be avoided. Others gave examples of female heroines to be admired and imitated. In Plate 5.10, three tall and triumphant women stand on dead or defeated enemies. On the left is Jael, who killed the Israelites' enemy leader, and on the right is Judith, who did the same. In the middle, the model for both, is Humility striking Pride in the breast. Clearly the cloistered twelfth-century virgin was justified in considering herself, as Peregrinus said, "an example of disdain for the present life and a model of desire for heavenly things."[14]

★ ★ ★ ★ ★

In the twelfth century, Europe was coming into its own. Growing population and the profitable organization of the countryside promoted cities, trade, and wealth. Townspeople created new institutions of self-regulation and self-government. Kings and popes found new ways to exert their authority and test its limits. Scholars mastered the knowledge of the past and put it to use in classrooms, royal courts, papal offices, and the homes of the sick. Monks who fled the world ended up in positions of leadership; the great entrepreneurs of the twelfth century were the Cistercians; Saint Bernard was the most effective preacher of the Second Crusade.

The power of communities was recognized in the twelfth century: the guilds and communes depended on this recognition. So too did the new theology of the time. In his theological treatise *Why God Became Man*, Saint Anselm put new emphasis on Christ's humanity: Christ's sacrifice was that of one human being for another. The Cistercians spoke of God's mothering. Historians are in this sense right to speak of the importance of "humanism"—with its emphasis on the dignity of human beings, the splendor of the natural world, and the nobility of reason—in the twelfth century. Yet the stress on the loving bonds that tied Christians together also led to the persecution of others, like Jews and Muslims, who lived outside the Christian community. In the next century European communities would become more ordered, regulated, and incorporated. By the same token, they became even more exclusive.

Plate 5.10 (facing page): Jael, Humility, and Judith (*c.*1140). In this early manuscript of the extremely popular *Mirror of Virgins*, exemplary women triumph over evil. Humility (in Latin, *humilitas*, a feminine noun) was the key virtue of the monastic life. Before she killed Holofernes, enemy of the Israelites, Judith prayed to God, reminding him that "the prayer of the humble and the meek hath always pleased thee" (Judith 9:16).

fruct' fpecter ut<g>. ¶ Attendo quide qd excollatione diffimilu fa
nif intellectib magnu pofuerif inctatniu 7 qdda pfpicuu odif
intuentiu fpeculu S; adhec quif ydone? Quid antiq colubro
forti inmalicia aftutia quid fubtili' cui furie pfcripte copen
dent. qs omif uincere. eog e pcipue. qs armat fex uirilif 7 menf
fubnixa fapientie. ¶ An ignoraf ut omitta milia feminarum
fublege t fub gra uiref hofticaf eneruantiu. qd iudith in olofne
que dice poffum? totu infernu. qsi q nihil fupnu habeat. quid
iahel in fifara madianitaru pncipe fecerit. que ualentia
fex infirmiorif nihil aluid e n qd humilitaf femp pualet
fupbie inquacuq. secog pfeffione:

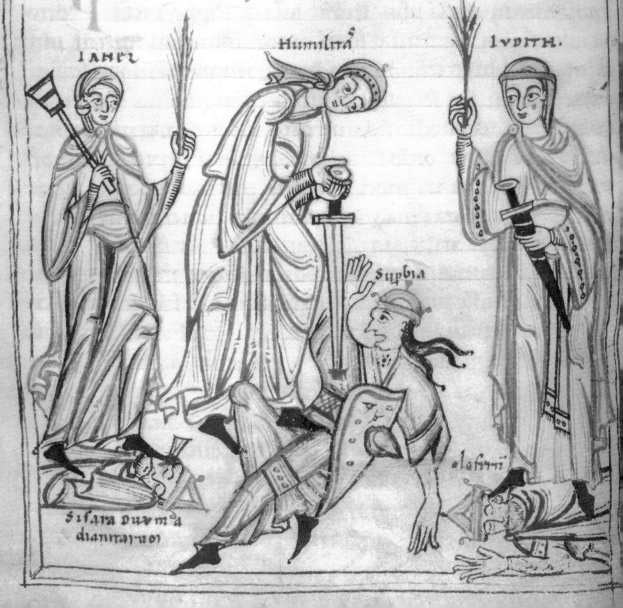

1049–1054	Papacy of Leo IX
1066	Norman Conquest of England by William of Normandy
1071	Battle of Manzikert
1073–1085	Papacy of Gregory VII
1075–1122	Investiture Conflict
1081–1118	Reign of Alexius I Comnenus
1085	Conquest of Toledo by Alfonso VI
1086	Domesday Book
1094	Al-Andalus under Almoravid (Berber) control
1096–1099	The First Crusade
1097	Establishment of a commune at Milan
1099–1291	Crusader States in the Holy Land
1122	Concordat of Worms
c.1140	Publication of Gratian's *Decretum*
1142	Death of Peter Abelard
1147–1149	The Second Crusade
1153	Death of Saint Bernard

NOTES

1 *Frederick of Hamburg's Agreement with Colonists from Holland*, in *Reading the Middle Ages: Sources from Europe, Byzantium, and the Islamic World*, ed. Barbara H. Rosenwein, 2nd ed. (Toronto: University of Toronto Press, 2014), p. 254.

2 *Chronicle of Saint Bertin*, quoted in *Histoire de la France urbaine*, vol. 2: *La ville médiévale* (Paris: Éditions du Seuil, 1980), p. 71, here translated from the French by the volume editor.

3 Henry I, *Privileges for the Citizens of London*, in *Reading the Middle Ages*, p. 257.

4 *Cluny's Foundation Charter*, in *Reading the Middle Ages*, p. 177.

5 Pope Gregory VII, *Admonition to Henry*, in *Power and the Holy in the Age of the Investiture Conflict: A Brief History with Documents*, ed. and trans. Maureen C. Miller (Boston: Bedford, 2005), p. 85.

6 *Roman Lenten Synod*, in *The Correspondence of Pope Gregory VII: Selected Letters from the Registrum*, ed. and trans. Ephraim Emerton (New York: Columbia University Press, 1969), p. 91.

7 Rabbi Eliezer b. Nathan, *O God, Insolent Men*, in *Reading the Middle Ages*, p. 268.

8 Ibn al-Athir, *The First Crusade*, in *Reading the Middle Ages*, p. 277.

9 *Domesday Book*, in *Reading the Middle Ages*, p. 287.

10 Abelard, *Glosses on Porphyry*, in *Reading the Middle Ages*, p. 289.

11 *Constantine the African's translation of Johannitius's Isagoge*, in *Reading the Middle Ages*, p. 291.

12 Saint Bernard, *Apologia*, in *Reading the Middle Ages*, p. 300.

13 Bernard of Clairvaux, *On the Song of Songs*, vol. 1, trans. Kilian Walsh, Cistercian Fathers Series 4 (Kalamazoo, MI: Cistercian Publications, 1977), p. 58.

14 *Speculum Virginum*, trans. Barbara Newman, in *Listen, Daughter: The* Speculum Virginum *and the Formation of Religious Women in the Middle Ages*, ed. Constant J. Mews (New York: Palgrave Macmillan, 2001), p. 270.

FURTHER READING

Barber, Malcolm. *Crusader States*. New Haven, CT: Yale University Press, 2012.

Bell, Nicholas. *Music in Medieval Manuscripts*. Toronto: University of Toronto Press, 2001.

Burton, Janet, and Julie Kerr. *The Cistercians in the Middle Ages*. Woodbridge: Boydell, 2011.

Frankopan, Peter. *The First Crusade: The Call from the East*. Cambridge, MA: Harvard University Press, 2012.

Hamilton, Louis I. *A Sacred City; Consecrating Churches and Reforming Society in Eleventh-Century Italy*. Manchester: Manchester University Press, 2010.

Iogna-Prat, Dominique. *Order and Exclusion: Cluny and Christendom Face Heresy, Judaism, and Islam (1000–1150)*. Trans. Graham Robert Edwards. Ithaca, NY: Cornell University Press, 2002.

Lange, Christian, and Songül Mecit. *The Seljuqs: Politics, Society and Culture*. Edinburgh: Edinburgh University Press, 2011.

Little, Lester K. *Religious Poverty and the Profit Economy in Medieval Europe*. Ithaca, NY: Cornell University Press, 1978.

MacEvitt, Christopher. *The Crusades and the Christian World of the East: Rough Tolerance*. Philadelphia: University of Pennsylvania Press, 2008.

Messier, Ronald A. *The Almoravids and the Meanings of Jihad*. Santa Barbara, CA: Praeger, 2010.

Mews, Constant J. *Abelard and Heloise*. Oxford: Oxford University Press, 2005.

Miller, Maureen C. *Power and the Holy in the Age of the Investiture Conflict: A Brief History with Documents*. Boston: Bedford, 2005.

Noble, Thomas F.X. and John Van Engen, eds. *European Transformations: The Long Twelfth Century*. Notre Dame, IN: University of Notre Dame Press, 2012.

Robinson, Ian S. *Henry IV of Germany*. Cambridge: Cambridge University Press, 2000.

Rubenstein, Jay. *Armies of Heaven: The First Crusade and the Quest for Apocalypse*. New York: Basic Books, 2011.

Toman, Rolf, ed. *Romanesque: Architecture, Sculpture*. Cologne: Painting, 2010.

Unger, Richard W. *Beer in the Middle Ages and the Renaissance*. Philadelphia: University of Pennsylvania Press, 2004.

To test your knowledge of this chapter, please go to

www.utphistorymatters.com

for Study Questions.

SIX

INSTITUTIONALIZING ASPIRATIONS
(c. 1150–c. 1250)

THE LIVELY DEVELOPMENTS of early twelfth-century Europe were institutionalized in the next decades. Fluid associations became corporations. Rulers hired salaried officials to staff their administrations. Churchmen defined the nature and limits of religious practice. While the Islamic world largely went its own way, only minimally affected by European developments, Byzantium was carved up by its Christian neighbors.

THE ISLAMIC AND BYZANTINE WORLDS IN FLUX

Nothing could be more different than the fates of the Islamic world and of Byzantium at the beginning of the thirteenth century. The Muslims remained strong; the Byzantine Empire nearly came to an end.

Islam on the Move

Like grains of sand in an oyster's shell—irritating but also generative—the Christian states of the Levant and Spain helped spark new Islamic principalities, one based in the Maghreb, the other in Syria and Egypt. In the Maghreb, the Almohads, a Berber group espousing a militant Sunni Islam, combined conquest with a program to "purify" the morals of their fellow Muslims. In al-Andalus their appearance in 1147 induced some Islamic rulers to seek alliances with the Christian rulers to the north. But other Andalusian rulers joined forces with the Almohads, who replaced the Almoravids as rulers of the whole Islamic far west

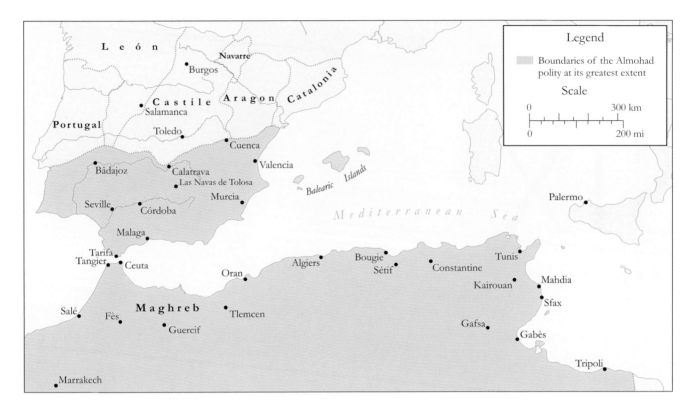

Map 6.1: The Almohads before the Battle of Las Navas de Tolosa (1212)

Map 6.2 (facing page): Saladin's Empire, *c.*1200

by 1172. (See Map 6.1.) At war continuously with Christian Spanish rulers, in 1212 they suffered a terrible defeat. For the Christian victors, the battle was known simply by its place name, Las Navas de Tolosa; but for the Almohads, it was known as "The Punishment." It was the beginning of the end of al-Andalus.

The Muslims were more successful in the shadow of the Crusader States. There, emboldened by the failure of the Second Crusade (see p. 173), Nur al-Din (r.1146–1174), son of Zangi, invaded Antioch. Soon his forces were occupying all the territory east of the Orontes River (see Map 5.4 on p. 173) and absorbing the entire county of Edessa. In 1154 he seized Damascus and began to carry out his goal of reuniting Syria and Egypt under his Sunni Muslim—rather than Fatimid Shi'ite—rule. During the 1160s, Nur al-Din's general Shirkuh led three successful military expeditions into Egypt accompanied by Shirkuh's nephew Saladin (r.1171–1193). In 1169, without formally deposing the Fatimid caliph, Shirkuh took over the powerful position of Egyptian vizier. Shortly thereafter, when Shirkuh died, Saladin succeeded him, and when in 1171 the Fatimid caliph died, Saladin simply had the name of the (more-or-less powerless, but Sunni) Abbasid caliph substituted for that of the Fatimid. Saladin was now ruler of Egypt, though ostensibly in the name of Nur al-Din.

Little wonder that when Nur al-Din died three years later, Saladin was ready to take over Syria. By 1183 he was master of Egypt, most of Syria, and part of Iraq. Like the Almohads, Saladin was determined to reform the faith along the Sunni model and to wage *jihad* against the Christian states in his backyard. Above all he wanted to recover Jerusalem, and in 1187, at the battle of Hattin, he succeeded. The Christian army was badly defeated, the Crusader States reduced to a few port cities. See Map 6.2. For about a half-century

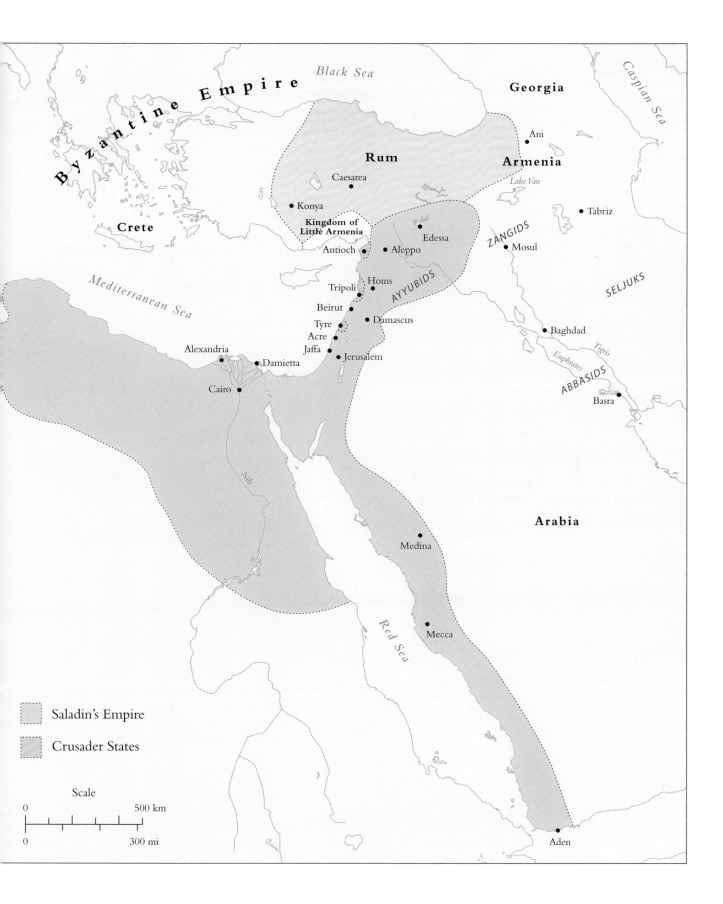

Black Sea

Caspian Sea

Byzantine Empire

Georgia

• Ani

Rum

Armenia

• Caesarea

Lake Van

• Tabriz

• Konya

**Kingdom of
Little Armenia**

ZANGIDS

• Edessa

Antioch •

• Mosul

• Aleppo

SELJUKS

Crete

Homs •

Tripoli •

AYYUBIDS

Mediterranean Sea

Beirut •

Tyre •

• Damascus

• Baghdad

Acre •

Euphrates

Tigris

Alexandria •

Jaffa •

• Jerusalem

ABBASIDS

• Damietta

• Cairo

• Basra

Nile

Arabia

• Medina

Red Sea

• Mecca

░░ Saladin's Empire

▓▓ Crusader States

Scale

0 ————————— 500 km

0 ————————— 300 mi

• Aden

thereafter, Saladin's descendants (the Ayyubids) held on to the lands he had conquered. Then the dynasty gave way (as we have often seen happen) to new military leaders. The chief difference this time was that these leaders were uniformly of Turkic slave and ex-slave origins—they were *mamluks*. The Mamluk Sultanate was exceptionally stable, holding on to Egypt and most of Syria until 1517.

The Undoing of Byzantium

In 1204 the leaders of the Fourth Crusade made a "detour" and conquered Constantinople instead. We shall later explore some of the reasons why they did so. But in the context of Byzantine history, the question is not why the Europeans attacked but rather why the Byzantines lost the fight.

Certainly the Byzantines themselves had no idea they were "in decline." Prior to 1204, they had reconquered some of Anatolia. In the capital, the imperial court continued to function; its bureaucracy and machinery of taxation were still in place; and powerful men continued to vie to be emperors—as if there were still power and glory in the position. Yet much had changed from the heyday of the Comneni.

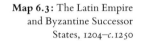

Map 6.3: The Latin Empire and Byzantine Successor States, 1204–*c*.1250

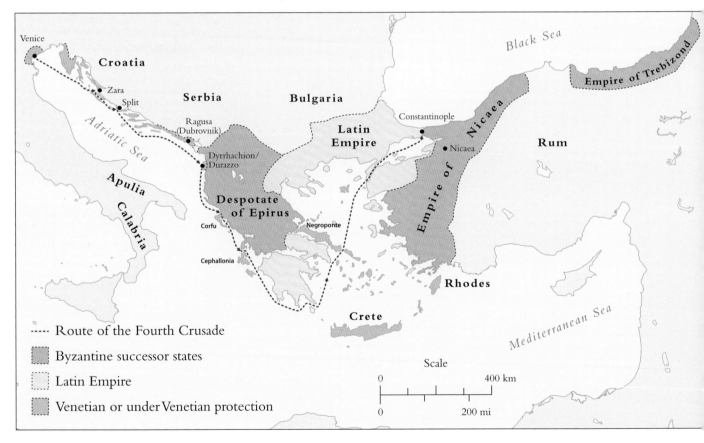

---- Route of the Fourth Crusade

Byzantine successor states

Latin Empire

Venetian or under Venetian protection

While the economy, largely based on peasant labor, boomed in the twelfth century, this ironically brought the peasants to their knees. Every landowner needed cultivators, but peasants had no way to bargain to improve their lot. Peasants worked for the state on imperial lands. They worked for military men when the emperors took to giving out *pronoiai*—grants of land to soldiers rather than wages in return for military service. Finally, peasants worked for the *dynatoi*, the great landowners who dominated whole regions. To all they paid taxes and rents. But there were only so many peasants, certainly not enough to cultivate all the land that the elites wanted to bring into production.

Manpower was scarce in every area of the economy. Skilled craftsmen, savvy merchants, and seasoned warriors were needed, but where were they to be found? Sometimes Jews were called upon; more often foreigners took up the work. Whole army contingents were made up of foreigners: Cumans, "Franks" (the Byzantine name for all Europeans), Turks. Forced to fight on numerous fronts, the army was not very effective; by the end of the twelfth century the Byzantines had lost much of the Balkans to what historians call the Second Bulgarian Empire.

Foreigners, mainly Italians, dominated Byzantium's long-distance trade. Italian neighborhoods (complete with homes, factories, churches, and monasteries) crowded the major cities of the empire. At the capital city itself, stretched along the Golden Horn like pearls on a string, were the Venetian Quarter, the Amalfitan Quarter, the Pisan Quarter, and the Genoese Quarter: these were the neighborhoods of the Italian merchants, exempt from imperial taxes and uniformly wealthy. (See Map 4.1 on p. 116.) They were heartily resented by the rest of Constantinople's restive and impoverished population, which needed little prodding to attack and loot the Italian quarters in 1182 and again in 1203, when they could see the crusaders camped right outside their city.

To be sure, none of this meant that Europeans had to take over. Yet in 1204, crusader armies breached the walls of Constantinople, encountered relatively little opposition, plundered the city for three days, and finally declared one of their leaders, Baldwin of Flanders, the new emperor. The Venetians gained the city harbor, Crete, and key Greek cities; other crusaders carved out other states. (See Map 6.3.) So did some Byzantines, however, and eventually, in 1261, their successors managed to recapture Constantinople and re-establish their empire until it fell for good in 1453 to the Ottoman Turks.

THE INSTITUTIONALIZATION OF GOVERNMENT IN THE WEST

While the Byzantine government was becoming more like those in the West—with emperors favoring family members and *dynatoi* creating regional dynasties—some Western polities were starting to look more Byzantine: more impersonal and bureaucratic. They entered a new phase of self-definition, codification, and institutionalization.

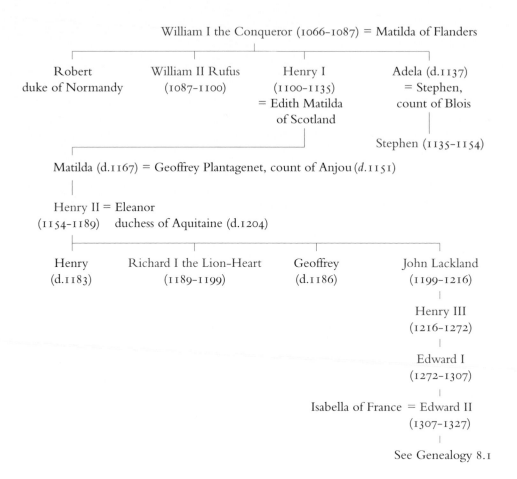

William I the Conqueror (1066-1087) = Matilda of Flanders

Robert
duke of Normandy

William II Rufus
(1087-1100)

Henry I
(1100-1135)
= Edith Matilda
of Scotland

Adela (d.1137)
= Stephen,
count of Blois

Stephen (1135-1154)

Matilda (d.1167) = Geoffrey Plantagenet, count of Anjou (*d.*1151)

Henry II = Eleanor
(1154-1189)   duchess of Aquitaine (d.1204)

Henry
(d.1183)

Richard I the Lion-Heart
(1189-1199)

Geoffrey
(d.1186)

John Lackland
(1199-1216)

Henry III
(1216-1272)

Edward I
(1272-1307)

Isabella of France = Edward II
(1307-1327)

See Genealogy 8.1

Genealogy 6.1: The Norman and Angevin Kings of England

Law, Authority, and the Written Word in England

One good example is England. The king hardly needed to be present: the government functioned by itself, with its own officials to handle administrative matters and record keeping. The very circumstances of the English king favored the growth of an administrative staff: his frequent travels to and from the Continent meant that officials needed to work in his absence, and his enormous wealth meant that he could afford them.

True, a long period of civil war (1135–1154) between the forces of two female heirs to the Norman throne (Matilda, daughter of Henry I, and Adela, Henry's sister) threatened royal power. As in Germany during the Investiture Conflict, so in England the barons and high churchmen consolidated their own local lordships during the war; private castles, symbols of their independence, peppered the countryside. But the war ended when Matilda's son, Henry of Anjou, ascended the throne as the first "Angevin" king of England.[1] (See Genealogy 6.1: The Norman and Angevin Kings of England.) Under Henry II (r.1154–1189), the institutions of royal government in England were extended and strengthened.

THE REFORMS OF HENRY II

Henry was count of Anjou, duke of Normandy, and overlord of about half the other counties of northern France. He was also duke of Aquitaine by his marriage to Eleanor, heiress of that vast southern French duchy. As for his power in the British Isles: the princes of Wales swore him homage and fealty; the rulers of Ireland were forced to submit to him; and the king of Scotland was his vassal. Thus Henry exercised sometimes more, sometimes less power over a realm stretching from northern England to the Pyrenees. (See Map 6.4 on p. 206.) For his Continental possessions, he was vassal of the king of France.

Once on the English throne, Henry destroyed or confiscated the private castles built during the civil war and regained the lands that had belonged to the crown. Then he proceeded to extend his power, above all by imposing royal justice. Already the Anglo-Saxon kings had claimed rights in local courts, particularly in capital cases, even though powerful men largely independent of royal authority dominated those courts. The Norman kings added to Anglo-Saxon law in the area of landholding. Henry built on these institutions, regularizing, expanding, and systematizing them. The Assize of Clarendon in 1166 recorded that the king

> decreed that inquiry shall be made throughout the several counties and throughout the several hundreds … whether there be … any man accused or notoriously suspect of being a robber or murderer or thief…. And let the justices inquire into this among themselves and sheriffs among themselves.[2]

"Throughout the several counties and throughout the several hundreds": these were the districts into which England had long been divided. Henry aimed to apply a *common* law regarding chief crimes—a law applicable throughout England—to all men and women in the land. Moreover, he meant his new system to be habitual and routine. There had always been justices to enforce the law, but under Henry, there were many more of them; they were trained in the law and required to make regular visitations to each locality, inquiring about crimes and suspected crimes. (They were therefore called "itinerant justices"—from *iter*, Latin for journey. The local hearing that they held was called an "eyre," also from *iter*.) The king required twelve representatives of the local knightly class—the middling aristocracy, later on known as the "gentry"—to meet during each eyre and either give the sheriff the names of those suspected of committing crimes in the vicinity or arrest the suspects themselves and hand them over to the royal justices. While convicted members of the knightly class often got off with only a fine, hanging or mutilation were the normal penalties for criminals. Even if acquitted, people "of ill repute" were to be exiled from England.

Henry also exercised new control over cases that we would call "civil," requiring all cases of property ownership to be authorized by a royal writ. Unlike the Angevin reforms of criminal law, this requirement affected only the class of free men and women—a minority. While often glad to have the king's protection, they grumbled at the expense and time required to obtain writs. Consider Richard of Anstey's suit to gain his uncle's property: over the course of five years, he paid out a great deal of money for royal writs; for journeys to line up witnesses and to visit various courts; for the expenses of his clerical staff; and for gifts to numerous officials. Yet it was all worthwhile in the end, for "*at length* by grace of the lord king and by the judgment of his court my uncle's land was adjudged to me."[3]

The whole system was no doubt originally designed to put things right after the civil war. Although these law-and-order measures were initially expensive for the king—he had to build many new jails, for example—they ultimately served to increase royal income and power. Fines came from condemned criminals and also from knightly representatives who failed to show up at the eyre when summoned; revenues poured in from the purchase of writs. The exchequer, as the financial bureau of England was called, recorded all the fines paid for judgments and the sums collected for writs. The amounts, entered on parchment leaves sewn together and stored as rolls, became the Receipt Rolls and Pipe Rolls, the first of many such records of the English monarchy and an indication that writing had become a tool to institutionalize royal rule in England.

Perhaps the most important outcome of this expanded legal system was the enhancement of royal power and prestige. The king of England touched (not personally but through men acting in his name) nearly every man and woman in the realm. However, the extent of royal jurisdiction should not be exaggerated. Most petty crimes did not end up in royal courts but rather in more local ones under the jurisdiction of a lord. Thus the case of Hugh Tree came before a manorial court run by officials of the monastery of Bec. They held that he was "in mercy [liable to a fine] for his beasts caught in the lord's garden."[4] He had to pay six pence to his lord (in this case the monastery); no money went to the king. This helps explain why manorial lords—barons, knights, bishops, and monasteries like Bec—held on tenaciously to their local prerogatives.

In addition to local courts were those run by and for the clergy. Had Hugh Tree committed murder, he would have come before a royal court. Had he been a homicidal cleric, however, he would have come before a church court, which could be counted on to give him a mild punishment. No wonder that churchmen objected to submitting to the jurisdiction of Henry II's courts. But Henry insisted—and not only on that point, but also on the king's right to have ultimate jurisdiction over church appointments and property disputes. The ensuing contest between the king and his appointed archbishop, Thomas Becket (1118–1170), became the greatest battle between the church and the state in the twelfth century. At a meeting held at Clarendon in 1164, Becket agreed, among other things, that clerics "cited and accused of any matter shall, when summoned by the king's justice, come before the king's court to answer there."[5] But Becket soon thereafter clashed with Henry over the rights of the church of Canterbury—Becket's church—to recover or alienate its own property. The conflict mushroomed to include control over the English church, its property, and its clergy. Soon the papacy joined, with Becket its champion. King and archbishop remained at loggerheads for six years, until Henry's henchmen murdered Thomas, unintentionally turning him into a martyr. Although Henry's role in the murder remained ambiguous, public outcry forced him to do public penance for the deed. In the end, the struggle made both institutions stronger. In particular, both church and royal courts expanded to address the concerns of an increasingly litigious society.

DEFINING THE ROLE OF THE ENGLISH KING

Henry II and his sons Richard I the Lion-Heart (r. 1189–1199) and John (r. 1199–1216) were English kings with an imperial reach. Richard was rarely in England, since half of France was his to subdue (see Map 6.4, paying attention to the areas in various shades of peach). Responding to Saladin's conquest of Jerusalem, Richard went on the abortive Third Crusade (1189–1192), capturing Cyprus on the way and arranging a three-year truce with Saladin before rushing home to reclaim his territory from his brother, John, and the French king, Philip II (r. 1180–1223). (His haste did him no good; he was captured by the duke of Austria and released only upon payment of a huge ransom, painfully squeezed out of the English people.)

When Richard died in battle in 1199, John took over. But if he began with an imperial reach, John must have felt a bit like the Byzantine emperor in 1204, for in that very year the king of France, Philip II, said that John had defied his overlordship—and promptly confiscated John's northern French territories. It was a purely military victory, and John set out to win the territories back by gathering money wherever and however he could in order to pay for an abler military force. He forced his barons and many members of the gentry to pay him "scutage"—a tax—in lieu of army service. He extorted money in the form of "aids"—the fees that his barons and other vassals ordinarily paid on rare occasions, such as the knighting of the king's eldest son. He compelled the widows of his barons and other vassals to marry men of his choosing or pay him a hefty fee to remain single. With the wealth pouring in from these effective but unpopular measures, John was able to pay for a navy and hire mercenary troops.

But all was to no avail. A broad coalition of German and Flemish armies led by Emperor Otto IV of Brunswick and masterminded by John was soundly defeated at the battle of Bouvines in 1214. It was a defining moment, not so much for English rule on the Continent (which would continue until the fifteenth century) as for England itself, where the barons—supported by many members of the gentry and the towns—organized, rebelled, and called the king to account. At Runnymede, just south of London, in June 1215, John was forced to agree to the charter of baronial liberties called Magna Carta, or "Great Charter," so named to distinguish it from a smaller charter issued around the same time concerning royal forests.

Magna Carta was intended to be a conservative document defining the "customary" obligations and rights of the nobility and forbidding the king to break from these without consulting his barons. Beyond this, it maintained that all free men in England had certain customs and rights in common that the king was obliged to uphold. "To no one will we sell, to no one will we refuse or delay right or justice."[6] In this way, Magna Carta documented the subordination of the king to written provisions; it implied that the king was

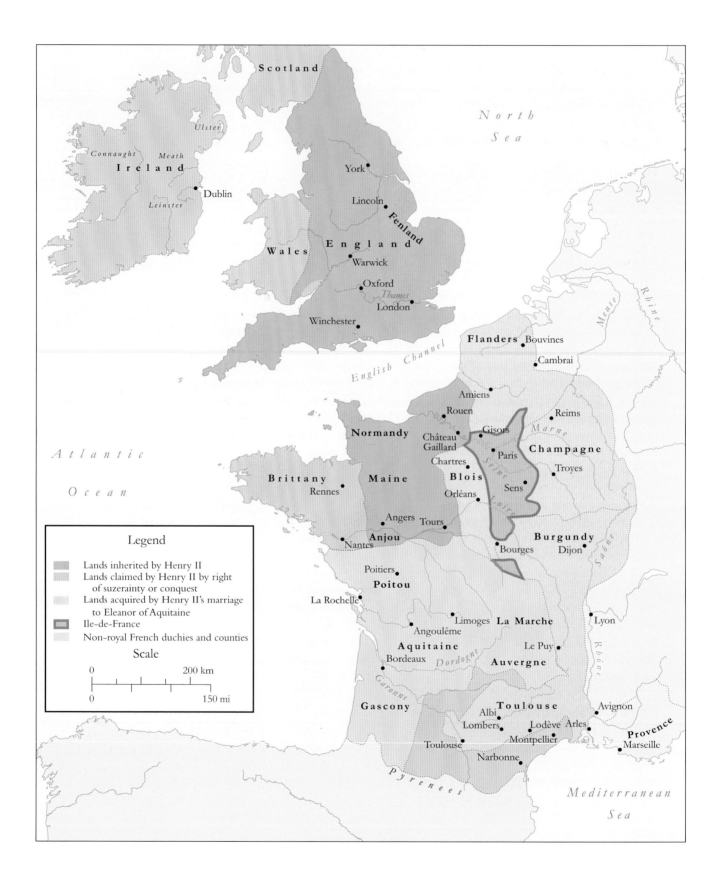

Scotland

Ireland
Ulster
Connaught   *Meath*
Leinster
• Dublin

Wales

England
• York
• Lincoln
Fenland
• Warwick
• Oxford
Thames
• London
• Winchester

North Sea

English Channel

Flanders Bouvines
• Cambrai

Atlantic Ocean

Normandy
• Amiens
• Rouen
Château • Gisors
Gaillard
• Chartres
• Paris
Champagne
• Reims
Marne
Blois
• Sens
Seine
• Troyes

Brittany
• Rennes

Maine

• Orléans
Loire

• Angers • Tours
Anjou
• Nantes

• Bourges
Burgundy
• Dijon
Saône

Poitou
• Poitiers

• La Rochelle

• Limoges
La Marche
• Lyon

Aquitaine
• Angoulême

• Le Puy
Rhône

• Bordeaux
Dordogne
Auvergne

Garonne

Gascony

Toulouse
• Albi
• Lombers
• Lodève
• Arles
• Avignon

• Montpellier
Provence
• Marseille

• Toulouse
• Narbonne

Pyrenees

Meuse   *Rhine*

Mediterranean Sea

Legend

Lands inherited by Henry II

Lands claimed by Henry II by right of suzerainty or conquest

Lands acquired by Henry II's marriage to Eleanor of Aquitaine

Ile-de-France

Non-royal French duchies and counties

Scale

0 ———————— 200 km

0 ———————— 150 mi

not above the law. Copies of the charter were sent to sheriffs and other officials, to be read aloud in public places. Everyone knew what it said, and later kings continued to issue it—and have it read out—in one form or another. Though not a "constitution," nevertheless Magna Carta was an important step in the institutionalization of the English government.

Spain and France in the Making

Two states—Spain and France—started small and beleaguered but slowly grew to embrace the territory we associate with them today. In Spain, the *reconquista* was the engine driving expansion. Like the king of England, the kings from northern Spain came as conquerors. But unlike England, Christian Spain had numerous kings who competed with one another. By the mid-thirteenth century, Spain had the threefold political configuration that would last for centuries (compare Map 6.1 on p. 198 with Map 7.5 on p. 253 and Map 8.5 on p. 298): to the east was the kingdom of Aragon; in the middle was Castile; and in the southwest was Portugal.

Map 6.4 (facing page): The Angevin and Capetian Realms in the Late Twelfth Century

All of the Spanish kings appointed military religious orders similar to the Templars to form permanent garrisons along their ever-moving frontier with al-Andalus. But how were the kings to deal with formerly Muslim-controlled lands? When he conquered Cuenca in 1177, King Alfonso VIII of Castile (r.1158–1214) established a bishopric and gave the city a detailed set of laws (*fueros*) that became the model for other conquests. Confiding enforcement to local officials, the king issued the *fueros* to codify, as its preface puts it, "judicial institutions in behalf of safeguarding peace and the rights of justice between clergy and laity, between townsmen and peasants, among the needy and the poor."[7] The preface might have added that the laws also regulated relations between local Christians, Muslims, and Jews.

The kingdom of France was smaller and more fragile than Spain; it was lucky that it did not confront an Islamic frontier or competing royal neighbors (though a glance at Map 6.4 shows that it was surrounded by plenty of independent counts and dukes). When Philip II (r.1180–1223) came to the throne at the age of fifteen, his kingdom consisted largely of the Ile-de-France, a dwarf surrounded by giants. Philip seemed an easy target for the ambitions of English king Henry II and the counts of Flanders and Champagne. Philip, however, played them off against one another. Through inheritance he gained a fair portion of the county of Flanders in 1191. Soon his military skills came to the fore as he wrenched Normandy from the king of England in 1204. This was the major conquest of his career, and in its wake he soon forced the lords of Maine, Anjou, and Poitou, once vassals of the king of England, to submit to him. A contemporary chronicler dubbed him Philip Augustus, recalling the expansionist first Roman emperor.

Indeed Philip did more than expand; he integrated his Norman conquest into his kingdom. Norman nobles promised him homage and fealty, while Philip's royal officers went about their business in Normandy—taxing, hearing cases, careful not to tread on local customs, but equally careful to enhance the flow of income into the French king's treasury. Gradually the Normans were brought into a new "French" orbit just beginning to take shape, constructed partly out of the common language of French and partly out of a new notion of the king as ruler of all the people in his territory.

Although there was never a French "common law" to supersede local ones, the French king, like the Spanish and English, succeeded in extending royal power through governmental bureaucracy. After 1194, Philip had all his decrees written down, establishing permanent repositories in which to keep them. Like the Angevin kings of England, Philip relied on members of the lesser nobility—knights and clerics, most of them educated in the city schools—to do the work of government. They served as officers of his court; as *prévôts*, officials who oversaw the king's estates and collected his taxes; and as *baillis* (or, in some places, seneschals) who not only supervised the *prévôts* but also functioned as judges, presiding over courts that met monthly, making the king's power felt locally as never before.

Of Empires and City-States

Smaller states were the norm. In that sense the empire ruled by the German king—spanning both Germany and Italy—was an oddity. In its embrace of peoples of contrasting traditions, it was more like Byzantium than like England. The location of the papacy made the empire different as well. Every other state was a safe distance away from the pope; but the empire had the pope in its throat. Tradition, prestige, and political self-respect demanded that the German king also be the emperor: Conrad III (r.1138–1152), though never actually crowned at Rome, nevertheless delighted in calling himself "August Emperor of the Romans" (while demeaning the Byzantine emperor as "King of the Greeks"). But being emperor meant controlling Italy and Rome. The difficulty was not only the papacy, defiantly opposed to another major power in Italy, but also the northern Italian communes, independent city-states in their own right.

THE REVIVAL AND DETERIORATION OF THE EMPIRE

Like the Angevin Henry II of England, Frederick I Barbarossa (r.1152–1190) came to the throne after a long period of bitter civil war between families. In Frederick's case, the feud, spawned in the wake of the Investiture Conflict, was between the Staufen and the Welfs. Contemporaries hailed Frederick as a reconciler of enemies: he was Staufen on his father's side and Welf on his mother's. (See Genealogy 6.2: Rulers of Germany and Sicily.) Again like the English king, Frederick held a kingdom and more. But he lacked Henry's wealth. As a result he was forced to rely on personal loyalties, not salaried civil servants. He could not tear down princely castles as Henry had done. Instead, he conceded the German princes their powers, requiring them in turn to recognize him as the source of those powers, and committing them to certain obligations, such as attending him at court and providing him with troops.

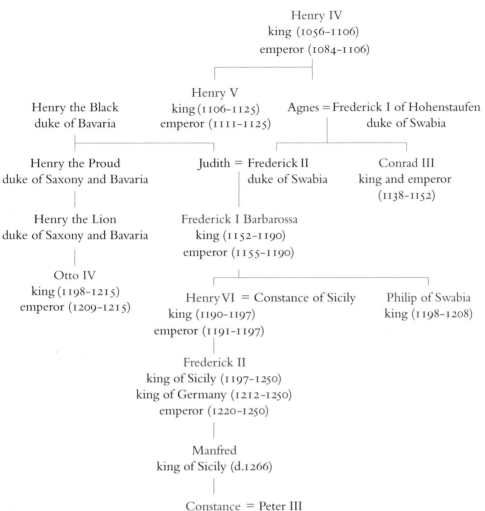

Genealogy 6.2: Rulers of Germany and Sicily

Frederick had to deal with more than the princes. He had to confront the papacy. In 1157, at the diet (assembly) of Besançon, Pope Adrian IV sent Frederick a letter that coyly referred to the imperial crown as the pope's *beneficium*—"benefit" or, more ominously, "fief." "A great tumult and uproar arose from the princes of the realm at so insolent a message," wrote Rahewin, a cleric who had access to many of the documents and people involved at the time. "It is said that one of the [papal] ambassadors, as though adding sword to flame, inquired: 'From whom then does he have the empire, if not from our lord the pope?' Because of this remark, anger reached such a pitch that one of [the princes] … threatened the ambassador with his sword."[8]

Frederick calmed his supporters, but in the wake of this incident, he countered the "holy church" by coining an equally charged term for his empire: *sacrum imperium*—the "sacred

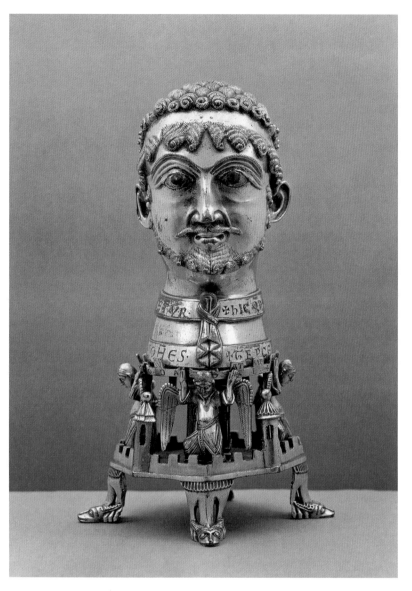

empire." The idea of "holiness" extended to the emperor as well. In 1165 Frederick exhumed the body of Charlemagne, enclosed the dead emperor's arm in a beautiful reliquary casket, and set the wheels of canonization in motion. Soon thereafter, Pascal III, Frederick's antipope, declared Charlemagne a saint. (See the list of Popes and Antipopes to 1500 on p. 341 to see the many competing popes of Barbarossa's reign.)

Finally, Frederick had to deal with Italy. As emperor, he had claims on the whole peninsula, but he had no hope—or even interest—in controlling the south. By contrast, northern Italy beckoned: added to his own inheritance in Swabia (in southwestern Germany), its rich cities promised to provide him with both a compact power base and the revenues that he needed.

Taking northern Italy was, however, nothing like, say, Philip's conquest of Normandy, which was used to ducal rule. The communes of Italy were themselves states (autonomous cities, yes, but each also with a good deal of surrounding land, their *contado*), jealous of their liberties, rivalrous, and fiercely patriotic. Frederick made no concessions to their sensibilities. Emboldened by theories of sovereignty that had been elaborated by the revival of Roman law, he marched into Italy and, at the diet of Roncaglia (1158), demanded imperial rights to taxes and tolls. He brought the Four Doctors (see p. 179) from Bologna to Roncaglia to hear court cases. Insisting that the conquered Italian cities be governed by his own men, Frederick appointed *podestà* (city managers) who were often German-speaking and heavy-handed. No sooner had the *podestà* at Milan taken up his post, for example, than he immediately ordered an inventory of all taxes due the emperor and levied new and demeaning labor duties. He even demanded that the Milanese carry the wood and stones of their plundered city to Pavia, to build new houses there. This was a double humiliation: Milan had been at war with Pavia. (For all of these cities, see Map 6.5.) Expressing his imperial might in material form, Frederick commissioned a bust of himself in the guise of a Roman emperor; supported by angels, his head towered over a representation of a city, probably Rome. (See Plate 6.1.)

By 1167, most of the cities of northern Italy had joined with Pope Alexander III (1159–1181) to form the Lombard League against Frederick. Defeated at the battle of Legnano in 1176, Frederick agreed to the Peace of Venice the next year and withdrew most of his forces from the region. But his failure in the north led him to try a southern strategy. By marrying his son Henry VI (r.1190–1197) to Constance, heiress of the Kingdom of Sicily, Frederick Barbarossa linked the fate of his dynasty to a well-organized monarchy that commanded dazzling wealth.

As we saw (p. 158), the Kingdom of Sicily had been created by Normans. In theory, it was held as a fief from the pope, who, in the treaty of Benevento (1156), recognized Norman sovereignty over a territory that extended from Sicily all the way to the southern edge of the papal states. Both multilingual and multi-religious, the Kingdom of Sicily embraced Jews, Muslims, Greeks, and Italians. Indeed, the Normans saw themselves as heirs to the Byzantines and Muslims and frequently came close to conquering Byzantium and North Africa. Taking over the Byzantine and Islamic administrative apparatuses already in place in their kingdom, they crafted a highly centralized government, with royal justices circuiting the kingdom and salaried civil servants drawn from the level of knights and townsmen.

Frederick II (1194–1250), the son of Henry VI and Constance, tried to unite Sicily, Italy, and Germany into an imperial unit. He failed: the popes, eager to carve out their own well-ordered state in the center of Italy, could not allow a strong monarch to encircle them. Declaring war on Frederick, the papacy not only excommunicated him several times but also declared him deposed and accused him of heresy, a charge that led to declaring a crusade against him in the 1240s. These were fearsome actions. The king of France urged negotiation and reconciliation, but others saw in Frederick the devil himself. In the words of one chronicler, Frederick was "an evil and accursed man, a schismatic, a heretic, and an epicurean, who 'defiled the whole earth' (Jer. 51:25)" because he sowed the seeds of division and discord in the cities of Italy.[9]

This was one potent point of view. There were others, more admiring. Frederick was a poet, a patron of the arts, and the founder of the first state-supported university, which he built at Naples. His administrative reforms in Sicily were comparable to Henry II's in England: he took what he found and made it routine. In the *Constitutions of Melfi* (1231) he made sure that his salaried officials worked according to

Plate 6.1 (facing page): Bust of Frederick Barbarossa (1165). Made in Aachen, and thus associated with Charlemagne, this bronze-gilt bust of Frederick shows him wearing an imperial fillet on his short curly hair. (You can see such fillets on the heads of the figures in Plate 3.1 on p. 85.) The inscriptions were added later, when Frederick gave the bust to his godfather, Otto. Transforming the bust into a reliquary to hold a hair of Saint John the Evangelist, Otto gave it to a religious house that he had co-founded and eventually led.

Map 6.5: Italy in the Age of Frederick Barbarossa

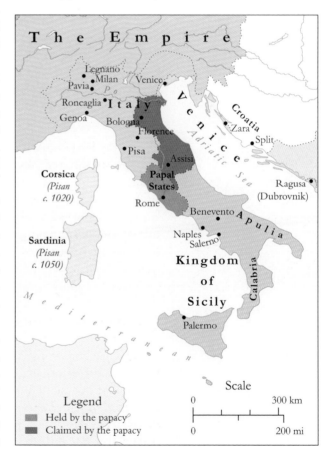

uniform procedures, required nearly all litigation to be heard by royal courts, regularized commercial privileges, and set up a system of royal taxation.

The struggle with the papacy obliged Frederick to grant enormous concessions to the German princes to give himself a free hand. In effect, he allowed the princes to turn their territories into independent states. Until the nineteenth century, Germany was a mosaic, not of city-states like Italy, but of principalities. Between 1254 and 1273 the princes, split into factions, kept the German throne empty by electing two different foreigners who spent their time fighting each other. Strangely enough, it was during this low point of the German monarchy that the term "Holy Roman Empire" was coined. In 1273, the princes at last united and elected a German, Rudolf I (r.1273–1291), whose family, the Habsburg, was new to imperial power. Rudolf used the imperial title to help him gain Austria for his family. But he did not try to assert his power in Italy. For the first time, the word "emperor" was freed from its association with Rome.

The Kingdom of Sicily was similarly parceled out. The papacy tried to ensure that the Staufen dynasty would never rule there again by calling upon Charles of Anjou, brother of the king of France, to take it over in 1263. Undeterred, Frederick's granddaughter, Constance, married to the King of Aragon (Spain), took the proud title "Queen of Sicily." In 1282, the Sicilians revolted against the Angevins in the uprising known as the "Sicilian Vespers," begging the Aragonese for aid. Bitter war ensued, ending only in 1302, when the Kingdom of Sicily was split: the island became a Spanish outpost, while its mainland portion (southern Italy) remained under Angevin control.

A HUNGARIAN MINI-EMPIRE

Unlike the Kingdom of Sicily, the Kingdom of Hungary reaped the fruits of a period of expansion. In the eleventh century, having solidified their hold along the Danube River (the center of their power), the kings of Hungary moved north and east. In an arc ending at the Carpathian Mountains, they established control over a multi-ethnic population of Germans and Slavs. In the course of the twelfth century, the Hungarian kings turned southward, taking over Croatia and fighting for control over the coastline with the powerful Republic of Venice. They might have dominated the whole eastern Adriatic had not the Kingdom of Serbia re-established itself west of its original site, eager for its own share of seaborne commerce.

THE TRIUMPH OF THE CITY-STATES

That Venice was strong enough to rival Hungary in the eastern Adriatic was in part due to the confrontations between popes and emperors in Italy, which weakened both sides. The winners of those bitter wars were not the papacy, not the Angevins, not even the Aragonese, and certainly not the emperors. The winners were the Italian city-states. Republics in the sense that a high percentage of their adult male population participated in their government, they were also highly controlling. For example, to feed themselves, the communes prohibited the export of grain while commanding the peasants in the *contado* to bring a certain amount of grain to the cities by a certain date each year. City governments told the peasants which crops to grow and how many times per year they should plow the land. The state controlled commerce as well. At Venice, exceptional in lacking a *contado* but controlling a vast maritime empire instead, merchant enterprises were state run, using state ships. When Venetians went off to buy cotton in the Levant, they all had to offer the same price, determined by their government back home.

Italian city-state governments outdid England, Sicily, and France in their bureaucracy and efficiency. While other governments were still taxing by "hearths," the communes devised taxes based on a census (*catasto*) of property. Already at Pisa in 1162 taxes were being raised in this way; by the middle of the thirteenth century, almost all the communes had such a system in place. But even efficient methods of taxation did not bring in enough money to support the two main needs of the commune: paying their officials and, above all, waging war. To meet their high military expenses, the communes created state loans, some voluntary, others forced. They were the first in Europe to do so.

CULTURE AND INSTITUTIONS IN TOWN AND COUNTRYSIDE

Organization and accounting were the concerns of lords outside Italy as well. But no one adopted the persona of the business tycoon; the prevailing ideal was the chivalrous knight. Courts were aristocratic centers, organized not only to enhance but also to highlight the power of lord and lady. Meanwhile, in the cities, guilds constituted a different kind of enclave, shutting out some laborers and women but giving high status to masters. Universities, too, were a sort of guild. Artistic creativity, urban pride, and episcopal power were together embodied in Gothic cathedrals.

Inventorying the Countryside

Not only kings and communes but also great lords everywhere hired literate agents to administer their estates, calculate their profits, draw up accounts, and make marketing decisions. Money financed luxuries, to be sure, but even more importantly it enhanced aristocratic honor, so dependent on personal generosity, patronage, and displays of wealth. In the late twelfth century, when some townsmen could boast fortunes that rivaled the riches of the landed nobility, noble extravagance tended to exceed income. Most aristocrats went into debt.

The nobles' need for money coincided with the interests of the peasantry, whose numbers were expanding. The solution was the extension of farmland. By the middle of the century, isolated and sporadic attempts to bring new land into cultivation had become regular and coordinated. Great lords offered special privileges to peasants who would do the backbreaking work of plowing marginal land. In 1154, for example, the bishop of Meissen (in Germany) proclaimed a new village and called for peasants from Flanders to settle there. Experts in drainage, the colonists received rights to the swampland they reclaimed. They owed only light monetary dues to the bishop, who nevertheless expected to reap a profit from their tolls and tithes. Similar encouragement came from lords throughout Europe, especially in northern Italy, England, Flanders, and Germany. In Flanders, where land was regularly inundated by seawater, the great monasteries sponsored drainage projects, and canals linking the cities to the agricultural hinterlands let boats ply the waters to virtually every nook and cranny of the region.

Sometimes free peasants acted on their own to clear land and relieve the pressure of overpopulation, as when the small freeholders in England's Fenland region cooperated to build banks and dikes to reclaim the land that led out to the North Sea. Villages were founded on the drained land, and villagers shared responsibility for repairing and maintaining the dikes even as each peasant family farmed its new holding individually.

On old estates, the rise in population strained to its breaking point the manse organization that had developed in Carolingian Europe, where each household was settled on the land that supported it. Now, in the twelfth century, many peasant families might live on what had been, in the ninth century, the manse of one family. Labor services and dues had to be recalculated, and peasants and their lords often turned services and dues into money rents, payable once a year. With this change, peasant men gained more control over their plots—they could sell them, will them to their sons, or even designate a small portion for their daughters. However, for these privileges they had either to pay extra taxes or, like communes, join together to buy their collective liberty for a high price, paid out over many years to their lord. Peasants, like town citizens, gained a new sense of identity and solidarity as they bargained with a lord keen to increase his income at their expense.

The Culture of the Courts

Great lords needed money to support their courtiers. When they traveled, they did so with a whole retinue of relatives, vassals, officials, priests, knights, probably a doctor, and very likely an entertainer. In the south of France a considerable number of men and women made their way as court troubadours (or, in the case of women, *trobairitz*). They were both poets and musicians, singing in Old Occitan, the vernacular of the region. Duke William IX of Aquitaine (1071–1126) is usually considered the first of the troubadours. But there were certainly people singing his kind of poetry in both Arabic and Hebrew in al-Andalus, which, as we have seen, was just at this time regularly coming into contact (mainly violently, to be sure) with the cultures of the north. By the twelfth century there were many troubadours; they were welcomed at major courts as essential personnel.

Bernart de Ventadorn (*fl. c.*1147–1170) was among them. Here is one of his verses:

Qan vei la lauzeta mover	When I see the lark beat his wings
de joi sas alas contra·l rai,	With joy in the rays of the sun
que s'oblid'e·is laissa cazer	and forget himself and fall
per la doussor c'al cor li vai,	In the warmth that fills his heart,
ai! Tant grans enveia m'en ve	Oh, I feel so great an envy
de cui que veia jauzion,	Of one I see who's merry
meravillas ai car desse	I wonder that my heart
lo cors de desirier no·m fon.	Does not melt with desire.[10]

The rhyme scheme *seems* simple: *mover* goes with *cazer*, *rai* with *vai*. Then comes a new pattern: *ve* rhymes with *desse* and *jauzion* with *fon*. But consider that all seven verses that come after this one have that same *-er*, *-ai*, *-e*, *-on* pattern. Enormous ingenuity is required for such a feat. In fact the poem is extremely complex and subtle, not only in rhyme and meter but also in word puns and allusions, essential skills for a poet whose goal was to dazzle his audience with brilliant originality.

In rhyme and meter, troubadour songs resembled Latin liturgical chants of the same region and period. Clearly, lay and religious cultures overlapped. They overlapped in musical terms as well, in the use, for example, of plucking and percussive instruments. Above all, they overlapped in themes: they spoke of love. The monks (as we have seen with the Cistercians, on p. 189) thought about the love between God and mankind; the troubadours thought about erotic love. Yet the two were deliciously entangled. The verse in which Bernart envies the lark continues:

Oh, I thought I knew so much
About love, but how little I know!
I cannot stop loving her
Though I know she'll never love me.
…
I get no help with my lady
From God or mercy or right.[11]

Putting his lady in the same stanza as God elevated her to the status of a religious icon, but at the same time it degraded God: should the Lord really help Bernart with his seduction? Finally, it played with the association of "my lady" with the Virgin Mary, the quintessential "our Lady."

Female troubadours, the *trobairitz*, flirted with the same themes. La Comtessa de Dia (*fl.* late 12th-early 13th cent.) sang,

I've been in heavy grief
For a knight that once was mine,
And I want it to be forever known
That I loved him too much.

> I see now that I'm betrayed
> For not giving him my love.
> Bemused, I lie in bed awake;
>   Bemused, I dress and pass the day.[12]

As with the *adab* literature of the Islamic world (see p. 91), the ideals of such courtly poetry emphasized refinement, feeling, and wit, all summed up in the word *cortezia*, "courtliness" or "courtesy."

Historians and literary critics used to use the term "courtly love" to emphasize one of the themes of this literature: the poet expressing overwhelming love for a beautiful married noblewoman who is far above him and utterly unattainable. But this was only one of the many sorts of loves that the troubadours sang about: some boasted of sexual conquests; others played with the notion of equality between lovers; still others preached that love was the source of virtue. The real theme of these poems was not courtly love; it was the power of women. No wonder southern French aristocratic women patronized the troubadours: they enjoyed the image that it gave them of themselves. Nor was this image a delusion. There were many powerful female lords in southern France. They owned property, commanded vassals, led battles, decided disputes, and entered into and broke political alliances as their advantage dictated. Both men and women appreciated troubadour poetry, which recognized and praised women's power even as it eroticized it.

From southern France, Catalonia, and northern Italy, the lyric love song spread to northern France, England, and Germany. Here Occitan was a foreign language, so other vernaculars were used: the *minnesinger* (literally, "love singer") sang in German; the *trouvère* sang in the Old French of northern France. In northern France another genre of poetry grew up as well, poking fun at nobles, priests, and pretentiousness and stupidity in general. This was the *fabliau* (pl. *fabliaux*), which boasted humbler folk as its protagonists:

> Long ago
> There lived a peasant who had wed
> A maiden courteous, well bred,
> Wise, beautiful, of goodly birth.
> He cherished her for all his worth
> And did his best to keep her pleased.
> The lady loved the parish priest,
> Who was her only heart's desire.
> The priest himself was so afire
> With love for her that he decided
> To tell his love and not to hide it.[13]

The priest tricked the peasant, had a rollicking love-making session with the peasant's wife, and left the house with the peasant none the wiser.

Some troubadours, like the poet Bertran de Born (*fl.* 2nd half of 12th cent.), wrote about war, not love:

> Trumpets, drums, standards and pennons
> And ensigns and horses black and white
> Soon we shall see, and the world will be good.[14]

But warfare was more often the subject of another kind of poem, the *chanson de geste*, "song of heroic deeds." Long recited orally, these vernacular poems appeared in written form at about the same time as troubadour poetry and, like them, the *chansons de geste* played with aristocratic codes of behavior, in this case on the battlefield rather than at court.

The *chansons de geste* were responding to social and military transformations. By the end of the twelfth century, nobles and knights had begun to merge into one class, threatened from below by newly rich merchants and from above by newly powerful kings. At the same time, the knights' importance in battle—unhorsing one another with lances and long swords and taking prisoners rather than killing their opponents—was waning in the face of mercenary infantrymen who wielded long hooks and knives that ripped easily through chain mail, killing their enemies outright. A knightly ethos and sense of group solidarity emerged within this changed landscape. Like Bertran de Born, the *chansons de geste* celebrated "trumpets, drums, standards and pennons." But they also examined the moral issues that confronted knights, taking up the often contradictory values of their society: love of family vied with fealty to a lord; desire for victory clashed with pressures to compromise.

The *chansons de geste*, later also called "epics," focused on battle; other long poems, later called "romances," explored relationships between men and women. Enormously popular in the late twelfth and early thirteenth centuries, romances took up such themes as the tragic love between Tristan and Isolde and the virtuous knight's search for the Holy Grail. Above all, romances were woven around the many fictional stories of King Arthur and his court. In one of the earliest, Chrétien de Troyes (*fl. c.*1150–1190) wrote about the noble and valiant Lancelot, in love with Queen Guinevere, wife of Arthur. Finding a comb bearing some strands of her radiant hair, Lancelot is overcome:

> He gently removed the queen's
> Hair, not breaking a single
> Strand. Once a man
> Has fallen in love with a woman
> No one in all the world
> Can lavish such wild adoration
> Even on the objects she owns,
> Touching them a hundred thousand
> Times, caressing with his eyes,

His lips, his forehead, his face.
And all of it brings him happiness,
Fills him with the richest delight;
He presses it into his breast,
Slips it between his shirt
And his heart—worth more than a wagon-
Load of emeralds or diamonds,
Holy relics that free him
Of disease and infection: no powdered
Pearls and ground-up horn
And snail shells for him! No prayers
To Saints Martin and James: his faith
In her hair is complete, he needs
        No more.[15]

By making Guinevere's hair an object of adoration, a sort of secular relic, Chrétien here not only conveys the depths of Lancelot's feeling but also pokes a bit of fun at his hero. When Lancelot is on the point of killing an evil opponent, he overhears Guinevere say that she wishes the "final blow be withheld." Then

Nothing in the world could have made him
Fight, or even move,
No matter if it cost his life[16]

Such perfect obedience and self-restraint even in the middle of a bloody battle was part of the premise of "chivalry." The word, deriving from the French *cheval* ("horse"), emphasized above all that the knight was a horseman, a warrior of the most prestigious sort. Perched high in the saddle, his heavy lance couched in his right arm, the knight was an imposing and menacing figure. Chivalry made him gentle, gave his battles a higher meaning, whether for love of a lady or of God. The chivalric hero was constrained by courtesy, fair play, piety, and devotion to an ideal. Did real knights live up to these ideals? They knew perfectly well that they could not and that it would be absurd if they tried to do so in every particular. But they loved playing with the idea. They were the poets' audience, and they liked to think of themselves as fitting into the tales. When William the Marshal, advisor of English kings, died in 1219, his biographer wrote of him as a model knight, courteous with the ladies, brave on the battlefield.

Urban Guilds Incorporated

Courtly "codes" were poetic and playful. City codes were drier but no less compelling. In the early thirteenth century, guilds drew up statutes to determine dues, regulate working hours, fix wages, and set standards for materials and products. Sometimes they came into conflict with town government; this happened, for example, to some bread-bakers' guilds in Italy, where communes considered bread too important a commodity to be left to its producers. At other times, the communes supported guild efforts to control wages, reinforcing guild regulations with statutes of their own. When great lords rather than communes governed a city, they too tried to control and protect the guilds. King Henry II of England, for example, eagerly gave some guilds in his Norman duchy special privileges so that they would depend on him.

There was nothing democratic about guilds. To make cloth, the merchant guild that imported the raw wool was generally the overseer of the other related guilds—the shearers, weavers, fullers (the workers who beat the cloth to shrink it and make it heavier), and dyers. In Florence, professional guilds of notaries and judges ranked in prestige and power above craft guilds. Within each guild was another kind of hierarchy. Apprentices were at the bottom, journeymen and -women in the middle, and masters at the top. Young boys and occasionally girls were the apprentices; they worked for a master for room and board, learning a trade. An apprenticeship in the felt-hat trade in Paris, for example, lasted seven years. After their apprenticeship, men and women often worked many years as day laborers, hired by a master when he needed extra help. Some men, but almost no women, worked their way up to master status. They were the ones who dominated the offices and set guild policies.

The codification of guild practices and membership tended to work against women, who were slowly being ousted from the world of workers during the late twelfth century. In Flanders, for example, as the manufacture of woolen cloth shifted from rural areas to cities, and from light to heavy looms, women were less involved in cloth production than they had been on traditional manors. Similarly, water- and animal-powered mills took the place of female hand labor to grind grain into flour—and most millers were male. Nevertheless, at Paris, guild regulations for the silk fabric makers assumed that the artisans would be women:

> No journeywoman maker of silk fabric may be a mistress [the female equivalent of "master"] of the craft until she has practiced it for a year and a day.... No mistress of the craft may weave thread with silk, or foil with silk.... No mistress or journeywoman of the craft may make a false hem or border.[17]

By contrast, universities were all-male guilds. (The word *universitas* is Latin for "guild.") Referring at first to organizations of masters and students, the term eventually came to apply to the school itself. At the beginning of the thirteenth century, the universities regulated student discipline, scholastic proficiency, and housing while determining the masters' behavior in equal detail. At the University of Paris, for example, the masters were required to wear long black gowns, follow a particular order in their lectures, and set the standards by which students could become masters themselves. The University of Bologna was unique in having two guilds, one of students and one of masters. At Bologna, the students participated in the appointment, payment, and discipline of the masters.

The University of Bologna was unusual because it was principally a school of law, where the students were often older men, well along in their careers (often in imperial service) and used to wielding power. At the University of Paris, young students predominated, drawn by its renown in the liberal arts and theology. The universities of Salerno (near Naples) and Montpellier (in southern France) specialized in medicine. Oxford, once a sleepy town where students clustered around one or two masters, became a center of royal administration; its university soon developed a reputation for teaching the liberal arts, theology, science, and mathematics.

The curriculum of each university depended on its specialty and its traditions. At Paris in the early thirteenth century, students spent at least six years studying the liberal arts before gaining the right to teach. If they wanted to specialize in theology, they attended lectures on the subject for at least another five years. With books both expensive and hard to find, lectures were the chief method of communication. These were centered on important texts: the master read an excerpt aloud, delivered his commentary on it, and disputed any contrary commentaries that rival masters might have proposed. Students committed the lectures to memory.

Within the larger association of the university, students found more intimate groups with which to live: "nations," linked to the students' place of origin. At Bologna, for example, students belonged to one of two nations, the Italians and the non-Italians. Each nation protected its members, wrote statutes, and elected officers.

Both masters and students were considered part of another group: clerics. This was an outgrowth of the original, church-related, purposes of the schools, and it had two important consequences. First, there were no university women. And second, university men were subject to church courts rather than the secular jurisdiction of towns or lords. Many universities could also boast generous privileges from popes and kings, who valued the services of scholars. The combination of clerical status and special privileges made universities virtually self-governing corporations within the towns. This sometimes led to friction. When the townsmen of Oxford tried to punish a student suspected of killing his mistress, the masters protested by refusing to teach and leaving the city. Such disputes are called "town against gown" struggles because students and masters wore gowns (the distant ancestors of today's graduation gowns). But since university towns depended on scholars to patronize local taverns, shops, and hostels, town and gown normally learned to negotiate with one another to their mutual advantage.

Gothic Style

Certainly town and gown agreed on building style: by *c.*1200, "Gothic" (the term itself comes from the sixteenth century) was the architecture of choice. Beginning as a variant of Romanesque in the Ile-de-France, Gothic style quickly took on an identity of its own.

Gothic architects tried to eliminate heavy walls by enlivening them with sculpture or piercing them with glass, creating a soaring feel by using pointed arches. Suger, abbot of Saint-Denis and the promoter of Capetian royal power (see p. 176), was the style's first sponsor. When he rebuilt portions of his church around 1135, he tried to meld royal and ecclesiastical interests and ideals in stone and glass. At the west end of his church, the point where the faithful entered, Suger decorated the portals with figures of Old Testament kings, queens, and patriarchs, signaling the links between the present king and his illustrious predecessors. Rebuilding the interior of the east end of his church as well, Suger used pointed arches and stained glass to let in light, which Suger believed to be God's own "illumination," capable of transporting the worshiper from the "slime of earth" to the "purity of Heaven."

Gothic was an urban architecture, reflecting—in its grand size, jewel-like windows, and bright ornaments—the aspirations, pride, and confidence of rich and powerful merchants, artisans, and bishops. The Gothic cathedral, which could take centuries to complete, was often the religious, social, and commercial focal point of a city. Funds for these buildings might come from the bishop himself, from the canons (priests) who served his cathedral, or from townsmen. Notre Dame of Paris (Plate 6.2) was begun in 1163 by Bishop Maurice de Sully, whose episcopal income from estates, forests, taxes, and Parisian properties gave him plenty of money to finance the tallest church of its day. Under his successors, the edifice took shape with three stories, the upper one filled with stained glass. Bristling on the outside with flying buttresses—the characteristic "look" of a French Gothic church—it gave no hint of the light and calm order within (see Plate 6.3, p. 224). But at Mantes-la-Jolie (about 25 miles west of Paris), it was the merchant guild and the Capetian king together—rather than a bishop—who sponsored the building of the new collegiate church.

However financed, Gothic cathedrals were community projects, enlisting the labor and support of a small army of quarrymen, builders, carpenters, and glass cutters. Houses of relics, they attracted pilgrims as well. At Chartres Cathedral, proud home of the Virgin's tunic, crowds thronged the streets, the poor buying small lead figures of the Virgin, the rich purchasing wearable replicas of her tunic.

The technologies that made Gothic churches possible were all known before the twelfth century. The key elements included ribbed vaulting, which could give a sense of precision and order (as at Notre Dame; consider Plate 6.3 again, concentrating on the orderly rhythm of piers and ribs) or of richness and playful inventiveness (as at Lincoln Cathedral in England: see Plate 6.4, p. 225). Flying buttresses took the weight of the vault off the walls, allowing most of the wall to be cut away and the open spaces filled by glass. (See Figure 6.1.) Pointed arches made the church appear to surge heavenward.

By the mid-thirteenth century, Gothic architecture had spread to most of Europe. Yet the style varied by region, most dramatically in Italy. San Francesco in Assisi is an example

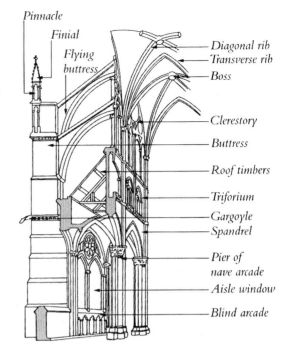

Figure 6.1: Elements of a Gothic Church. This drawing of a section through the nave at Amiens shows the most important features of a Gothic church.

Following pages:

Plate 6.2: Notre Dame of Paris, Exterior (begun 1163). To take the weight of the vault off the walls and open them to glass and light, the architects of Gothic churches such as Notre Dame used flying buttresses, which sprang from the top of the exterior wall. In this photograph they look rather like oars jutting out from the church. You can most easily see them on the apse, to the right.

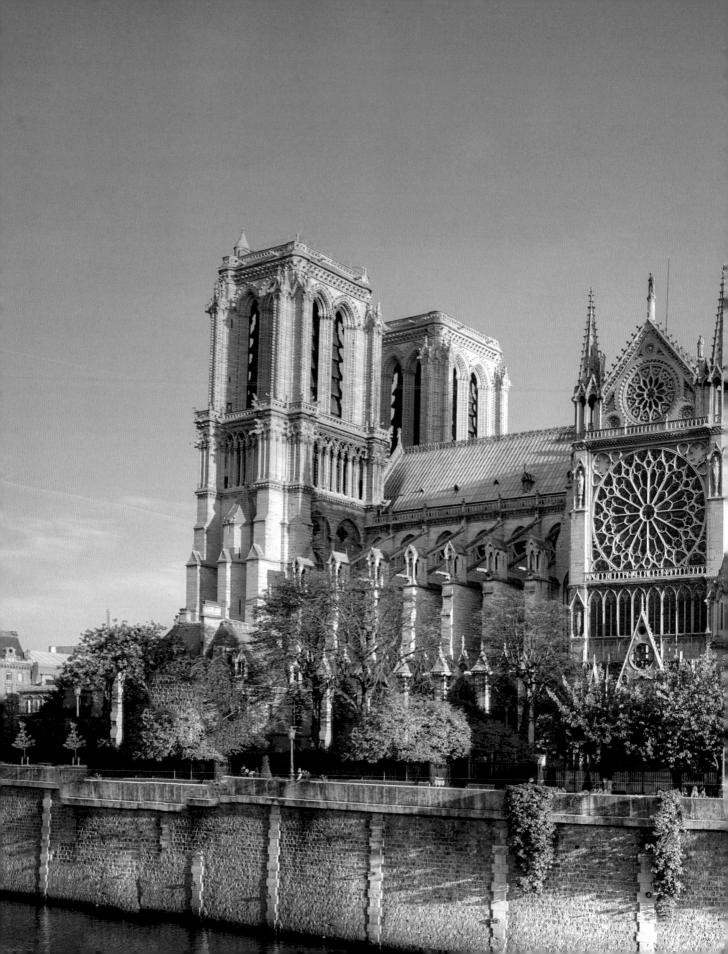

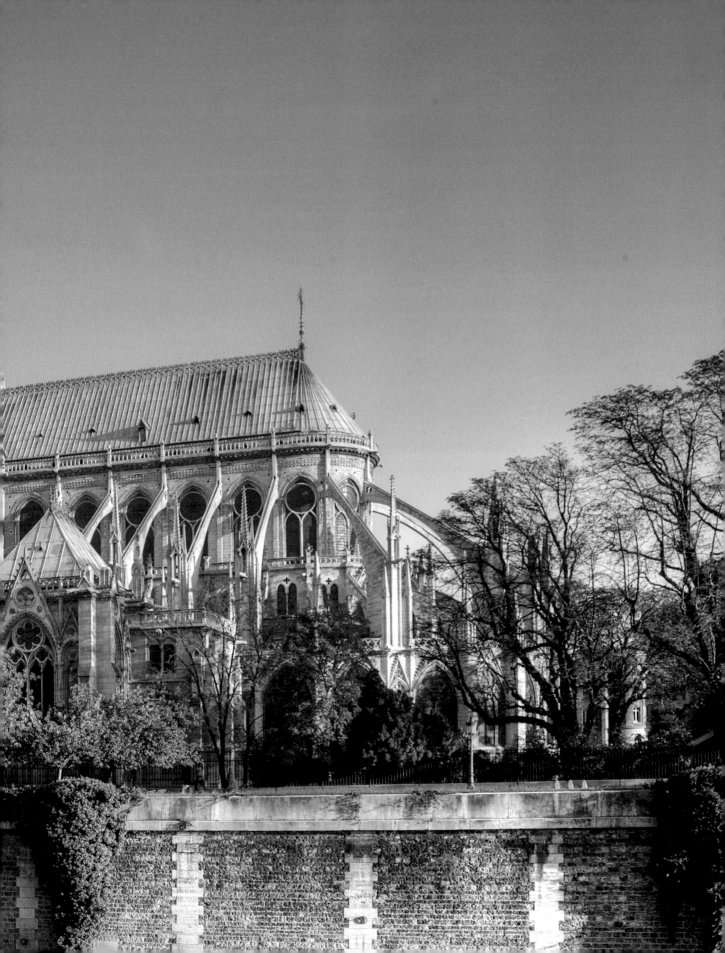

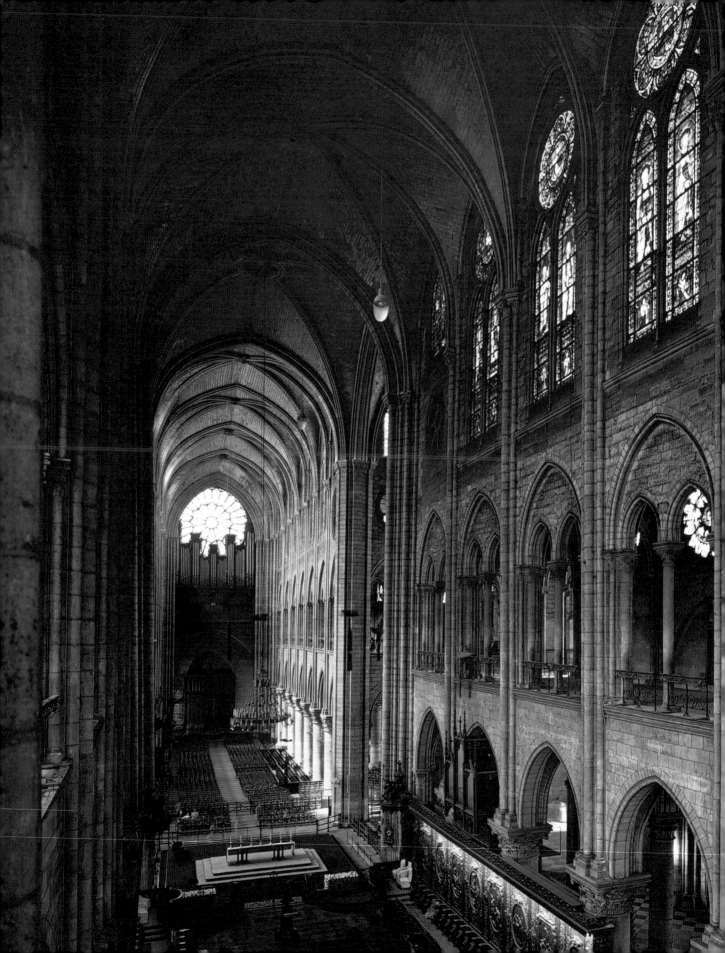

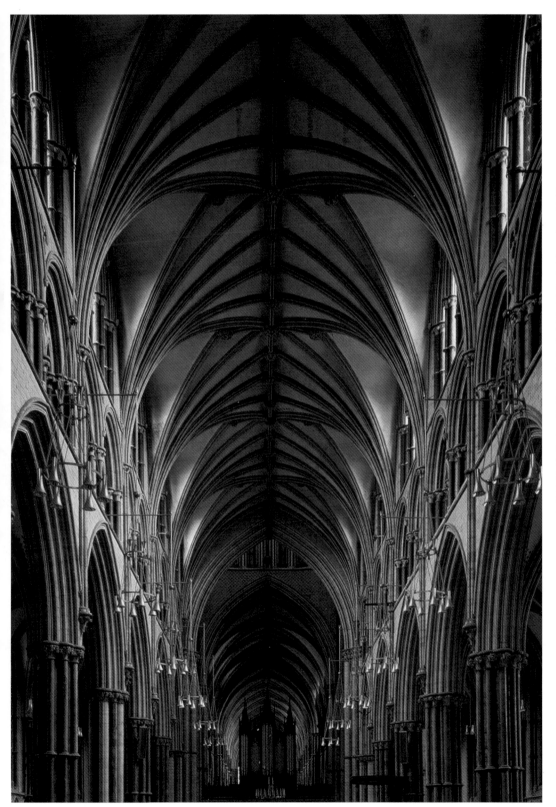

Plate 6.3 (facing page): Notre Dame of Paris, Interior (begun 1163). Compare this interior with that of Autun in Plate 5.6 (p. 185). Autun, a typical Romanesque church, has a barrel vault (though slightly pointed) and small windows at the top. By contrast, the Gothic cathedral of Notre Dame (shown here) has a pointed ribbed vault that soars above the nave, while light from large stained-glass windows suffuses the interior.

Plate 6.4: Lincoln Cathedral, Interior (choir begun 1192, nave begun 1225). Many English Gothic cathedrals emphasized surface ornament. Here the ribs, which spring from carved moldings on the walls of the nave, are splayed into fans on the vault. What other elements are decorative?

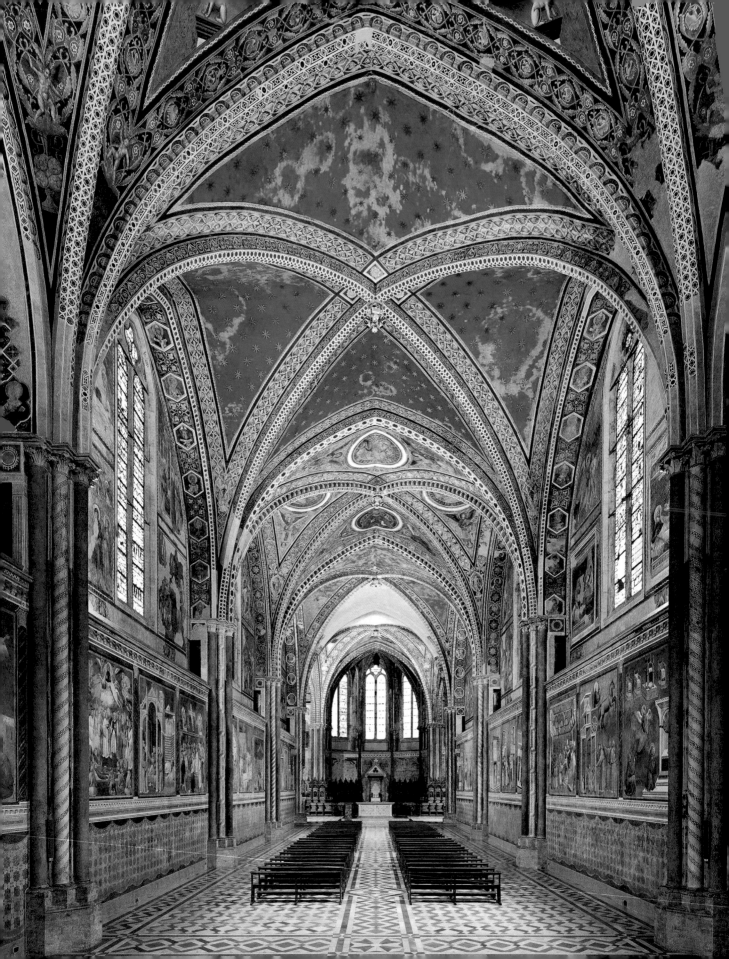

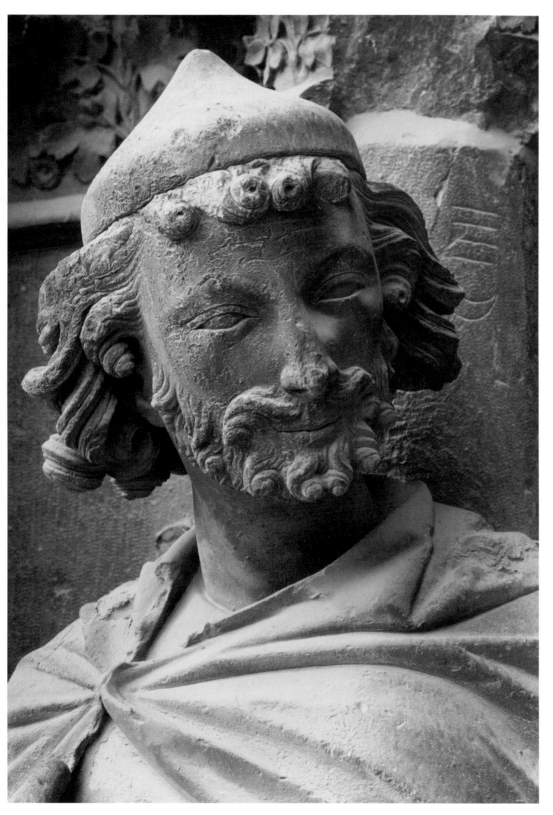

Plate 6.5 (facing page): San Francesco at Assisi (upper church; completed by 1253). Influenced by French Gothic, this church of the Franciscan Order in Assisi nevertheless asserts a different aesthetic. Compare it with Notre Dame in Plate 6.3, where the piers and ribs mark off units of space (called "bays"). By contrast, San Francesco presents a unified space. Notre Dame celebrated its soaring height; San Francesco balanced its height by its generous width. Unlike French Gothic, Italian Gothic churches gloried in their walls; at San Francesco they were decorated in the 1280s and 1290s with frescoes, the most famous of which illustrated the life and legend of Saint Francis (for whom see below, p. 231).

Plate 6.6: Reims Cathedral, West Portal, Saint Joseph (*c.*1240). Compare Saint Joseph on this Gothic portal with the portrayal of Eve on the Romanesque lintel at Autun in Plate 5.7. Forgetting, for the moment, the differences in subject matter, note the change in style: Eve's body adheres to the flat surface behind her and conforms to its shape. By contrast, Joseph breaks away from the column behind him and is carved fully in the round.

of what *Italian* architects meant by a Gothic church. It has high stained glass windows and a pointed, ribbed vault (see Plate 6.5.) But the focus is not on light and height but on walls, painted decoration, and well-proportioned space. With flying buttresses rare and portal sculpture unobtrusive, Italian Gothic churches convey a spirit of spare and quiet beauty.

Gothic art, both painting and sculpture, echoed and decorated the Gothic church. While Romanesque sculpture played upon a flat surface, Gothic figures were liberated from their background, turning, bending, and interacting. At Reims Cathedral the figure of Saint Joseph on the west portal, elegant and graceful, reveals a gentle smile. (See Plate 6.6.) Above his head is carved foliage of striking naturalness. Portals like this were meant to be "read" for their meaning. Joseph is not smiling for nothing; in the original arrangement of the portal he was looking at the figure of a servant while, further to his left, his wife, Mary, presented the baby Jesus in the temple. This was the New Testament story brought to life.

WORLDLY CONCERNS IN AND OUT OF CHURCH

The depiction of Joseph in the guise of proud father reflected a new and widespread sensibility among the educated elites: interest in the joys and woes of everyday life. This was as true at the basic level of bodily health as it was at the more rarified heights of religious behavior and belief. To care for the ill were doctors, trained in medical schools and ready to prescribe remedies according to the most up-to-date theories. To mold religious behavior and belief were churchmen, trained in both law and theology and determined to impose clear obligations on all Christians—and to rid Christendom of those who did not conform.

Caring for the Body

Around 1151, Peter the Venerable, the abbot of Cluny, wrote to a Doctor Bartholomew (probably the famous physician Bartholomew of Salerno) for help:

> For almost a year I have been repeatedly afflicted with the disease called catarrh [a head cold]; I have had it twice already, once in the summer and once in the winter or around that time. This year I came down with it at the end of summer and beginning of autumn. Prior to this, [because of business] ... I was forced to postpone much longer than usual my customary bloodletting, which I normally have at the end of every second month. And because the disease that I mentioned came upon me during that delay in bloodletting, I did not dare to go ahead with it the way I normally would.[18]

In fact Peter had been advised by local doctors that he might lose his voice (and possibly even his life!) if he had his blood let. He held off for four months, and then tried bloodletting again. It was no use: he lost his voice and coughed up phlegm for months thereafter. He needed advice. Should he let more blood or not? He ended his letter by politely excusing Bartholomew from making a house call himself; but would he send his student Bernard? Bartholomew wrote back to say that he was indeed dispatching Bernard. Meanwhile, even without seeing the patient, he had advice for Peter based on the very best knowledge of Galenic medicine as taught at Salerno. Peter should not proceed with bloodletting, Bartholomew said, because of Peter's unbalanced constitution. Galenic theory held that the physiological basis of human life rested on four humors: blood, yellow bile, phlegm, and black bile. Health depended on their balance. Bartholomew had observed on a previous visit that Peter had an excess of phlegm. It made little sense to drain the blood. The remedy, rather, was to apply heat and to use dry medications against the excess of phlegm, which was cold and wet.

When Bernard visited Peter, he no doubt gave similar advice. In doing so, he probably followed one of the advice manuals for good bedside manners that were beginning to proliferate at this time. In one of them, attributed to one "Archimatthaeus," the doctor was to enter the sickroom with a humble demeanor. Seated by the patient,

> ask him how he feels and reach out for his arm, and all that we shall say is necessary so that through your entire behavior you obtain the favor of the people who are around the sick. And because the trip to the patient has sharpened your sensitivity, and the sick rejoices at your coming or because he has already become stingy and has various thoughts about the fee, therefore by your fault as well as his the pulse is affected, is different and impetuous from the motion of the spirits.[19]

Here the doctor revealed himself to be both an astute politician (thinking about making a good impression) and a successful businessman (whose fee was hefty). But he was also a savvy physician who knew that his patient's pulse might be elevated not by his illness but from the emotions surrounding the doctor's visit itself.

The Fourth Lateran Council (1215)

Physicians like Bartholomew were professionals; increasingly, so too were the popes. Innocent III (1198–1216) studied theology at the University of Paris and trained in law at the University of Bologna. The mix allowed him to think that he ruled in the place of Christ the King; secular kings and emperors existed simply to help the pope, who was the real lawmaker—the maker of laws that would lead to moral reformation. The council that Innocent convened at the Lateran Palace at Rome in 1215 produced a comprehensive set of canons—most of them prepared by the pope's committees beforehand—to reform both clergy and laity. It defined Christianity—embracing some doctrines while rejecting others—and turned against Jews and Muslims with new vigor.

For laymen and -women perhaps the most important canons concerned the sacraments. The Fourth Lateran Council required Christians to take Communion—i.e., receive the Eucharist—at Mass and to confess their sins to a priest at least once a year. Marriage was declared a sacrament, and bishops were assigned jurisdiction over marital disputes. Forbidding secret marriages, the council expected priests to uncover evidence that might impede a marriage. There were many impediments: people were not allowed to marry their cousins, nor anyone related to them by godparentage, nor anyone related to them through a former marriage. Children conceived within clandestine or forbidden marriages were to be considered illegitimate; they could not inherit property from their parents, nor could they become priests.

Like the code of chivalry, the rules of the Fourth Lateran Council about marriage worked better on parchment than in life. Well-to-do London fathers included their bastard children in their wills. On English manors, sons conceived out of wedlock regularly took over their parents' land. The prohibition against secret marriages was only partially successful. Even churchmen had to admit that the consent of both parties made a marriage valid.

The most important sacrament was the Mass, the ritual in which the bread and wine of the Eucharist was transformed into the flesh and blood of Christ. In the twelfth century a newly rigorous formulation of this transformation declared that Christ's body and blood were truly present in the bread and wine on the altar. The Fourth Lateran Council not only adopted this as church doctrine but also explained it by using a technical term coined by twelfth-century scholars. The bread and wine were "transubstantiated": although the Eucharist continued to *look* like bread and wine, after the consecration during the Mass the bread became the actual body and the wine the real blood of Christ. The council's emphasis on this potent event strengthened the role of the priest, for only he could celebrate this mystery (the transformation of ordinary bread and wine into the flesh of Christ) through which God's grace was transmitted to the faithful.

The Embraced and the Rejected

As the Fourth Lateran Council provided rules for good Christians, it turned against all others. Some canons singled out Jews and heretics for special punitive treatment; others were directed against Byzantines and Muslims. These laws were of a piece with wider movements. With the development of a papal monarchy that confidently declared a single doctrine and the laws pertaining to it, dissidence was perceived as heresy, non-Christians seen as treacherous.

NEW GROUPS WITHIN THE FOLD

The Fourth Lateran Council prohibited the formation of new religious orders. It recognized that the trickle of new religious groups—the Carthusians is one example—of the early twelfth century had become a torrent by 1215. Only a very few of the more recent movements were accepted into the church, among them the Dominicans, the Franciscans, and the Beguines.

Saint Dominic (1170–1221), founder of the Dominican order, had been a priest and regular canon (following the *Rule* of Saint Augustine) in the cathedral church at Osma, Spain. On an official trip to Denmark, while passing through southern France in 1203, Dominic and his companion, Diego, reportedly converted a heretic with whom they lodged. This was a rare success; most anti-heretic preachers were failing miserably around this time. Richly clad, riding on horseback, and followed by a retinue, they had no moral standing. Dominic, Diego, and their followers determined to reject material riches. Gaining a privilege from the pope to preach and teach, they went about on foot, in poor clothes, and begged for their food. They took the name "friars," after the Latin word for "brothers." Because their job was to dispute, teach, and preach, the Dominicans quickly became university men. Even in their convents (where they adopted the *Rule* of Saint Augustine), they established schools requiring their recruits to follow a formal course of studies. Already by 1206 they had established the first of many Dominican female houses. Most of these also followed the *Rule* of Saint Augustine, but their relationship to the Dominican Order was never codified. Married men and women associated themselves with the Dominicans by forming a "Tertiary" Order.

Unlike Dominic, Saint Francis (1181/1182–1226) was never a priest. Indeed, he was on his way to a promising career as a cloth merchant at Assisi when he experienced a complete conversion. Clinging to poverty as if, in his words, "she" were his "lady" (thus borrowing the vocabulary of chivalry), he accepted no money, walked without shoes, wore only one coarse tunic, and refused to be confined even in a monastery. He and his followers (who were also called "friars") spent their time preaching, ministering to lepers, and doing manual labor. In time they dispersed, setting up fraternal groups throughout Italy, France, Spain, the Crusader States, and later Germany, England, Scotland, Poland, and elsewhere. Always they were drawn to the cities. Sleeping in "convents" on the outskirts of the towns, the Franciscans became a regular part of urban community life as they preached to crowds and begged their daily bread. Early converts included women: in 1211 or 1212 Francis converted the young noblewoman Clare. She joined a community of women at San Damiano, a church near Assisi. Clare wanted the Damianites to follow the rule and lifestyle of the friars. But the church disapproved of the women's worldly activities, and the many sisters following Francis—by 1228 there were at least 24 female communities inspired by him in central and northern Italy—were confined to cloisters under the *Rule* of Saint Benedict. In the course of the thirteenth century laypeople, many of them married, formed their own Franciscan order, the "Tertiaries." They dedicated themselves to works of charity and to daily church attendance. Eventually the Franciscans, like the Dominicans, added learning and scholarship to their mission, becoming part of the city universities.

The Beguines were even more integral to town life. In the cities of northern France, the Low Countries, and Germany, these women worked as launderers, weavers, and spinners. (Their male counterparts, the "Beghards," were far less numerous.) Choosing to live together in informal communities, taking no vows, and being free to marry if they wished, they dedicated themselves to simplicity and piety. If outwardly ordinary, however, inwardly their religious lives were often emotional and ecstatic. Some were mystics, seeking union with God. Mary of Oignies (1177–1213), for example, imagined herself with the Christ-child, who "nestled between her breasts like a baby.... Sometimes she kissed him as though He were a little child and sometimes she held Him on her lap as if He were a gentle lamb."[20]

DEFINING THE OTHER

The heretical groups that Dominic confronted in southern France were derisively called Albigensians or Cathars by the church. But they referred to themselves, among other things, as "good men" and "good women." Particularly numerous in urban, highly commercialized regions such as southern France, Italy, and the Rhineland, the good men were dissatisfied with the reforms achieved by the Gregorians and resented the church's newly centralized organization. Precisely what these dissidents believed may be glimpsed only with difficulty, largely through the reports of those who questioned and persecuted them. At a meeting in Lombers in 1165 to which some of them apparently voluntarily agreed to come, they answered questions put to them by the bishop of Lodève. Asked about the Eucharist, for example, "they answered that whoever consumed it worthily was saved, but the unworthy gained damnation for themselves; and they said that it could be consecrated [that is, transformed into Christ's body and blood] by a good man, whether clerical or lay." When questioned about whether "each person should confess his sins to priests and ministers of the church—or to any layman," they responded that it "would suffice if they confessed to whom they wanted." On this and other questions, then, the good men of Lombers had notions at variance with the doctrines that the post-Gregorian church was proclaiming. Above all, their responses downgraded the authority and prerogatives of the clergy. When the bishop at Lombers declared the good men heretics, "the heretics answered that the bishop who gave the sentence was the heretic and not they, that he was their enemy and a rapacious wolf and a hypocrite...."[21]

By the time that Dominic confronted the southern French heretics, the hostility of these dissidents toward church leaders had created the sense of a major threat. The church termed them all "dualists" who believed that the world was torn between two great forces, one good and the other evil. Dualism was well known to well-educated churchmen; Saint Augustine (see p. 9) had briefly flirted with the dualists of his own day before decisively breaking with them. Moreover, some dualist groups flourished in the Byzantine Empire, which was increasingly being vilified in the West. Classifying heretics as such created a powerful new tool of persecution and coercion that came to be used by both ecclesiastical and secular rulers.

There is no doubt that some of the good men were dualists. But there were many shades of dualism—many "catharisms"—ranging from the innocuous notion that spiritual things were pure and eternal, while materials things were not, to the radical claim that the devil had created the world and all that was in it, including man. The Christianity espoused by the church hierarchy itself had many dualist elements. In some ways, therefore, the issue of the good men's dualism overlooked the most important point for them: that their doctrine was largely a by-product of their determination to pursue poverty and simplicity—to live like the apostles—and to adhere literally to the teachings of Christ as contained in the Gospels.

Other heretical groups were condemned not on doctrinal grounds but because they allowed their lay members to preach, assuming for themselves the privilege of bishops. At Lyon (in southeastern France) in the 1170s, for example, a rich merchant named Waldo decided to take literally the Gospel message, "If you wish to be perfect, then go and sell everything you have, and give to the poor" (Matt. 19:21). The same message had inspired countless monks and would worry the church far less several decades later, when Saint Francis established his new order. But when Waldo went into the street and gave away his belongings, announcing, "I am not out of my mind, as you think,"[22] he scandalized not only the bystanders but the church as well. Refusing to retire to a monastery, Waldo and his followers, men and women called Waldensians, lived in poverty and went about preaching, quoting the Gospel in the vernacular so that everyone would understand them. But the papacy rejected Waldo's bid to preach freely; and the Waldensians—denounced, excommunicated, and expelled from Lyon—wandered to Languedoc, Italy, northern Spain, and the Mosel valley, just east of France.

EUROPEAN AGGRESSION WITHIN AND WITHOUT

Jews, heretics, Muslims, Byzantines, and pagans: all felt the heavy hand of Christian Europeans newly organized, powerful, and zealous. Meanwhile, even the undeniable Catholicism of Ireland did not prevent its takeover by England.

The Jews

Prohibited from joining guilds, Jews increasingly were forced to take the one job Christians could not have: lending on credit. Even with Christian moneylenders available (for some existed despite official prohibitions), lords borrowed from Jews. Then, relying on dormant anti-Jewish feeling, they sometimes "righteously" attacked their creditors. This happened in 1190 at York, for example, where local nobles orchestrated a brutal attack on the Jews of the city to rid themselves of their debts and the men to whom they owed money. Kings claimed the Jews as their serfs and Jewish property as their own. In England a special royal exchequer of the Jews was created in 1194 to collect unpaid debts due after the death of Jewish creditors. In France, Philip Augustus expelled the Jews from the Ile-de-France in 1182, confiscating their houses, fields, and vineyards for himself. He allowed them to return—minus their property—in 1198.

Attacks against Jews were inspired by more than resentment against Jewish money or desire for power and control. They grew out of the codification of Christian religious doctrine. The newly rigorous definition of the Eucharist as the true body and blood of Christ meant to some that Christ, wounded and bleeding, lay upon the altar. Miracle tales sometimes reported that the Eucharist bled. Reflecting Christian anxieties about real flesh upon the altar, sensational stories, originating in clerical circles but soon widely circulated, told of Jews who secretly sacrificed Christian children in a morbid revisiting of the crucifixion of Jesus. This charge, called "blood libel" by historians, led to massacres of Jews in cities in England, France, Spain, and Germany. In this way, Jews became convenient and vulnerable scapegoats for Christian guilt and anxiety about eating Christ's flesh.

After the Fourth Lateran Council, Jews were easy to spot as well. The council required all Jews to advertise their religion by some outward sign, some special dress. Local rulers enforced this canon with zeal, not so much because they were anxious to humiliate Jews as because they saw the chance to sell exemptions to Jews eager to escape the requirement. Nonetheless, sooner or later Jews almost everywhere had to wear something to advertise their second-class status: in southern France and Spain they had to wear a round badge; in Vienna they were forced to wear pointed hats.

Crusades

Attacks against Jews coincided with vigorous crusades. A new kind of crusade was launched against the heretics in southern France; along the Baltic, rulers and crusaders redrew Germany's eastern border; and the Fourth Crusade was rerouted and took Constantinople.

Against the Albigensians in southern France, Innocent III demanded that northern princes take up the sword, invade Languedoc, wrest the land from the heretics, and populate it with orthodox Christians. This Albigensian Crusade (1209–1229) marked the first time the pope had offered warriors who were fighting an enemy within Christian Europe all the spiritual and temporal benefits of a crusade to the Holy Land. In the event, the political ramifications were more notable than the religious results. After twenty years of fighting, leadership of the crusade was taken over in 1229 by the Capetian kings. Southern resistance was broken and Languedoc was brought under the control of the French crown. (On Map 6.4, p. 206, the area taken over by the French crown corresponds more or less with the region of Toulouse.)

Like Spain's southern boundary, so too was Europe's northeast a moving frontier, driven ever farther eastward by crusaders and settlers. By the twelfth century, the peoples living along the Baltic coast—partly pagan, mostly Slavic- or Baltic-speaking—had learned to make a living and even a profit from the inhospitable soil and climate. Through fishing and trading, they supplied the rest of Europe and Rus' with slaves, furs, amber, wax, and dried fish. Like the earlier Vikings, they combined commercial competition with outright raiding, so the Danes and the Saxons (i.e., the Germans in Saxony) both benefited and suffered from their presence. It was Saint Bernard (see p. 192) who, while preaching the Second Crusade in Germany, urged one to the north as well. Thus began the Northern Crusades, which continued intermittently until the early fifteenth century.

In key raids in the 1160s and 1170s, the king of Denmark and Henry the Lion, the duke of Saxony, worked together to bring much of the region between the Elbe and Oder Rivers under their control. They took some of the land outright, leaving the rest in the hands of the Baltic princes, who surrendered, converted, and became their vassals. Churchmen arrived: the Cistercians built their monasteries right up to the banks of the Vistula River, while bishops took over newly declared dioceses. In 1202 the "bishop of Riga"—in fact he had to bring some Christians with him to his lonely outpost amidst the Livs—founded a military/monastic order called the Order of the Brothers of the Sword. The monks soon became a branch of the Teutonic Knights (or Teutonic Order), a group originally founded in the Crusader States and vowed to a military and monastic rule like the Templars. The Knights organized crusades, defended newly conquered regions, and launched their own holy wars against the "Northern Saracens." By the end of the thirteenth century, they had brought the lands from Prussia to Estonia under their sway. (See Map 6.6.) Meanwhile German knights, peasants, and townspeople streamed in, colonists of

Map 6.6: German Settlement in the Baltic Sea Region, Twelfth to Fourteenth Centuries

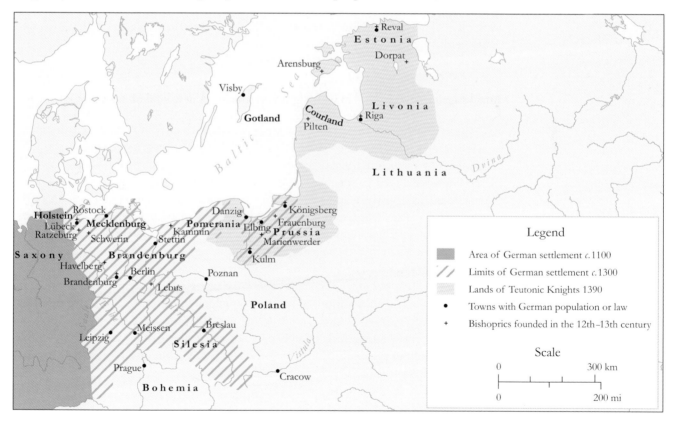

the new frontier. Although less well known than the crusades to the Levant, the Northern Crusades had more lasting effects, settling the Baltic region with a German-speaking population that brought its western institutions—cities, laws, guilds, universities, castles, manors, vassalage—with it.

Colonization was the unanticipated consequence of the Fourth Crusade as well. Called by Innocent III, who intended it to re-establish the Christian presence in the Holy Land, the crusade was diverted when the organizers overestimated the numbers joining the expedition. The small army mustered was unable to pay for the large fleet of ships that had been fitted out for it by the Venetians. Making the best of adversity, the Venetians convinced the crusaders to "pay" for the ships by attacking Zara (today Zadar), one of the coastal cities that Venice disputed with Hungary. Then, taking up the cause of one claimant to the Byzantine throne, the crusaders turned their sights on Constantinople. We already know the political results. The religious results were more subtle. Europeans disdained the Greeks for their independence from the pope; on the other hand, they considered Constantinople a treasure trove of the most precious of relics, including the True Cross. When, in the course of looting the city, one crusader, the abbot of a German Cistercian monastery, came upon a chest of relics, he "hurriedly and greedily thrust in both hands."[23] There was a long tradition of relic theft in the West; it was considered pious, a sort of holy sacrilege. Thus, when the abbot returned to his ship to show off his booty, the crusaders shouted, "Thanks be to God." In this sense Constantinople was taken so that the saints could get better homes.

Ireland

In 1169 the Irish king of Leinster, Diarmait Mac Murchada (Dermot MacMurrough), enlisted some lords and knights from England to help him first keep, then expand, his kingdom. The English fighters succeeded all too well; when Diarmait died in 1171, some of the English decided to stay, claiming Leinster for themselves. The king of England, Henry II, reacted swiftly. Gathering an army, he invaded Ireland in 1171. The lords of the 1169 expedition recognized his overlordship almost immediately, keeping their new territories, but now redefined as fiefs from the king. Most of the native Irish kings submitted in similar manner. The whole of one kingdom, Meath, was given to one of Henry's barons.

The English came to stay, and more—they came to put their stamp on the Irish world. It became "English Ireland": England's laws were instituted; its system of counties and courts was put in place; its notions of lordship (in which the great lords parceled out some of their vast lands to lesser lords and knights) prevailed. Small wonder that Gerald of Wales (d.1223) could see nothing good in native Irish culture: "they are uncultivated," he wrote, "not only in the external appearance of their dress, but also in their flowing hair and beards. All their habits are the habits of barbarians."[24]

★　　　★　　　★　　　★　　　★

In the fifty years before and after 1200, Europe, aggressive and determined, pushed against its borders. Whether gaining territory from the Muslims in Spain and Sicily, colonizing the Baltic region and Ireland, or creating a Latin empire at Constantinople, Europeans accommodated the natives only minimally. For the most part, they imposed, with enormous self-confidence, their institutions and their religion.

Self-confidence also led lords and ladies to pay poets to celebrate their achievements and bishops and townspeople to commission architects to erect towering Gothic churches in their midst. Similar certainties lay behind guild statutes, the incorporation of universities, the development of common law, and the Fourth Lateran Council's written definitions of Christian behavior and belief.

An orderly society would require institutions so fearlessly constructed as to be responsive to numerous individual and collective goals. But in the next century, while harmony was the ideal and sometimes the reality, discord was an ever-present threat.

CHAPTER SIX KEY EVENTS

1152–1190	Frederick Barbarossa (king of Germany and emperor from 1155)
1154–1189	King Henry II of England
1170	Murder of Thomas Becket
1171	Henry II conquers Ireland
1171–1193	Saladin's rule
1176	Battle of Legnano
1187	Battle of Hattin
1189–1192	Third Crusade
1194–1250	Frederick II
1198–1216	Pope Innocent III
1202–1204	Fourth Crusade
1204	Fall of Constantinople to Crusaders
1204	Philip II of France takes King John of England's northern French possessions
1212	Battle of Las Navas de Tolosa
1214	Battle of Bouvines
1215	Magna Carta
1215	Fourth Lateran Council
1226	Death of Saint Francis
1261	Constantinople again Byzantine
1273	Election of Rudolf of Habsburg as Holy Roman Emperor

NOTES

1 Henry's father, Geoffrey of Anjou, was nicknamed Plantagenet from the *genêt*, the name of a shrub ("broom" in English) that he liked. Historians sometimes use the sobriquet to refer to the entire dynasty, so Henry II was the first "Plantagenet" as well as the first "Angevin" king of England.

2 *The Assize of Clarendon*, in *Reading the Middle Ages: Sources from Europe, Byzantium, and the Islamic World*, ed. Barbara H. Rosenwein, 2nd ed. (Toronto: University of Toronto Press, 2014), p. 311.

3 *The Costs of Richard of Anstey's Law Suit*, in *Reading the Middle Ages*, p. 314.

4 *Proceedings for the Abbey of Bec*, in *Reading the Middle Ages*, p. 321.

5 *Constitutions of Clarendon*, in *Reading the Middle Ages*, p. 331.

6 *Magna Carta*, in *Reading the Middle Ages*, p. 340.

7 *The Laws of Cuenca*, in *Reading the Middle Ages*, p. 315.

8 *Diet of Besançon*, in *Reading the Middle Ages*, p. 335.

9 *The Chronicle of Salimbene de Adam*, ed. and trans. Joseph L. Baird, Giuseppe Baglivi, and John Robert Kane, Medieval & Renaissance Texts & Studies 40 (Binghamton, NY: MRTS, 1986), p. 5.

10 Bernart de Ventadorn, *When I see the lark*, in *Reading the Middle Ages*, p. 348.

11 Ibid., pp. 348–49.

12 La Comtessa de Dia, *I have been in heavy grief*, in *Reading the Middle Ages*, p. 349.

13 *The Priest Who Peeked*, in *Reading the Middle Ages*, p. 352.

14 Bertran de Born, *Half a sirventés I'll sing*, in *Reading the Middle Ages*, p. 351.

15 Chrétien de Troyes, *Lancelot*, in *Reading the Middle Ages*, p. 360.

16 Ibid., p. 362.

17 *Guild Regulations of the Parisian Silk Fabric Makers*, in *Reading the Middle Ages*, p. 322.

18 Peter the Venerable, *Letter to Doctor Bartholomew*, in *Reading the Middle Ages*, p. 342.

19 *Advice from "Archimatthaeus,"* in *Reading the Middle Ages*, p. 346.

20 Jacques de Vitry, *The Life of Mary of Oignies*, in *Reading the Middle Ages*, p. 372.

21 Edition of the text in Pilar Jiménez Sánchez, *L'évolution doctrinale du catharisme, XIIe-XIIIe siècle*, 3 vols., Ph.D. Diss, University of Toulouse II, 2001, Annex 1: Actes de Lombers.

22 *The Chronicle of Laon*, in *Reading the Middle Ages*, p. 369.

23 Gunther of Pairis, *Hystoria Constantinopolitana*, in *The Capture of Constantinople*, ed. and trans. Alfred J. Andrea (Philadelphia: Scholarly Book Services, 2007), p. 111.

24 Gerald of Wales, *The History and Topography of Ireland*, trans. John O'Meara (London: Penguin, 1982), p. 102.

FURTHER READING

Abulafia, David. *Frederick II: A Medieval Emperor*. London: Oxford University Press, 1988.

Angold, Michael. *The Byzantine Empire, 1025–1204*. 2nd. ed. London: Longman, 1997.

Baldwin, John. *The Government of Philip Augustus: Foundations of French Royal Power in the Middle Ages*. Berkeley: University of California Press, 1986.

Bartlett, Robert. *England under the Norman and Angevin Kings, 1075–1225*. Oxford: Oxford University Press, 2000.

———. *The Making of Europe: Conquest, Colonization and Cultural Change, 950–1350*. Princeton, NJ: Princeton University Press, 1993.

Christiansen, Eric. *The Northern Crusades*. 2nd ed. London: Penguin, 1997.

Clanchy, Michael T. *From Memory to Written Record, 1066–1307*. 3rd ed. Oxford: John Wiley & Sons, 2012.

Cobb, Paul M. *Usama ibn Munqidh: Warrior-Poet of the Ages of Crusades*. Oxford: Oneworld, 2005.

Duggan, Anne. *Thomas Becket*. London: Arnold, 2004.

Eddé, Anne-Marie. *Saladin*. Translated by Jane Marie Todd. Cambridge, MA: Belknap Press, 2011.

Frame, Robin. *Colonial Ireland*. Dublin: Four Courts Press, 2012.

———. *The Political Development of the British Isles, 1100–1400*. Oxford: Oxford University Press, 1990.

Gaunt, Simon, and Sarah Kay, eds. *The Troubadours: An Introduction*. Cambridge: Cambridge University Press, 1999.

Haverkamp, Alfred. *Medieval Germany, 1056–1273*. Trans. Helga Braun and Richard Mortimer. Oxford: Oxford University Press, 1988.

Lawrence, C.H. *The Friars: The Impact of the Early Mendicant Movement on Western Society*. London: Longman, 1994.

Moore, R.I. *The War on Heresy*. Cambridge, MA: Belknap Press, 2012.

Mayr-Harting, Henry. *Religion, Politics and Society in Britain 1066–1272*. Harlow, U.K.: Pearson, 2011.

Pegg, Mark Gregory. *The Corruption of Angels: The Great Inquisition of 1245–1246*. Princeton, NJ: Princeton University Press, 2001.

Şenocak, Neslihan. *The Poor and the Perfect: The Rise of Learning in the Franciscan Order, 1209–1310*. Ithaca, NY: Cornell University Press, 2012.

Taylor, Claire. *Heresy, Crusade and Inquisition in Medieval Quercy*. Woodbridge: Boydell, 2011.

Tyerman, Christopher. *God's War: A New History of the Crusades*. Cambridge, MA: Belknap Press, 2006.

Vauchez, André. *Francis of Assisi: The Life and Afterlife of a Medieval Saint*. Trans. Michael F. Cusato. New Haven, CT: Yale University Press, 2012.

To test your knowledge of this chapter, please go to
www.utphistorymatters.com
for Study Questions.

SEVEN

DISCORDANT HARMONIES (*c.*1250–*c.*1350)

IN THE SHADOW of a great Mongol empire that, for about a century, stretched from the East China Sea to the Black Sea and from Moscow to the Himalayas, Europeans were bit players in a great Eurasian system tied together by a combination of sheer force and open trade routes. Taking advantage of the new opportunities for commerce and evangelization offered by the mammoth new empire, Europeans ventured with equal verve into experiments in their own backyards: in government, thought, and expression. Above all, they sought to harmonize disparate groups, ideas, and artistic modes. At the same time, unable to force everything into unified and harmonious wholes and often confronted instead with discord and strife, the directing classes—both secular and ecclesiastical—tried to purge their society of deviants of every sort.

THE MONGOL HEGEMONY

The Mongols, like the Huns and Seljuks before them, were pastoralists. Occupying the eastern edge of the great steppes that stretch west to the Hungarian plains, they herded horses and sheep while honing their skills as hunters and warriors. Believing in both high deities and slightly lower spirits, the Mongols were also open to other religious ideas, easily assimilating Buddhism, Islam, and even some forms of Christianity. Their empire, in its heyday stretching about 4,000 miles from east to west, was the last to be created by the nomads from the steppes.

The Contours of the Mongol Empire

The Mongols formed under the leadership of Chinghis (or Genghis) Khan (c.1162–1227). Fusing together various tribes of mixed ethnic origins and traditions, Chinghis created a highly disciplined, orderly, and sophisticated army. Impelled out of Mongolia in part by new climatic conditions that threatened their grasslands, the Mongols were equally inspired by Chinghis's vision of world conquest. All of China came under their rule by 1279; meanwhile, the Mongols were making forays to the west as well. They took Rus' in the 1230s, invaded Poland and Hungary in 1241, and might well have continued into the rest of Europe, had not unexpected dynastic disputes and insufficient pasturage for their horses drawn them back east. In the end, the borders of their European dominion rolled back east of the Carpathian Mountains.

Something rather similar happened in the Islamic world, where the Mongols took Seljuk Rum, the major power in the region, by 1243. They then moved on to Baghdad (putting an end to the caliphate there in 1258) and Syria (1259–1260), threatening the fragile Crusader States a few miles away. Yet a few months later the Mongols withdrew their troops from Syria, probably (again) because of inadequate grasslands and dynastic problems. The Mamluks of Egypt took advantage of the moment to conquer Syria. This

Map 7.1: The Mongol Empire, *c.*1260–1350

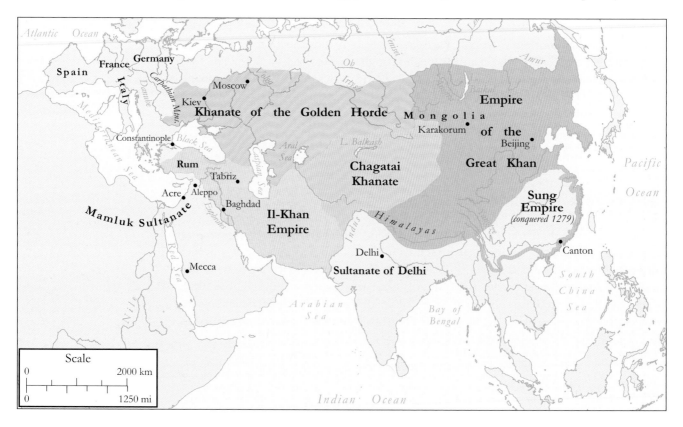

effectively ended the Mongol push across the Islamic world. It was the Mamluks, not the Mongols, who took Acre in 1291, snuffing out the last bit of the original Crusader States.

By the middle of the thirteenth century, the Mongol Empire had taken on the contours of a settled state. (See Map 7.1.) It was divided into four regions, each under the rule of various progeny of Chinghis. The westernmost quadrant was dominated by the rulers of Rus', the so-called Golden Horde ("horde" derived from the Turkic word for "court"). Settled along the lower Volga River valley, the Mongols of the Golden Horde combined traditional pastoralism with more settled activities. They founded cities, fostered trade, and gradually gave up their polytheism in favor of Islam. While demanding regular and exactly calculated tribute, troops, and recognition of their overlordship from the indigenous Rus rulers, they nevertheless allowed the princes of Rus' considerable autonomy. Their policy of religious toleration allowed the Orthodox Church to flourish, untaxed, and willing in turn to offer up prayers for the soul of the Mongol khan (ruler). Kiev-based Rus', largely displaced by the Mongols, gave way to the hegemony of northern Rus princes centered in the area around Moscow. As Mongol rule fragmented, in the course of the fifteenth century, Moscow-based Russia emerged.

From Europe to China

The Mongols taught Europeans to think globally. Once settled, the Mongols sent embassies west, welcomed Christian missionaries, and encouraged European trade. For their part, Europeans initially thought that the Mongols must be Christians; news of Mongol onslaughts in the Islamic world gave ballast to the myth of a lost Christian tribe led by a "Prester John" and his son "King David." Even though Europeans soon learned that the Mongols were not Christians, they dreamed of new triumphs: they imagined, for example, that Orthodox Christians under the Golden Horde would now accept papal protection (and primacy); they flirted with the idea of a Mongol-Christian alliance against the Muslims; and they saw the advent of the "new" pagans as an opportunity to evangelize. Thus in the 1250s the Franciscan William of Rubruck traveled across Asia to convert the Mongols in China; on his way back he met some Dominicans determined to do the same. European missions to the East became a regular feature of the West's contact with the Mongol world.

Such contact was further facilitated by trade. European caravans and ships crisscrossed the Mongol world, bringing silks, spices, ceramics, and copper back from China, while exporting slaves, furs, and other commodities. (See Map 7.2.) The Genoese, who allied with the Byzantines to overthrow the Latin Empire of Constantinople in 1261, received special trading privileges from both the newly installed Byzantine emperor, Michael VIII Paleologus (r.1259–1282), and the khans of the Golden Horde. Genoa, which set up a permanent trading post at Caffa (today Feodosiya), on the Black Sea, was followed by Venice, which established its own trade-stations at Tana and Tabriz. These were sites well poised to exploit overland routes. Other European traders and missionaries traveled

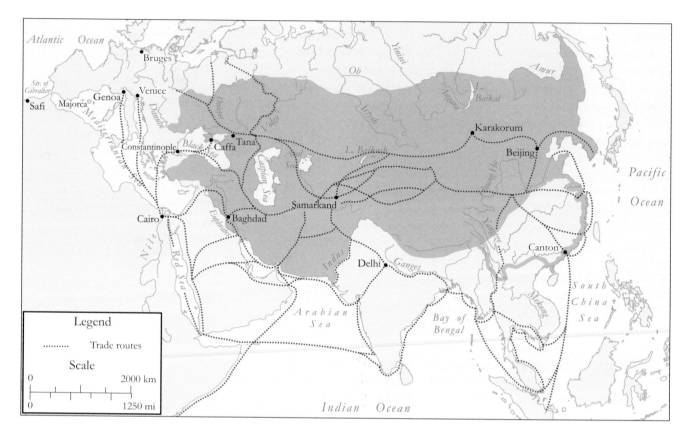

Map 7.2: Mongol-European Trade Routes, *c.*1350

arduous sea routes, setting sail from the Persian Gulf (controlled by the Mongols) and rounding India before arriving in China. Marco Polo (1254–1324) was the most famous of the travelers to the East only because he left a fascinating travel book. His descriptions of the fabulous wealth of the orient fired up new adventurers. In a sense, the Mongols initiated the search for exotic goods and missionary opportunities that culminated in the European "discovery" of a new world, the Americas.

THE MATURATION OF THE EUROPEAN ECONOMY

The pull of the East on the trade of the great Italian maritime cities was part of a series of shifts in Europe's commercial patterns. Another one, even more important, was toward the Atlantic. At the same time, new roads and bridges within Europe made land trade both possible and profitable. The need for large-scale payments meant the introduction of new sorts of coins. Europeans now had access to material goods of every sort, but wealth also heightened social tensions, especially within the cities.

New Routes

The first ships to ply the Atlantic's waters in regular trips were the galleys of Genoese entrepreneurs. By the 1270s they were leaving the Mediterranean via the Strait of Gibraltar,
stopping to trade at various ports along the Spanish coast, and then making their way north
to England and northern France. (See Map 7.3 on p. 246.) In the western Mediterranean,
Majorca, recently conquered by the king of Aragon, sent its own ships to join the Atlantic
trade at about the same time. Soon the Venetians began state-sponsored Atlantic expeditions using new-style "great galleys" that held more cargo yet required fewer oarsmen.
Eventually, as sailing ships—far more efficient than any sort of galley—were developed
by the Genoese and others, the Atlantic passage replaced older overland and river routes
between the Mediterranean and Europe's north.

Equally important for commerce were new initiatives in North Africa. As the Almohad
Empire collapsed, weak successor states allowed Europeans new elbow room. Genoa had
outposts in the major Mediterranean ports of the Maghreb and new ones down the Atlantic
coast, as far south as Safi (today in Morocco). Pisa, Genoa's traditional trade rival, was
entrenched at Tunis. Catalonia and Majorca, by now ruled by the king of Aragon, found
their commercial stars rising fast. Catalonia established its own settlements in the port
cities of the Maghreb; Majorcans went off to the Canary Islands. Profits were enormous.
Besides acting as middlemen, trading goods or commodities from northern Europe, the
Italian cities had their own products to sell (Venice had salt and glass products, Pisa had
iron) in exchange for African cotton, linen, spices, and, above all, gold. In the mid-thirteenth century, Genoa and Florence were minting coins from gold panned on the upper
Niger River, while Venice began minting gold ducats in 1284.

At the same time as Genoa, Pisa, Venice, Majorca, and Catalonia were forging trade
networks in the south, some cities in the north of Europe were creating their own marketplace in the Baltic Sea region. Built on the back of the Northern Crusades, the Hanseatic
League was created by German merchants, who, following in the wake of Christian
knights, hoped to prosper in cities such as Danzig (today Gdansk, in Poland), Riga, and
Reval (today Tallinn, in Estonia). Lübeck, founded by the duke of Saxony, formed the
Hansa's center. Formalized through legislation, the association of cities agreed that

> Each city shall ... keep the sea clear of pirates.... Whoever is expelled from one city
> because of a crime shall not be received in another ... If a lord besieges a city, no
> one shall aid him in any way to the detriment of the besieged city.[1]

There were no mercantile rivalries here, unlike the competition between Genoa and Pisa
in the south. But there was also little glamor. Pitch, tar, lumber, furs, herring: these were
the stuff of northern commerce.

The opening of the Atlantic and the commercial uniting of the Baltic were dramatic
developments. Elsewhere the pace of commercial life quickened more subtly. By 1200
almost all the cities of pre-industrial Europe were in existence. By 1300 they were connected

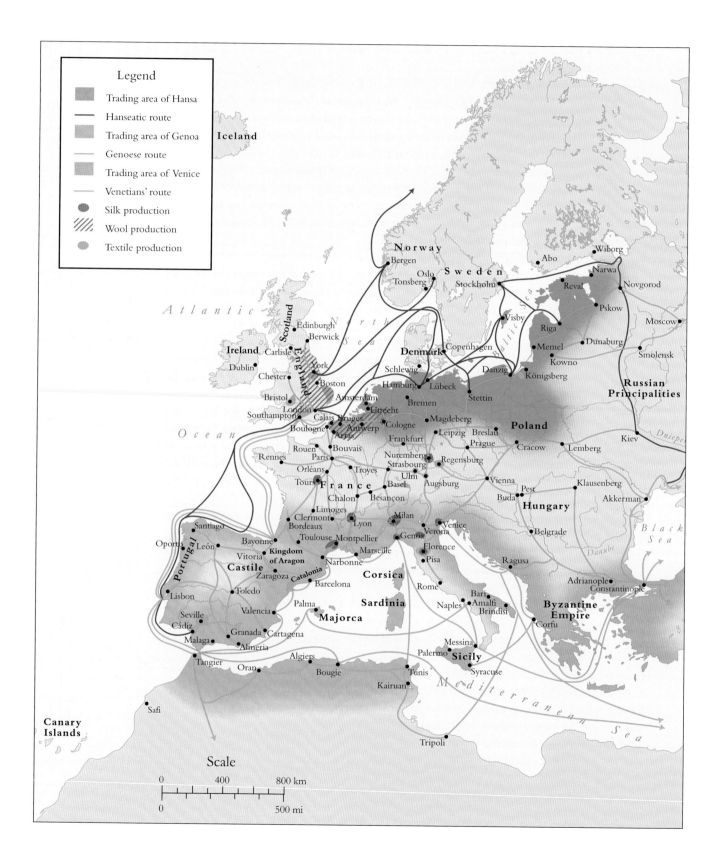

Legend

Trading area of Hansa

Hanseatic route

Trading area of Genoa

Genoese route

Trading area of Venice

Venetians' route

Silk production

Wool production

Textile production

Iceland

Atlantic

Ocean

North Sea

Baltic Sea

Norway
Bergen
Oslo
Tonsberg

Sweden
Stockholm

Abo
Wiborg
Narwa
Reval
Novgorod
Pskow
Moscow
Riga
Dunaburg
Smolensk
Memel
Kowno
Königsberg
Danzig

Scotland
Edinburgh
Berwick

Ireland
Dublin
Carlisle
Chester

England
York
Boston

Bristol
London
Southampton
Calais
Boulogne
Amsterdam
Bruges
Utrecht
Arras
Antwerp

Denmark
Schlewig
Copenhagen

Hamburg
Lübeck
Stettin
Bremen
Magdeberg
Cologne
Leipzig
Breslau
Frankfurt
Prague

Poland

Cracow
Lemberg
Kiev

Dnieper

**Russian
Principalities**

Rouen
Bouvais
Paris
Rennes
Orléans
Troyes
Nuremberg
Strasbourg
Regensburg
Tours
France
Chalon
Basel
Ulm
Augsburg
Vienna
Besançon
Limoges
Clermont
Lyon
Milan
Verona
Venice
Belgrade
Klausenberg
Akkerman
Pest
Buda
Hungary

Danube

Black Sea

Santiago
Oporto
León
Bayonne
Bordeaux
Toulouse
Montpellier
Marseille
Genoa
Florence
Ragusa
Adrianople
Constantinople

Vitoria
**Kingdom
of Aragon**
Narbonne
Pisa
Rome

Portugal

Castile
Zaragoza
Catalonia
Barcelona

Corsica

Lisbon
Toledo
Valencia
Palma
Sardinia
Majorca

Seville
Cádiz
Granada
Cartagena
Malaga
Almeria
Tangier
Oran
Algiers
Bougie

Naples
Bari
Amalfi
Brindisi
**Byzantine
Empire**
Corfu

Safi

**Canary
Islands**

Messina
Palermo
Sicily
Syracuse
Tunis
Kairuan
Mediterranean
Sea

Tripoli

Scale

0   400   800 km

0   500 mi

by a spider's web of roads that brought even small towns of a few thousand inhabitants into wider networks of trade. To be sure, some old trading centers declined: the towns of Champagne, for example, had been centers of major fairs—periodic but intense commercial activity. By the mid-thirteenth century the fairs' chief functions were as financial markets and clearing houses. On the whole, however, urban centers grew and prospered. As the burgeoning population of the countryside fed the cities with immigrants, the population of many cities reached their medieval maximum: in 1300 Venice and London each had perhaps 100,000 inhabitants, Paris an extraordinary 200,000. Many of these people became part of the urban labor force, working as apprentices or servants; but others could not find jobs or became disabled and could not keep them. The indigent and sick posed new challenges for urban communities. To be sure, rich townspeople and princes alike supported the building of new charitable institutions: hospices for the poor, hospitals for the sick, orphanages, refuges for penitent prostitutes. But in big cities the numbers that these could serve were woefully inadequate. Beggars (there were perhaps 20,000 in Paris alone) became a familiar sight, and not all prostitutes could afford to be penitent.

Map 7.3 (facing page): European Trade Routes, c.1300

New Money

Workers were paid in silver pennies; the burgeoning economy demanded a lot of coins. Silver mines were discovered and exploited to provide them. At Freiburg, in northern Germany, such mines meant a jump in the number of mints from nine (in 1130) to twenty-five in 1197. Small workshop mints, typical before the thirteenth century, gave way to mint factories run by profit-minded entrepreneurs. Princes added to their power by making sure that the coins of one mint under their control would prevail in their region. Thus the bishops of Maguelonne, who also were the counts of Melgueil, issued coins that supplanted most of the others in southern France.

But large-scale transactions required larger coins than pennies. Between the early thirteenth and mid-fourteenth centuries, new, heavier silver coins were struck. Under Doge Enrico Dandolo (r.1192–1205), Venice began to strike great silver coins, *grossi* ("big ones" in Italian), in order to make convenient payments for the Fourth Crusade. (To be sure, Venice's little silver coins, the *piccoli*, continued to be minted.) Soon Venice's commercial rival Genoa produced similarly large coins, and the practice quickly spread to other cities in northern Italy, Tuscany, and southern France. In 1253, Rome doubled the size of the *grossi*, a coinage model that was followed in Naples and Sicily. The practice of minting these heavy silver coins spread northward.

Heavy silver was one answer to the problem of paying for large transactions. Gold coins were another. They were certainly common in the Islamic and Mediterranean worlds. In Europe before the mid-thirteenth century, though, they were limited to the regions that bordered on those worlds, like Sicily and Spain. Gold panned on the upper Niger River in Africa and wrested from mines in Hungary helped infuse Europe with the precious metal. In 1252 Genoa and Florence struck gold coins for the first time. The practice spread, profiting above all Italy and East Central Europe. In fact, the kings of Hungary and Bohemia formed an alliance to control the flow of gold, enhance their purchasing power, and increase trade.

New Inter-city Conflicts

The most commercialized regions were the most restive. This was certainly true in Flanders, where the urban population had grown enormously since the twelfth century. Flemish cities depended on England for wool to supply their looms and on the rest of Europe to buy their finished textiles. But Flemish workers were unhappy with their town governments, run by wealthy merchants, the "patricians," whose families had held their positions for generations. When, in the early 1270s, England slapped a trade embargo on Flanders, discontented laborers, now out of work, struck, demanding a role in town government. While most of these rebellions resulted in few political changes, workers had better luck early in the next century, when the king of France and the count of Flanders went to war. The workers (who supported the count) defeated the French forces at the battle of Courtrai in 1302. Thereafter the patricians, who had sided with the king, were at least partly replaced by artisans in the apparatus of Flemish town governments. In the early fourteenth century, Flemish cities had perhaps the most inclusive governments of Europe.

Map 7.4 (facing page): Piacenza, Late Thirteenth Century

Similar population growth and urban rebellions beset the northern Italian cities. (See Map 7.4 for the ballooning of the walls at Piacenza, a fair measure of its expanding population. Each successive wall meant in large measure the dismantling of the older one.) Italian cities were torn into factions that defined themselves not by loyalties to a king or a count (as in Flanders) but rather by adherence to either the pope or the emperor. "Outsiders," they nevertheless affected inter-urban politics. City factions often fought under the party banners of the Guelfs (papal supporters) or the Ghibellines (imperial supporters), even though for the most part they were waging very local battles. As in the Flemish cities, the late thirteenth century saw a movement by the Italian urban lower classes to participate in city government. The *popolo* ("people") who demanded the changes was in fact made up of many different groups, including crafts and merchant guildsmen, fellow parishioners, and even members of the commune. The *popolo* acted as a sort of alternative commune within the city, a sworn association dedicated to upholding the interests of its members. Armed and militant, the *popolo* demanded a say in matters of government, particularly taxation.

While no city is "typical," the case of Piacenza may serve as an example. Originally dominated by nobles, the commune of Piacenza granted the *popolo*—led by a charismatic nobleman from the Landi family—a measure of power in 1222, allowing the *popolo* to take over half the governmental offices. A year later the *popolo* and the nobles worked out a plan to share the election of their city's *podestà*, or governing official. Even so, conflict flared up periodically: in 1224, 1231, and again in 1250, when a grain shortage provoked protest:

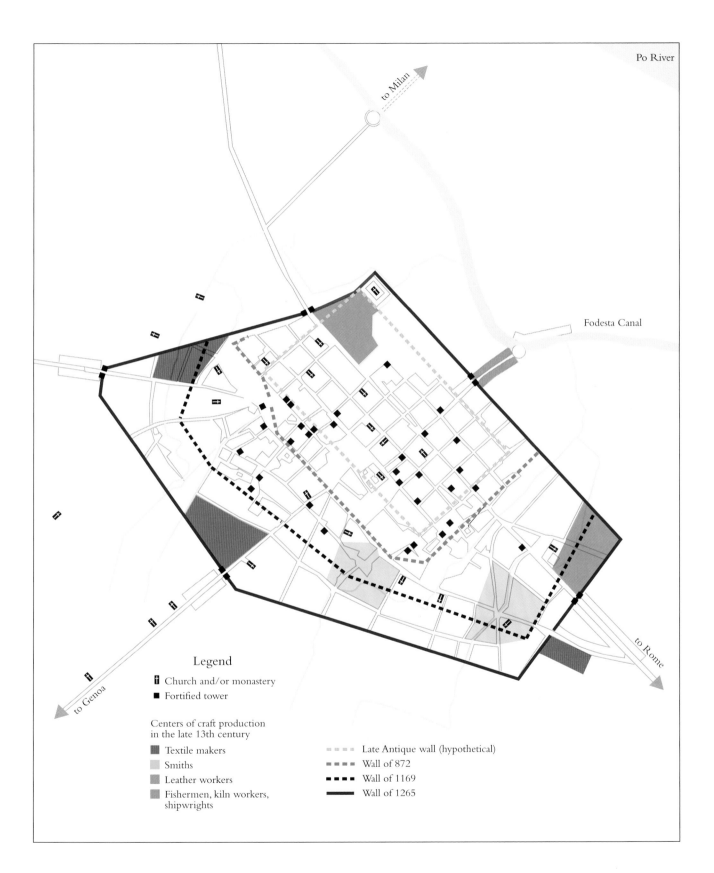

Po River

to Milan

Fodesta Canal

to Genoa

to Rome

Legend

🏛 Church and/or monastery

■ Fortified tower

Centers of craft production
in the late 13th century

▦ Textile makers

▦ Smiths

▦ Leather workers

▦ Fishermen, kiln workers,
  shipwrights

▰ ▰ ▰ Late Antique wall (hypothetical)

▰ ▰ ▰ Wall of 872

▰ ▰ ▰ Wall of 1169

━━━ Wall of 1265

In 1250 the common people of Piacenza saw that they were being badly treated regarding foodstuffs: first, because all the corn [grain] that had been sent from Milan, as well as other corn in Piacenza, was being taken to Parma ... [and] second because the Parmesans were touring Piacentine territory buying corn from the threshing floors and fields.... The Parmesans could do this in safety because Matteo da Correggio, a citizen of Parma, was podestà of Piacenza.[2]

In this case, too, members of noble families took the lead in the uprising, but this time the *popolo* of Piacenza divided into factions, each supporting a different competing leader. Eventually one came to the fore—Alberto Scotti, from a family deeply immersed in both commerce and landholding. In 1290 he took over the city, gaining the grand title of "defender and rector of the commune and the society of merchants and craft guilds and of all the *popolo*."[3] He was, in short, a lord, a *signore* (pl. *signori*). Map 7.4 shows some of the features of Piacenza in his day: concentrated centers of craft production, a new wall built in 1265 to enclose most of the population, an impressive number of churches and monasteries, and a generous sprinkling of private towers put up by proud and often warring members of the nobility.

A similar evolution—from commune to the rule of the *popolo* and then to the rule of a *signore*—took place in cities throughout northern Italy and in much of Tuscany as well. It was as if the end of imperial rule in Italy, marked by the fall of Frederick II, ironically brought in its train the creation of local monarchs—the *signori*, who maintained order at the price of repression. By 1300 the commune had almost everywhere given way to the *signoria* (a state ruled by a *signore*), with one family dominating the government.

XENOPHOBIA

Urban discord was fairly successfully defused in Flanders, fairly well silenced in Italy. In neither instance was pluralism valued. Europeans had no interest in hearing multiple voices; rather, they were eager to purge and purify themselves of the pollutants in their midst.

Driving the Jews from the Ile-de-France in the twelfth century (see p. 233) was a dress rehearsal for the expulsions of the thirteenth. In England during the 1230s and 1250s, local lords and municipal governments expelled the Jews from many cities. At the same time, King Henry III (r.1216–1272) imposed unusually harsh taxes on them. (For the English kings of this period, see Genealogy 6.1 on p. 202.) By the end of Henry's reign, the Jews were impoverished and their numbers depleted. There were perhaps 3,000 Jews in all of England when King Edward I (r.1272–1307) drew up the *Statute of the Jewry* in 1275, stipulating that they end the one occupation that had been left open to them: moneylending. They were expected to "live by lawful trade and by their labor."[4] But, as the Jews responded in turn, they would be forced to buy and sell at higher prices than Christians, and thus would sell nothing. Fifteen years later Edward expelled them from England entirely.

The story was similar in France. (For the French kings, see Genealogy 8.1 on p. 291.) King Louis IX (r.1226–1270), later canonized as Saint Louis, reportedly could not bear to look at a Jew and worried that their "poison" might infect his kingdom. In 1242, he presided over the burning of two dozen cartloads of the ancient rabbinic Bible commentaries known as the Talmud. Actively promoting the conversion and baptism of Jews, Louis offered converts pensions, new names, and an end to special restrictions. His grandson, Philip IV ("The Fair") (r.1285–1314), gave up on conversion and expelled the Jews from France in 1306. By contrast with England, the French Jewish population had been large; after 1306, perhaps 125,000 French men, women, and children became refugees in the Holy Roman Empire, Spain, and Italy. The few who were later allowed to return were wiped out in popular uprisings in the early 1320s.

Some anti-Jewish movements linked the Jews with lepers. Occupying a profoundly ambivalent place in medieval society, lepers were both revered and despised. Saint Louis used to feed the lepers who came to him, and he supported *leprosaria*, houses to care for them. Saint Francis was praised for ministering to lepers and was admired for kissing them on their hands and mouths. Yet at the same time, lepers were thought to be tainted by horrible sin; they were made to carry a bell as they moved about to alert everyone to their ominous presence; their rights to private property were restricted; and, through rituals of expulsion, they were condemned to live apart from normal people, never "to eat or drink in any company except that of lepers."[5] In the south of France in the 1320s, lepers were accused of horrific crimes: of poisoning the wells and streams, like Jews, to whom they gave consecrated hosts for their wicked rites. Hauled in by local officials, the lepers were tortured, made to confess, and then burned.

Only by comparison with lepers does the revulsion against beggars seem mild. Like leprosy, poverty too was thought to have its social uses. Certainly the mendicants like the Franciscans and Dominicans, who went about begging, were understood to be exercising the highest vocation. And even involuntary beggars were thought (and expected) to pray for the souls of those who gave them alms. Nevertheless the sheer and unprecedented number of idle beggars led to calls for their expulsion.

No group, however, suffered social purging more than heretics. Beginning in the thirteenth century, church inquisitors, aided by secular authorities, worked to find and extirpate heretics from Christendom. The inquisition was a continuation (and expansion) of the Albigensian Crusade by other means. Working in the south of France, the mid-Rhineland, and Italy, the inquisitors began their scrutiny in each district by giving a sermon and calling upon heretics to confess. Then the inquisitors granted a grace period for heretics to come forward. Finally, they called suspected heretics and witnesses to inquests, where they were interrogated:

> Asked if she had seen Guillaume [who was accused of being a heretic] take communion [at Mass] or doing the other things which good and faithful Christians are accustomed to do, [one of Guillaume's neighbors] responded that for the past twelve years she had lived in the village of Ornolac and she had never seen Guillaume take communion.[6]

Often imprisonment, along with both physical and mental torture, was used to extract a confession. Then penalties were assigned. Bernard Gui, an inquisitor in Languedoc from 1308 to 1323, gave out 633 punishments; nearly half involved imprisonment. A few heretics were required to go on penitential pilgrimages. Forty-one people (6.5 per cent of those punished by Bernard) were burned alive. Many former heretics were forced to wear crosses sewn to their clothing, rather like Jews, but shamed by a different marker.

STRENGTHENED MONARCHS AND THEIR ADAPTATIONS

The impulse behind "purification" was less hatred than the exercise of power. Expelling the Jews meant confiscating their property and calling in their loans while polishing an image of zealous religiosity. Burning lepers was one way to gain access to the assets of *leprosaria* and claim new forms of hegemony. Imprisonment and burning put heretics' property into the hands of secular authorities. Yet even as kings and other great lords manipulated the institutions and rhetoric of piety and purity for political ends, they learned how to adapt to, mollify, and use—rather than stamp out—new and up-and-coming classes. As their power increased, they came to welcome the broad-based support that representative institutions afforded them.

All across Europe, from Spain to Poland, from England to Hungary, rulers summoned parliaments. Growing out of ad hoc advisory sessions that kings and other rulers held with the most powerful people in their realms, parliaments became solemn and formal assemblies in the thirteenth century, moments when rulers celebrated their power and where the "orders"—clergy, nobles, and commons—assented to their wishes. Eventually parliaments became organs through which groups not ordinarily at court could articulate their interests.

The orders (or "estates") were based on the traditional division of society into those who pray, those who fight, and those who work. Unlike modern classes, defined largely by economic status, medieval orders cut across economic boundaries. The clerics, for example, included humble parish priests as well as archbishops; the commons included wealthy merchants as well as impoverished peasants. That, at least, was the theory. In practice, rulers did not so much command representatives of the orders to come to court as they summoned the most powerful members of their realm, whether clerics, nobles, or important townsmen. Above all they wanted support for their policies and tax demands.

Spanish *Cortes*

The *cortes* of the Spanish kingdoms of Castile and León were among the earliest representative assemblies called to the king's court and the first to include townsmen. (For these kingdoms, see Map 7.5, but by the date of that map, *c.*1300, Castile and León had been united (1230) and was known as Castile.) As the *reconquista* pushed southward across the Iberian peninsula, Christian kings called for settlers to occupy the new frontiers. Enriched by plunder, fledgling villages soon burgeoned into major commercial centers. Like the cities of Italy, Spanish towns dominated the countryside. Their leaders—called *caballeros villanos*, or "city horsemen," because they were rich enough to fight on horseback—monopolized municipal offices. In 1188, when King Alfonso IX (r.1188–1230) summoned townsmen to the *cortes* for the first time on record, the city *caballeros* served as their representatives, agreeing to Alfonso's plea for military and financial support and for help in consolidating his rule. Once convened at court, these wealthy townsmen joined bishops and noblemen in formally counseling the king and assenting to royal decisions. Beginning with Alfonso X (r.1252–1284), Castilian monarchs regularly called on the *cortes* to participate in major political and military decisions and to assent to new taxes to finance them.

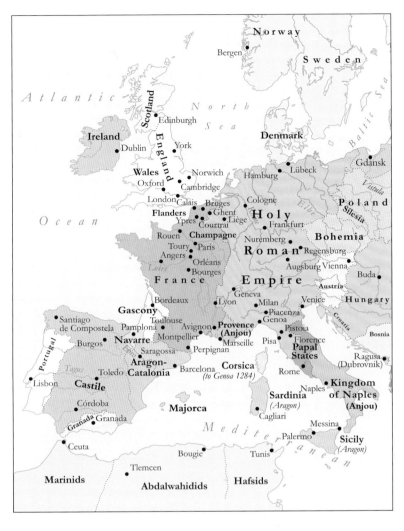

Map 7.5: Western Europe, *c.*1300

Local Solutions in the Empire

In 1356 the so-called Golden Bull freed imperial rule from the papacy but at the same time made it dependent on the German princes. The princes had always had a role in ratifying the king and emperor; now seven of them were given the role and title of "electors." When a new emperor was to be chosen, each prince knew in which order his vote would be called, and a majority of votes was needed for election.

After the promulgation of the Golden Bull, the royal and imperial level of administration was less important than the local. Yet every local ruler had to deal with the same two classes on the rise: the townsmen (as in Castile and elsewhere) and a group particularly important in Germany, the ministerials. The ministerials were legally serfs whose services—collecting taxes, administering justice, and fighting wars—were so honorable as to garner them both high status and wealth. By 1300 they had become "nobles" in every way but one: marriage. In the 1270s at Salzburg, for example, the archbishop required his ministerials to swear that they would marry within his lordship or at least get his permission to marry a woman from elsewhere. Apart from this indignity (which itself was not always imposed), the ministerials, like other nobles, profited from German colonization to become enormously wealthy landowners. Some held castles, and many controlled towns. They became counterweights to the territorial princes who, in the wake of the downfall of the Staufen, had expected to rule unopposed. In Lower Bavaria in 1311, for example, when the local duke was strapped for money, the nobles, in tandem with the clergy and the townsmen, granted him his tax but demanded in return recognition of their collective rights. The privilege granted by the duke was a sort of Bavarian Magna Carta. By the middle of the fourteenth century, princes throughout the Holy Roman Empire found themselves negotiating periodically with various noble and urban leagues.

English Parliament

In England, the consultative role of the barons at court had been formalized by the guarantees of Magna Carta. When Henry III (r.1216–1272) was crowned at the age of nine, a council consisting of a few barons, professional administrators, and a papal legate governed in his name. Although not quite "rule by parliament," this council set a precedent for baronial participation in government. Once grown up and firmly in the royal saddle, Henry so alienated barons and commoners alike by his wars, debts, favoritism, and lax attitude toward reform that the barons threatened rebellion. At Oxford in 1258, they forced Henry to dismiss his foreign advisers (he had favored the Lusignans, from France). He was henceforth to rule with the advice of a Council of Fifteen, chosen jointly by the barons and the king, and to limit the terms of his chief officers. Yet even this government was riven by strife, and civil war erupted in 1264. At the battle of Lewes in the same year, the leader of the baronial opposition, Simon de Montfort (c.1208–1265), routed the king's forces, captured the king, and became England's *de facto* ruler.

By Simon's time the distribution of wealth and power in England had changed from the days of Magna Carta. Well-to-do merchants in the cities could potentially buy out most knights and even some barons many times over. Meanwhile, in the rural areas, the "knights of the shire" as well as some landholders below them were rising in wealth and standing. These ancestors of the English gentry were politically active: the knights of the shire attended local courts and served as coroners, sheriffs, and justices of the peace, a new office that gradually replaced the sheriff's. The importance of the knights of the shire was clear to Simon de Montfort, who called a parliament in 1264 that included them; when he summoned another parliament in 1265, he added, for the first time ever, representatives of the towns—the "commons." Even though Simon's brief rule ended that very year and Henry's son Edward I (r.1272–1307) became a rallying point for royalists, the idea of representative government in England had emerged, born of the interplay between royal initiatives and baronial revolts. Under Edward, parliament met fairly regularly, a by-product of the king's urgent need to finance his wars against France, Wales, and Scotland. "We strictly require you," he wrote in one of his summonses to the sheriff of Northamptonshire, to cause two knights from [Northamptonshire], two citizens from each city in the same county, and two burgesses from each borough, of those who are especially discreet and capable of laboring, to be elected without delay, and to cause them to come to us [at Westminster].[7]

French Monarchs and the "Estates"

French King Louis IX, unlike Henry III, was a born reformer. He approached his kingdom as he did himself: with zealous discipline. As an individual, he was (by all accounts) pious, dignified, and courageous. He attended church each day, diluted his wine with water, and cared for the poor and sick (we have already seen his devotion to lepers). Hatred of Jews and heretics followed as a matter of course. Twice Louis went on crusade, dying on the second expedition.

Generalized and applied to the kingdom as a whole, Louis's discipline meant doling out proper justice to all. As the upholder of right in his realm, Louis pronounced judgment on some disputes himself—most famously under an oak tree in the Vincennes forest, near his palace. This personal touch polished Louis's image, but his wide-ranging administrative reforms were more fundamentally important for his rule. Most cases that came before the king were not, in fact, heard by him personally but rather by professional judges in the *Parlement*, a newly specialized branch of the royal court.[8] Louis also created a new sort of official, the *enquêteurs*: like the *missi dominici* of Charlemagne's day, they traveled to the provinces to hear complaints about the abuses of royal administrators. At the same time, Louis made the seneschals and *baillis*, local officials created by Philip Augustus, more accountable to the king by choosing them directly. They called up the royal vassals for military duty, collected the revenues from the royal estates, and acted as local judges. For the administration of the city of Paris, which had been lax and corrupt, Louis found a solution in the joint rule of royal officials and citizens.

There were discordant voices in France, but they were largely muted and unrecognized. Paris may have been governed by a combination of merchants and royalists, but at the level of the royal court no regular institution spoke for the different orders. This began to change only under Louis's grandson, Philip IV the Fair (r.1285–1314). When Philip challenged the reigning pope, Boniface VIII (1294–1303), over rights and jurisdictions (see below for the issues), he felt the need to explain, justify, and propagandize his position. Summoning representatives of the French estates—clergy, nobles, and townspeople—to Paris in 1302, Philip presented his case in a successful bid for support. In 1308 he called another representative assembly, this time at Tours, to ratify his actions against the Templars—the crusading order that had served as *de facto* bankers for the Holy Land. Philip had accused the Templars of heresy, arrested their members, and confiscated their wealth. He wanted the estates to applaud him, and he was not disappointed. These assemblies, ancestors of the French Estates General, were convened sporadically until the

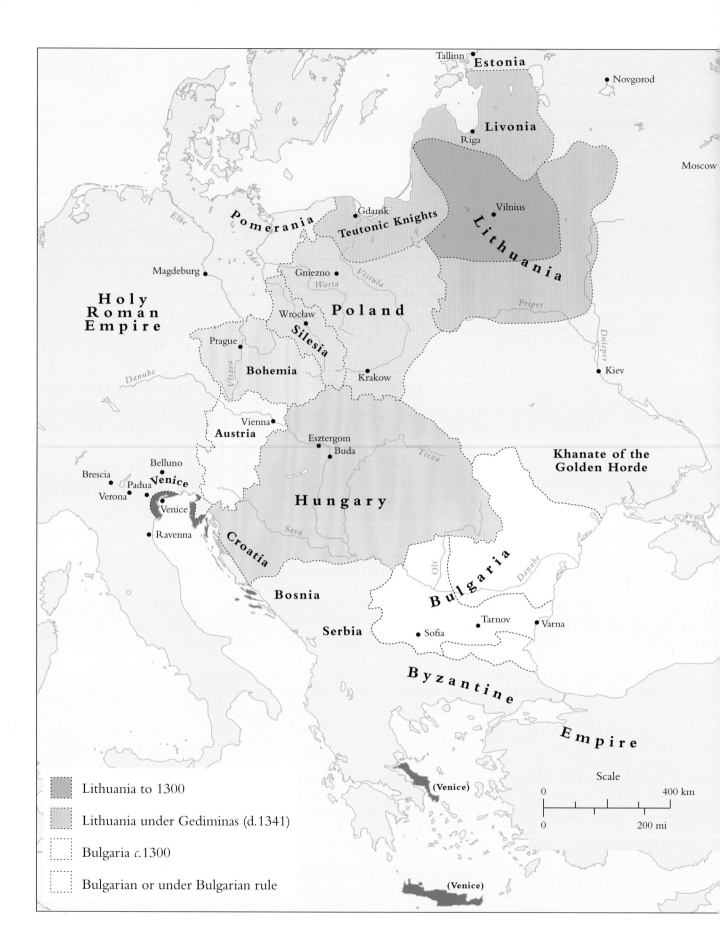

Tallinn

Estonia

Novgorod

Livonia

Riga

Moscow

Pomerania

Gdansk

Teutonic Knights

Vilnius

Lithuania

Elbe

Oder

Vistula

Warta

Magdeburg

Gniezno

Holy
Roman
Empire

Wrocław

Poland

Pripet

Silesia

Prague

Dnieper

Bohemia

Krakow

Danube

Vltava

Kiev

Vienna

Austria

Esztergom

Buda

Khanate of the
Golden Horde

Belluno

Tisza

Brescia

Venice

Padua

Verona

Venice

Hungary

Ravenna

Croatia

Sava

Olt

Bulgaria

Danube

Bosnia

Serbia

Tarnov

Varna

Sofia

Byzantine

Empire

Scale

0

400 km

(Venice)

0

200 mi

Lithuania to 1300

Lithuania under Gediminas (d.1341)

Bulgaria c.1300

Bulgarian or under Bulgarian rule

(Venice)

Revolution of 1789 overturned the monarchy. Yet representative institutions were never fully or regularly integrated into the pre-revolutionary French body politic.

New Formations in East Central Europe

Like a kaleidoscope—the shards shuffling before falling into place—East Central Europe was shaken by the Mongol invasions and then stabilized in a new pattern. (See Map 7.6.) In Hungary, King Béla IV (r.1235–1270) complained that the invaders had destroyed his kingdom: "most of the kingdom of Hungary has been reduced to a desert by the scourge of the Tartars," he wrote, begging the pope for help.[9] But the greatest danger to his power came not from the outside but from the Hungarian nobles, who began to build castles for themselves—in a move reminiscent of tenth-century French castellans. The nobles eventually elected an Angevin—Charles Robert, better known as Carobert (r.1308–1342)—to be their king. Under Carobert, Hungary was very large, even though the region controlled by the king was quite small.

Bulgaria and Poland experienced similar fragmentation in the wake of the Mongols. At the end of the twelfth century, Bulgaria had revolted against Byzantine rule and established the Second Bulgarian Empire. Its ruler, no longer harking back to the khans, took the title tsar, Slavic for "emperor." He wanted his state to rival the Byzantines in other ways as well. In the early thirteenth century, for example, when crusaders had taken Constantinople and Byzantine power was at a low ebb, Tsar Ivan Asen II (r.1218–1241) expanded his hegemony over neighboring regions. Making a bid for enhanced prestige, he seized the relics of the popular Byzantine saint Paraskeve and brought them to his capital city. She became the patron saint of Bulgaria, where she was known as Saint Petka: "The great Tsar Ivan Asen," wrote Petka's admiring biographer, "heard about the miracles of the saint and strongly desired to transport the body of the saint to his land. … He wanted neither silver nor precious stones, but set off with diligence and carried the saintly body to his glorious [imperial city of] Tarnov."[10] It was a great triumph. But the Mongol invasions hit Bulgaria hard, and soon its neighbors were gnawing away at its borders. Meanwhile, its nobles—the boyars—began to carve out independent regional enclaves for themselves. Nevertheless, by the early fourteenth century agreements with the Byzantines and Mongols brought territories both north and south back under Bulgarian control.

In Poland, as one author put it, "as soon as the pagans [the Mongols] entered this land, and did much in it that was worthy of lament, and after the celebrated Duke [Henry II] was killed, this land was dominated by knights, each of whom seized whatever pleased him from the duke's inheritances."[11] The author was abbot of a monastery in Silesia, which in his day—the mid-thirteenth century—was ruled by a branch of the Piast ducal dynasty, as were other Polish territories. He looked back with nostalgia to the days of Henry II, when one Piast duke ruled over all. In fact, a centralized Poland was gradually reconstructed, not least by Casimir III the Great (r.1333–1370), but this time it looked eastward to Rus' and Lithuania rather than westward to Silesia and Bohemia.

Map 7.6 (facing page):
East Central Europe, *c.*1300

It made sense to veer in Lithuania's direction: there Duke Gediminas (r.c.1315/1316–1341), while he himself had not formally converted, favored Christian missionaries and encouraged merchants from Germany and Rus' to settle in his duchy and build churches representing both Roman and Byzantine forms of worship. Declaring war against the Teutonic Knights, he took Riga and pressed yet farther eastward and southward. By the time of his death, Lithuania was the major player in Eastern Europe. Gediminas's heirs (known as the Jagiellon dynasty) expanded still further into Rus'.

On the other, western edge of East Central Europe, Bohemia, too, became a power-house. Taking advantage of the weak position of the German emperors, Bohemia's rulers now styled themselves "king." Ottokar II (r.1253–1278) and his son Vaclav II (r.1283–1305) welcomed settlers from Germany and Flanders and took advantage of newly discovered silver mines to consolidate their rule. Charles IV (r.1347–1378) even became Holy Roman Emperor. At the same time, however, Czech nobles, who had initially worked as retainers for the dukes and depended on ducal largesse, now became independent lords who could bequeath both castles and estates to their children.

Despite their differences, the polities of East Central Europe c.1300 were all (some more, some less so) starting to resemble Western European states. They had begun to rely on written laws and administrative documents; their nobles were becoming landlords and castellans; their economies were increasingly urban and market-oriented; their consti-tutions were defined by charters reminiscent of Magna Carta; and their kings generally ruled with the help of representative institutions of one sort or another. All—except for Lithuania until Gediminas's death—were officially Christian, and even Lithuania under Gediminas supported Christian institutions like monasteries, churches, and friaries. Universities, the symbolic centers of Western European culture, were transplanted east-ward in quick succession: one was founded at Prague in 1348, another at Krakow in 1364, and a third at Vienna in 1365.

THE CHURCH MILITANT, HUMILIATED, AND REVAMPED

On the surface, the clash between Philip the Fair and Boniface VIII seemed yet one more episode in the ongoing struggle between medieval popes and rulers for power and authority. But by the end of the thirteenth century the tables had turned: the kings had more power than the popes, and the confrontation between Boniface and Philip was one sign of the dawning new principle of national sovereignty.

The Road to Avignon

The issue that first set Philip and Boniface at loggerheads involved the English king Edward I as well: taxation of the clergy. Eager to finance new wars, chiefly against one another but also elsewhere (Edward, for example, conquered Wales and tried, unsuccessfully, to subdue Scotland), both monarchs needed money. When the kings financed their wars by taxing the clergy along with everyone else (as if they were going on crusade), Boniface reacted. In the bull *Clericis laicos* (1296), he declared that all clerics who paid and all laymen who imposed payments without prior authorization from the pope "shall, by the very act, incur the sentence of excommunication."[12]

Reacting swiftly, the kings soon forced Boniface to back down. But in 1301, testing his jurisdiction in southern France by arresting Bernard Saisset, the bishop of Pamiers, on a charge of treason, Philip precipitated another crisis. Boniface responded with outrage, but we already know (see p. 255) how Philip adroitly rallied public opinion in his favor by calling the Estates together. After Boniface issued the bull *Unam sanctam* (1302), which declared that "it is altogether necessary to salvation for every human being to be subject to the Roman Pontiff,"[13] Philip's agents invaded Boniface's palace at Anagni (southeast of Rome) to capture the pope, bring him to France, and try him for heresy. Although the citizens of Anagni drove the agents out of town, Philip's power could not be denied. A month later, Boniface died, and the next two popes quickly pardoned Philip and his agents.

The papacy was never quite the same thereafter. In 1309, forced from Rome by civil strife, the popes settled at Avignon, a Provençal city administered by the Angevins of Naples but very much under the influence of the French crown. There they remained until 1377. The Avignon Papacy, largely French, established a sober and efficient organization that took in regular revenues and gave the papacy more say than ever before in the appointment of churchmen and the distribution of church benefices and revenues. Its authority grew: it became the unchallenged judge of sainthood. And the Dominicans and Franciscans became its foot soldiers in the evangelization of the world and the purification of Christendom. These were tasks that required realistic men. When a group of Franciscans objected to their fellows building convents and churches within the cities, the popes condemned them. The Spirituals, as they were called, cultivated a piety of poverty and apocalypticism, believing that Saint Francis had ushered in a new Age of the Holy Spirit. But the popes interpreted the Franciscan rule differently. They advocated the repression of the Spirituals and even had a few burned at the stake.

In some ways, the papacy had never been as powerful as it was at Avignon. On the other hand, it was mocked and vilified by contemporaries, especially Italians, whose revenues suffered from the popes' exile from Rome. Petrarch (Francesco Petrarca, 1304–1374), one of the great literary figures of the day, called the Avignon Papacy the "Babylonian Captivity," referring to 2 Kings 25:11, when the ancient Hebrews were exiled and held captive in Babylonia. Pliant and accommodating to the rulers of Europe, especially the kings of France, the popes were slowly abandoning the idea of leading all of Christendom and were coming to recognize the right of secular states to regulate their internal affairs.

Following page:

Plate 7.1: Chalice (*c.*1300). This gilded silver chalice, one of a pair made in the Rhineland, graphically shows the connection between the wine of the Eucharist and Christ's blood. On a large knob just below the cup, the goldsmith has placed medallions stamped with Christ's head alternating with rosettes that represent the five wounds of Christ. Each rosette sprouts a vine tendril that spreads its leaves on the base of the chalice, reminding communicants of the grapes that were pressed into the wine.

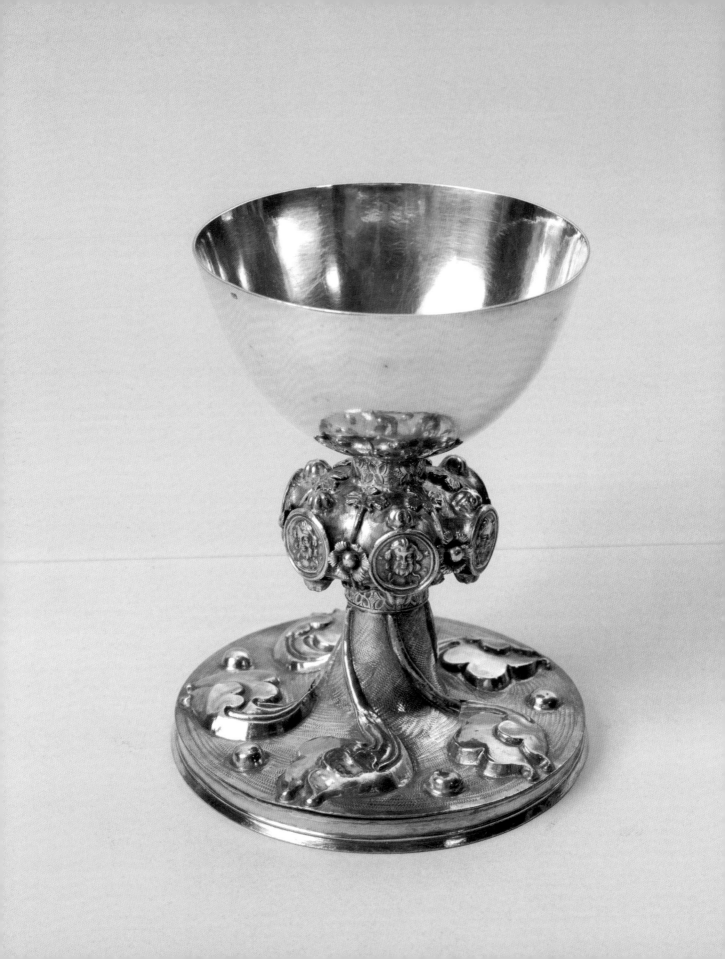

Lay Religiosity

Secular states, yes; but their populations took religion very seriously. With the doctrine of transubstantiation (see p. 230), Christianity became a religion of the body: the body of the wafer of the Mass, the body of the communicant who ate it, and equally the body of the believers who celebrated together in the feast of Corpus Christi (the Body of Christ). Eucharistic piety was already widespread in the most urbanized regions of Europe, when Juliana of Mont Cornillon (1193–1258), prioress of a convent in the Low Countries, announced that Christ himself wanted a special day set aside to celebrate his Body and Blood. Taken up by the papacy and promulgated as a universal feast, Corpus Christi was adopted throughout Western Europe. Cities created new processions for the day. Fraternities dedicated themselves to the Body of Christ, holding their meetings on the feast day, focusing their regular charity on bringing the *viaticum* (or final Eucharist) to the dying. Dramas were elaborated on the theme. Artists decorated the chalices used in the Mass with symbols that made the connection between the wine and the very blood that Christ had shed on the cross. (See Plate 7.1.)

Along with new devotion to the flesh of Christ came devotion to his mother. In the hands of the Sienese painter Pietro Lorenzetti (*c.*1280/90–1348), for example, Mary's life took on lively detail. In Plate 7.2, an altarpiece depicting the Birth of the Virgin, two servants—one probably the midwife—tenderly wash the infant Mary. Her mother, clearly modeled on the mistress of a well-to-do Italian household, sits up in bed, gazing at the child with dreamy eyes, while, in another room, a little serving boy whispers news of the birth to the expectant father.

Both publicly, in feasts dedicated to the major events in Mary's life, and privately, in small and concentrated images made to be contemplated by individual viewers, the Virgin was the focus of intense religious feeling. As mother of God, she was popularly carved to show the Godhead in her very womb. Called "Vièrges Ouvrantes" in French (literally: virgins that open) and Shrine Madonnas in English, these objects were often used as aids to private devotion. (See Plate 7.3, Seeing the Middle Ages: A Shrine Madonna.)

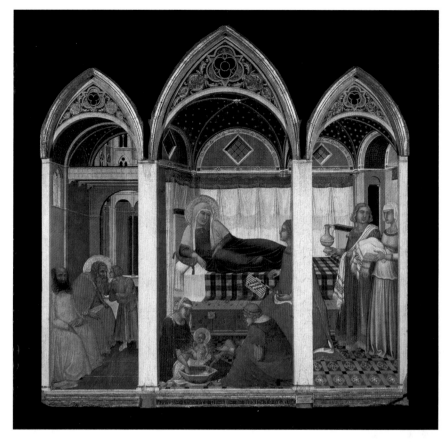

Plate 7.2: Pietro Lorenzetti, *Birth of the Virgin* (1342). This painted altarpiece creates an architectural space of real depth in which figures of convincing solidity act and interact; compare them with Saint Joseph in Plate 6.6, p. 227. Note how the ribs, rose windows, and arches of a Gothic church are used here as both decorative and unifying elements.

SEEING THE MIDDLE AGES

An outgrowth of the cult of the Virgin Mary, Shrine Madonnas became very popular throughout Europe in the later Middle Ages. Large ones stood on church altars; smaller versions, like the one here, which is about 14.5 inches high, were used as aids to private prayer and devotion. Certainly this example—from the Rhine Valley region and perhaps owned by a nun at a convent in Cologne—offers much to contemplate. Closed, it depicts at first glance a simple scene: Mary nursing the Christ Child. But Mary wears a crown, signaling that she is no ordinary mother but rather Queen of Heaven, while Christ holds a dove, the symbol of the Holy Spirit. That the statue is "about" the harmony of flesh

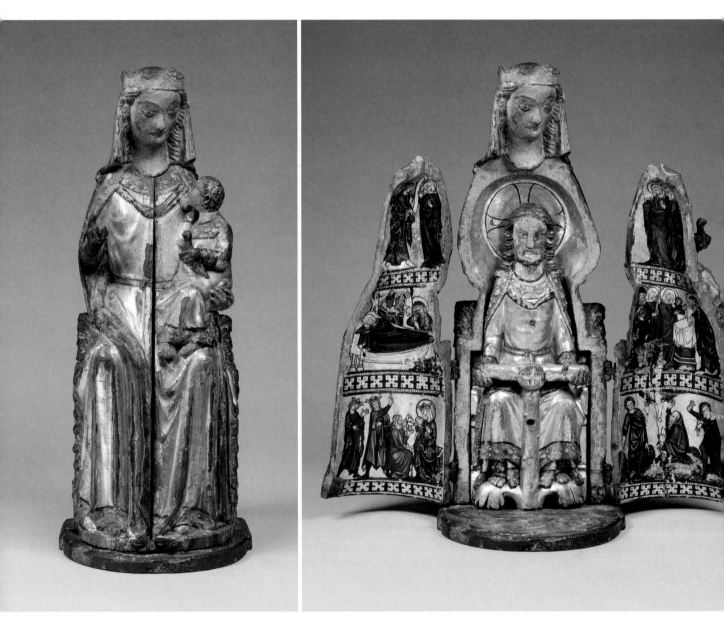

Plate 7.3: A Shrine Madonna (*c.*1300)

and spirit becomes clear when the Virgin's body is opened, revealing a seated God the Father holding a cross. The original sculpture would have included (where there are now only holes) the figure of the crucified Christ on the cross and, above him, a dove signifying the Holy Spirit. The three together—the Father, the Son, and the Holy Spirit—formed the Trinity, called, in this form, the Throne of Mercy. Flanking Christ's throne are six painted scenes of his infancy.

The statue embodies an idea that was echoed in contemporary prayers, hymns, and poetry: that Mary was not just the mother of Christ but the bearer of the entire Trinity. "Hail, mother of piety and of the whole Trinity," went one popular prayer. The Shrine Madonna physically placed the Trinity in Mary's very womb. Just as her inward parts consisted of a large central area flanked by three "compartments" on each side (the painted depictions of Christ's infancy), so, too, late medieval representations divided the womb into seven cells: a large one at the center and three small cells on each side. In Guido da Vigevano's fourteenth-century diagram of the female anatomy, for example, the uterus looks rather like a Christmas tree—or like the open Madonna.

However, Guido's conception was not nearly as complex as the Rhineland Madonna. For the side cells of *her* innards were painted with narratives that made her seem much like an "open book." On the left are, reading from top to bottom, the Annunciation (when the angel Gabriel told Mary she would give birth to God's son), the Nativity (Christ's birth), and the Adoration of the Magi. On the right are the Visitation (when the pregnant Virgin visited the equally pregnant Saint Elizabeth, mother of John the Baptist), the Presentation in the Temple (when Joseph and Mary brought Jesus to the temple to be "consecrated to the Lord"), and the Annunciation to the Shepherds. Like viewers of the fourteenth century, we are reminded not only of Christ's human beginnings on earth but also, in glancing at the central throne, of his equally divine nature. Moreover, the "cells" are in dialogue with one another across that central image. For example, the scene of the Nativity, which shows Mary stretched out on the bed on which she will give birth to Jesus, is directly opposite the Presentation, which depicts Christ lifted over an altar as he is given to Simeon. Thus the birth of Christ is paired with Christ as the "bread of life," the Eucharist of the altar. In these ways, the Shrine Madonna literally holds the Trinity in all its complexity in her very womb.

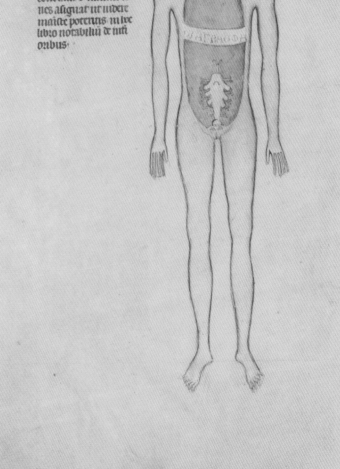

Guido da Vigevano, "The Seven Cells of the Uterus" (1345). One of many anatomical drawings in a book that offered extracts from Galen's medical works, this page represents the uterus as a self-contained organ.

Plate 7.4: *Hours of Jeanne d'Evreux* (c.1325–1328). Meant for private devotion, this Book of Hours was lavishly illustrated, probably by Jean Pucelle (c.1300–1355). Scenes from the life of Christ, the Virgin, and King Louis IX (Jeanne's great-grandfather) contrast with delicate illustrations at the foot of each page. On the left-hand side of the two pages illustrated here is Christ's Betrayal, the moment when Judas brings soldiers and priests to capture Jesus, while Peter cuts off the ear of Malchus, the high priest's slave. This horrific moment is juxtaposed on the right with the promise of the Annunciation. Below, in delicate line-drawings, the frivolity of the world is highlighted: on the left a man on a ram and another on a goat practice jousting with a barrel; on the right, young people play a game of "frog in the middle."

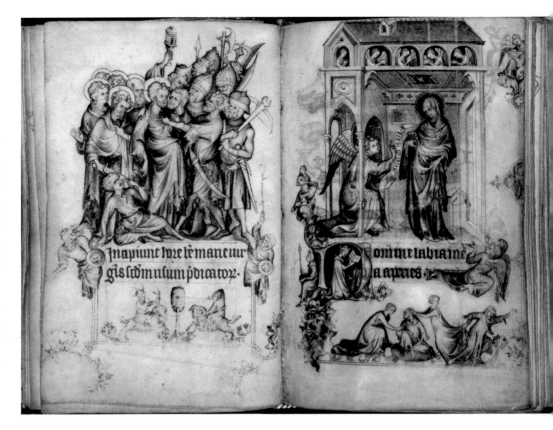

Books of Hours—small prayer books for laymen and (especially) -women—almost always included images of the Virgin for worshippers to contemplate. In Plate 7.4, on the right-hand side, Jeanne d'Evreux (1301–1371), queen of France and the original owner of this Book of Hours, is shown kneeling in prayer within the initial D. This is the first letter of "Domine," "Lord," the opening word of the first prayer of the Office of the Virgin Mary. Above Jeanne is the Annunciation, when Gabriel tells Mary that she will bear the Savior.

That worship could be a private matter was part of larger changes in the ways in which people negotiated the afterlife while here on earth. The doctrine of Purgatory, informally believed long before it was declared dogma in 1274, held that the Masses and prayers of the living could shorten the purgative torments that had to be suffered by the souls of the dead. Soon families were endowing special chapels for themselves, private spaces for offering private Masses on behalf of their own members. High churchmen and wealthy laymen and -women insisted that they and members of their family be buried within the walls of the church rather than outside of it, reminding the living—via their effigies—to pray for them. Typical is the tomb of Robert d'Artois (d.1317), commissioned by his mother, Countess Mahaut d'Artois (in northern France). (See Plate 7.5.)

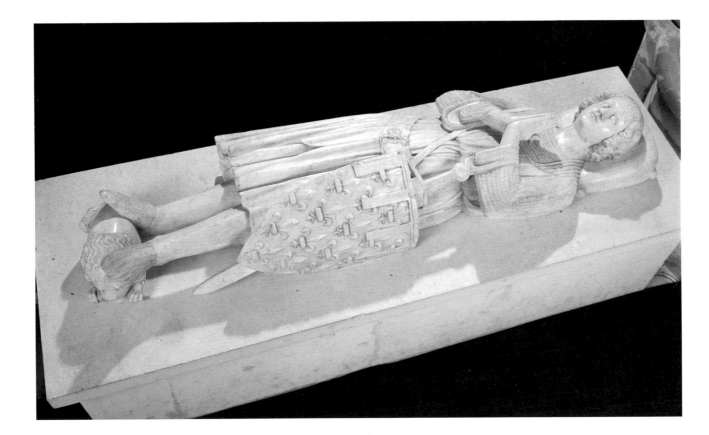

THE SCHOLASTIC SYNTHESIS AND ITS FRAYING

Widespread religiosity went hand-in-hand with increasing literacy. In some rural areas, schools for children were attached to monasteries or established in villages. In the south of France, where the church still feared heresy, preachers made sure that they taught children how to read along with the tenets of the faith. In the cities, all merchants and most artisans had some functional literacy: they had to read and write to keep accounts, and, increasingly, they owned religious books for their private devotions. In France, Books of Hours were most fashionable; Psalters were favored in England.

The broad popularity of the friars fed the institutions of higher education. Franciscans and Dominicans now established convents and churches *within* cities; their members attended the universities as students, and many went on to become masters. By the time the other theologians at the University of Paris saw the danger to their independence, the friars were too entrenched to be budged. Besides, the friars—men like Thomas Aquinas (*c.*1225–1274) and Bonaventure (*c.*1217–1274)—were unarguably the greatest of the scholastics, the scholars who mastered the use of logic to summarize and reconcile all knowledge and use it in the service of contemporary society.

Plate 7.5: Tomb and Effigy of Robert d'Artois (1317). Although Robert was only seventeen years old when he died, the sculptor of his tomb effigy, Jean Pépin de Huy, gave him a sword and buckler (the accoutrements of a knight) and placed a tame lion at his feet (the symbol of his power). At the same time, his prayerful pose and the lion alert viewers to the life to come: his uplifted hands signify Robert's piety, while the lion (mother lions were believed to waken their still-born cubs to life by their roars) recalls the hope of resurrection.

The Dominican Thomas Aquinas's *summae* (sing. *summa*)—long, systematic treatises that attempted to sum up all knowledge—were written to harmonize matters both human and divine. Using the technique of juxtaposing opposite positions, as Abelard had done in his *Sic et non*, Aquinas (unlike Abelard) carefully explained away or reconciled contradictions, using Aristotelian logic as his tool for analysis and exposition. Aquinas wanted to reconcile faith with reason, to demonstrate the harmony of belief and understanding even though (in his view) faith ultimately surpassed reason in knowing higher truths. Thomas's *Summa against the Gentiles*, for example, written as a guide for missionaries attempting to convert the Muslims, tried to demonstrate the truths of Christian practice and religion through natural reason to the extent possible, taking up questions ranging from the principles of the Christian religion to mundane matters. Are God's words contrary to reason? Should marriage be between one man and one woman only? Is simple fornication a sin? In the work of Albertus Magnus (*c.*1200–1280), Aquinas's teacher, the topics ranged from biology and physics to theology. In the writings of the Franciscan Saint Bonaventure, for whom Augustine replaced Aristotle as the key philosopher, the topics as such were secondary to an overall vision of the human mind as the recipient of God's beneficent illumination. For Bonaventure, minister general of the Franciscan Order, spirituality was the font of theology. Yet it was the Spiritual Franciscan Peter Olivi (1248–1298) who first defined the very practical word "capital": wealth with the potential to generate more wealth.

The scholastics' teachings were preached to townsmen by the friars as a matter of course. They came as well to permeate the thought of the reclusive contemplatives in the cities of Italy, the Netherlands, and the Rhineland, who absorbed the vocabulary of the schools from their confessors. The Dominican Meister Eckhart (d.1327/1328), who studied at Paris before beginning a career of teaching and preaching in Germany, and who enriched the German language with new words for the abstract ideas of the schools, was himself a contemplative: a mystic who saw union with God as the goal of human life.

These thirteenth-century scholastics united the secular realm with the sacred in apparent harmony. But at the end of the century, fissures began to appear. In the writings of the Franciscan John Duns Scotus (1265/1266–1308), for example, the world and God were less compatible. As with Bonaventure, so too with Duns Scotus: human reason could know truth only by divine illumination. But Duns Scotus argued that this illumination came not as a matter of course but only when God chose to intervene. He saw God as willful rather than reasonable; the divine will alone determined whether human reason could soar to knowledge. Further unraveling the knot tying reason and faith together was William of Ockham (d.1347/1350), another Franciscan who nevertheless disputed Duns Scotus vigorously. For Ockham, reason was unable to prove the truths of faith; it was apt only for things human and worldly, where, in turn, faith was of no use. Ockham himself turned his attention to the nature of government, arguing the importance of the state for human society. But several of his contemporaries looked at the physical world: Nicole Oresme (*c.*1320–1382), for example, following Ockham's view that the simplest explanation was the best, proposed that the sun, not the earth, was the center of the heavens.

HARMONY AND DISSONANCE IN WRITING, MUSIC, AND ART

On the whole, writers, musicians, architects, and artists, like scholastics, presented complicated ideas and feelings in harmony. Writers explored the relations between this world and the next; musicians found ways to bridge sacred and secular genres of music; artists used fleshy, natural forms to evoke the divine.

Vernacular Literature

In the hands of Dante Alighieri (1265–1321), vernacular poetry expressed the order of the scholastic universe, the ecstatic union of the mystic's quest, and the erotic and emotional life of the troubadour. His *Commedia*—later known as the *Divine Comedy*—presents Dante (writing in the first person) as a traveler who passes through Hell, Purgatory, and Paradise, and yet the poem is fixed on locations in this world. For example, when Dante asks a soul in Hell to introduce herself, she begins with her hometown: "The city where I was born lies on that shore where the Po descends."[14] Dante himself was a child of the Arno, the river that flows through Florence. An ardent Florentine patriot and member of the "Whites" party, the faction that opposed papal intervention in Tuscany, he was condemned to death and expelled from the city by the "Blacks" after their victory in 1301. The *Commedia* was written during Dante's bitter exile. It was peopled with his friends, lovers, enemies, and the living and dead whom he admired and reviled.

At the same time, it was a parable about the soul seeking and finding God in the blinding light of love. Just as Thomas Aquinas used Aristotle's logic to lead him to important truths, Dante used the pagan poet Virgil as his guide through Hell and Purgatory. And just as Aquinas believed that faith went beyond reason to even higher truths, Dante found a new guide, Beatrice, representing earthly love, to lead him through most of Paradise. But only faith, in the form of the divine love of the Virgin Mary, could bring Dante to the culmination of his journey, the inexpressible and ravishing vision of God.

In other writers, the harmony of heaven and earth was equally sought, if differently expressed. In the anonymous prose *Quest of the Holy Grail* (*c*.1225), the adventures of the knights of King Arthur's Table were turned into a fable to teach the doctrine of transubstantiation and the wonder of the vision of God. In *The Romance of the Rose*, begun by one author (Guillaume de Lorris, a poet in the romantic tradition) and finished by another (Jean de Meun, a poet in the scholastic tradition), a lover seeks the rose, his true love, but is continually thwarted by personifications of love, shame, reason, abstinence, and so on. They present him with arguments for and against love, but in the end, erotic love is embraced in the divine scheme—and the lover plucks the rose.

The Motet

Plate 7.6 (facing page):
The Motet *S'Amours* (c.1300).
Like the composer of
S'Amours, the artist of this
page (painted not long after
the music itself was written)
weaves together three separate
stories. In the S of the word
"S'Amours," which is sung
by the disconsolate lover (the
top voice), the artist presents,
by contrast with the text,
two very contented lovers
petting both animals and each
other. To the right of this
happy scene is the initial A,
the first letter of the word
"Au," which is sung by the
victorious lover of the middle
voice. Again ironically, *this*
figure is sad and lonely. By
reversing the moods of the
two voices with his pictures,
is the artist commenting
on the fickleness of love?
Beneath the "Ecce" of the
third voice is a hunting scene,
complete with stag, hound,
and hawk. The hunt was
often used as a metaphor for
amorous relations.

Already by the tenth century, the chant in unison had been joined by a chant of many voices: polyphony. Initially voice met voice in improvised harmony, but in the twelfth century polyphony was increasingly composed as well. In the thirteenth century its most characteristic form was the motet. Created at Paris, probably in the milieus of the university and the royal court, the motet harmonized the sacred with the worldly, the Latin language with the vernacular.

Two to four voices joined together in a motet. The most common sort from the second half of the thirteenth century had three voices. The lowest, often taken from a liturgical chant, generally consisted of one or two words, suggesting that it was normally played on an instrument (such as a vielle or lute) rather than sung. The second and third voices had different texts and melodies, sung simultaneously. The form allowed for the mingling of religious and secular motives. Very likely motets were performed by the clerics who formed the entourages of bishops or abbots—or by university students—for their entertainment and pleasure. In the motet *S'Amours*, whose opening music is pictured in Plate 7.6, the top voice complains (in French): "If Love had any power, I, who have served it all my life with a loyal heart, should surely have noticed." By contrast, the middle voice, also singing in French, rejoices in Love's rewards: "At the rebirth of the joyous season, I must begin a song, for true Love, whom I desire to serve, has given me a reason to sing." Meanwhile the lowest voice sings the Latin word "Ecce"—"Behold!"[15]

Complementing the motet's complexity was the development of new schemes to indicate rhythm. The most important, that of Franco of Cologne in his *Art of Measurable Song* (c.1260), used different shapes to mark the number of beats for which each note should be held. (See Figure 7.1; the music in Plate 7.6 uses a similar rhythmic system.) Allowing for great flexibility and inventiveness in composition, Franco's scheme became the basis of modern musical notation.

Figure 7.1: Single Notes and Values of Franconian Notation

Name and shape of note		Value (in beats)	Modern equivalent
Duplex long		6	𝅝.
Perfect long		3	𝅗𝅥.
Imperfect long		2	𝅗𝅥
Breve		1	♩
Semibreve			
Minor + major		⅓ + ⅔	♪ ♩ (3)
Three minor		⅓ + ⅓ + ⅓	♫♪ 3

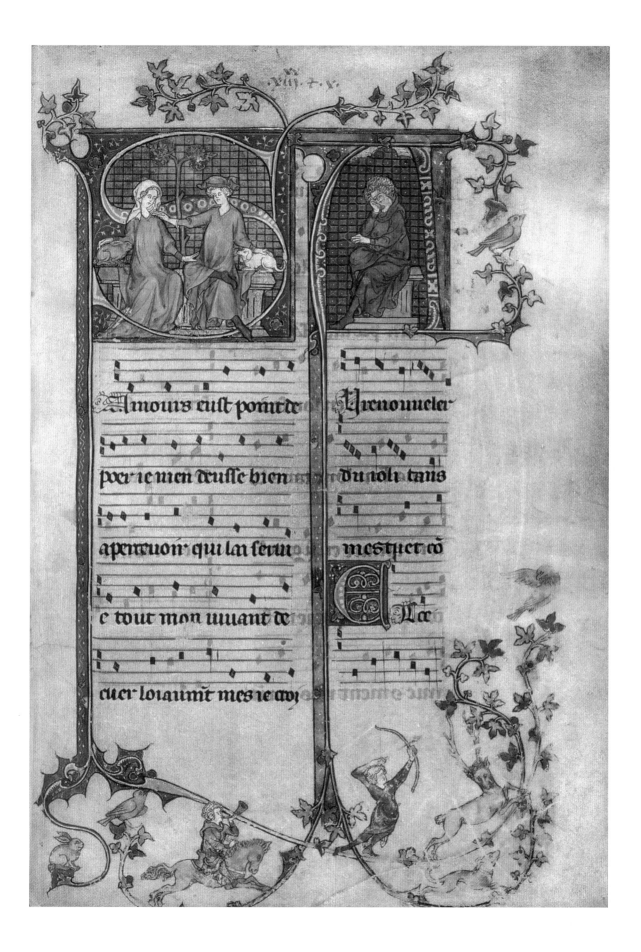

Amours eust point de
Yrenoueler
poer ie mien deusse bien
du ioli tans
a peroon qui lai serui
mest iet co
e tout mon uuant de
ee
cuer loiaumt mes ie ao

New Currents in Art

Plate 7.7 (facing page):
Saint John, "Dominican" Bible (mid-13th cent.). The graceful and elegant S-curve of these depictions of Saint John is characteristic of late Gothic figural style. Here the evangelist bisects the first letter of the first word—"senior," or "elder"—of two of his own texts, 2 John and 3 John.

Flexibility and inventiveness describe the art of Franco's time as well. It had new patrons to serve: the urban elite. In the Paris of Saint Louis's day, for example, wealthy merchants coveted illuminated law books and romances; rich students prized illustrated Bibles as essential fashion accessories; churchmen wanted beautiful service books; the royal family wanted lavishly illustrated Bibles, Psalters, and Books of Hours; and the nobility aspired to the same books as their sovereigns. The old-fashioned *scriptoria* that had previously produced books, with scribes and artists working in the same place, gave way to specialized workshops, often staffed by laypeople. Some workshops produced the raw materials: the ink, gold leaf, or parchment; others employed scribes to copy the texts; a third kind was set up for the illuminators; and a fourth did nothing but bind the finished books. This was not mass production, however, and the styles of different artists are clear, if subtle. In Plate 7.7, the artist of one workshop has made the apostle John conform to the shape of an S, his body out of joint yet utterly elegant. But another Parisian artist working at about the same time, in a different shop and on a different book, painted a thinner John, almost ramrod straight, with a flaming head of hair. (See Plate 7.8.)

Meanwhile, in Italy, sculptors, also working in shops, were melding the sort of Gothic naturalism exemplified by Saint Joseph of Reims in Plate 6.6 (on p. 227) with the classical style of Roman sculpture we saw on the Roman sarcophagus relief of Meleager in Plate 1.4 (on p. 15). For the Duomo of Siena, for example, Nicola Pisano (d. before 1284) and his assistants created a baptistery pulpit composed of eight panels. The Adoration of the Magi, the panel shown in Plate 7.9, has the same dense crowds as the Meleager sarcophagus. Today all the color is gone, but originally Nicola painted the backgrounds and gilded the hemlines with gold, emphasizing details that brought the event "to life," melding the everyday world of thronging people and animals with the mystery of the divine incarnation.

Within a half-century the weighty, natural forms of the sculptors found a home in painting as well, above all in the paintings of Giotto (1266/1267–1337). In one of his commissions to decorate the private chapel of the richest man in Padua, for example, Giotto filled the walls with frescoes narrating humanity's redemption through Christ, culminating in the Final Judgment. (See Plate 7.10 on p. 274.) Throughout, Giotto experimented with the illusion of depth, weight, and volume, his figures expressing unparalleled emotional intensity as they reacted to events in the world-space created by painted frames. In the *Raising of Lazarus*, a story told in John 11:1–46 and depicted in Plate 7.11, we see the moment just after Christ has performed his miracle: Lazarus stands up, white as a sheet after four days in the grave, still bound in his winding sheet, his eyes still unseeing. Compare this depiction of the story with the one in Plate 4.2 (p. 142). As in the Ottonian portrayal, some of the Jews hold their noses and Mary and Martha bow down before Christ. But in Giotto's fresco, the figures interact as well as gesture; they operate within a fully realized landscape; and Lazarus's miracle does not undo the order of nature: he still looks dead.

maligno positus ē. Et scimus
qm̄ filius dei uenit: et dedit
nob sensū ut cognoscam̄ uer
dm̄ τ simus in uero filio eius.
hic ē uerꝰ dꝰ τ uita etn̄a. Fi
lioli custodite uos a simulacris
cris. amen. Explic epl̄a iohīs ī.

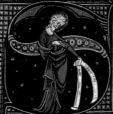

enior Incipit
electe dn̄e et filiis
τ natis eius
qs̄ ego diligo
in ueritate: τ nō
ego solus sꝫ τ os̄ q̄ cognoueꝛt
ueritatē ꝓpꞇ ueritatē q̄ ꝑmanet
in nob et nobcū erit in eꞇn̄m;
sit nobiscū gꞃa mia pax a dō
pꞃe τ a xp̄o ihu filio pꞃis in ueri
tate τ caritate. Gauisus sum
ualde qm̄ inueni de filiis tuis
ambulantes in ueritate. sic ma
datū accepim̄ a pꞃe. Et nc̄ rogo
te dn̄a. nō tāqm̄ mandatū
nouū scribens tibi sꝫ qd̄ habu
imus ab initio ut diligamus
alter utrū. Et hec ē caritas: ut
ambulem̄ sctm̄ mandata eius
hoc ē eni mandatū ut quemad
modū audistis ab initio in
eo ambuletis; qm̄ multi se
ductores exierūt in mundo. qui
nō confitetur ihm̄ xp̄m uenisse
in carne: hic ē seductor τ antixp̄s

videre nos metipos ne ꝑdatis
qd̄ operati estis: sꝫ ut mecedē ple
nā accipiatis. Omn̄s qui rece
dit τ nō ꝑmanet in doctrina xp̄i
dm̄ nō hꞇ. Qui ꝑmanet in doc
trina xp̄i: hic τ filiū τ pꞃem hꞃꝫ
Si quis uenit ad uos τ hanc
doctrinā nō affert: nolite eū recipe
cipe in domū nec aue ei dixe
ritis. Qui eni dicit ei aue: comu
nicat operibꝫ eius malignis. Ec
ce ꝓdixi uobis ut in diē dn̄i nr̄i
ihu xp̄i nō confundamini. Plu
ra habui uob scribe: nolui ꝑ car
tā τ atramentū. spero eni me
futurū ad uos. τ os ad os loq̄
ut gaudiū urm̄ sit plenū.
Salutāt te filii sororis tue e
lecte amen. Explic epl̄a iohīs ij.

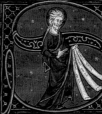

enior scribit tua
gaio kmō q̄
ego diligo in
ueritate. kme
de omnibꝫ oꞃa
ne facio ꝓspere te ingredi
τ ualere sicut ꝓspe agit aia
tua. Gauisus sū ualde ue
nientibꝫ frib; τ testimoniū
ꝑhibentibꝫ ueritati tue: sicut
tu in ueritate ambulas. Maio
rem hac nō habeo leticiā: qm̄
ut audiā filios meos in ueri

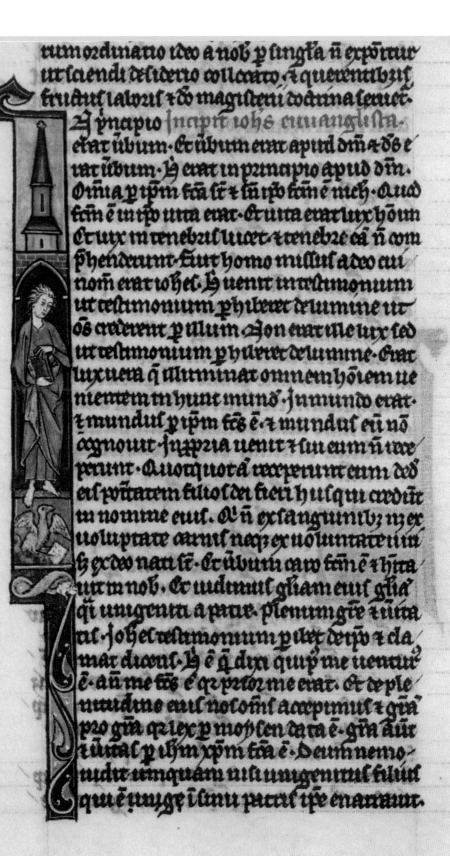

Plate 7.8: Saint John, "Aurifaber" Bible (mid-13th cent.). An artist working at another workshop at about the same time as the artist of Plate 7.7 produced a very different Saint John, hardly curved at all. He stands in a miniature church, while beneath him is his symbol, an eagle holding a book.

Plate 7.9 (facing page): Nicola Pisano, Pulpit (1266–1268). *The Adoration of the Magi,* the scene on this panel of the Siena pulpit, was a very traditional Christian theme (see an early representation on the Franks Casket, Plate 2.8, pp. 70–71), but here the sculptor, Nicola Pisano, has imagined it as a crowd scene and filled it with little details—like the camels—to make it "come to life."

Following page:

Plate 7.10: Giotto, Scrovegni Chapel, Padua (1304–1306). Giotto organized the Scrovegni Chapel paintings like scenes in a comic book, to be read from left to right, with the Last Judgment over the entryway.

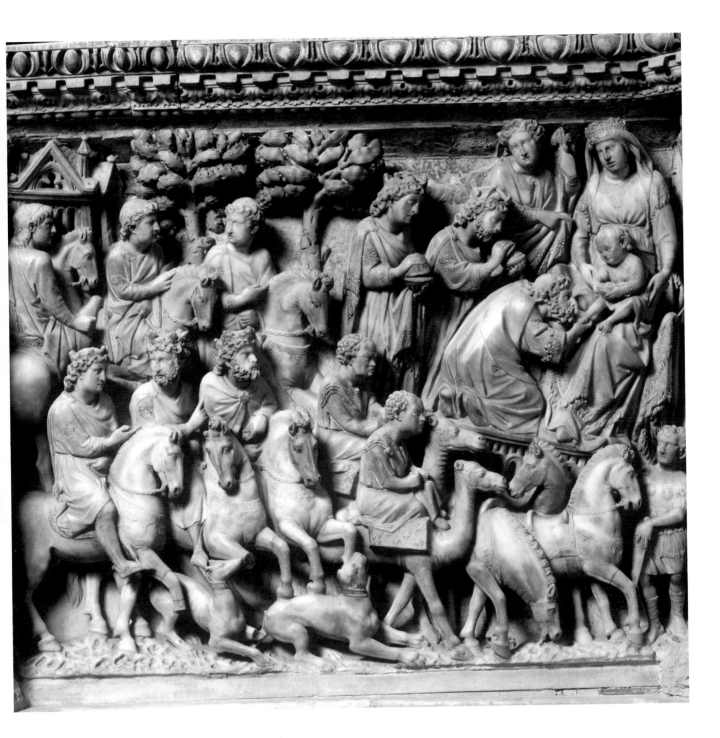

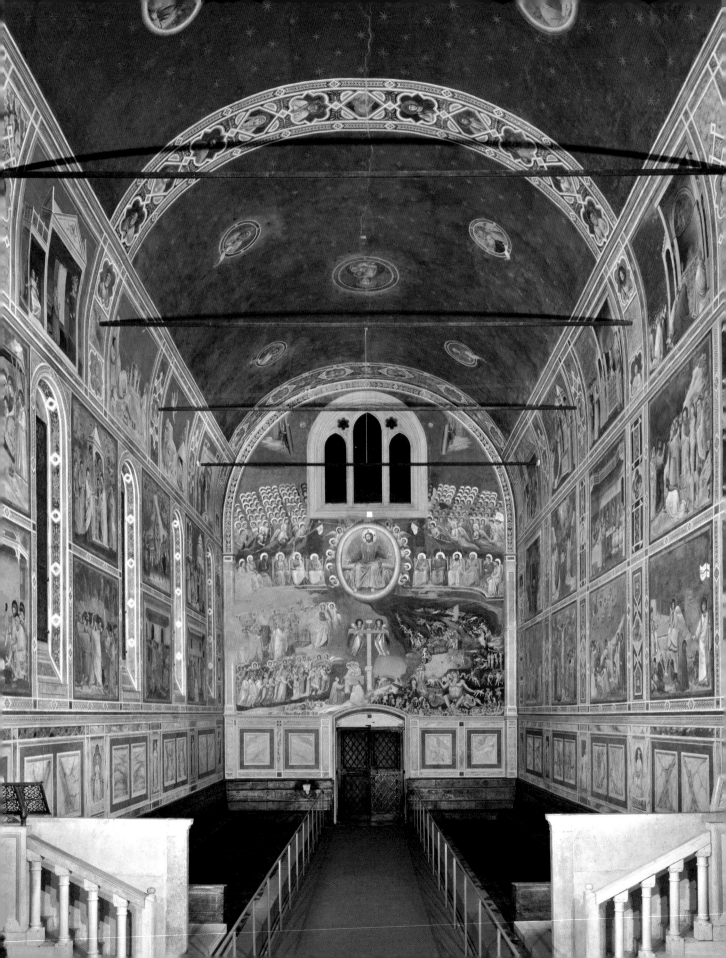

Just as Italian art was influenced by northern Gothic style, so in turn the new Italian currents went north. In France, for example, illuminators for the royal court made miniature spaces for figures in the round, creating illusions of depth. Have another look at the *Hours of Jeanne d'Evreux* (Plate 7.4 on p. 264). In the picture of Christ's Betrayal on the left-hand side, the old S-shape figures are still favored, but the soldiers who crowd around Christ are as dense and dramatic as the crowd that reacts to Lazarus in Giotto. On the right-hand page Mary, surprised by the angel of the Annunciation, sits in a space as deep as the landscape in Plate 7.11. Influenced perhaps by the look of sculpted figures such as those of ancient monuments like the Meleager Sarcophagus (Plate 1.4 on p. 15), the artist painted in *grisaille*, a bare gray highlighted by light tints of color.

Plate 7.11: Giotto, *Raising of Lazarus*, Scrovegni Chapel (1304–1306). Giotto brought to painting the sensibilities of a sculptor. Just as Nicola Pisano's figures (see Plate 7.9) had depth, weight, and roundness, so did Giotto's painted ones. And just as Nicola used telling details to humanize scenes from the Bible, Giotto's painting suggests the weight of the tomb cover and the varying emotions of the people at the scene.

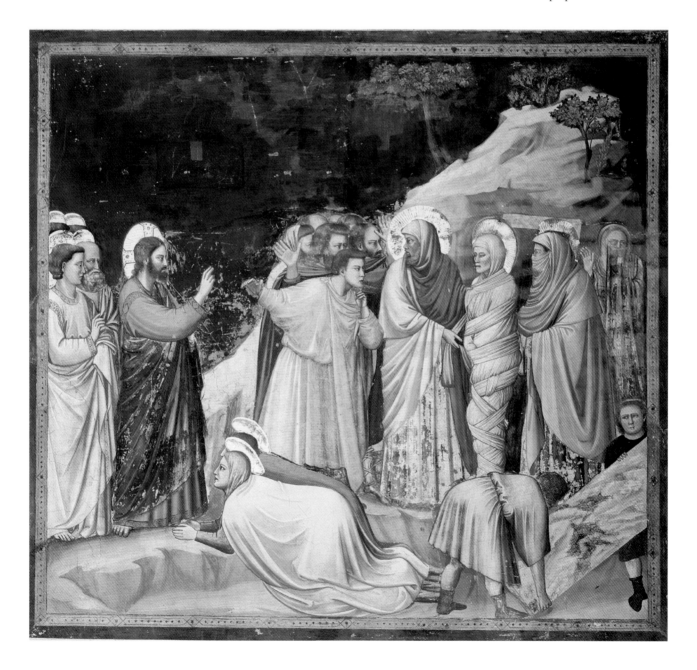

AN AGE OF SCARCITY?

The *Hours of Jeanne d'Evreux* were created not long after the horrific event that historians call the Great Famine (1315–1317), one of many waves of food shortages that shook the medieval world on either side of the year 1300. The chief causes of such scarcity have traditionally been sought in demographics and declining food production. But newer research pins the blame not so much on natural factors as on human action—and inaction.

Overpopulation, Undersupply

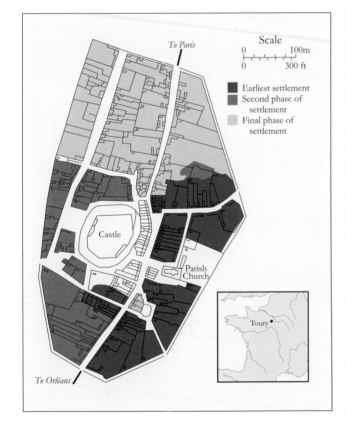

Map 7.7: The Village of Toury, Fourteenth and Fifteenth Centuries

Map 7.8 (facing page): The Lands of Toury, Fourteenth and Fifteenth Centuries

There is certainly much to be said for the demographic argument. While around the year 1300 farms were producing more food than ever before, population growth meant that families had more hungry mouths to feed. One plot that had originally supported a single family in England was, by the end of the thirteenth century, divided into twenty tiny parcels for the progeny of the original peasant holder.

Land was similarly subdivided in France. Consider the village of Toury, about 45 miles south of Paris (Map 7.7). It originally consisted of a few peasant habitations (their houses and gardens) clustered around a central enclosure belonging to the lord, in this case the monastery of Saint-Denis (see p. 221). Nearby, across the main route that led from Paris to Orléans, was a parish church. In 1110 Suger, then a monk at Saint-Denis and provost of Toury, constructed a well-fortified castle on the site of the enclosure. In the course of the thirteenth century, encouraged both by Saint-Denis's policy of giving out lots in return for rents and by a market granted by the king, the village grew rapidly, expanding to the east, then to the west, and finally (by the fourteenth century) to the north. Meanwhile the lands cultivated by the villagers—once called upon to support only a small number of householders—were divided into more than 5,000 parcels, which appear as tiny rectangles on Map 7.8.

In general, population growth seems to have leveled off by the mid-thirteenth century, but climatic changes wrought their own havoc. A mini ice age took hold in the north of Europe (though not in the south), leading to wheat shortages. In 1309 the cold weather was joined by an extremely wet growing season that ruined the harvest in southern and western Germany; the towns, to which food had to be imported, were hit especially hard. And yet the towns were themselves overpopulated, swollen by immigrants from the overcrowded countryside.

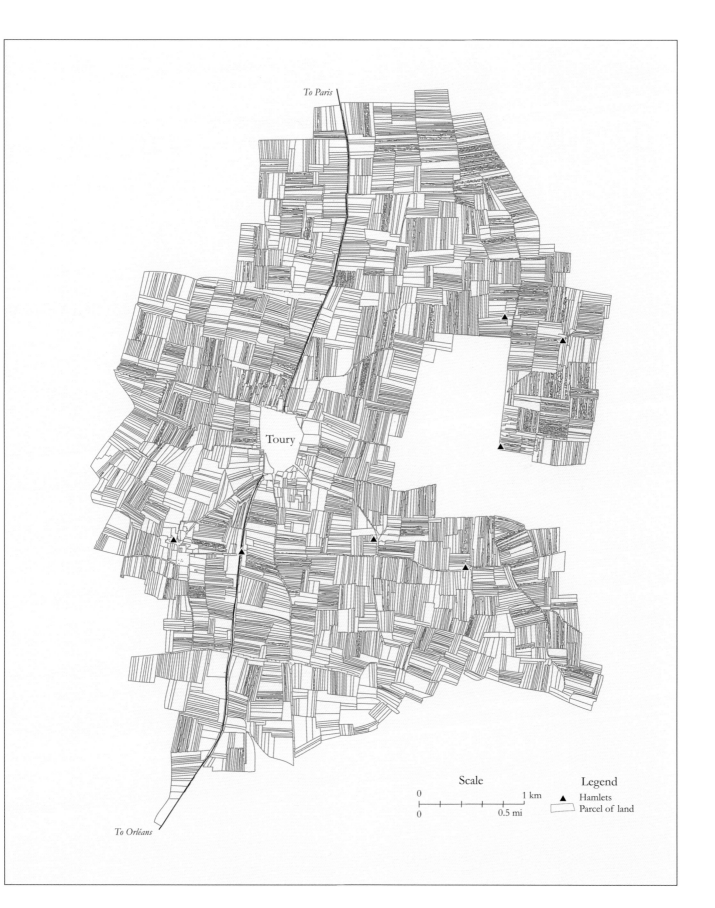

To Paris

Toury

To Orléans

Scale

0   1 km

0   0.5 mi

Legend

▲ Hamlets

Parcel of land

Human Manipulation of Supply and Demand

Yet scarcity and famine were hardly inevitable, and in some places they were not evident at all. Often human actions were responsible for aggravating food shortages across Europe. Warfare, for example, took a major toll on economic life. As states grew in power, rulers hired soldiers—mercenaries—and depended less on knights. But these troops were paid such poor wages that they plundered the countryside even when they were not fighting. Warring armies had always disrupted farms, ruining the fields as they passed by, but in the thirteenth century burning became a battle tactic, used both to devastate enemy territory and to teach the inhabitants a lesson. Towns were as vulnerable as the countryside. They could defend their walls against roving troops, but they could not easily stop the flow of refugees who sought their safety. Lille's population, for example, nearly doubled as a result of the wars between Flanders and France during the first two decades of the thirteenth century. Like other Flemish cities, Lille was obliged to impose new taxes on its population to pay for its huge war debts.

Pressed by such debts as well as the desire for gain, landlords and town officials alike strove to get more money. Everywhere, customary and other dues were deemed inadequate. In 1315 the king of France offered liberty to all his serfs, mainly to assess a new war tax on all free men. In other parts of France, lords imposed a *taille*, an annual money payment, and many peasants had to go into debt to pay it. Some lost their land entirely. To enforce their new taxes, great lords, both lay and ecclesiastical, installed local agents. Living near villages in fortified houses, these officials kept account books and carefully computed their profits and their costs.

But great lords, rulers, and merchants did not simply keep records of agricultural production; they planned ahead and manipulated the markets. At Constantinople at the beginning of the fourteenth century, the patriarch noticed a marked increase in beggars on the street. Moved by their plight, he wrote to the emperor: "everyone entreats me piteously that [the grain] not leave the capital, and [they] bind me with oaths to put before any other request to your divine majesty a petition about the grain." His letter was clear about both the problem and the solution: "a few gifts and bribes triumph over [your] good qualities, and drive the grain we yearn for out of the city as should not happen."[16] He was right: merchants from Genoa and Venice were bribing the emperor to allow them first to import into Constantinople grain from the Black Sea region and then to export it to Italy, where they could make handsome profits.

Merchants like these were participating in far-flung markets that extended from the Black Sea to England. Italian cities no longer fed themselves from nearby farms: they relied on imports. Florentines got their grain from Sicily, Genoa (as we have seen) from as far away as the Black Sea. Controlling these imports were the cities themselves, which functioned like mini-states. Great merchants (like those at Byzantium) worked in collusion with the political powers in place. In England, major landowners were now as much agri-businessmen as they were feudal lords.

Anticipating food shortages, middlemen hoarded food stocks until prices rose steeply. Rulers were torn by their desire to make money and their duty to the common good. The kings of Aragon (in Spain) prohibited the export of wheat in times of scarcity, but they also sold special licenses to individuals, allowing them to ignore the law. City governments found themselves in a balancing act: they could store food in reserve to sell at below-market cost to the needy, but they also wanted to please their merchants.

Peasants were not passive in the face of the new conditions. They too were involved in markets—not in the grand long-distance networks of Venetian and Genoese traders, but in small-scale exchanges among local hamlets and villages. The countryside had its own sort of commerce, petty but active. The little Provençal village of Reillane, for example, with a population of 2,400, supported 13 cloth makers. Such merchants might also sell meat or extend credit, on the side, to the local peasantry. The Mediterranean region—Italy, Spain, southern France, and Provence—boasted more diversified crops than the north: this meant that, when wheat harvests were poor, peasants could survive on chestnuts and millet. Or they could relocate to regions better suited to their needs. When peasants in Navarre found that they could not afford to pay their lord his dues, they moved to the Ebro valley, where they found a place in the flourishing commercial economy there. All was not bleak in the age of the Great Famine; much depended on who and where you were—and on how fair the markets were.

★ ★ ★ ★ ★

In the second half of the thirteenth century, Europeans found ways to mesh their institutions of commerce and religion with those of the vast Mongol empire to their east. In many ways medieval Europe reached the zenith of its prosperity, certainly of its population, during the century bisected by 1300. The cities became the centers of culture and wealth. Universities took wing, producing scholasticism, a "scientific revolution" in logical and systematic thought. The friars, among the most prominent of the scholastics, and ministering to an attentive, prosperous, increasingly literate laity, installed themselves right in the center of towns.

Harmony was often achieved through clashes. The synthesis of a scholastic *summa* was possible only when opposite ideas were faced and sorted out. The growth of representative institutions nearly always entailed accommodating the demands of the discontented with the enlightened self-interest of rulers. The great artistic innovations of the day involved reconciling classical with Gothic styles. Poems and musical compositions worked to assimilate the secular order with the divine.

The harmonies were not always sweet, but sweetness need not be a value, in music or in life. More ominous were the attempts to sound single notes: to suppress the voices of the Jews and the heretics, to silence the bells of the lepers. Cities tried to close their gates to beggars. In the next century terrible calamities would construct new arenas for discord and creativity.

1188	King Alfonso IX (r.1188–1230) summons townsmen to the *cortes*
1222	*Popolo* at Piacenza wins role in government
c.1225–1274	Thomas Aquinas
1226–1270	King Louis IX (Saint Louis) of France
1230s	Mongols conquer Rus'
1252	Genoa and Florence begin minting gold coins
1265	Commons included in English Parliament
1266/1267–1337	Giotto
1279	Mongols conquer China
1284	Gold ducats first minted at Venice
1290	Jews expelled from England
1291	End of the Crusader States
1309–1377	Avignon Papacy (so-called Babylonian Captivity)
1315–1317	Great Famine
1321	Death of Dante
1341	Death of Lithuanian Duke Gediminas
1356	Golden Bull promulgated in Germany

NOTES

1 *Decrees of the [Hanseatic] League*, in *Reading the Middle Ages: Sources from Europe, Byzantium, and the Islamic World*, ed. Barbara H. Rosenwein, 2nd ed. (Toronto: University of Toronto Press, 2014), p. 400.

2 *The Ghibelline Annals of Piacenza*, in *Reading the Middle Ages*, p. 398.

3 Quoted in Riccardo Rao, *Signori di popolo. Signoria cittadina e società comunale nell'Italia nord-occidentale, 1275–1350* (Milan: FrancoAngeli, 2011), p. 42.

4 *Statute of the Jewry*, in *Reading the Middle Ages*, p. 414.

5 *Sarum manual*, in *Reading the Middle Ages*, p. 413.

6 Jacques Fournier, *Episcopal Register*, in *Reading the Middle Ages*, pp. 405–6.

7 *Summons of Representatives of Shires and Towns to Parliament*, in *Reading the Middle Ages*, p. 423.

8 Despite the similarity between the terms *Parlement* and Parliament, both deriving from French *parler*, "to talk," the two institutions were different. The former was the central French court of law, the latter the English representative institution. It is true that the English Parliament did hear legal cases, but it also discussed foreign affairs, published royal statutes, and (above all) granted taxes to the king.

9 Béla IV, *Letter to Pope Innocent IV*, in *Reading the Middle Ages*, p. 382.

10 *The Short Life of St Petka (Paraskeve) of Tarnov*, in *Reading the Middle Ages*, p. 396.

11 *The Henryków Book*, in *Reading the Middle Ages*, p. 385.

12 Boniface VIII, *Clericis laicos*, in *Reading the Middle Ages*, p. 424.

13 Boniface VIII, *Unam sanctam*, in *Reading the Middle Ages*, p. 426.

14 Dante, *Inferno, Canto V (Paolo and Francesca)*, in *Reading the Middle Ages*, p. 434.

15 *The Montpellier Codex*, part IV: *Text and Translations*, trans. Susan Stakel and Joel C. Relihan, in *Recent Researches in the Music of the Middle Ages and Early Renaissance* 8 (Middleton, WI: A-R Editions, 1985), p. 81.

16 Athanasius I, *Letter*, in *Reading the Middle Ages*, p. 401.

FURTHER READING

Abulafia, David, ed. *Italy in the Central Middle Ages*. Short Oxford History of Italy. Oxford: Oxford University Press, 2004.

Given, James B. *Inquisition and Medieval Society: Power, Discipline, and Resistance in Languedoc*. Ithaca, NY: Cornell University Press, 1997.

Glick, Leonard B. *Abraham's Heirs: Jews and Christians in Medieval Europe*. Syracuse, NY: Syracuse University Press, 1999.

Jackson, Peter. *The Mongols and the West, 1221–1410*. Harlow: Pearson, 2005.

Jobson, Adrian. *The First English Revolution: Simon de Montfort, Henry III and the Barons' War*. London: Bloomsbury, 2012.

Jones, P.J. *The Italian City-State: From Commune to Signoria*. Oxford: Oxford University Press, 1997.

Jordan, William Chester. *The French Monarchy and the Jews: From Philip Augustus to the Last Capetians*. Philadelphia: University of Pennsylvania Press, 1989.

Kitsikopoulos, Harry, ed. *Agrarian Change and Crisis in Europe, 1200–1500*. New York: Routledge, 2012.

Klápště, Jan. *The Czech Lands in Medieval Transformation*. Ed. Philadelphia Ricketts. Trans. Sean Mark Miller and Kateřina Millerová. Leiden: Brill, 2012.

Martin, Janet. *Medieval Russia, 980–1584*. Cambridge: Cambridge University Press, 1995.

Mundill, Robin R. *England's Jewish Solution: Experiment and Expulsion, 1262–1290*. Cambridge: Cambridge University Press, 1998.

Nirenberg, David. *Communities of Violence: Persecution of Minorities in the Middle Ages*. Princeton, NJ: Princeton University Press, 1996.

O'Callaghan, Joseph F. *The Cortes of Castile-León, 1188–1350*. Philadelphia: University of Pennsylvania Press, 1989.

Pegg, Mark Gregory. *The Corruption of Angels: The Great Inquisition of 1245–1246*. Princeton, NJ: Princeton University Press, 2001.

Rubin, Miri. *Corpus Christi: The Eucharist in Late Medieval Culture*. Cambridge: Cambridge University Press, 1991.

Spufford, Peter. *Money and Its Use in Medieval Europe*. Cambridge: Cambridge University Press, 1988.

Strayer, Joseph R. *The Reign of Philip the Fair*. Princeton, NJ: Princeton University Press, 1980.

Vallerani, Massimo. *Medieval Public Justice*. Trans. Sarah Rubin Blanshei. Washington, DC: Catholic University of America Press, 2012.

Watts, John. *The Making of Polities: Europe, 1300–1500*. Cambridge: Cambridge University Press, 2009.

White, John. *Art and Architecture in Italy, 1250–1400*. 3rd ed. New Haven, CT: Yale University Press, 1993.

To test your knowledge of this chapter, please go to

www.utphistorymatters.com

for Study Questions.

EIGHT

CATASTROPHE AND CREATIVITY

(*c.1350–c.1500*)

STRUCK BY A PLAGUE that carried off between a fifth and a half of its population, shaken by Ottoman Turks who conquered Constantinople and moved into the Balkans, buffeted by internal wars that threatened the very foundations of its political life, Europe shuddered. Soon, however, it shrugged and forged ahead. Those who survived war and disease enjoyed a higher standard of living than before; new-style political entities gained powers that the old had never had; and new-rigged sailing ships, manned by hopeful adventurers and financed by rich patrons, plied the seas east- and westwards. By 1500, Europe was poised to conquer the globe.

CRISES AND CONSOLIDATIONS

In the 1340s, the first pandemic since the Plague of Justinian (see p. 29) made swift inroads into Europe even while France and England were waging a long and debilitating Hundred Years' War. Popular revolts and insurrections, the bitter harvest of war and economic contraction, rocked both town and countryside. Meanwhile a schism within the church—setting first two, then three popes against one another—shattered all illusions of harmony within Christendom. At the same time, however, smaller units gained apparent cohesion under new-style princes.

The Black Death

The Black Death (1346–1353), so named by later historians looking back on the disease, was caused by *Yersinia pestis*, the bacterium of the plague. Its symptoms, as an eye witness reported, included "tumorous outgrowths at the roots of thighs and arms and simultaneously bleeding ulcerations, which, sometimes the same day, carried the infected rapidly out of this present life."[1]

New research on the DNA of the microbe suggests that the disease began in China, arriving in the West along well-worn routes of trade with the Mongols. Caffa, the Genoese trading post on the northern shore of the Black Sea, was hit in 1347. From there the plague traveled to Europe and the Middle East, immediately striking Constantinople and Cairo and soon leaving the port cities for the hinterlands. In early 1348 the citizens of Pisa and Genoa, fierce rivals on the seas, were being felled without distinction by the disease. Early spring of the same year saw the Black Death at Florence; two months later it had hit Dorset in England. Dormant during the winter, it revived the next spring to infect French ports and countryside, moving on swiftly to Germany. By 1351 it was at Moscow, where it stopped for a time, only to recur in ten- to twelve-year cycles throughout the fourteenth century. (Only the attack of 1346–1353 is called the Black Death.) The disease continued to strike, though at longer intervals, until the eighteenth century. Typical was the experience of Esteve Beyneyc, a well-to-do burgher at Limoges (in southern France), who in 1426 drew up a grim list of his children's and wife's recent deaths:

> Mathivot, my son, was born Sunday evening the 16th day of the month of August in the year 1424. And Mathieu de Julien held him [over the baptismal font as godfather]. And his godmother was Valeria, my niece…. And he went to Paradise Friday morning, the 30th day of the month of August in the year 1426. And there was in that year great mortality. And at that same time my wife, his mother—may God pardon her—died there, and many [other] people. Valeria, my daughter, was born on Friday the 16th day of the month of June in the year 1424. And my son Guilhoumot held her [over the baptismal font]. And she went to Paradise on Wednesday, the 24th day of the month of July in the year 1426. And there was then great mortality.[2]

The effect on Europe's population was immediate and devastating. At Paris, by no means the city hardest hit, about half the population died, mainly children and poor people. In eastern Normandy, perhaps 70 to 80 per cent of the population succumbed. At Bologna, even the most robust—men able to bear arms—were reduced by 35 per cent in the course of 1348. Demographic recovery across Europe began only in the second half of the fifteenth century.

Deaths, especially of the poor, led to acute labor shortages in both town and country. In 1351, King Edward III (r.1327–1377) of England issued the *Statute of Laborers*, forbidding workers to take pay higher than pre-plague wages and fining employers who offered more. Similar laws were promulgated—and flouted—elsewhere. In the countryside, landlords

Plate 8.1 (facing page): Corpses Confront the Living (*c*.1441). This unusual illustration shows not only the physical confrontations between the dead and the living but also verbal exchanges written on scrolls in front of each protagonist. For example, the king (top right), proudly faces the viewer and boasts, "I am the king and the emperor and a lover of delights." But the corpse calls his bluff: "Once you ruled over nations; now you are conquered by worms."

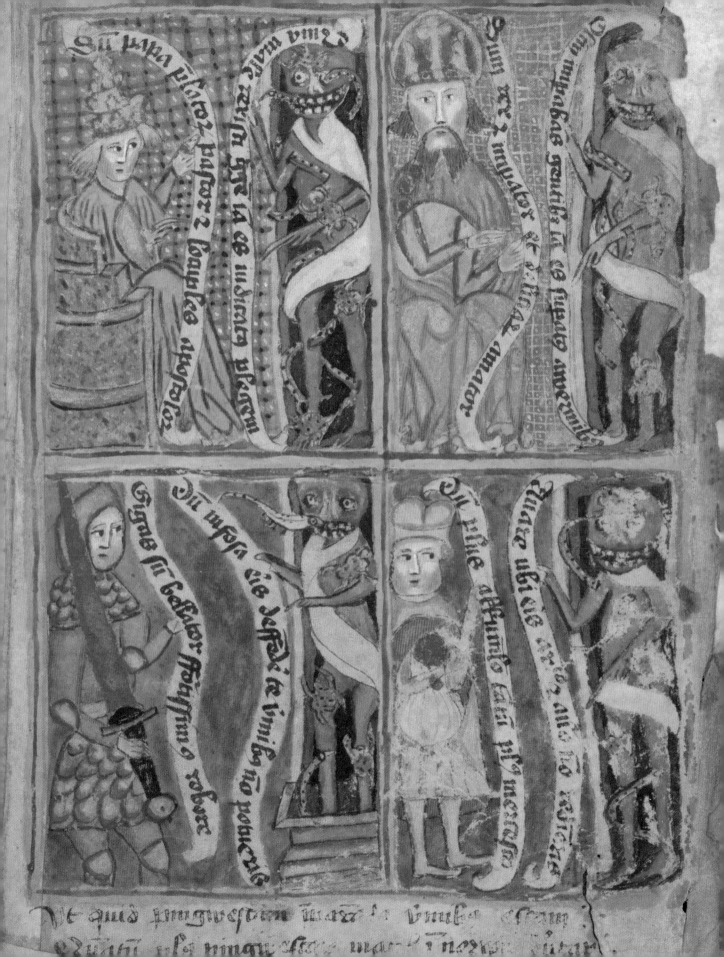

needed to keep their profits up even as their workforce was decimated. They were obliged to strike bargains with enterprising peasants, furnishing them, for example, with oxen and seed; or they turned their land to new uses, such as pasturage. In the cities, the guilds and other professions recruited new men, survivors of the plague. Able to marry and set up households at younger ages, these *nouveaux riches* helped reconstitute the population. Although many widows were now potentially the heads of households, deeply rooted customs tended to push them either into new marriages (in northern Europe) or (in southern Europe) into the house of some male relative, whether brother, son, or son-in-law.

The plague affected both desires and sentiments. Upward mobility in town and country meant changes in consumption patterns, as formerly impoverished groups found new wealth. They chose silk clothing over wool, beer over water. In Italy, where a certain theoretical equality within the communes had restrained consumer spending, cities passed newly toughened laws to restrict finery. In Florence in 1349, for example, a year after the plague first struck there, the town crier roamed the city shouting out new or renewed prohibitions: clothes could not be adorned with gold or silver; capes could not be lined with fur; the wicks of funeral candles had to be made of cotton; women could wear no more than two rings, only one of which could be set with a precious stone; and so on. As always, such sumptuary legislation affected women more than men.

Small wonder that eventually death became an obsession and a cult. A newly intense interest in the macabre led to new artistic themes. Plate 8.1 shows one side of a manuscript folio that illustrated the various people whom death would visit sooner or later. In each of the four frames Death, personified by a corpse (outlined by its coffin and covered with the lizards, snakes, worms, maggots, and frogs that were consuming its flesh), confronts a living person. A pope is in the first box, an emperor in the next, below left is a knight, below right a burgher. On the other side of the folio page (not shown here) the corpses meet a young woman, a young man, an astrologer, and a shepherd.

Similarly, in the artistic and literary genre known as the Dance of Death, life itself became a dance with death, as men and women from every class were escorted—sooner or later—to the grave by ghastly skeletons. Blaming their own sins for the plague, penitent pilgrims, occasionally bearing whips to flagellate themselves, crowded the roads. Rumors flew, accusing the Jews of causing the plague by poisoning the wells. The idea spread from southern France and northern Spain (where, as we have seen [p. 251], similar charges had already been leveled in the 1320s) to Switzerland, Strasbourg, and throughout Germany. At Strasbourg more than 900 Jews were burned in 1349, right in their own cemetery.

Upheavals of War

"And westward, look! Under the Martian Gate," wrote the English poet Geoffrey Chaucer (*c.*1340–1400) in *The Canterbury Tales*, continuing,

Arcita and his hundred knights await,
And now, under a banner of red, march on.
And at the self-same moment Palamon
Enters by Venus' Gate and takes his place
Under a banner of white, with cheerful face.
You had not found, though you had searched the earth,
Two companies so equal in their worth.[3]

Chaucer's association of war with "cheer" and "valor" was a central conceit of chivalry, giving a rosy tint to the increasingly "total" wars that engulfed even civilian populations in the fourteenth and fifteenth centuries. In the East, the Ottoman Turks took the Byzantine Empire by storm; in the West, England and France fought a bitter Hundred Years' War. Dynastic feuds and princely encroachments marked a tumultuous period in which the map of Europe was remade.

THE OTTOMAN EMPIRE

The establishment of a new Islamic empire—the Ottoman—just south of the Danube River marked an astonishing transformation of Europe's southeast. (See Map 8.1.) It began very gradually in the thirteenth century, as Turkish tribal leaders carved out ephemeral principalities for themselves in the interstices between Mongol-ruled Rum and the Byzantine Empire. At the beginning of the fourteenth century, Othman (d.1324/1326), after whom the Ottomans were named, took the lead. (See the list of Ottoman Emirs and Sultans on p. 343.) About 150 years later the chronicler Ashikpashazade, looking back on Othman's achievements, stressed his wisdom, his cunning, and, above all, his legitimacy by right of *jihad*: "What does the sultan [the last Seljuk ruler of Rum] have to do with it?" the chronicler has Othman ask those who want the sultan's permission before appointing a religious leader. "It is true that the sultan endowed me with this banner. But it is I who carried the banner into battle with the infidels!"[4]

Attracting other Turkish princes to fight alongside him, Othman carved out a principality in Byzantium's backyard. But rather than unite in the face of these developments, rival factions within the Byzantine state tried to make use of the Ottomans. It was as ally to one claimant for the Byzantine throne that Ottoman troops arrived in Gallipoli in 1354. They remained long after their welcome had run out. In the 1360s they took Thrace, and then, under the energetic leadership of Bayezid I (r.1389–1402), they conquered much of the Balkans, taking Serbia (at the battle of Kosovo) in 1389 and Bulgaria in 1393.

To the east, the Ottoman advance was aided by the weakening of Mongol power, which began in China with the overthrow of the khanate there. To be sure, the Ottomans were halted by Timur the Lame (Tamerlane) (1336–1405), a warrior leader from the region of Samarkand, who saw himself as restoring the Mongol Empire. But with Timur's death, the Ottomans slowly regained their hold, in part because of the superiority of their elite

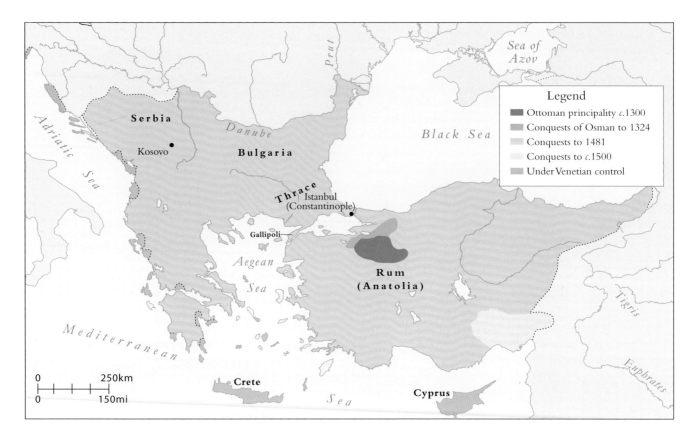

Map 8.1: The Ottoman Empire, *c.*1500

troops, the janissaries, professional soldiers of slave origin. Adopting the new military hardware of the west—cannons and harquebuses (heavy matchlock guns)—the Ottomans retook Anatolia and the Balkans. Under Mehmed II the Conqueror (r.1444–1446, 1451–1481), their cannons accomplished what former sieges had never done, breaching the thick walls of Constantinople in 1453 and bringing the Byzantine Empire to an end.

The new Ottoman state had come to stay. Its rise was due to its military power and the weakness of its neighbors. But its longevity—it did not begin to decline until the late seventeenth century—was due to more complicated factors. Building on a theory of absolutism that echoed similar ideas in the Christian West, the Ottoman rulers acted as the sole guarantors of law and order; they considered even the leaders of the mosques to be their functionaries, soldiers without arms. Prospering from taxes imposed on their relatively well-to-do peasantry, the new rulers spent their money on roads to ease troop transport and a navy powerful enough to oust the Italians from their eastern Mediterranean outposts. Eliminating all signs of rebellion (which meant, for example, brutally putting down Serb and Albanian revolts), the Ottomans created a new world power.

The Ottoman state eventually changed Europe's orientation. Europeans could—and did—continue to trade in the Mediterranean. But on the whole they preferred to treat the Ottomans as a barrier to the Orient. Not long after the fall of Constantinople, as we shall see, the first transatlantic voyages began as a new route to the East.

THE HUNDRED YEARS' WAR

Although in the seventeenth century English rulers would set their sights on the Americas and the Indies, between 1350 and 1500 they were still preoccupied with older claims. The Hundred Years' War (in fact fought sporadically over more than a century, from 1337 to 1453) was the English king's bid to become ruler of France. Beyond this dynastic dispute were England's long-standing claims to Continental lands, many of which had been confiscated by Philip II of France and the rest by Philip VI in 1337. (See Map 8.2, paying particular attention to English possessions in 1337.) Beyond that were Flemish–English economic relations, to which English prosperity and taxes were tied. Ultimately, the war was not so much between England and France as between two conceptions of France: one, a centralized monarchy, the other, an association of territories ruled by counts and dukes.

As son of Isabella, the last living child of French king Philip the Fair, Edward III of England was in line for the French throne when Charles IV died in 1328. The French nobles awarded it, instead, to Philip VI, the first Valois king of France. (See Genealogy 8.1: Kings of France and England and the Dukes of Burgundy during the Hundred Years' War.) Edward's claims led to the first phase of the Hundred Years' War. Looking back on it, the chronicler Froissart tried to depict its knightly fighters as gallant protagonists:

> As soon as Lord Walter de Manny discovered ... that a formal declaration of war had been made ... he gathered together 40 lances [each lance being a knight, a servant, and two horses], good companions from Hainaut and England ... [because] he had vowed in England in the hearing of ladies and lords that, "If war breaks out between my lord the king of England and Philip of Valois who calls himself king of France, I will be the first to arm himself and capture a castle or town in the kingdom of France."[5]

In fact knights like Walter de Manny and his men were outmoded; the real heroes of the war were the longbowmen—non-knightly fighters who, by wielding a new-style bow and arrows that flew far and penetrated deeply, gave English troops the clear advantage. By 1360, the size of English possessions in southern France was approximately what it had been in the twelfth century. (Look at Map 8.2 again, this time considering "English Possessions in 1360," and compare it with Map 6.4 on p. 206.)

English successes were nevertheless short-lived. Harrying the border of Aquitaine, French forces chipped away at it in the course of the 1380s. Meanwhile, sentiments for peace were gaining strength in both England and France; a treaty to put an end to the fighting for a generation was drawn up in 1396. Yet the "generation" was hardly grown when Henry V (r.1413–1422) came to the throne and revived England's Continental claims. Demanding nearly all of the land that the Angevins had held in the twelfth century, he

Following pages:

Map 8.2: The First Phase of the Hundred Years' War, 1337–1360

Genealogy 8.1: Kings of France and England and the Dukes of Burgundy during the Hundred Years' War

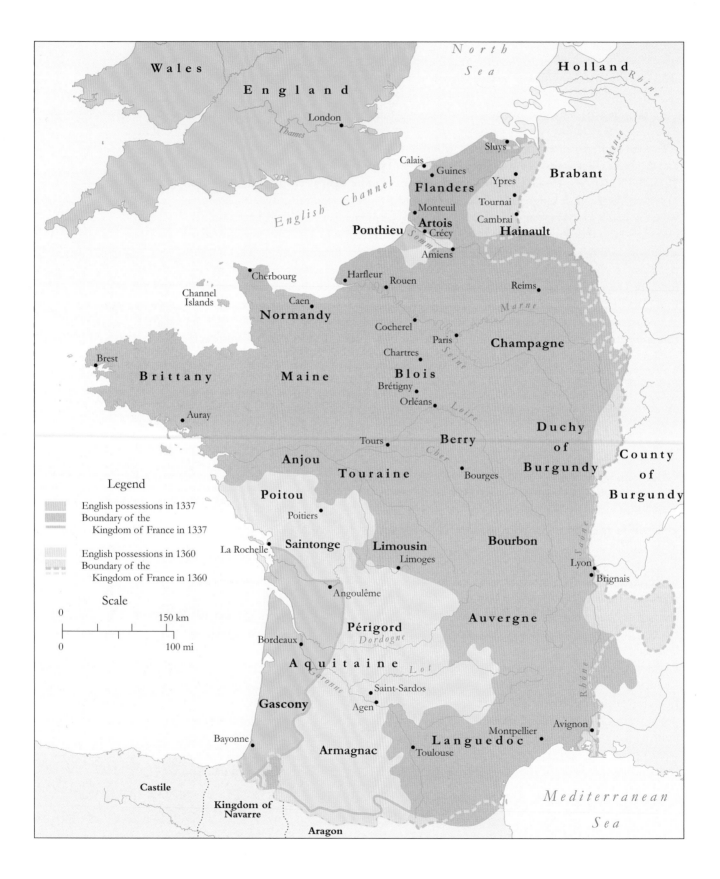

Wales

England

London

Thames

North Sea

Holland

Rhine

Meuse

Sluys

Calais

Guines

Flanders

Ypres

Brabant

Monteuil

Tournai

Cambrai

Artois

Ponthieu

Crécy

Hainault

Somme

Amiens

English Channel

Cherbourg

Harfleur

Rouen

Reims

Channel Islands

Caen

Normandy

Marne

Cocherel

Paris

Chartres

Seine

Champagne

Brest

Brittany

Maine

Blois

Brétigny

Orléans

Loire

Duchy of Burgundy

County of Burgundy

Auray

Tours

Berry

Anjou

Touraine

Cher

Bourges

Poitou

Poitiers

La Rochelle

Saintonge

Limousin

Limoges

Bourbon

Lyon

Saône

Brignais

Angoulême

Auvergne

Périgord

Dordogne

Bordeaux

Garonne

Aquitaine

Lot

Saint-Sardos

Gascony

Agen

Bayonne

Armagnac

Languedoc

Toulouse

Montpellier

Avignon

Rhône

Castile

Kingdom of Navarre

Aragon

Mediterranean Sea

Legend

English possessions in 1337
Boundary of the
  Kingdom of France in 1337

English possessions in 1360
Boundary of the
  Kingdom of France in 1360

Scale

0   150 km

0   100 mi

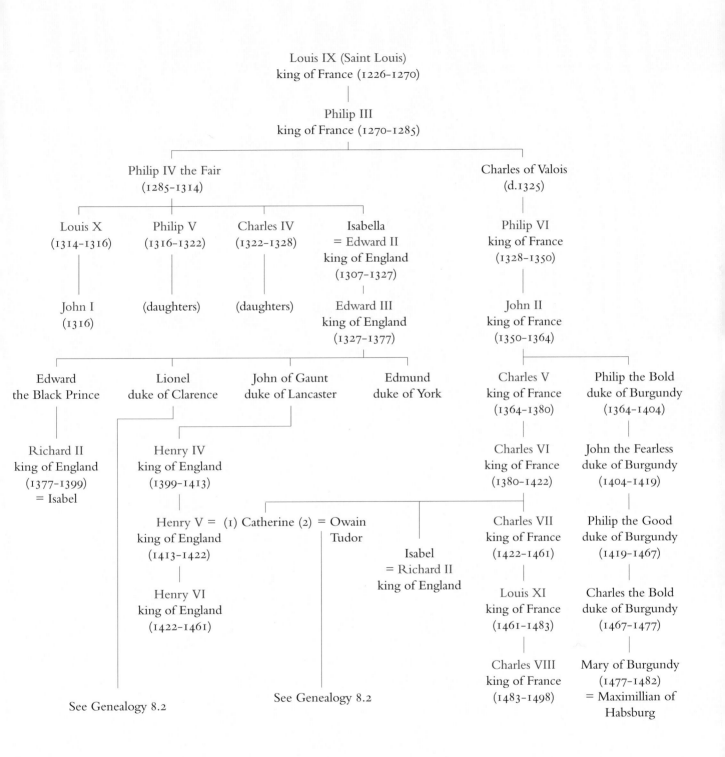

Louis IX (Saint Louis)
king of France (1226-1270)

Philip III
king of France (1270-1285)

Philip IV the Fair
(1285-1314)

Charles of Valois
(d.1325)

Louis X
(1314-1316)

Philip V
(1316-1322)

Charles IV
(1322-1328)

Isabella
= Edward II
king of England
(1307-1327)

Philip VI
king of France
(1328-1350)

John I
(1316)

(daughters)

(daughters)

Edward III
king of England
(1327-1377)

John II
king of France
(1350-1364)

Edward
the Black Prince

Lionel
duke of Clarence

John of Gaunt
duke of Lancaster

Edmund
duke of York

Charles V
king of France
(1364-1380)

Philip the Bold
duke of Burgundy
(1364-1404)

Richard II
king of England
(1377-1399)
= Isabel

Henry IV
king of England
(1399-1413)

Charles VI
king of France
(1380-1422)

John the Fearless
duke of Burgundy
(1404-1419)

Henry V = (1) Catherine (2) = Owain
king of England   Tudor
(1413-1422)

Isabel
= Richard II
king of England

Charles VII
king of France
(1422-1461)

Philip the Good
duke of Burgundy
(1419-1467)

Henry VI
king of England
(1422-1461)

Louis XI
king of France
(1461-1483)

Charles the Bold
duke of Burgundy
(1467-1477)

See Genealogy 8.2

See Genealogy 8.2

Charles VIII
king of France
(1483-1498)

Mary of Burgundy
(1477-1482)
= Maximillian of
Habsburg

struck France in 1415 in a concerted effort to conquer both cities and countryside. Soon Normandy was Henry's, and, determined to keep it, he forced all who refused him loyalty into exile, confiscating their lands and handing the property over to his own followers. (See Map 8.3.)

Henry's plans were aided by a new regional power: Burgundy. A marvel of shrewd marriage alliances, canny purchases, and outright military conquests, the Duchy of Burgundy forged by Philip the Bold (r.1364–1404) was a cluster of principalities with one center at Dijon (the traditional Burgundy) and another at Lille, in the north (the traditional Flanders). The only unity in these disparate regions was provided by the dukes themselves, who traveled tirelessly from one end of their duchy to the other, participating in elaborate ceremonies—lavish entry processions into cities, wedding and birth festivities, funerals—and commissioning art and music that both celebrated and justified their power. (See Map 8.4.)

Map 8.3 (facing page): English and Burgundian Hegemony in France, *c*.1430

Like the kings of France, Philip the Bold was a Valois, but his grandson, Philip the Good (r.1419–1467), decided to link his destiny with England, long the major trading partner of Flanders. Thus, with the support of the Burgundians, the English easily marched into Paris, inadvertently helped by the French king, Charles VI (r.1380–1422), whose frequent bouts of insanity created a vacuum at the top of France's leadership. The Treaty of Troyes (1420) made Henry V the heir to the throne of France.

Had Henry lived, he might have made good his claim. But he died in 1422, leaving behind an infant son to take the crown of France under the regency of the duke of Bedford. Meanwhile, with Charles VI dead the same year, Charles VII, the French "dauphin," or crown prince, was disheartened by defeats. Only in 1429 did his mood change: Jeanne d'Arc (Joan of Arc), a sixteen-year-old peasant girl from Domrémy (part of a small enclave in northern France still loyal to the dauphin), arrived at Chinon, where Charles was holed up, to convince him and his theologians that she had been divinely sent to defeat the English. As she wrote in an audacious letter to the English commanders, "The Maid [as she called herself] has come on behalf of God to reclaim the blood royal. She is ready to make peace, if you [the English] are willing to settle with her by evacuating France."[6]

In effect, Jeanne inherited the moral capital that had been earned by the Beguines and other women mystics. When the English forces laid siege to Orléans (the prelude to their moving into southern France—see Map 8.3), Jeanne not only wrote the letter to the English quoted above but was allowed to join the French army. Its "miraculous" defeat of the English at Orléans (1429) turned the tide. "Oh! What an honor for the feminine sex!" wrote the poet Christine de Pisan (*c*.1364–*c*.1431), continuing,

> It is obvious that God loves it
> That all those vile people,
> Who had laid the whole kingdom to waste—
> By a woman this realm is now made safe and sound,
> Something more than five thousand men could not have done—
> And those traitors purged forever![7]

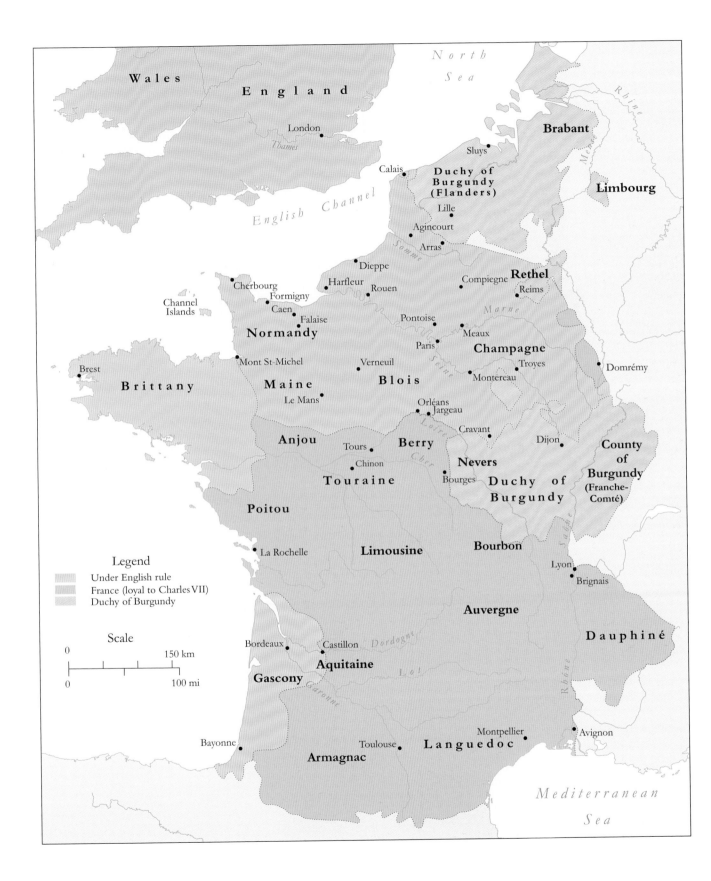

Wales

England

London

Thames

North Sea

English Channel

Calais

Sluys

Brabant

Duchy of Burgundy (Flanders)

Lille

Agincourt

Arras

Limbourg

Meuse

Rhine

Dieppe

Cherbourg

Formigny

Harfleur

Rouen

Somme

Compiegne

Rethel

Reims

Channel Islands

Caen

Falaise

Pontoise

Marne

Paris

Meaux

Champagne

Troyes

Domrémy

Normandy

Brest

Mont St-Michel

Verneuil

Blois

Montereau

Seine

Brittany

Maine

Le Mans

Orléans

Jargeau

Cravant

Dijon

Anjou

Tours

Berry

Loire

Nevers

County of Burgundy (Franche-Comté)

Chinon

Bourges

Duchy of Burgundy

Touraine

Cher

Poitou

La Rochelle

Limousine

Bourbon

Lyon

Brignais

Saône

Legend

Under English rule

France (loyal to Charles VII)

Duchy of Burgundy

Auvergne

Dauphiné

Scale

0

150 km

0

100 mi

Bordeaux

Castillon

Dordogne

Aquitaine

Lot

Gascony

Garonne

Bayonne

Toulouse

Armagnac

Montpellier

Avignon

Rhône

Languedoc

Mediterranean Sea

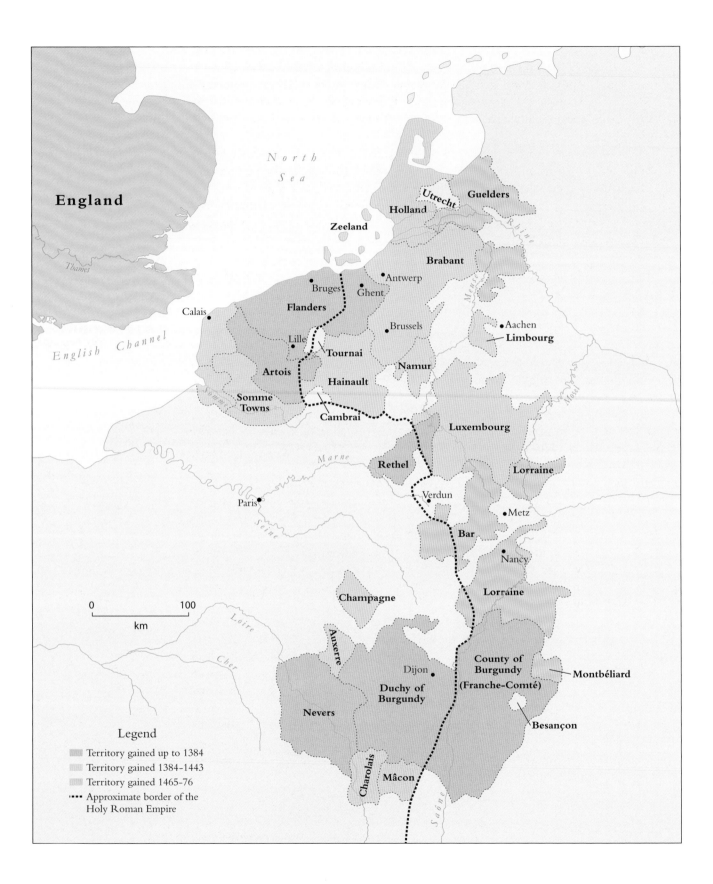

England

North
Sea

Thames

Calais

English Channel

Somme

Marne

Paris

Seine

0   100
km

Loire

Cher

Zeeland

Bruges
Ghent
Antwerp

Flanders

Lille
Tournai

Artois
Hainault

Somme
Towns

Cambrai

Rethel

Verdun

Bar

Holland

Utrecht

Guelders

Brabant

Brussels

Namur

Rhine

Meuse

Aachen
Limbourg

Luxembourg

Lorraine

Metz

Moselle

Nancy

Lorraine

Champagne

Auxerre

Dijon

Duchy of
Burgundy

Nevers

County of
Burgundy
(Franche-Comté)

Montbéliard

Besançon

Charolais
Mâcon

Saône

Legend

Territory gained up to 1384
Territory gained 1384–1443
Territory gained 1465–76
Approximate border of the
Holy Roman Empire

Soon thereafter Jeanne led Charles to Reims, deep in English territory, where he was anointed king. Captured by Burgundians in league with the English in 1430, Jeanne was ransomed by the English and tried as a heretic the following year. Found guilty, she was famously burned, eventually becoming a symbol of martyrdom as well as triumphant French resistance.

In fact it took many more years, indeed until 1453, for the French to win the war. One reason for the French triumph was their systematic use of gunpowder-fired artillery: in one fifteen-month period around 1450, the French relied heavily on siege guns such as cannons to capture more than seventy English strongholds. Diplomatic relations helped the French as well: after 1435, the duke of Burgundy abandoned the English and supported the French, at least in lukewarm fashion.

The Hundred Years' War devastated France in the short run. During battles, armies destroyed cities and harried the countryside, breaking the morale of the population. Even when not officially "at war," bands of soldiers—"Free Companies" of mercenaries that hired themselves out to the highest bidder, whether in France, Spain, or Italy—roved the countryside, living off the gains of pillage. Nevertheless, soon after 1453, France began a long and steady recovery. Merchants invested in commerce, peasants tilled the soil, and the king exercised more power than ever before. A standing army was created, trained, billeted, and supplied with weapons, including the new "fiery" artillery, all under royal command.

Map 8.4 (facing page): The Duchy of Burgundy, 1363–1477

Burgundy, so brilliantly created a century earlier, fell apart even more quickly: Charles the Bold's expansionist policies led to the formation of a coalition against him, and he died in battle in 1477. His daughter Mary, his only heir, tried to stave off French control by quickly marrying Maximilian of Habsburg. This was only partly successful: while she brought the County of Burgundy and most of the Low Countries to the Holy Roman Empire, the French kings were able to absorb the southern portions of the duchy of Burgundy as well as the Somme Towns in the north. Soon (in 1494) France was leading an expedition into Italy, claiming the crown of Naples.

In England, the Hundred Years' War brought about a similar political transformation. Initially France's victory affected mainly the topmost rank of the royal house itself. The progeny of Edward III formed two rival camps, York and Lancaster (named after some of their lands in northern England). (See Genealogy 8.2: York and Lancastrian [Tudor] Kings.) Already in 1399, unhappy with Richard II, who had dared to disinherit him, the Lancastrian Henry had engineered the king's deposition and taken the royal scepter himself as Henry IV. But when his grandson Henry VI lost the war to France, the Yorkists quickly took advantage of the fact. A series of dynastic wars—later dubbed the "Wars of the Roses" after the white rose badge of the Yorkists and the red of the Lancastrians—was fought from 1455 to 1487. In 1461, Edward of York deposed Henry, becoming Edward IV. Upon his death in 1483 there was further intrigue as his brother, Richard III, seized the eleven-year-old Edward V and his brother, packing them off to the Tower of London, where they were soon murdered. Two years later, Richard himself was dead on the fields of Bosworth, and Henry VII, the first Tudor king, was on the throne.

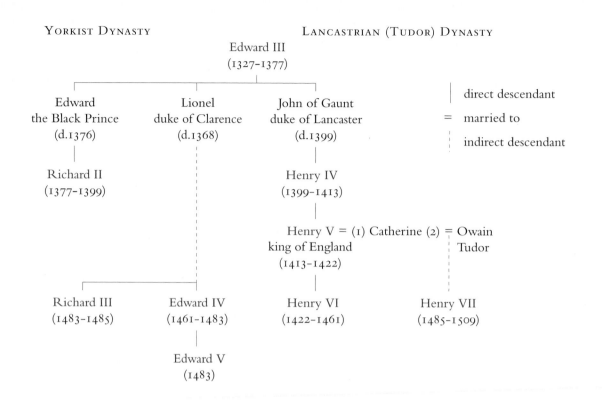

Edward III
(1327–1377)

Edward
the Black Prince
(d.1376)

Lionel
duke of Clarence
(d.1368)

John of Gaunt
duke of Lancaster
(d.1399)

direct descendant

= married to

indirect descendant

Richard II
(1377–1399)

Henry IV
(1399–1413)

Henry V = (1) Catherine (2) = Owain
king of England   Tudor
(1413–1422)

Richard III
(1483–1485)

Edward IV
(1461–1483)

Henry VI
(1422–1461)

Henry VII
(1485–1509)

Edward V
(1483)

Genealogy 8.2: York and Lancastrian (Tudor) Kings

All of this would later be grist for Shakespeare's historical dramas, but at the time it was more the stuff of tragedy, as whole noble lines were killed off, Yorkist lands were confiscated for the crown, and people caught in the middle longed for a strong king who would keep the peace. When the dust settled, the Tudors were far more powerful than previous English kings had ever been.

Princes, Knights, and Citizens

The Hundred Years' War, the Wars of the Roses, and other, more local wars of the fifteenth century brought to the fore a kind of super-prince: mighty kings (as in England, Scotland, and France), dukes (as in Burgundy), and *signori* (in Italy). All were supported by mercenary troops and up-to-date weaponry, putting knights and nobles in the shade. Yet the end of chivalry was paradoxically the height of the chivalric fantasy. We have already seen how delighted Froissart was by Walter de Manny's chivalric vow. Heraldry, a system of symbols that distinguished each knight by the sign on his shield, came into full flower around the same time. Originally meant to advertise the fighter and his heroic deeds on the battle-field, it soon came to symbolize his family, decorating both homes and tombs. Kings and other great lords founded and promoted chivalric orders with fantastic names—the Order of the Garter, the Order of the Golden Buckle, the Order of the Golden Fleece. All had mainly social and honorific functions, sponsoring knightly tournaments and convivial feasts precisely when knightly jousts and communal occasions were no longer useful for war.

While super-princes were the norm, there were some exceptions. In the mountainous terrain of the alpine passes, a coalition of members of urban and rural communes along with some lesser nobles promised to aid one another against the Habsburg emperors. Taking advantage of rivalries within the Holy Roman Empire, the Swiss Confederation created *c.*1500 a militant state of its own. Structured as a league, the Confederation put power into the hands of urban citizenry and members of peasant communes. The nobility gradually disappeared as new elites from town and countryside took over. Unlike the great European powers in its "republican" organization, Switzerland nevertheless conveniently served as a reservoir of mercenary troops for its princely neighbors.

Venice maintained its own republicanism via a different set of compromises. It was dominated by a Great Council from whose membership many of the officers of the state were elected, including the "doge," a life-long position. Between 1297 and 1324 the size of the Council grew dramatically: to its membership of 210 in 1296, more than a thousand new names were added by 1340. At the same time, however, the Council was gradually closed off to all but certain families, which were in this way turned into a hereditary aristocracy. Accepting this fact constituted the compromise of the lower classes. Its counterpart by the ruling families was to suppress (in large measure) their private interests in favor of the general welfare of the city. That welfare depended mainly on the sea for both necessities and wealth. Only at the end of the fourteenth century did the Venetians begin to expand within Italy itself, becoming a major land power in the region. But as it gobbled up Bergamo and Verona, Venice collided with the interests of Milan. Wars between the two city-states ended only with the Peace of Lodi in 1454. Soon the three other major Italian powers—Florence, the papacy, and Naples—joined Venice and Milan in the Italic League. (See Map 8.5.) The situation in Naples eventually brought this status quo to an end. Already in 1442 Alfonso V of Aragon had entered Naples as Alfonso I, ending Angevin rule there. A half century later, the Valois king of France's desire to reinstate French rule over Naples helped fuel his invasion of Italy in 1494.

Revolts in Town and Country

While power at the top consolidated, discontent seethed from below. Throughout the fourteenth century popular uprisings across Europe gave vent to discontent. The "popular" component of these revolts should not be exaggerated, as many were led by petty knights or wealthy burghers. But they also involved large masses of people, some of whom were very poor indeed. Although at times articulating universal principles, these revolts were nevertheless deeply rooted in local grievances.

Long accustomed to a measure of self-government in periodic assemblies that reaffirmed the customs of the region, the peasants of Flanders reacted boldly when the count's officials began to try to collect new taxes. Between 1323 and 1328, Flemish peasants drove out the officials and their noble allies, redistributing the lands that they confiscated. The peasants set up an army, established courts, collected taxes, and effectively governed themselves.

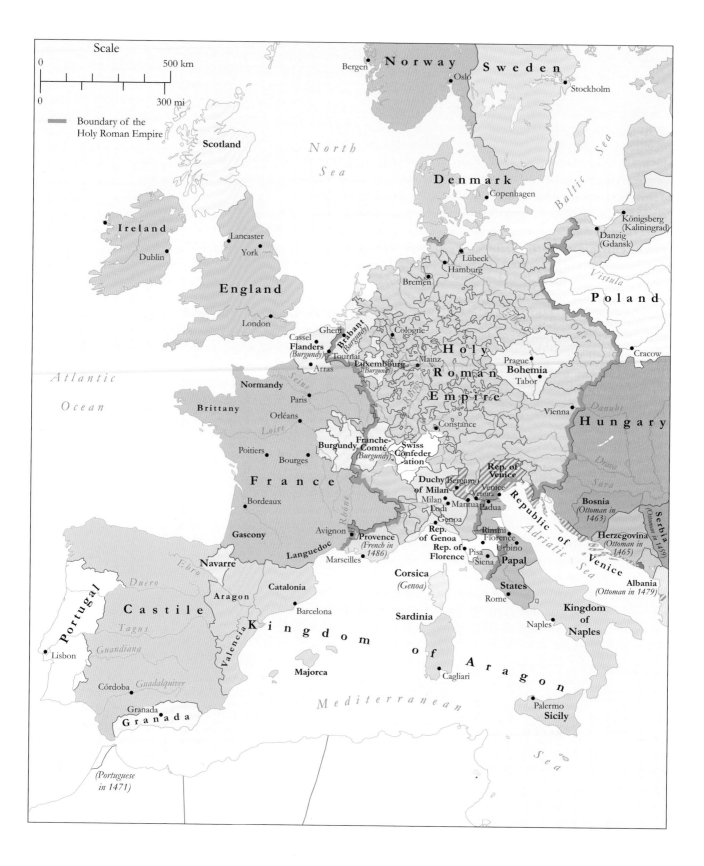

Scale

0   500 km

0   300 mi

Boundary of the
Holy Roman Empire

North
Sea

Scotland

Ireland

Lancaster
York

Dublin

England

London

Atlantic

Ocean

Cassel
Ghent
Brabant
(Burgundy)
Flanders
(Burgundy)
Tournai
Arras
Luxembourg
(Burgundy)

Normandy

Seine
Paris

Brittany

Orléans

Loire

Poitiers
Bourges

France

Bordeaux

Gascony

Avignon

Languedoc

Marseilles

Navarre

Portugal

Castile

Lisbon

Córdoba

Granada

Granada

Duero

Tagus

Guandiana

Guadalquiver

Aragon

Catalonia

Barcelona

Valencia

Kingdom

Majorca

Ebro

(Portuguese
in 1471)

Norway   Sweden

Bergen

Oslo

Stockholm

Baltic

Sea

Denmark

Copenhagen

Königsberg
(Kaliningrad)

Danzig
(Gdansk)

Lübeck
Hamburg

Bremen

Cologne

Holy

Roman

Empire

Mainz

Vistula

Poland

Cracow

Prague
Bohemia
Tabor

Vienna

Constance

Danube

Hungary

Franche-
Comté
(Burgundy)

Burgundy

Swiss
Confeder-
ation

Drava

Provence
(French in
1486)

Duchy
of Milan

Milan
Lodi
Genoa

Rep.
of Genoa

Rep. of
Florence

Corsica
(Genoa)

Bergamo
Mantua
Padua

Rep. of
Venice

Venice
Verona

Sava

Bosnia
(Ottoman in
1463)

Republic of

Adriatic

Rimini
Florence
Pisa
Siena

Urbino

Papal

States

Rome

Sardinia

Cagliari

Herzegovina
(Ottoman in
1465)

Venice

Serbia
(Ottoman in 1459)

Albania
(Ottoman in 1479)

Kingdom
of
Naples

Naples

of   Aragon

Majorca

Mediterranean

Palermo
Sicily

Sea

The cities of Flanders, initially small, independent pockets outside of the peasants' jurisdiction, soon followed suit, with the less wealthy citizens taking over city government. It took the combined forces of the rulers of France and Navarre plus a papal declaration of crusade to crush the peasants at the battle of Cassel in 1328.

Anti-French and anti-tax activities soon resumed in Flanders, however, this time at Ghent, where the weavers had been excluded from city government since 1320. When England prepared for the opening of the Hundred Years' War, it cut off wool exports to Flanders, putting the weavers (who depended on English wool) out of work. At Ghent the weavers took the hint and rallied to the English cause. Led by Jacob van Artevelde, himself a landowner but now spokesman for the rebels, the weavers overturned the city government. By 1339, Artevelde's supporters dominated not only Ghent but also much of northern Flanders. A year later, he was welcoming the English king Edward III to Flanders as king of France. Although Artevelde was assassinated in 1345 by weavers who thought he had betrayed their cause, the tensions that brought him to the fore continued. The local issues that pitted weavers against the other classes in the city were exacerbated by the ongoing hostility between England and France. Like a world war, the Hundred Years' War engulfed its bystanders.

Map 8.5 (facing page): Western Europe, *c*.1450

In France, uprisings in the mid-fourteenth century signaled further strains of the war. At the disastrous battle of Poitiers (1356), King John II of France was captured and taken prisoner. The Estates General, which prior to the battle had agreed to heavy taxes to counter the English, met in the wake of Poitiers to allot blame and reform the government. When the new regent (the ruler in John's absence) stalled in instituting the reforms, Étienne Marcel, head of the merchants of Paris, led a plot to murder some royal councilors and take control of Paris. But the presence of some Free Company troops in Paris led to disorder there, and some of Marcel's erstwhile supporters blamed him for the riots, assassinating him in 1358.

Meanwhile, outside Paris, the Free Companies harried the countryside. In 1358 a peasant movement formed to resist them. Called the Jacquerie by dismissive chroniclers (probably after their derisive name for its leader, Jacques Bonhomme—Jack Goodfellow), it soon turned into an uprising against the nobility, failures as knights (in the eyes of the peasants) because of their loss at Poitiers and their inability to defend the rural peace. The revolt was depicted in sensationally gory detail: "Those evil men," wrote Froissart, "pillaged and burned everything and violated and killed all the ladies and girls without mercy, like mad dogs."[8] Perhaps. But the repression of the Jacquerie was at least equally brutal and, in most places, quicker.

More permanent in their consequences were peasant movements in England; Wat Tyler's Rebellion of 1381 is the most famous. During this revolt, groups of "commons" (in this case mainly country folk from southeast England) converged on London to demand an end to serfdom: "And they required that for the future no man should be in serfdom, nor make any manner of homage or suit to any lord, but should give a rent of 4 pennies an acre for his land."[9] Most immediately, the revolt was a response to a poll tax of one shilling per person, the third fiscal imposition in four years passed by Parliament to recoup the expenses of war. More profoundly, it was a clash between new expectations of freedom (in the wake of the Black Death, labor was worth much more) and old obligations of servitude. The egalitarian chant of the rebels signaled a growing sense of their own power:

When Adam delved [dug] and Eve span [spun],
Who then was the gentleman?

Although Tyler, the leader of the revolt, was soon killed and the rest of the commons dispersed, the death knell of serfdom in England had in fact been sounded, as the rebels went home to bargain with their landlords for new-style leases.

In the decades just before this in a number of Italian cities, cloth workers chafed under regimes that gave them no say in government. At Florence in 1378, matters came to a head as a coalition of wool workers (most of whom were barred from any guild), small businessmen, and some disaffected guild members challenged the ruling elites. The *ciompi* (wool-carders) rebellion, as the movement was called, succeeded briefly in taking over the Florentine government and permitting some new guilds to form there. But the movement soon splintered, and, strapped for money, it resorted to forced loans, an expedient that backfired. By 1382, the old elite was back in power, determined not to let the lower classes rise again; in the next century, the Florentine republic gave way to rule by a powerful family of bankers, the Medici.

Economic Contraction

While the Black Death was good for the silk trade, and the Hundred Years' War stimulated the manufacture of arms and armor, in other spheres economic contraction was the norm. After 1340, with the disintegration of the Mongol Empire, easy trade relations between Europe and the Far East were destroyed. Within Europe, rulers' war machines were fueled by new taxes and loans—some of them forced. At times, rulers paid back the loans; often they did not. The great import-export houses, which loaned money as part of their banking activities, found themselves advancing too much to rulers all too willing to default. In the 1340s the four largest firms went bankrupt, producing, in domino effect, the bankruptcies of hundreds more.

War did more than gobble up capital. Where armies raged, production stopped. Even in intervals of peace, Free Companies attacked not only the countryside but also merchants on the roads. To ensure its grain supply, Florence was obliged to provide guards all along the route from Bologna. Merchants began investing in insurance policies, not only against losses due to weather but also against robbers and pirates.

Meanwhile, the plague dislocated normal economic patterns. Urban rents fell as houses went begging for tenants, while wages rose as employers sought to attract scarce labor. In the countryside, whole swathes of land lay uncultivated. The monastery of Saint-Denis, so rich and powerful under Abbot Suger in the twelfth century, lost more than half its income from land between 1340 and 1403. As the population fell and the demand for grain decreased, the Baltic region—chief supplier of rye to the rest of Europe—suffered badly; by the fifteenth century, some villages had disappeared.

Yet, as always, the bad luck of some meant the prosperity of others. While Tuscany lost its economic edge, cities in northern Italy and southern Germany gained new muscle, manufacturing armor and fustian (a popular textile made of cotton and flax) and distributing their products across Europe. The center of economic growth was in fact shifting northwards, from the Mediterranean to the European heartlands. There was one unfortunate exception: the fourteenth century saw the burgeoning of the slave trade in southern Europe. Girls, mainly from the Mongol world but also sometimes Greeks or Slavs (and therefore Christians), were herded onto ships; those who survived the harrowing trip across the Mediterranean were sold on the open market in cities such as Genoa, Florence, and Pisa. They were high-prestige purchases, domestic "servants" with the allure of the Orient.

THE CHURCH DIVIDED

The fourteenth and fifteenth centuries saw deep divisions within the church. Popes fought over who had the right to the papacy, and ordinary Catholics disputed about that as well as the very nature of the church itself.

The Great Schism

Between 1378 and 1409, rival popes—one line based in Avignon, the other in Rome—claimed to rule as vicar of Christ; from 1409 to 1417, a third line based in Bologna joined them. (See the list of Popes and Antipopes to 1500 on p. 341.) The popes at each venue excommunicated the others, surrounded themselves with their own college of cardinals, and commanded loyal followers. The Great Schism (1378–1417)—as this period of popes and antipopes is called—was both a spiritual and a political crisis.

Exacerbating political tensions, the schism fed the Hundred Years' War: France supported the pope at Avignon, England the pope at Rome. In some regions the schism polarized a single community: for example, around 1400 at Tournai, on the border of France and Flanders, two rival bishops, each representing a different pope, fought over the diocese. Portugal, more adaptable and farther from the fray, simply changed its allegiance four times.

The crisis began with the best of intentions. Stung by criticism of the Avignon papacy, Pope Gregory XI (1370–1378) left Avignon to return to Rome in 1377. When he died a year later, the cardinals elected an Italian as Urban VI (1378–1389). Finding Urban high-handed, however, the French cardinals quickly thought better of what they had done. At Anagni, declaring Urban's election invalid and calling on him to resign, they elected Clement VII, who installed himself at Avignon. The papal monarchy was now split. The group that went to Avignon depended largely on French resources to support it; the group at Rome survived by establishing a *signoria*, complete with mercenary troops to collect its taxes and fight its wars. Thus Urban's successor, Boniface IX (1389–1404), reconquered the papal states and set up governors (many of them his family members) to rule them. Desperate for more revenues, the popes turned all their prerogatives into sources of income. Boniface, for example, put church benefices on the open market and commercialized "indulgences"—acts of piety (such as viewing a relic or attending a special church feast) for which people were promised release from Purgatory for a specific number of days. Now money payments were declared equivalent to performing the acts. Many people willingly made such purchases; others were outraged that Heaven was for sale.

Solutions to end the schism eventually coalesced around the idea of a council. The "conciliarists"—those who advocated the convening of a council that would have authority over even the pope—included both university men and princes anxious to flex their muscles over the church. At the Council of Pisa (1409), which neither of the popes attended, the delegates deposed them both and elected a new man. But the two deposed popes refused to budge: there were now *three* popes, one at Avignon, one at Rome, and a third at Bologna. The successor of the newest one, John XXIII, turned to the emperor to arrange for another council.

The Council of Constance (1414–1418) met to resolve the papal crisis as well as to institute church reforms. In the first task it succeeded, deposing the three rivals and electing Martin V as pope. In the second, it was less successful, for it did not end the fragmentation of the church. National, even nationalist, churches had begun to form, independent of and sometimes in opposition to papal leadership. Meanwhile the conciliar movement continued, developing an influential theory that held that church authority in the final instance resided in a corporate body (whether representing prelates or more broadly the community of the faithful) rather than the pope.

Popular Religious Movements in England and Bohemia

While the conciliarists worried about the structure of the church, many men and women thought more about their personal relationship with Christ. *The Book of Margery Kempe* is about an English woman (presumably Margery Kempe, though she calls herself "the creature" throughout the book) who had long conversations with the Lord. In "contemplation" she traveled back in time to serve Mary, the mother of Jesus:

> [Mary said to Margery], "follow me, your service pleases me well." Then [Margery] went forth with our Lady [i.e. Mary] and with Joseph [Mary's husband], bearing with her a vessel of sweetened and spiced wine. Then they went forth to Elizabeth, Saint John the Baptist's mother, and, when they met together, both of them worshipped each other, and so they dwelled together with great grace and gladness

twelve weeks.... And then [Margery] went forth with our Lady to Bethlehem and purchased her lodging every night with great reverence, and our Lady was received with a glad manner. Also she begged for our Lady fair white clothes and kerchiefs to swaddle her son when he was born, and, when Jesus was born, she prepared bedding for our Lady to lie in with her blessed son.[10]

This was the Gospel story (see, for example, Luke 1:39–40 and 2:4–7) with a new protagonist!

Others began to rethink the role of the church. In England, the radical Oxford-trained theologian John Wyclif (c.1330–1384), influenced in part by William of Ockham (see p. 266), argued for a very small sphere of action for the church. In his view, the state alone should concern itself with temporal things, the pope's decrees should be limited to what was already in the Gospels, the laity should be allowed to read and interpret the Bible for itself, and the church should stop promulgating the absurd notion of transubstantiation. At first the darling of the king and other powerful men in England (who were glad to hear arguments on behalf of an expanded place for secular rule), Wyclif appealed as well (and more enduringly) to the gentry and literate urban classes. Derisively called "lollards" (idlers) by the church and persecuted as heretics, the followers of Wyclif were largely, though not completely, suppressed in the course of the fifteenth century.

Considerably more successful were the Bohemian disciples of Wyclif. In Bohemia, part of the Holy Roman Empire but long used to its own monarchy (see above, p. 145), the disparities between rich and poor helped create conditions for a new vision of society in which religious and national feeling played equal parts. There were at least three inequities in Bohemia: the Germans held a disproportionate share of its wealth and power, even though Czechs constituted the majority of the population; the church owned almost a third of the land; and the nobility dominated the countryside and considered itself the upholder of the common good. In the hands of Jan Hus (1369/71–1415), the writings of Wyclif were transformed into a call for a reformed church and laity. All were to live in accordance with the laws of God, and the laity could disobey clerics who were more interested in pomp than the salvation of souls. Hus translated parts of the Bible into Czech while encouraging German translations as well. Furthering their vision of equality within the church, Hus's followers demanded that all the faithful be offered not just the bread but also the consecrated wine at Mass. (This was later called Utraquism, from the Latin *sub utraque specie*—communion "in both kinds.") In these ways, the Hussites gave shape to their vision of the church as the community of believers—women and the poor included. Hus's friend Jerome of Prague identified the whole reform movement with the good of the Bohemian nation itself, appropriating the traditional claim of the nobility.

Burned as a heretic at the Council of Constance, Hus nevertheless inspired a movement that transformed the Bohemian church. The Hussites soon disagreed about demands and methods (the most radical, the Taborites, set up a sort of government in exile in southern Bohemia, pooling their resources while awaiting the Second Coming), but most found willing protectors among the Bohemian nobility. In the struggle between these groups and imperial troops—backed by a papal declaration of crusade in Bohemia—a peculiarly Bohemian church was created, with its own special liturgy for the Mass.

Churches under Royal Leadership: France and Spain

"National" churches did not need popular revolts to spark them. Indeed, in France and Spain they were forged in the crucible of growing royal power. In the Pragmatic Sanction of Bourges (1438), Charles VII surveyed the various failings of the church in France and declared himself the guarantor of its reform. Popes were no longer to appoint French prelates nor grant benefices to churchmen; these matters now came under the jurisdiction of the king.

The crown in Spain claimed similar rights about a half-century later, when the marriage of Ferdinand (r.1479–1516) and Isabella (r.1474–1504)—dubbed the "Catholic Monarchs" by the pope—united Aragon and Castile. In their hands, Catholicism became an instrument of militant royal sovereignty. King and queen launched an offensive against the Muslims in Granada (conquering the last bit in 1492). In 1502 the remaining Muslims were required to convert to Christianity or leave Spain. Many chose to convert (coming to be known as *moriscos*), but they were never integrated into the mainstream and were expelled from the kingdom in the early seventeenth century.

The Jews suffered a similar fate even earlier—in fact, right after the 1492 conquest of Granada. Their persecution had deep roots. The relatively peaceful co-existence of Christians and Jews in most of Spain during the twelfth and thirteenth centuries ended in the fourteenth. Virulent anti-Jewish pogroms in 1391 led many Spanish Jews to convert to Christianity (gaining the name *conversos*). But the subsequent successes of the *conversos*—some of whom obtained civil and church offices or married into the nobility—stirred resentment among the "Old Christians." Harnessing popular resentments, the Catholic Monarchs received a papal privilege to set up their own version of the Inquisition in 1478. Under the friar-inquisitor Tomás de Torquemada (1420–1498), wholesale torture and public executions became the norm for disposing of "crypto-Jews." After they conquered Grenada, the monarchs demanded that all remaining Jews convert or leave the country. Many chose exile over *conversos* status. Soon the newly "purified" church of Spain was extended to the New World as well, where papal concessions gave the kings control over church benefices and appointments.

DEFINING STYLES

Everywhere, in fact, kings and other rulers were intervening in church affairs, wresting military force from the nobility, and imposing lucrative taxes to be gathered by their zealous and efficient salaried agents. All of this was largely masked, however, behind brilliant courts that employed every possible means to burnish the image of the prince.

Renaissance Italy

In 1416, taking a break from their jobs at the Council of Constance, three young Italians went off on a "rescue mission." One of them, Cincius Romanus (d. 1445) described the escapade to one of his Latin teachers back in Italy:

> In Germany there are many monasteries with libraries full of Latin books. This aroused the hope in me that some of the works of Cicero, Varro, Livy, and other great men of learning, which seem to have completely vanished, might come to light, if a careful search were instituted. A few days ago, [we] went by agreement to the town of St. Gall. As soon as we went into the library [of the monastery there], we found *Jason's Argonauticon*, written by C. Valerius Flaccus in verse that is both splendid and dignified and not far removed from poetic majesty. Then we found some discussions in prose of a number of Cicero's orations…. In fact we have copies of all these books. But when we carefully inspected the nearby tower of the church of St. Gall in which countless books were kept like captives and the library neglected and infested with dust, worms, soot, and all the things associated with the destruction of books, we all burst into tears.[11]

Cicero, Varro, Livy: these provided the models of Latin and the rules of expression that Cincius and his friends admired. To them the monks of St. Gall were "barbarians" for not wholeheartedly valuing ancient Latin rhetoric, prose, and poetry over all other writings. In the course of the fourteenth century Italian intellectuals turned away from the evolved Latin of their contemporaries to find models in the ancients. Already in 1333 the young Petrarch (1304–1374) had traveled through the Low Countries looking for manuscripts of the ancient authors; he discovered Cicero's *Pro Archia*, a paean to poetry, and carefully copied it out.

Petrarch's taste for ancient eloquence and his ability to write in a new, elegant, "classical" style (whether in Latin or in the vernacular) made him a star. But he was not alone, as Cincius' letter proves; he was simply one of the more famous exemplars of a new group calling themselves "humanists." There had been humanists before: we have seen Saint Anselm's emphasis on Christ's saving humanity, Saint Bernard's evocation of human religious emotion, and Thomas Aquinas's confidence in human reason to scale the heights of truth (see pp. 192 and 266). But the new humanists were more self-conscious about their calling, and they tied it to the cultivation of classical literature.

As Cincius' case also shows, if the humanists' passion was antiquity, their services were demanded with equal ardor by ecclesiastical and secular princes. Cincius worked for Pope John XXIII. Petrarch was similarly employed by princes: for several years, for example, he worked for the Visconti family, the rulers of Milan. As Italian artists associated themselves with humanists, working in tandem with them, they too became part of the movement.

Historians have come to give the name Renaissance to this era of artists and humanists. But the Renaissance was not so much a period as a program. It made the language and art of the ancient past the model for the present; it privileged classical books as "must" reading for an eager and literate elite; and it promoted old, sometimes crumbling, and formerly little-appreciated classical art, sculpture, and architecture as inspiring models for Italian artists and builders. Meanwhile, it downgraded the immediate past—the last thousand years!—as a barbarous "Middle" Age. Above all, the Renaissance gave city communes and wealthy princes alike a new repertory of vocabulary, symbols, and styles, drawn from a resonant and heroic past, with which to associate their present power.

At Florence, for example, where the Medici family held sway in the fifteenth century behind a façade of communal republicanism, the sculptor Donatello (1386–1466) cast a gilded bronze figure of Judith beheading the tyrant Holofernes (Plate 8.2). Commissioned, probably in the 1420s, for the private garden of the Medici Palace, the heroic woman paired with the drunk and groggy Holofernes was meant to present the Medicis as glorious defenders of liberty. An inscription added about forty years later by Piero de' Medici made the symbolism clear: "Kingdoms fall through luxury, cities rise through virtue; behold the neck of pride severed by the hand of humility…. Piero, son of Cosimo Medici has dedicated the statue of this woman to that liberty and fortitude bestowed on the republic by the invincible and constant spirit of the citizens."[12] The unabashed fleshiness and dramatic gestures of the figures were reminiscent of ancient Roman art (see, for example, Plate 1.4 on p. 15) but had many more recent precedents as well (see, for example, Plates 7.9 on p. 273 and 7.11 on p. 275).

The Medici were not the only Florentines who commissioned the new-style art. So did other wealthy merchants and aristocrats, rivalrous neighborhood churches, and confraternities. The painting of *Venus, Cupid, and Mars* by Piero di Cosimo (1462–1522) in Plate 8.3 was probably made as a wedding gift for a wealthy client. It echoed not only a popular theme of ancient art (see Plate 1.1 on p. 12) but also key elements of the classical style: figures with substance and volume, a recognizable natural world in which the figures move (or, in this case, rest), and hints of a private world into which the viewer is intruding.

Renaissance artists did not just imitate ancient models; they also strove to surpass them. Consider the new dome for the cathedral at Florence (Plate 8.4 on p. 310). The Florentine Opera del Duomo, which was responsible for the upkeep of Florence's cathedral, held a competition to decide who would span the huge octagonal opening above the church. The winner was Filippo Brunelleschi (1377–1446). Later one of his many admirers, Leon Battista Alberti, himself an architect, dedicated his book *On Painting* to Brunelleschi, praising the dome as "an enormous structure towering over the skies, and wide enough to cast its shadow all over the Tuscan people, made as it is without any beam or abundance of wooden supports, surely hard to believe as an artifice that it was done at this time when nothing of the kind was ever to have been seen in antiquity."[13]

The Renaissance flourished in many Italian cities besides Florence, among them Rome, Urbino, Mantua, Venice, Milan, and Perugia. A Perugian noblewoman, Atalanta Baglioni, for example, commissioned the artist Raphael (1483–1520) to paint an altarpiece for her private chapel to commemorate the death of her son, Grifonetto. In his *Entombment of Christ* (see Plate 8.5 on p. 311), Raphael joined religious piety to family feeling and admiration for classical themes and representations. The piety and family feeling are obvious: the altar was meant to serve as the backdrop for commemorative masses on behalf of Grifonetto's soul and for Atalanta herself when she died. Viewers would have associated her with the Virgin, mother of the crucified Christ, who appears in the painting fainting with grief. Raphael's reliance on classical precedents is perhaps less evident here than in, say, Piero's painting of Venus. But compare the limp figure of Christ and his straining corpse-bearers with the group carrying the lifeless Meleager in Plate 1.4 on p. 15. It is likely that this ancient sarcophagus, which was well known and admired in Raphael's day, inspired his modeling of Christ and his bearers.

At Milan, Duke Ludovico il Moro (r.1494–1499) gave Leonardo da Vinci (1452–1519) numerous commissions, including painting *The Last Supper* (see Plate 8.6 on pp. 312–13) on one of the walls of the dining hall of a Dominican convent. Here Leonardo demonstrated his mastery of the relatively new science of linear perspective: the hall sheltering Christ and his disciples seems to recede as its walls approach a vanishing point. On the opposite side of the hall, Leonardo added a fresco (now nearly obliterated) of his patron: Ludovico, his wife, and their two children kneeling before an image of the Crucifixion.

These were religious themes, but Ludovico sponsored classical ones as well, some woven into the very fabric of courtly life. At one of his banquets in 1491, for example, boiled fish were presented under covers consisting "of a model of the Coliseum lavishly decorated with gold and mottoes," while a dessert arrived under "ornate lids in gold, in the Royal manner, depicting Rome triumphant with an ox, who together vow never to part, and this represents justice, temperance and great friendship, and many verses testifying to this are recited."[14] No doubt many humanists in Ludovico's employ were kept busy writing the verses.

Plate 8.2 (facing page):
Donatello, *Judith and Holofernes* (c.1420–1430). The dense symbolism of this sculpture allows it to be used for many purposes. Taken literally, it illustrates the moment in the biblical Book of Judith (13:4–10) when "Holofernes lay on his bed, fast asleep, being exceedingly drunk," while Judith, strengthened by prayer, grabbed his sword and "took him by the hair of his head ... struck twice upon his neck, and cut off his head." The Medici took it to justify their extraordinary role in Florence's political life. But in 1494, when the Medici were expelled (temporarily, as it turned out) from the city, and the sculpture was transferred from the private space of the Medici garden to the publically accessible Piazza della Signoria, it signified the triumph of the citizens. How did Judith's image change from that expressed in the *Mirror of Virgins* of the twelfth century in Plate 5.10 on p. 193? What similarities nevertheless remained?

Following pages:

Plate 8.3: Piero di Cosimo, *Venus, Cupid, and Mars* (c.1495–1505). For Florentines steeped in Neo-Platonic ideas, Venus and Mars represented not just ancient mythological lovers but an allegory of the marriage of opposites—in this case peace and war—that harmonized apparent opposites into one perfect form: harmony. Here the wakeful Venus's seduction of Mars has put war to sleep. At the same time, Piero's painting spoke to more earthly concerns: women were said to conceive more beautiful children if they gazed at beautiful forms.

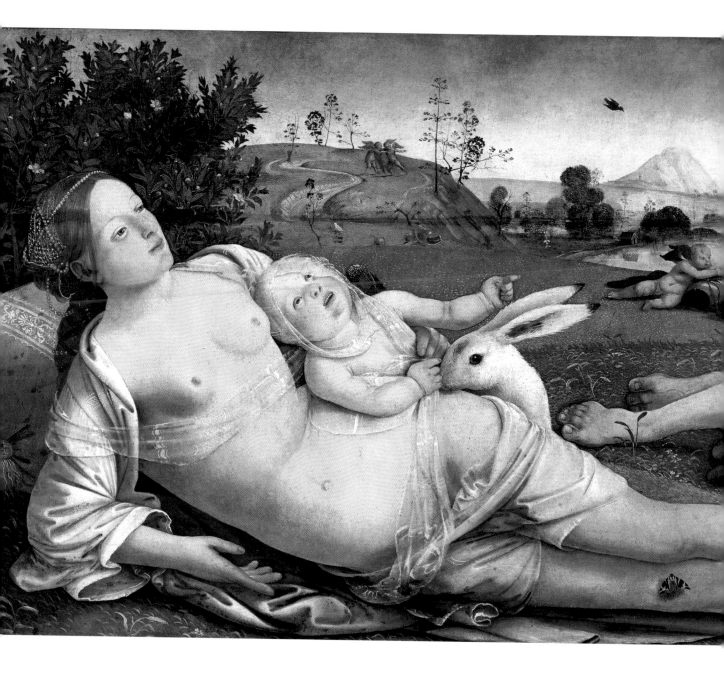

308 EIGHT: CATASTROPHE AND CREATIVITY (*c*.1350–*c*.1500)

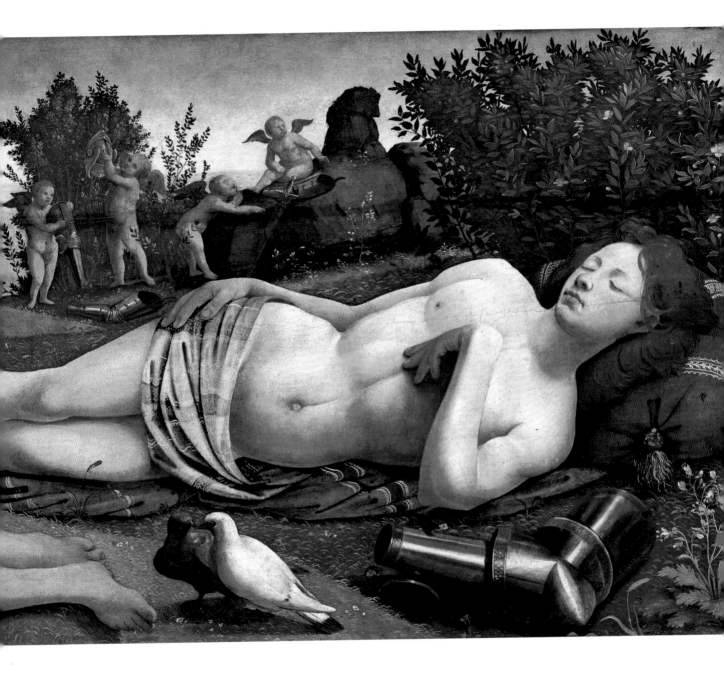

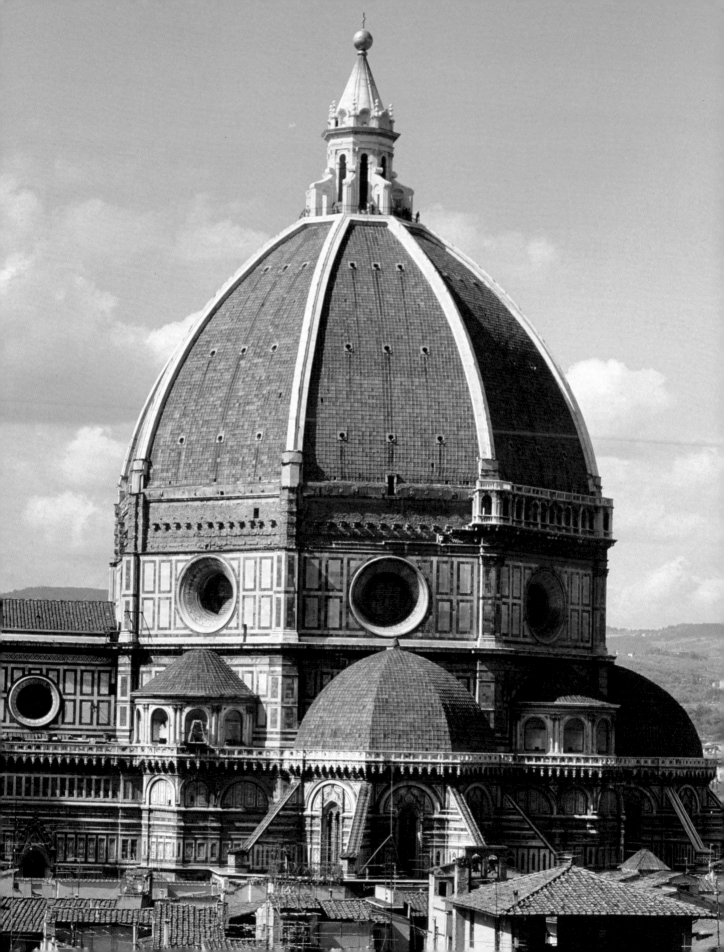

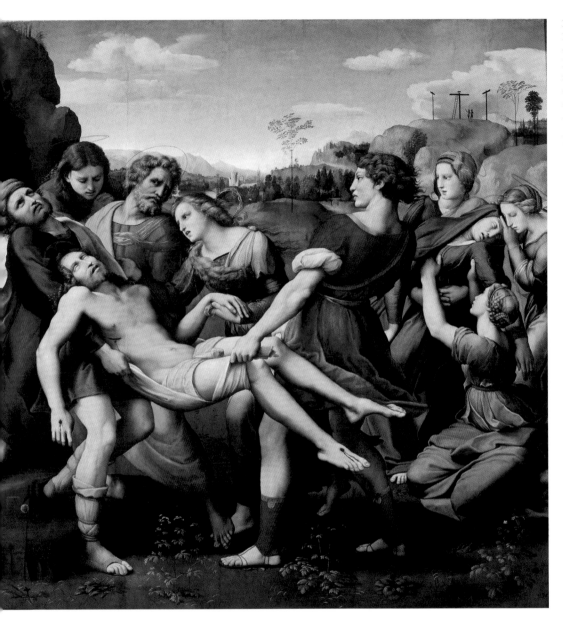

Plate 8.4 (facing page):
Filippo Brunelleschi, Florence Cathedral Dome (1418–1436). It was a major engineering feat to span the 42-meter (46-yard) octagonal space over the cathedral with a dome. Brunelleschi solved the problem by an ingenious use of ribs. He also designed the scaffolding that was necessary to build the dome and the hoisting equipment for the building materials. No wonder that Brunelleschi became a "star" —the first celebrity architect.

Plate 8.5: Raphael, *Entombment of Christ* (1507). Not so much about Christ's entombment as it is about carrying Christ, this central altarpiece panel should be read from right to left. First comes Christ's mother, the Virgin, her face white as a sheet, swooning into the arms of the three Maries (Holy Women mentioned in the Gospels). To their left are two men straining to bear Christ to his tomb, which is indicated by a cave-like opening. Mary Magdalene, one of the Maries, is there as well, lifting Christ's head and hand.

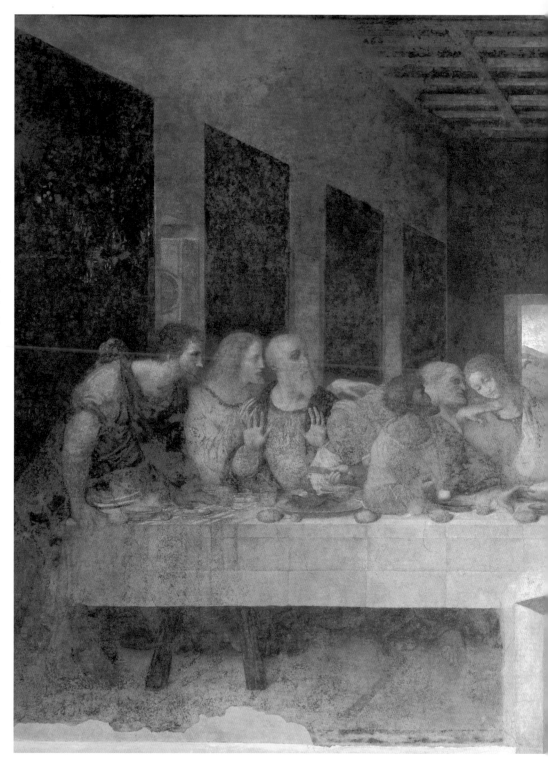

Plate 8.6: Leonardo da Vinci, *The Last Supper* (1494–1497). Leonardo first made his reputation with this painting, which evokes the precise moment when Christ said to his feasting apostles, "One of you is about to betray me." All the apostles react with horror and surprise, but the guilty Judas recoils, his face in shadows. Compare this depiction with the same moment in the Romanesque painting of Plate 5.4 on p. 183.

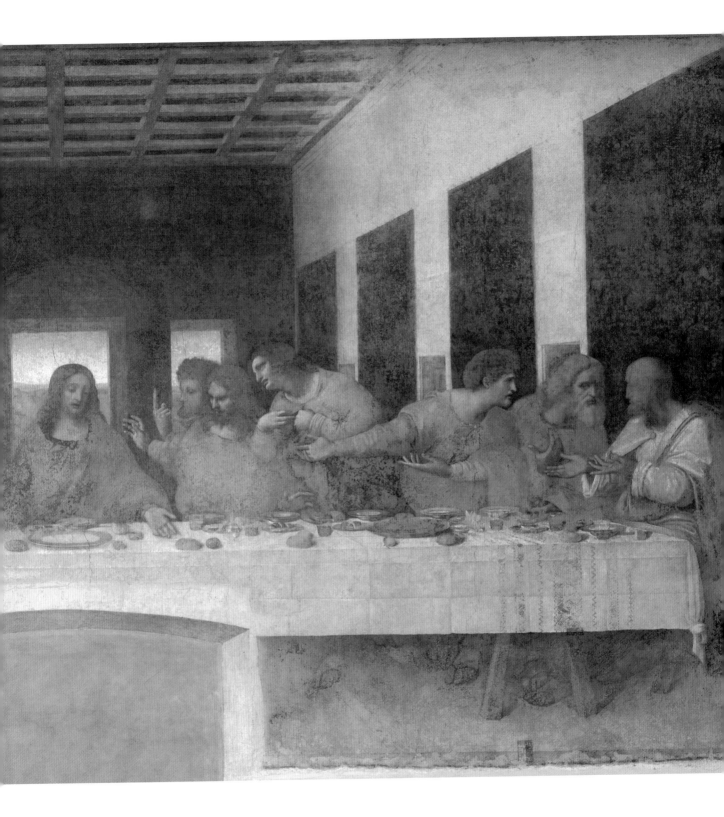

The Ottoman Court

Some of Ludovico's dinner presentations acted out a different preoccupation—the power of the new Ottoman state. When a whole roasted capon was brought in for each guest, it was accompanied by a little drama:

> A bull is presented by Indians and brought in by slaves of the Sultan in a most elaborately decorated procession of gold and silver with two little moors who sing very elaborately and an ambassador with an interpreter, who translates the words of the embassy.[15]

Here the Ottoman sultan was depicted as the lackey of Duke Ludovico, in a pageant that was meant to be very exotic and in need of "translation" (even though Ludovico himself was dubbed "il Moro," the Moor, because of his swarthy complexion). But imagine that the real sultan—the Ottoman ruler—held his own banquet at the same time: at *his* dinner, the lackey would be an *Italian*, and the sultan would have understood his language. For the Ottomans considered the Renaissance court to be their own as well. They had taken Byzantium, purified it of its infidel past (turning its churches into mosques), and reordered it along fittingly traditional lines. Although in popular speech Constantinople became Istanbul (meaning "the city"), its official name remained "Qustantiniyya"—the City of Constantine. The Ottoman sultans claimed the glory of Byzantium for themselves.

Thus Mehmed II continued to negotiate with Genoese traders, while he "borrowed" Gentile Bellini (*c.*1429–1507) from Venice to be his own court artist. In 1479, he posed for his portrait (see Plate 8.7), only a few decades after the genre of portrait painting itself had been "invented" in Europe. On the walls of his splendid Topkapi palace, he displayed tapestries from Burgundy portraying the deeds of Alexander the Great, each no doubt something like the tapestry illustrated in Plate 8.8, discussed below. Just as a statue of Judith gave glory to the Medici family, so Alexander burnished the image of the sultan. The tapestries were themselves trophies of war: a failed Burgundian crusade against the Ottomans in 1396 had ended in the capture of Duke John the Fearless; his ransom was the Alexander tapestries.

Learning as well as art was key to the sultans' notions of power. Mehmed and his successors staffed their cities with men well schooled in Islamic administration and culture and set up *madrasas* to teach the young. For himself, Mehmed commissioned a copy of Homer's *Iliad* in Greek, epic poetry in Italian, and other literary works by Turkish, Persian, and European writers. His zeal for scholarship was on a lesser scale but not very different in kind from that of the Florentine ruler Cosimo de' Medici (1389–1464), who in the mid-fifteenth century took over the nearly one thousand volumes of ancient Greek and Latin texts that had been collected with painstaking care by the humanist Niccolò Niccoli (1364–1437). Open to all, the Medici library became the model for princely bibliophiles throughout Italy and elsewhere. Calls for further crusades against the infidel Turks (in 1455 and 1459, for example) were in this sense "family disputes," attempts to contest the East's right to common notions of power and legitimacy.

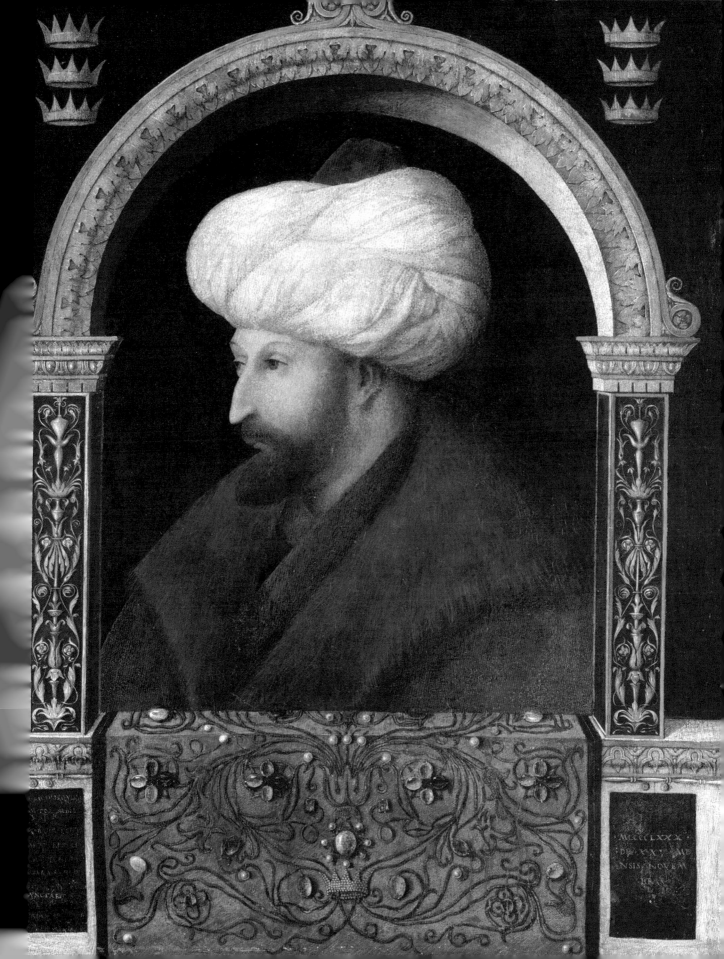

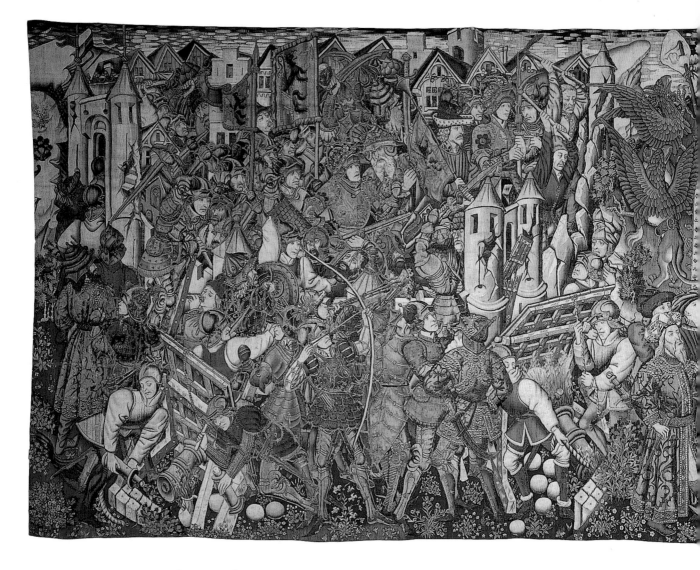

The Northern Renaissance

Northern Europe shared the same notions, but here the symbols of authority and piety were even more eclectic. Burgundy—an hourglass with its top in Flanders, its bottom just above the Alps—embraced nearly all the possibilities of Renaissance culture. Although Gothic style persisted in northern Europe, especially in architecture, the Greco-Roman world also beckoned. Ancient themes—especially the deeds of heroes, whether real or mythical—were depicted on tapestries that provided lustrous backdrops for rulers of every stripe. The dukes of Burgundy traveled from one end of their dominions to the other with such tapestries in tow. Weavings lined their tents during war and their boats during voyages. In 1459 Philip the Good bought a series of fine tapestries—woven in silk spiced with gold and silver threads—depicting the *History of Alexander the Great* (see Plate 8.8).

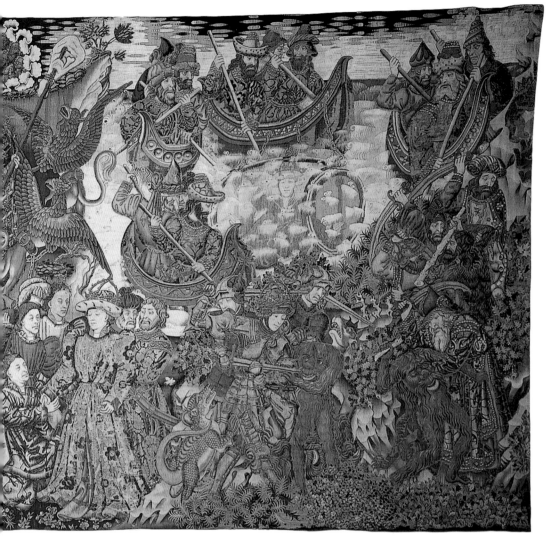

Plate 8.8: *History of Alexander the Great*, Tapestry (*c.*1459). To the right of the depiction of his ascent into the air, Alexander appears surrounded by his courtiers. Next he explores the underwater world: seated in a glass bell, he is encircled by sea creatures. Below, now returned to land, Alexander and his men fight dragons and monsters, one of whom is pierced by the hero's sword. The tapestry was commissioned by Philip the Good for 500 gold pieces and created by the master weaver of Tournai in silk, wool, and real gold thread. Alexander's adventures were recounted in vernacular romances; the text that probably directly inspired this tapestry was *The Book of the Conquests and Deeds of Alexander the Great* by Jean Wauquelin (d.1452), a copy of which was owned by the duke of Burgundy.

Following pages:

Plate 8.9: Rogier van der Weyden, *Columba Altarpiece* (1450s). Depicting three standard scenes from Christ's childhood—the Annunciation, the Adoration of the Magi, and the Presentation in the Temple—the *Columba Altarpiece* subtly introduces new themes alongside the old. For example, Christ's death is suggested by the crucifix above Mary in the central panel, while the present time (the fifteenth century) is suggested by the cityscape in the background, which probably represents Cologne, the native city of the man who commissioned the altar and the proud home of the relics of the Magi.

Reading this tapestry from left to right, we see a city besieged, the trumpeters, archers, and artillerymen and soldiers reflecting the realities of fifteenth-century warfare. At the center, Alexander rises to the sky in a decorated metal cage lifted by four winged griffons. The weaving was the perfect stage setting for the performance of ducal power. No wonder European rulers—from English kings to Italian *signori* (and on to Ottoman sultans)—all wanted tapestries from Burgundy for *their* palaces.

At the same time, dukes and other northern European patrons favored a new style of art that emphasized devotion, sentiment, and immediacy. (This style would later be one of the inspirations for Raphael's *Entombment* in Plate 8.5.) Painted in oil-based pigments, capable of showing the finest details and the subtlest shading, Netherlandish art was valued above all for its true-to-life expressivity. In the *Columba Altarpiece* (Plate 8.9) by Rogier van der Weyden—likely commissioned by Johann Dasse, a wealthy merchant from Cologne

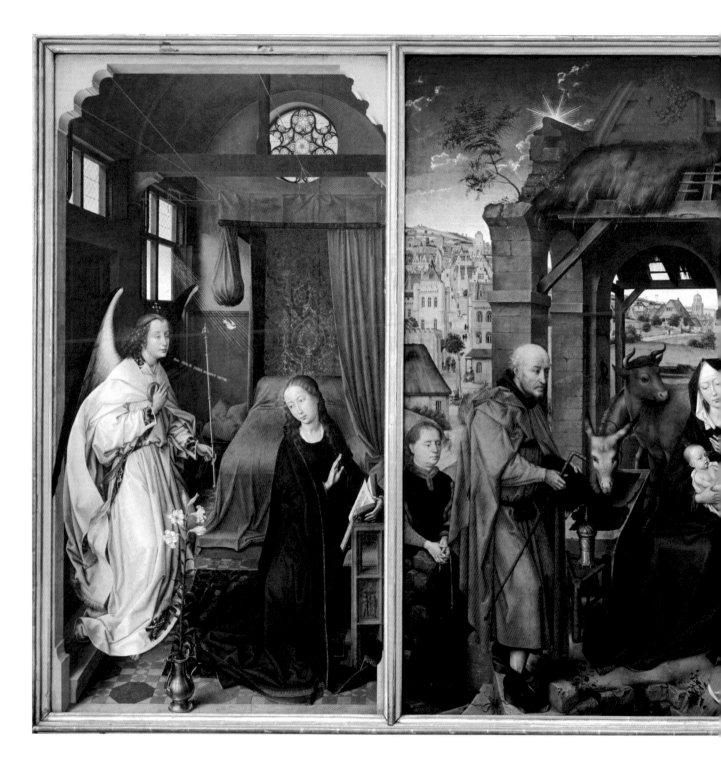

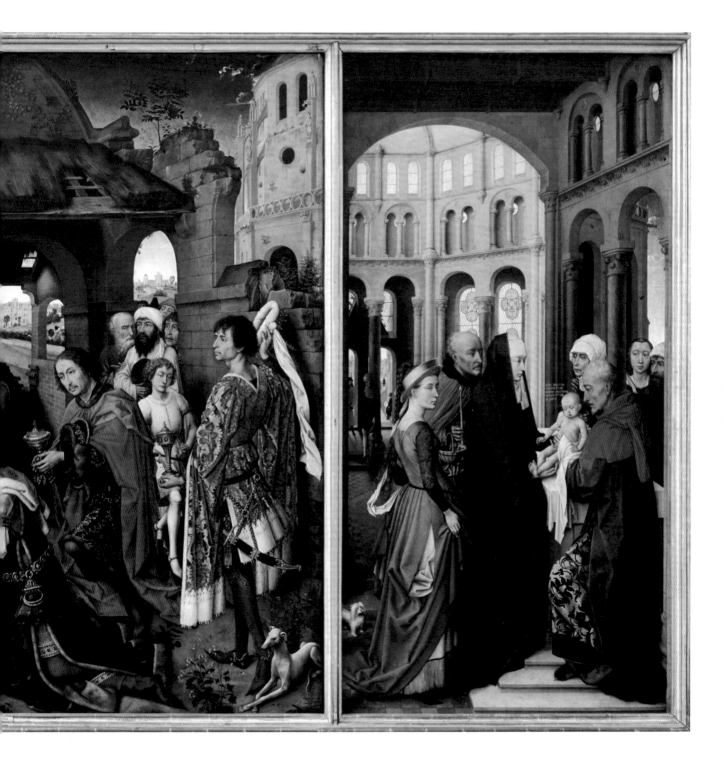

Plate 8.10 (facing page): Jan
van Eyck, *Man in a Red Turban*
(1433). Compare this head
with that of the idealized Mars
from imperial Rome (Plate 1.1
on p. 12), the gesturing Saint
John of the Carolingians
(Plate 3.8 on p. 110), the jovial
Saint Joseph of a Gothic
cathedral (Plate 6.6 on p. 227),
and the beautiful young Mars
of the Italian Renaissance
(Plate 8.3 on p. 309). Only van
Eyck paints his anonymous
subject without idealizing or
beautifying him; the man's
worth and dignity derive only
(but importantly) from his
individuality.

(Germany)—the donor himself is depicted, hat in hand (to the left in the central panel), humbly witnessing the visit of the Magi. Time itself is compressed in this picture, as the immediacy of the painting—its here-and-now presence—belies the historical reality: like Margery Kempe at the birth of Christ (see above, p. 302), so also here: no one from the fifteenth century could possibly have been at the scene.

The emphasis on the natural details of the moment was equally striking in secular paintings from the Netherlands. In *Man in a Red Turban* (see Plate 8.10) by Jan van Eyck (*c*.1390–1441), we even see the stubble of the man's beard. Yet this entirely secular theme—a man in stylish red headgear (evidence of the Turkish allure)—is infused with a quiet inner light that endows its subject with a kind of otherworldliness.

Both the Italian and Northern Renaissances cultivated music and musicians, above all for the aura that they gave rulers, princes, and great churchmen. In Italy, Isabella d'Este (1474–1539), marchesa of Mantua, employed her own musicians—singers, woodwind and string players, percussionists, and keyboard players—while her husband had his own band. In Burgundy the duke had a fine private chapel and musicians, singers, and composers to staff it. In England wealthy patrons founded colleges—Eton (founded by King Henry VI in 1440–1441) was one—where choirs offered up prayers in honor of the Virgin. Motets continued to be composed and sung, but now polyphonic music for larger groups became common as well. In the hands of a composer such as John Dunstable (d.1453), who probably worked for the duke of Bedford, regent for Henry VI in France during the Hundred Years' War, dissonance was smoothed out. In the compositions of Dunstable and his followers, harmonious chords that moved together even as they changed replaced the old juxtapositions of independent lines. Working within the old modal categories, composers made their mark with music newly sonorous and smooth.

NEW HORIZONS

Experiment and play within old traditions were thus the major trends of the period. They can be seen in explorations of interiority, in creative inventions, even in the conquest of the globe. Yet their consequences may fairly be said to have ushered in a new era.

Interiority

Donatello's Judith, intent on her single-minded task, and van Eyck's red-turbaned man, glowing from within, are similar in their self-involved interiority. Judith's self-centeredness is that of a hero; van Eyck's man's is that of any ordinary creature of God, the artist's statement about the holiness of nature.

These two styles of interiority were mirrored in religious life and expression. Saint Catherine of Siena (1347–1380) was a woman in Judith's heroic mold. A reformer with a

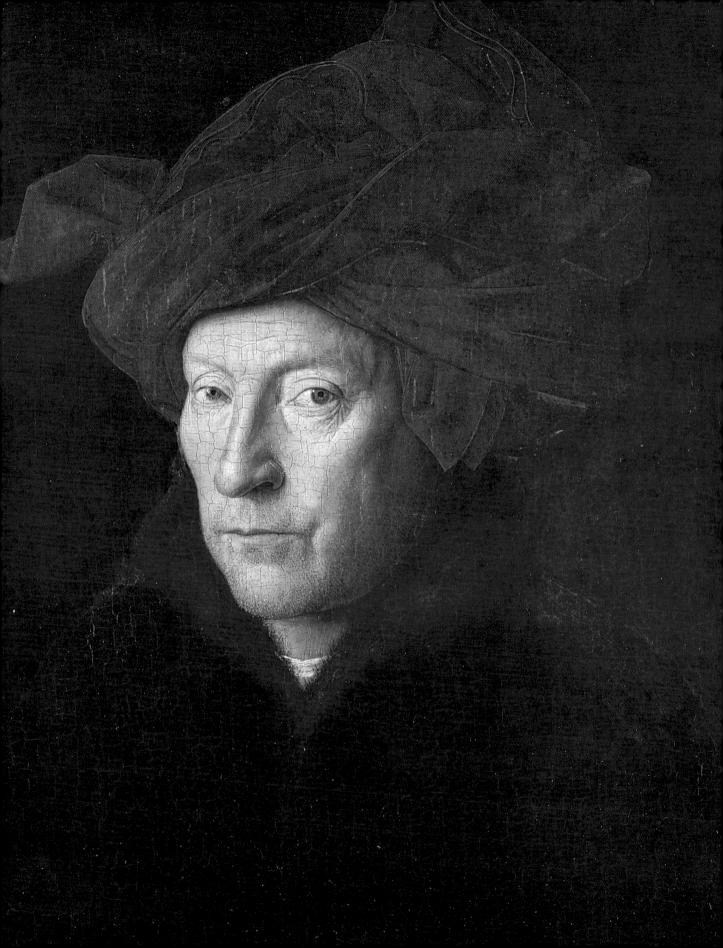

message, she was one of the first in a long line of women (Jeanne d'Arc is another example) to intervene on the public stage because of her private agonies. Writing (or rather dictating) nearly 400 letters to the great leaders of the day, she worked ceaselessly to bring the pope back to Rome and urged crusade as the best way to purge and revivify the church.

In the Low Countries, northern Germany, and the Rhineland, the *devotio moderna* (the "new devotion") movement found, to the contrary, purgation and renewal in individual reading and contemplation rather than in public action. Founded *c.*1380 by Gerhard Groote (1340–1384), the Brethren of the Common Life lived in male or female communities that focused on education, the copying of manuscripts, material simplicity, and individual faith. The Brethren were not quite humanists and not quite mystics, but they drew from both for a religious program that depended very little on the hierarchy or ceremonies of the church. Their style of piety would later be associated with Protestant groups.

Inventions

The enormous demand for books—whether by ordinary lay people, adherents of the *devotio moderna*, or humanists eager for the classics—made printed books a welcome addition to the repertory of available texts, though manuscripts were neither quickly nor easily displaced. The printing press, however obvious in thought, marked a great practical breakthrough: it depended on a new technique to mold metal type. This was first achieved by Johann Gutenberg at Mainz (in Germany) around 1450. The next step was getting the raw materials that were needed to ensure ongoing production. Paper required water mills and a steady supply of rag (pulp made of cloth); the metal for the type had to be mined and shaped; ink had to be found that would adhere to metal letters as well as spread evenly on paper.

By 1500 many European cities had publishing houses, with access to the materials that they needed and sufficient clientele to earn a profit. Highly competitive, the presses advertised their wares. They turned out not only religious and classical books but whatever the public demanded. Martin Luther (1483–1546) may not in fact have nailed his 95 Theses to the door of the church at Wittenberg in 1517, but he certainly allowed them to be printed and distributed in both Latin and German. Challenging prevailing church teachings and practice, the Theses ushered in the Protestant Reformation. The printing press was a powerful instrument of mass communication.

More specialized, yet no less decisive for the future, were new developments in navigation. Portolan maps charted the shape of the Mediterranean coastline through accurate measurements from point to point.[16] Compasses, long known in China but newly adopted in the West, provided readings that were noted down in nautical charts; sailors used them alongside maps and written information about such matters as harbors, political turmoil, and anchorage. But navigating the Atlantic depended on more; it required methods for exploiting the powerful ocean wind systems. New ship designs—the light caravel, the heavy galleon—featured the rigging and sails needed to harness the wind.

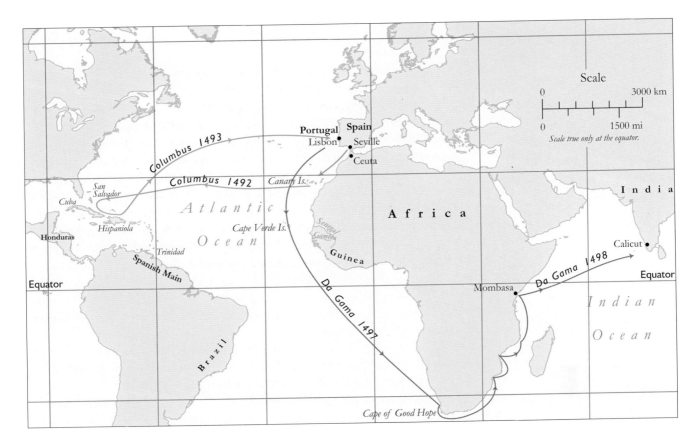

Voyages

As we have seen (p. 245), already in the thirteenth century merchants and missionaries from Genoa and Majorca were making forays into the Atlantic. In the fifteenth century the initiative that would eventually take Europeans around the Cape of Good Hope in one direction and to the Americas in the other came from the Portuguese royal house. The enticements were gold and slaves as well as honor and glory. Under King João I (r.1385–1433) and his successors, Portugal extended its rule to the Muslim port of Ceuta and a few other nearby cities. (See Map 8.6.) More importantly, João's son Prince Henry "the Navigator" (1394–1460) sponsored expeditions—mainly by Genoese sailors—to explore the African coast: in the mid-1450s they reached the Cape Verde Islands and penetrated inland via the Senegal and Gambia rivers. A generation later, Portuguese explorers were working their way far past the equator; in 1487 Bartholomeu Dias (d.1500) rounded the southern tip of Africa (soon thereafter named the Cape of Good Hope), opening a new route that Vasco da Gama sailed about ten years later all the way to Calicut (today Kozhikode) in India. In his account of the voyage he made no secret of his methods: when he needed water, he landed on an island and bombarded the inhabitants, taking "as much water as we wanted."[17]

Da Gama's cavalier treatment of the natives was symptomatic of a more profound development: European colonialism. Already in the 1440s, Henry was portioning out the uninhabited islands of Madeira and the Azores to those of his followers who promised to find peasants to settle them. The Azores remained a grain producer, but, with financing by the Genoese, Madeira began to grow cane sugar. The product took Europe by storm. Demand was so high that a few decades later, when few European settlers could be found to work sugar plantations on the Cape Verde Islands, the Genoese Antonio da Noli, discoverer and governor of the islands, brought in African slaves instead. Cape Verde was a microcosm of later European colonialism, which depended on just such slave labor.

Portugal's successes and pretensions roused the hostility and rivalry of Castile. Ferdinand and Isabella's determination to conquer the Canary Islands was in part their "answer" to Portugal's Cape Verde. When, in 1492, they half-heartedly sponsored the Genoese Christopher Columbus (1451–1506) on a westward voyage across the Atlantic, they knew that they were playing Portugal's game.

Although the conquistadores confronted a New World, they did so with the expectations and categories of the Old. When the Spaniard Hernán Cortés (1485–1547) began his conquest of Mexico, he boasted in a letter home that he had reprimanded one of the native chiefs for thinking that Mutezuma, the Aztec emperor who ruled much of Mexico at the time, was worthy of allegiance:

> I replied by telling him of the great power of Your Majesty [Emperor Charles V, who was also king of Spain] and of the many other princes, greater than Mutezuma, who were Your Highness's vassals and considered it no small favor to be so; Mutezuma also would become one, as would all the natives of these lands. I therefore asked him to become one, for if he did it would be greatly to his honor and advantage, but if, on the other hand, he refused to obey, he would be punished.[18]

The old values lived on.

★   ★   ★   ★   ★

Between the years 1350 and 1500, a series of catastrophes struck Europe. The Black Death felled at least a fifth of the population of Europe. The Hundred Years' War wreaked havoc when archers shot and cannons roared; it loosed armies of freebooters in both town and country during its interstices of peace. The Ottomans conquered Byzantium, took over the Balkans, and threatened Austria and Hungary. The church splintered as first the Great Schism and then national churches tore at the loyalties of churchmen and laity alike.

Yet these catastrophes were confronted, if not always overcome, with both energy and inventiveness. In England, peasants loosed the bonds of serfdom; in Portugal and Spain, adventurers discovered gold and land via the high seas; and everywhere bibliophiles and artists discovered wisdom and beauty in the classical past while princes flexed the muscles of sovereignty. History books normally divide this period into two parts, the crises going into a chapter on the Middle Ages, the creativity saved for a chapter on the Renaissance. But the two happened together, witness to Europe's aggressive resilience. Indeed, in the next century it would parcel out the globe.

CHAPTER EIGHT KEY EVENTS

1324/1326	Death of Othman, founder of Ottomans
1304–1374	Petrarch
c.1330–1384	John Wyclif
1337–1453	Hundred Years' War
c.1340–1400	Geoffrey Chaucer
1346–1353	Black Death
1351	Statute of Laborers in England
1358	Jacquerie in France
1369/1371–1415	Jan Hus
1378	Ciompi revolt in Florence
1378–1417	Great Schism of the papacy
1381	Wat Tyler's Rebellion
c.1390–1441	Jan van Eyck
1414–1418	Council of Constance
1429	Jeanne d'Arc leads French army to victory at Orléans
1438	Pragmatic Sanction of Bourges
1444–1446, 1451–1481	Rule of Mehmed II the Conqueror, Ottoman sultan
c.1450	Gutenberg invents the printing press
1452–1519	Leonardo da Vinci
1453	Ottoman conquest of Constantinople; end of Byzantine Empire
1454	Peace of Lodi in Northern Italy
1455–1487	Wars of the Roses
1477	Battle of Nancy; end of the Burgundian state
1492	Conquest of Granada; expulsion of Jews from Spain; first trans-Atlantic voyage of Columbus

NOTES

1 Nicephorus Gregoras, *Roman History*, in *Reading the Middle Ages: Sources from Europe, Byzantium, and the Islamic World*, ed. Barbara H. Rosenwein, 2nd ed. (Toronto: University of Toronto Press, 2014), p. 444.

2 Louis Guibert, ed. and trans., *Le livre de raison d'Etienne Benoist* (Limoges, 1882), p. 43.

3 Geoffrey Chaucer, *The Canterbury Tales*, trans. Nevill Coghill (Harmondsworth: Penguin, 1977), p. 88.

4 Ashikpashazade, *Othman Comes to Power*, in *Reading the Middle Ages*, p. 455.

5 Froissart, *Chronicles*, in *Reading the Middle Ages*, pp. 469–70.

6 Jeanne d'Arc, *Letter to the English*, in *Reading the Middle Ages*, p. 475.

7 Christine de Pisan, *The Tale of Joan of Arc*, quoted in Nadia Margolis, "The Mission of Joan of Arc," in *Medieval Hagiography: An Anthology*, ed. Thomas Head (New York: Routledge, 2000), p. 822.

8 Froissart, *Chronicles*, ed. and trans. Geoffrey Brereton (Harmondsworth: Penguin, 1968), p. 151.

9 *Wat Tyler's Rebellion*, in *Reading the Middle Ages*, p. 481.

10 *The Book of Margery Kempe*, in *Reading the Middle Ages*, p. 487.

11 Cincius Romanus, *Letter to His Most Learned Teacher Franciscus de Fiana*, in *Reading the Middle Ages*, p. 491.

12 Quoted in Evelyn Welch, *Art in Renaissance Italy, 1350–1500* (Oxford: Oxford University Press, 1997), p. 261.

13 Leon Battista Alberti, *On Painting*, in *Reading the Middle Ages*, pp. 493–94.

14 "A Sforza Banquet Menu (1491)," in *The Renaissance in Europe: An Anthology*, ed. Peter Elmer, Nick Webb, and Roberta Wood (New Haven, CT: Yale University Press, 2000), pp. 172–75.

15 Ibid., p. 173.

16 For an example, see *Reading the Middle Ages*, Plate 15, p. 252.

17 *A Journal of the First Voyage of Vasco da Gama, 1497–1499*, ed. and trans. E.G. Ravenstein (rpt. New York, 1964), p. 30.

18 Hernán Cortés, *The Second Letter*, in *Reading the Middle Ages*, p. 501.

FURTHER READING

Aberth, John. *From the Brink of the Apocalypse: Confronting Famine, War, Plague, and Death in the Later Middle Ages*. New York: Routledge, 2001.

Belozerskaya, Marina. *Rethinking the Renaissance: Burgundian Arts across Europe*. Cambridge: Cambridge University Press, 2002.

Blockmans, Wim, and Walter Prevenier. *The Promised Lands: The Low Countries under Burgundian Rule, 1369–1530*. Trans. Elizabeth Fackelman. Ed. Edward Peters. Philadelphia: University of Pennsylvania Press, 1999.

Blumenfeld-Kosinski, Renate. *Poets, Saints, and Visionaries of the Great Schism, 1378–1417*. University Park: Penn State Press, 2006.

Cerman, Markus. *Villages and Lords in Eastern Europe, 1300–1800*. New York: Palgrave Macmillan, 2012.

Curry, Ann. *The Hundred Years' War, 1337–1453*. Oxford: Osprey, 2002.

Fernández-Armesto, Felipe. *Pathfinders: A Global History of Exploration*. New York: Norton, 2006.

Goffman, Daniel. *The Ottoman Empire and Early Modern Europe*. Cambridge: Cambridge University Press, 2002.

Hudson, Anne. *The Premature Reformation: Wycliffite Texts and Lollard History*. Oxford: Oxford University Press, 1988.

Imber, Colin. *The Ottoman Empire, 1300–1650: The Structure of Power*. 2nd ed. New York: Palgrave Macmillan, 2009.

Jardine, Lisa, and Jerry Brotton. *Global Interests: Renaissance Art between East and West*. Ithaca, NY: Cornell University Press, 2000.

Johnson, Geraldine A. *Renaissance Art: A Very Short Introduction*. Oxford: Oxford University Press, 2005.

Karras, Ruth Mazo. *Unmarriages: Women, Men, and Sexual Unions in the Middle Ages*. Philadelphia: University of Pennsylvania Press, 2012.

Klassen, John Martin. *The Nobility and the Making of the Hussite Revolution*. New York: Columbia University Press, 1978.

McKitterick, David. *Print, Manuscript and the Search for Order, 1450–1830*. Cambridge: Cambridge University Press, 2003.

Parker, Geoffrey. *The Cambridge History of Warfare*. Cambridge: Cambridge University Press, 2005.

Patton, Pamela A. *Art of Estrangement: Redefining Jews in Reconquest Spain*. University Park: Penn State Press, 2012.

Small, Graeme. *Late Medieval France*. New York: Palgrave Macmillan, 2009.

Watts, John. *The Making of Polities: Europe, 1300–1500*. Cambridge: Cambridge University Press, 2009.

Wheeler, Bonnie, and Charles Wood, eds. *Fresh Verdicts on Joan of Arc*. New York: Routledge, 1996.

To test your knowledge of this chapter, please go to
www.utphistorymatters.com
for Study Questions.

EPILOGUE

Cortéz may have used the old vocabulary of vassalage when speaking of his conquests in the Americas, but clearly the *reality* was so changed that we are right to see the years around 1500 as the turning point between the Middle Ages and a new phase of history. The Middle Ages began when the Roman provinces came into their own. They ended as those provinces—now vastly expanded, rich, and powerful, now "Europe," in fact—became in turn a new imperial power, its tentacles in the New World, Asia, and Africa. In the next centuries, as Europeans conquered most of the world, they (as the Romans had once done) exported themselves, their values, cultures, diseases, inventions, and institutions, while importing, usually without meaning to, many of the people, ideas, and institutions of the groups they conquered. In another phase, one not yet ended, former European colonies—at least some of them—have become, in turn, the center of a new-style empire involving economic, cultural, and (occasionally) military hegemony. It remains to be seen if this empire, too, will eventually be overtaken by its peripheries.

Does anything now remain of the Middle Ages? Without doubt. Bits and pieces of the past are clearly embedded in the present: universities, parliaments, ideas about God and human nature, the papacy, Gothic churches. We cling to some of these bits with ferocious passion, while repudiating others and allowing still more to float in and out of our unquestioned assumptions. Many things that originated in the Middle Ages are now so transformed that only their names are still medieval. And beyond that? Beyond that, "persistence" is the wrong question. The past need not be replayed because it is "us" but rather because it is "not us," and therefore endlessly fascinating.

GLOSSARY

aids
  In England, this refers to payments made by vassals to their lords on important occasions.

The Annunciation
  See Virgin Mary (below).

antiking
  A king elected illegally.

antipope
  A pope elected illegally.

Book of Hours
  A prayer book for lay devotion, meant to be read eight times a day either at home or in church. It normally contained the church calendar; a lesson from each of the gospels; prayers and other readings in honor of the Virgin Mary (see below) based on simplified versions of the Divine Office (see Office below); the penitential psalms; the Office of the Dead; and prayers to saints. Some were lavishly illustrated, and even humble ones were usually decorated.

bull
  An official document issued by the papacy. The word derives from *bulla*, the lead impression of the pope's seal that was affixed to the document to validate it.

canon law
  The laws of the church. These were at first hammered out as need arose at various regional church councils and in rules issued by great bishops, particularly the pope. Early collections of canon law were incomplete and sometimes contradictory. Beginning in the ninth century, commentators began to organize and systematize them. The most famous of these treatises was the mid-twelfth-century *Decretum* of Gratian, which, although not an official code, became the basis of canon law training in the schools.

cathedral
  The principal church of a bishop or archbishop.

church
  To the Roman Catholics of the Middle Ages, this had two related meanings. It signified in the first place the eternal institution created by Christ, composed of the whole body

of Christian believers, and served on earth by Christ's ministers—priests, bishops, the pope. Related to the eternal church were individual, local churches (parish churches, cathedrals, collegiate churches, chapels) where the daily liturgy was carried out and the faithful received the sacraments.

cleric
A man in church orders.

collegiate church
A church for priests living in common according to a rule.

The Crucifixion
The execution of Jesus by hanging on a cross (*crux* in Latin). The scene, described in some detail in the Gospels, was often depicted in art; and free-standing crucifixes (crosses with the figure of Jesus on them) were often placed upon church altars.

diet
A formal assembly of German princes.

dogma
The authoritative truth of the church.

empire
Refers in the first instance to the Roman Empire. Byzantium considered itself the continuation of that empire. In the West, there were several successor empires, all ruled by men who took the title "emperor": there was the empire of Charlemagne, which included more or less what later became France, Italy, and Germany; it was followed in the tenth century (from the time of Otto I on) by the empire held (after a crowning at Rome) by the German kings. This could be complicated: a ruler like Henry IV was king of Germany in 1056 at the age of six, but, as a minor, his kingdom was ruled by his mother and others in his name. In 1065, at the age of 15, he became an adult and was able to take the reins of power. But he was not crowned emperor until 1084. Nevertheless, he *acted* as an emperor long before that. That "German" empire, which lasted until the thirteenth century, included Germany and (at least in theory) northern Italy. Some historians call all of these successor empires of Rome the "Holy Roman Empire," but in fact, although Barbarossa called his empire *sacer*, "holy," the full phrase "Holy Roman Empire" was not used until 1254. This empire, which had nothing to do with Rome, ended in 1806. By extension, the term empire can refer to other large realms, often gained through conquest, such as the Mongol Empire or the Ottoman Empire.

episcopal

As used for the Middle Ages, this is the equivalent of "bishop's." An "episcopal church" is the bishop's church; an "episcopal appointment" is the appointment of a bishop; "episcopal power" is the power wielded by a bishop.

excommunication

An act or pronouncement that cuts someone off from participation in the sacraments of the church and thus from the means of salvation.

fresco

A form of painting using pigments on wet plaster, frequently employed on the walls of churches.

gentry

By the end of the Middle Ages, English landlords consisted of two groups, lords and gentry. The gentry were below the lords; knights, squires, and gentlemen were all considered gentry. Even though the term comes from the Late Middle Ages, it is often used by historians as a rough and ready category for the lesser English nobility from the twelfth century onward.

grisaille

Painting in monochrome grays highlighted with color tints.

Guelfs and Ghibellines

Guelf was the Italian for Welf (the dynasty that competed for the German throne against the Staufen), while Ghibelline referred to Waiblingen (the name of an important Staufen castle). In the various conflicts between the popes and the Staufen emperors, the "Guelfs" were the factions within the Italian city-states that supported the papacy, while the "Ghibellines" supported the emperor. More generally, however, the names became epithets for various inter- and intra-city political factions that had little or no connection to papal/imperial issues.

illumination

The term used for paintings in medieval manuscripts. These might range from simple decorations of capital letters to full-page compositions. An "illuminated" manuscript is one containing illuminations.

layman/laywoman/laity

Men and women not in church orders, not ordained. In the early Middle Ages it was possible to be a monk and a layperson at the same time. But by the Carolingian period, most monks were priests, and although nuns were not, they were not considered part of the laity because they had taken vows to the church.

Levant
The lands that border the eastern shore of the Mediterranean; the Holy Land.

liturgy
The formal worship of the church, which included prayers, readings, and significant gestures at fixed times appropriate to the season. While often referring to the Mass (see below), it may equally be used to describe the Offices (see below).

The Madonna
See Virgin Mary (below).

Maghreb
A region of northwest Africa embracing the Atlas Mountains and the coastline of Morocco, Algeria, and Tunisia.

Mass
The central ceremony of Christian worship; it includes prayers and readings from the Bible and culminates in the consecration of bread and wine as the body and blood of Christ, offered to believers in the sacrament of the "Eucharist," or "Holy Communion."

New Testament
This work, a compilation of the second century, contains the four Gospels (accounts of the life of Christ) by Matthew, Mark, Luke, and John; the Acts of the Apostles; various letters, mainly from Saints Paul, Peter, and John to fledgling Christian communities; and the Apocalypse. It is distinguished from the "Old Testament" (see below).

Office
In the context of monastic life, the day and night were punctuated by eight periods in which the monks gathered to recite a precise set of prayers. Each set was called an "Office," and the cycle as a whole was called the "Divine Office." Special rites and ceremonies might also be called offices, such as the "Office of the Dead."

Old Testament
The writings of the Hebrew Bible that were accepted as authentic by Christians, though reinterpreted by them as prefiguring the coming of Christ; they were thus seen as the precursor of the "New Testament" (see above), which fulfilled and perfected them.

Presentation in the Temple
An event in the life of Christ and his mother. See The Virgin below.

referendary

A high Merovingian administrative official responsible for overseeing the issuing of royal documents.

relief

This has two separate meanings. In connection with medieval English government, the "relief" refers to money paid upon inheriting a fief. In the history of sculpture, however, "relief" refers to figures or other forms that project from a flat background. "Low relief" means that the forms project rather little, while "high relief" refers to forms that may be so three-dimensional as to threaten to break away from the flat surface.

sacraments

The rites of the church that (in its view) Jesus instituted to confer sanctifying grace. With the sacraments, one achieved salvation. Cut off from the sacraments (by anathema, excommunication, or interdict), one was damned.

scriptorium

(*pl.* scriptoria) The room of the monastery where parchment was prepared and texts were copied, illuminated, and bound.

summa

(*pl.* summae) A compendium or summary. A term favored by scholastics to title their comprehensive syntheses.

The Virgin/The Virgin Mary/The Blessed Virgin/The Madonna

The Gospels of Matthew (1:18–23) and Luke (1:27–35) assert that Christ was conceived by the Holy Spirit (rather than by a man) and born of Mary, a virgin. Already in the fourth century the Church Fathers stressed the virginity of Mary, which guaranteed the holiness of Christ. In the fifth century, at the Council of Chalcedon (451), Mary's perpetual (eternal) virginity was declared. Mary was understood as the exact opposite of (and antidote to) Eve. In the medieval church, Mary was celebrated with four feasts— her Nativity (birth), the Annunciation (when the Angel Gabriel announced to her that she would give birth to the Messiah), the Purification (when she presented the baby Jesus in the temple and was herself cleansed after giving birth), and her Assumption (when she rose to Heaven). (The Purification is also called the Presentation in the Temple.) These events were frequently depicted in paintings and sculpture, especially in the later Middle Ages, when devotion to Mary's cult increased and greater emphasis was placed on her role as intercessor with her son in Heaven.

APPENDIX: LISTS

LATE ROMAN EMPERORS
(Usurpers in Italics)

Maximinus Thrax (235–238)

Gordian I (238)

Gordian II (238)

Balbinus and Pupienus (238)

Gordian III (238–244)

Philip the Arab (244–249)

Decius (249–251)

Trebonianus Gallus (251–253)

Aemilian (253)

Valerian (253–260)

Gallienus (253–268)

Claudius II Gothicus (268–270)

Quintillus (270)

Aurelian (270–275)

Tacitus (275–276)

Florian (276)

Probus (276–282)

Carus (282–283)

In the West	*In the East*
Numerianus (283–284)	Carinus (283–285)

Diocletian (284–305)

Maximian (Augustus in the West) (286–305)

First Tetrarchy:*

Maximian (Augustus) (293–305)   Diocletian (Augustus) (293–305)

Constantius I (Caesar) (293–305)   Galerius (Caesar) (293–305)

Second Tetrarchy:

Constantius I (Augustus) (305–306)   Galerius (Augustus) (305–306)

Severus II (Caesar) (305–306)   Maximin (Caesar) (305–306)

Third Tetrarchy:

Severus II (Augustus) (306–307)   Galerius (Augustus) (306–307)

Constantine I (Caesar) (306–307)   Maximin (Caesar) (306–307)

Fourth Tetrarchy:

Licinius (Augustus) (308–311)   Galerius (Augustus) (308–311)

Constantine I (Caesar) (308–311)   Maximin (Caesar) (308–311)

Maxentius (in Italy) (306–312)

Constantine I (Augustus) (311–337), Licinius (Augustus) (311–324),
Maximin (Augustus) (311–313)

Constantine I and Licinius (313–324)

Constantine I (324–337)

Constantine II (Augustus) (337–340), Constans (Augustus) (337–350),
Constantius II (Augustus) (337–361)

Constans (340–350)   Constantius II (340–361)

Constantius II (350–361)

Magnentius (350–353)

Julian (361–363)

Jovian (363–364)

Valentinian I (364–375)   Valens (364–378)

Gratian (367–383)   Theodosius I (379–395)

Valentinian II (375–392)

Magnus Maximus (383–388) and Flavius Victor (384–388)

Eugenius (392–394)

---

*Dates refer to the duration of the tetrarchy.

Theodosius I (394–395)

Honorius I (395–423)
(Stilicho regent) (395–408)

Arcadius (395–408)

Theodosius II (408–450)

Constantius III (421)

John (423–425)

Valentian III (425–455)

Marcian (450–457)

Petronius Maximus (455)

Leo I (457–474)

Avitus (455–456)

Majorian (457–461)

Libius Severus (461–465)

Anthemius (467–472)

Olybrius (472)

Glycerius (473–474)

Julius Nepos (474–475)

Zeno (474–491)

Romulus Augustulus (475–476)

Anastasius I (491–518)

Justin I (518–527)

Justinian I (527–565)

BYZANTINE EMPERORS

Justinian I (527–565)
Justin II (565–578)
Tiberius I (578–582)
Maurice (582–602)
Phocas (602–610)
Heraclius (610–641)
Constantine III and Heraclius II
(Heraclonas) (641)
Constans II (641–668)
Constantine IV (668–685)
Justinian II (685–695)
Leontius (695–698)
Tiberius II (698–705)

Justinian II (again) (705–711)
Philippicus (711–713)
Anastasius II (713–715)
Theodosius III (715–717)
Leo III (717–741)
Constantine V (741–775)
Leo IV (775–780)
Constantine VI (780–797)
Irene (797–802)
Nicephorus I (802–811)
Stauracius (811)
Michael I (811–813)
Leo V (813–820)

Michael II (820–829)
Theophilus (829–842)
Michael III (842–867)

Macedonian Dynasty (867–1056)
Basil I (867–886)
Leo VI (886–912)
Alexander (912–913)
Constantine VII (913–959)
Romanus I (920–944)
Romanus II (959–963)
Nicephorus II (963–969)
John I (969–976)
Basil II (976–1025)
Constantine VIII (1025–1028)
Romanus III (1028–1034)
Michael IV (1034–1041)
Michael V (1041–1042)
Zoe and Theodora (1042)
Constantine IX (1042–1055)
Theodora (again) (1055–1056)

Michael VI (1056–1057)
Isaac I (1057–1059)
Constantine X (1059–1067)
Romanus IV (1068–1071)
Michael VII (1071–1078)
Nicephorus III (1078–1081)

Comnenian Dynasty (1081–1185)
Alexius I (1081–1118)
John II (1118–1143)
Manuel I (1143–1180)
Alexius II (1180–1183)
Andronicus I (1183–1185)

Isaac II (1185–1195)
Alexius III (1195–1203)
Isaac II (again) and Alexius IV (1203–1204)
Alexius V (1204)
Theodore I (1205–1221)
John III (1221–1254)
Theodore II (1254–1258)
John IV (1259–1261)

Palaiologan Dynasty (1259–1453)
Michael VIII (1259–1282)
Andronicus II (1282–1328)
Michael IX (1294/5–1320)
Andronicus III (1328–1341)
John V (1341–1391)
John VI (1347–1354)
Andronicus IV (1376–1379)
John VII (1390)
Manuel II (1391–1425)
John VIII (1425–1448)
Constantine XI (1449–1453)

POPES AND ANTIPOPES TO 1500* (Antipopes in Italics)

Peter (?–c.64)
Linus (c.67–76/79)
Anacletus (76–88 or 79–91)
Clement I (88–97 or 92–101)
Evaristus (c.97–c.107)
Alexander I (105–115 or 109–119)
Sixtus I (c.115–c.125)

Telesphorus (c.125–c.136)
Hyginus (c.136–c.140)
Pius I (c.140–155)
Anicetus (c.155–c.166)
Soter (c.166–c.175)
Eleutherius (c.175–189)
Victor I (c.189–199)

---

* Only since the ninth century has the title of "pope" come to be associated exclusively with the bishop of Rome.

Zephyrinus (c.199–217)

Calixtus I (Callistus) (217?–222)

Hippolytus (217, 218–235)

Urban I (222–230)

Pontian (230–235)

Anterus (235–236)

Fabian (236–250)

Cornelius (251–253)

Novatian (251)

Lucius I (253–254)

Stephen I (254–257)

Sixtus II (257–258)

Dionysius (259–268)

Felix I (269–274)

Eutychian (275–283)

Galus (283–296)

Marcellinus (291/296–304)

Marcellus I (308–309)

Eusebius (309/310)

Miltiades (Melchiades) (311–314)

Sylvester I (314–335)

Mark (336)

Julius I (337–352)

Liberius (352–366)

Felix II (355–358)

Damasus I (366–384)

Ursinus (366–367)

Siricius (384–399)

Anastasius I (399–401)

Innocent I (401–417)

Zosimus (417–418)

Boniface I (418–422)

Eulalius (418–419)

Celestine I (422–432)

Sixtus III (432–440)

Leo I (440–461)

Hilary (461–468)

Simplicius (468–483)

Felix III (or II) (483–492)

Gelasius I (492–496)

Anastasius II (496–498)

Symmachus (498–514)

Laurentius (498, 501–c.505/507)

Hormisdas (514–523)

John I (523–526)

Felix IV (or III) (526–530)

Dioscorus (530)

Boniface II (530–532)

John II (533–535)

Agapetus I (535–536)

Silverius (536–537)

Vigilius (537–555)

Pelagius I (556–561)

John III (561–574)

Benedict I (575–579)

Pelagius II (579–590)

Gregory I (590–604)

Sabinian (604–606)

Boniface III (607)

Boniface IV (608–615)

Deusdedit (also called Adeodatus I)
   (615–618)

Boniface V (619–625)

Honorius I (625–638)

Severinus (640)

John IV (640–642)

Theodore I (642–649)

Martin I (649–655)

Eugenius I (654–657)

Vitalian (657–672)

Adeodatus II (672–676)

Donus (676–678)

Agatho (678–681)

Leo II (682–683)

Benedict II (684–685)

John V (685–686)

Conon (686–687)

Sergius I (687–701)

Theodore (687)

Paschal (687)

John VI (701–705)

John VII (705–707)

Sisinnius (708)

Constantine (708–715)

Gregory II (715–731)

Gregory III (731–741)

Zacharias (Zachary) (741–752)

Stephen II (752–757)

Paul I (757–767)

Constantine (II) (767–768)

Philip (768)

Stephen III (768–772)

Adrian I (772–795)

Leo III (795–816)

Stephen IV (816–817)

Paschal I (817–824)

Eugenius II (824–827)

Valentine (827)

Gregory IV (827–844)

John (844)

Sergius II (844–847)

Leo IV (847–855)

Benedict III (855–858)

Anastasius (Anastasius the Librarian) (855)

Nicholas I (858–867)

Adrian II (867–872)

John VIII (872–882)

Marinus I (882–884)

Adrian III (884–885)

Stephen V (885–891)

Formosus (891–896)

Boniface VI (896)

Stephen VI (896–897)

Romanus (897)

Theodore II (897)

John IX (898–900)

Benedict IV (900–903)

Leo V (903)

Christopher (903–904)

Sergius III (904–911)

Anastasius III (911–913)

Lando (913–914)

John X (914–928)

Leo VI (928)

Stephen VII (929–931)

John XI (931–935)

Leo VII (936–939)

Stephen VIII (939–942)

Marinus II (942–946)

Agapetus II (946–955)

John XII (955–964)

Leo VIII (963–965)

Benedict V (964–966?)

John XIII (965–972)

Benedict VI (973–974)

Boniface VII (1st time) (974)

Benedict VII (974–983)

John XIV (983–984)

Boniface VII (2nd time) (984–985)

John XV (or XVI) (985–996)

Gregory V (996–999)

John XVI (or XVII) (997–998)

Sylvester II (999–1003)

John XVII (or XVIII) (1003)

John XVIII (or XIX) (1004–1009)

Sergius IV (1009–1012)

Gregory (VI) (1012)

Benedict VIII (1012–1024)

John XIX (or XX) (1024–1032)

Benedict IX (1st time) (1032–1044)

Sylvester III (1045)

Benedict IX (2nd time) (1045)

Gregory VI (1045–1046)

Clement II (1046–1047)

Benedict IX (3rd time) (1047–1048)

Damasus II (1048)

Leo IX (1049–1054)

Victor II (1055–1057)

Stephen IX (1057–1058)

Benedict (X) (1058–1059)

Nicholas II (1059–1061)

Alexander II (1061–1073)

Honorius (II) (1061–1072)

Gregory VII (1073–1085)

Clement (III) (1080–1100)
Victor III (1086–1087)
Urban II (1088–1099)
Paschal II (1099–1118)
Theodoric (1100–1102)
Albert (also called Aleric) (1102)
Sylvester (IV) (1105–1111)
Gelasius II (1118–1119)
Gregory (VIII) (1118–1121)
Calixtus II (Callistus) (1119–1124)
Honorius II (1124–1130)
Celestine (II) (1124)
Innocent II (1130–1143)
Anacletus (II) (1130–1138)
Victor (IV) (1138)
Celestine II (1143–1144)
Lucius II (1144–1145)
Eugenius III (1145–1153)
Anastasius IV (1153–1154)
Adrian IV (1154–1159)
Alexander III (1159–1181)
Victor (IV) (1159–1164)
Paschal (III) (1164–1168)
Calixtus (III) (1168–1178)
Innocent (III) (1179–1180)
Lucius III (1181–1185)
Urban III (1185–1187)
Gregory VIII (1187)
Clement III (1187–1191)
Celestine III (1191–1198)
Innocent III (1198–1216)
Honorius III (1216–1227)
Gregory IX (1227–1241)
Celestine IV (1241)
Innocent IV (1243–1254)
Alexander IV (1254–1261)
Urban IV (1261–1264)
Clement IV (1265–1268)
Gregory X (1271–1276)
Innocent V (1276)

Adrian V (1276)
John XXI (1276–1277)
Nicholas III (1277–1280)
Martin IV (1281–1285)
Honorius IV (1285–1287)
Nicholas IV (1288–1292)
Celestine V (1294)
Boniface VIII (1294–1303)
Benedict IX (1303–1304)
Clement V (at Avignon, from 1309)
   (1305–1314)
John XXII (at Avignon) (1316–1334)
Nicholas (V) (at Rome) (1328–1330)
Benedict XII (at Avignon) (1334–1342)
Clement VI (at Avignon) (1342–1352)
Innocent VI (at Avignon) (1352–1362)
Urban V (at Avignon) (1362–1370)
Gregory XI (at Avignon, then Rome from
   1377) (1370–1378)
Urban VI (1378–1389)
Clement (VII) (at Avignon) (1378–1394)
Boniface IX (1389–1404)
Benedict (XIII) (at Avignon) (1394–1417)
Innocent VII (1404–1406)
Gregory XII (1406–1415)
Alexander (V) (at Bologna) (1409–1410)
John (XXIII) (at Bologna) (1410–1415)
Martin V (1417–1431)
Clement (VIII) (1423–1429)
Eugenius IV (1431–1447)
Felix (V) (also called Amadeus VIII of Savoy)
   (1439–1449)
Nicholas V (1447–1455)
Calixtus III (Callistus) (1455–1458)
Pius II (1458–1464)
Paul II (1464–1471)
Sixtus IV (1471–1484)
Innocent VIII (1484–1492)
Alexander VI (1492–1503)

CALIPHS

Early Caliphs
Abu-Bakr (632–634)
Umar I (634–644)
Uthman (644–656)
Ali (656–661)

Umayyads
Mu'awiyah I (661–680)
Yazid I (680–683)
Mu'awiyah II (683–684)
Marwan I (684–685)
'Abd al-Malik (685–705)
al-Walid I (705–715)
Sulayman (715–717)
Umar II (717–720)
Yazid II (720–724)
Hisham (724–743)
al-Walid II (743–744)
Yazid III (744)
Ibrahim (744)
Marwan II (744–750)

Abbasids*
al-Saffah (750–754)
al-Mansur (754–775)
al-Mahdi (775–785)
al-Hadi (785–786)
Harun al-Rashid (786–809)
al-Amin (809–813)
al-Ma'mun (813–833)

al-Mu'tasim (833–842)
al-Wathiq (842–847)
al-Mutawakkil (847–861)
al-Muntasir (861–862)
al-Musta'in (862–866)
al-Mu'tazz (866–869)
al-Muhtadi (869–870)
al-Mu'tamid (870–892)
al-Mu'tadid (892–902)
al-Muqtafi (902–908)
al-Muqtadir (908–932)
al-Qahir (932–934)
al-Radi (934–940)

Fatimids
'Ubayd Allah (al-Mahdi) (909–934)
al-Qa'im (934–946)
al-Mansur (946–953)
al-Mu'izz (953–975)
al-'Aziz (975–996)
al-Hakim (996–1021)
al-Zahir (1021–1036)
al-Mustansir (1036–1094)
al-Musta'li (1094–1101)
al-Amir (1101–1130)
al-Hafiz (1130–1149)
al-Zafir (1149–1154)
al-Fa'iz (1154–1160)
al-'Adid (1160–1171)

---

* Abbasid caliphs continued at Baghdad—with, however, only nominal power—until 1258.
Thereafter, a branch of the family in Cairo held the caliphate until the sixteenth century.

OTTOMAN EMIRS AND SULTANS

Othman (Uthman) (d. 1324/1326)
Orkhan (1324/1326–1359/1360)
Murad I (1359/1360–1389)
Bayazid I (1389–1402)
Ottoman Civil War (1402–1413)

Mehmed I (1413–1421)
Murad II (1421–1444, 1446–1451)
Mehmed II the Conqueror (1444–1446,
    1451–1481)
Bayazid II (1481–1512)

SOURCES

MAPS

1.4 Tours, *c.*600. Copyright © Henri Galinié.

3.1 The Byzantine and Bulgarian Empires, *c.*920. Mark Whittow, "Imperial Territory and the Themes, c.917," *The Making of Orthodox Byzantium, 600–1025* (University of California Press, 1996), p. 166. Reproduced with permission of Palgrave Macmillan.

4.1 Constantinople, *c.*1100. Adapted from Linda Safran, editor, *Heaven on Earth: Art and the Church in Byzantium*, Maps 1.7 and 1.9, pp. 21 and 23, Copyright © 1998 by The Pennsylvania State University Press. Reprinted by permission of The Pennsylvania State University Press.

5.1 The Byzantine Empire and the Seljuk World, *c.*1090. Christophe Picard, "Byzantium and the Islamic World, *c.*1090," *Le monde musulman du XIe du XVe au siècle* (SEDES, 2000). Copyright © Armand Colin, 2000. Reproduced by permission.

6.6 German Settlement in the Baltic Sea Region, Twelfth to Fourteenth Centuries. From *Atlas of Medieval Europe* (Routledge, 2007). Reproduced by permission of Robert Bartlett.

7.7 The Village of Toury, Fourteenth and Fifteenth Centuries. Reproduced by permission of Samuel Leturcq.

7.8 The Lands of Toury, Fourteenth and Fifteenth Centuries. Reproduced by permission of Samuel Leturcq.

8.4 The Duchy of Burgundy, 1363–1477. From *Atlas of Medieval Europe* (Routledge, 2007). Reproduced by permission of Michael C.E. Jones.

PLATES

1.1 Mars and Venus, Pompeii (1st cent.). Fresco from House of Mars and Venus, Pompeii. 1st C. BCE–79 CE. Image source: Fotografica Foglia. Museo Archeologico Nazionale, Naples, Italy. Reprinted by permission of Scala / Art Resource, NY.

1.2 Landscape, Pompeii (1st cent.). The stray ram. Pompeiian fresco. Museo Archeologico Nazionale, Naples, Italy. Reprinted by permission of Scala / Art Resource, NY.

1.3 A City Scene, Boscoreale (1st cent. BCE). Cubiculum (bedroom) from the Villa of P. Fannius Synistor at Boscoreale (detail of left wall with urban scene). Roman, ca. 50–40 BCE. Second Style. Fresco. Rogers Fund, 1903 (03.14.13a-g). Image copyright © The Metropolitan Museum of Art, New York, NY, USA. Image source: Art Resource, NY.

1.4 Meleager on a Roman Sarcophagus (2nd cent.). Villa Doria Pamphili, Rome. Reprinted by permission of Ministero per i Beni e le Attività Culturali–Soprintendenza Speciale per i Beni Archeologici di Roma.

1.5 Venus and Two Nymphs, Britain (2nd or early 3rd cent.). Relief: Venus bathing with two attendant nymphs (1958.46.N). Great North Museum Hancock / NEWMA / The Bridgeman Art Library. Reproduced by permission.

1.6 Tombstone, near Carthage (2nd cent.?). Limestone stela with flat top and relief; Ghorfa; Carthage. Copyright © The Trustees of the British Museum. All rights reserved.

1.7 Decorated Coffer from Jerusalem (1st cent.?). Carved limestone ossuary decorated with incised floral, geometric and architectural designs, lid is decorated with an eight-arched arcade with rosettes in the centre of each arcade. Copyright © The Trustees of the British Museum. All rights reserved.

1.8 Base of the Hippodrome Obelisk (*c.*390). Emperor Theodosius, seated between his two sons, receives homage from vanquished enemy. Base of the Egyptian obelisk imported by Emperor Theodosius and erected in the Hippodrome in Constantinople. Reprinted by permission of SEF / Art Resource, NY.

1.9 Orant Fresco (2nd half of 4th cent.). SS. Giovanni e Paolo, Rome, view of confessio (late 4th c.). Reprinted by permission of the Ministero dell'Interno–Dipartimento per le Libertà civili e l'Immigrazione–Direzione Centrale per l'Amministrazione del Fondo Edifici di Culto.

1.10 Sarcophagus of Junius Bassus (359). Sarcophagus of Junius Bassus, Roman prefect. Museum of the Treasury, St. Peter's Basilica, Vatican State. Reprinted by permission of Scala / Art Resource, NY.

1.11 Reliquary of Theuderic (late 7th cent.). Merovingian. Gold-plated silver, pearls, precious stones. Treasury, Abbey, St. Maurice, Switzerland. Reprinted by permission of Erich Lessing / Art Resource, NY.

1.12 Mosaic from San Vitale, Ravenna (*c.*545–*c.*550). Emperor Justinian, 483–565, and his court, with Archbishop Maximian and General Belisarius in San Vitale, 6th century AD, Ravenna, Italy. Reprinted by permission of Alfredo Dagli Orti / The Art Archive at Art Resource, NY.

2.1 An Ivory Diptych of Christ and the Virgin (mid–6th cent.). Christ with Codex, Behind Him Saints Peter and Paul, and Mother of God. 546–556 CE. Panels of an ivory diptych, from Constantinople. 29 x 13 cm. Inv. 564 and 565. Photos: Juergen Liepe. Skulpturensammlung und Museum fuer Byzantinische Kunst, Staatliche Museen, Berlin, Germany. Reproduced by permission of bpk, Berlin / Skulpturensammlung und Museum fuer Byzantinische Kunst / Juergen Liepe / Art Resource, NY.

Seeing the Middle Ages: Panel from the consular diptych of Magnus. Flavius Magnus, Roman Consul in 518, sitting on a lion-legged throne. Panel of the diptych. Bibliotheque Nationale, Cabinet de Medailles, Paris. France. Reproduced by permission of Erich Lessing / Art Resource, NY.

2.2 Cross at Hagia Sophia (orig. mosaic 6th cent.; redone 768/769). Cross from South Tympanum, Hagia Sophia. The Courtauld Institute of Art, London. Photograph by Ernest Hawkins. Reproduced by permission.

2.3 Damascus Great Mosque Mosaic (706). Western portico, decoration detail. Reproduced by permission of Andrea Jemolo.

2.4 Belt Buckle from Sutton Hoo (early 7th cent.). Gold belt buckle from the ship-burial at Sutton Hoo. Anglo-Saxon, early 7th CE. From Mound 1, Sutton Hoo, Suffolk, England (l. 13.2cm; w. 5.6cm; weight 412.7 grams). Inv. PY 1939.1010.1. Copyright © The Trustees of the British Museum / Art Resource, NY.

2.5 Saint Luke, Lindisfarne Gospels (1st third of 8th cent.?). Cotton Nero D.IV fol. 137v. Copyright © The British Library Board. All Rights Reserved.

2.6 Carpet Page, Lindisfarne Gospels (1st third of 8th cent.?). Cotton Nero D.IV fol. 138v. Copyright © The British Library Board. All Rights Reserved.

2.7 First Text Page, Gospel of Saint Luke, Lindisfarne Gospels (1st third of 8th cent.?). Cotton Nero D.IV fol. 139. Copyright © The British Library Board. All Rights Reserved.

2.8 Franks Casket (1st half of 8th cent.). The Franks (Auzon) Casket. Anglo-Saxon, ca. 700 CE. Whalebone, 22.9 x 19 x 10.9 cm. Inv. PY 1867.0120.1. Copyright © The Trustees of the British Museum / Art Resource, NY.

3.1 The Empress Eudocia and Her Sons, *Homilies* of Gregory Nazianzus (*c.*880). Eudocie Ingerina et ses fils (879–882), fol. b. Reproduced by permission of the Bibliothèque nationale de France.

3.2 Ezekiel in the Valley of Dry Bones, *Homilies* of Gregory Nazianzus (*c.*880). Le prophete Ezechiel dans la vallée des ossements (879–882), fol. 438v. Reproduced by permission of the Bibliothèque nationale de France.

3.3 Water Pitcher in the Shape of an Eagle (796–797). 180 AH/796-797 Aquamanile in the Form of an Eagle; The State Hermitage Museum, St. Petersburg. Photograph © The State Hermitage Museum / photo by Vladimir Terebenin, Leonard Kheifets, Yuri Molodkovets.

3.4 Great Mosque, Córdoba (785–787). Interior of the mosque. Umayyad caliphate (Moorish), 10th c. Mosque, Cordoba, Spain. Reproduced by permission of Scala / Art Resource, NY.

3.5 Sacramentary of Saint-Germain-des-Prés (early 9th cent.). Sacramentarium Elnonense ad usum Parisiensem accommodatum. MS lat. 2291, fol. 14v. Reproduced by permission of the Bibliothèque nationale de France.

3.6 The Pleiades (2nd quarter, 9th cent.). MS VLQ 79, fol. 42v: Aratus, Phaenomena interprete Claudio Germanico Caesare. Reproduced by permission of Leiden University Library.

3.7 Psalter Page (2nd quarter, 9th cent.). *Psalter of Louis the German*, Saint-Omer (*c.* 850). MS Theol. lat. fol. 58, Bl. 3r. Reproduced by permission of bpk, Berlin / Staatsbibliothek zu Berlin / Art Resource, NY.

3.8 Saint John (2nd half, 9th cent.). Evangelia quattuor [Évangiles dits de François II]. MS lat. 257, fol. 147v. Reproduced by permission of the Bibliothèque nationale de France.

3.9 Utrecht Psalter (*c.*820–835). MS 323, fol. 4v. Reproduced by permission of Utrecht University Library.

4.1 Emperor Basil II (r.976–1025). Gilded miniature from a psalter. MS gr. z 17, fol. 111r, Biblioteca Marciana, Venice, Italy. Reproduced by permission of Erich Lessing / Art Resource, NY.

4.2 The Raising of Lazarus, Egbert Codex (985–990). MS 24 fol. 5v. Photograph by Anja Runkel. Reproduced by permission of Stadtbibliothek/Stadtarchiv Trier.

4.3 Christ Asleep, Hitda Gospels (c. 1000–c. 1020). MS 1640, fol. 117r. Hessische Landes- und Hochschulbibliothek Darmstadt. Reproduced by permission of Universitäts- und Landesbibliothek Darmstadt.

4.4 Saint Luke, Gospel Book of Otto III (998–1001). Bayerische Staatsbibliothek München, Clm 4453, fol. 139v. Reproduced by permission.

Seeing the Middle Ages: Otto III Enthroned, Aachen Gospels (c.996). Apotheosis of Otto III (from the Ottonian Book of Gospels). Photo by Ann Münchow. Copyright © Domkapitel Aachen. Reproduced by permission.

5.1 San Miniato Cathedral (late 12th cent.). View of the facade. Cathedral, San Miniato, Italy. Reproduced by permission of Scala / Art Resource, NY.

5.2 Bowl, North Africa (late 12th cent.). San Miniato, Museo Diocesano, bacino ceramico, prov. Cattedrale S. Maria Assunta (AFSPI n. 88904). Reprinted by permission of MiBAC/Soprintendenza Pisa, prot. 10902 del 15/07/2013.

5.3 Durham Cathedral, Interior (1093–1133). Nave looking east. Cathedral, Durham, Great Britain. Reproduced by permission of Anthony Scibilia / Art Resource, NY.

5.4 Sant Tomàs de Fluvià, The Last Supper, Painted Vault (early 12th cent.). Sant Tomàs de Fluvià (Toroella). Photograph by Heinz Hebeisen. Reproduced by permission of Iberimage.

5.5 Cathedral Complex, Pisa (11th–12th cent.). Courtesy of Barbara H. Rosenwein.

5.6 Saint-Lazare of Autun, Nave (1120–1146). Copyright © Emmanuel PIERRE / Romanes.com. Reproduced by permission.

5.7 Autun, Eve (12th cent.). Relief from Autun Cathedral, Saint Lazare, 1130 (stone) / Cathedral of St. Lazare, Autun, France / The Bridgeman Art Library. Reproduced by permission.

5.8 Carthusian Diurnal from Lyon (12th cent.). Add 17302, fol. 52r. Copyright © The British Library Board. All Rights Reserved.

5.9 Fontenay Abbey Church, Interior (1139–1147). Nave looking east. Abbey, Fontenay, France. Reproduced by permission of Anthony Scibilia / Art Resource, NY.

5.10 Jael, Humility, and Judith (c.1140). Arundel 44, fol. 34v. Copyright © The British Library Board. All Rights Reserved.

6.1 Bust of Frederick Barbarossa (1165). Reliquary bust of Frederick I (c.1123–1190) made in Aachen, 1155–71 (gilded bronze), German School, (12th century) / Church of St. Johannes, Cappenberg, Germany / The Bridgeman Art Library. Reproduced by permission.

6.2 Notre Dame of Paris, Exterior (begun 1163). Reproduced by permission of Stan Parry.

6.3 Notre Dame of Paris, Interior (begun 1163). Central nave toward the altar. Reproduced by permission of Scala / Art Resource, NY.

6.4 Lincoln Cathedral, Interior (choir begun 1192, nave begun 1225). Center nave of Lincoln Cathedral, looking east. 2nd quarter 13th c. Reproduced by permission of Erich Lessing / Art Resource, NY.

6.5 San Francesco at Assisi (upper church; completed by 1253). The interior of the Upper Basilica, S. Francesco, Assisi, Italy, from the east, after the earthquake of 1997. Photo: Ghigo Roli, 2002. Reproduced by permission of Alinari / Art Resource, NY.

6.6 Reims Cathedral, West Portal, Saint Joseph (*c.*1240). Martin Hurliman, "Saint Joseph" (Reims Cathedral), 1967. Copyright © Estate of Martin Hurliman / SODRAC (2013).

7.1 Chalice (*c.*1300). Copyright © Rheinisches Bildarchiv Koln, rba_c007428. Rhineland, in 1300, silver, gold, H 15.7 cm, Inv. No. G 12.

7.2 Pietro Lorenzetti, *Birth of the Virgin* (1342). Lorenzetti, Pietro (fl. c. 1306–1345). Birth of the Virgin. Museo dell'Opera Metropolitana, Siena, Italy. Reproduced by permission of Scala / Art Resource, NY.

7.3 A Shrine Madonna (*c.*1300). Shrine of the Virgin. Ca. 1300. German, made in Rhine Valley. Oak, linen covering, polychromy, gilding, gesso. Overall: 14 1/2 x 13 5/8 x 5 1/8 in. Closed: w. 5 in. Gift of J. Pierpont Morgan, 1917 (17.190.185). Image copyright The Metropolitan Museum of Art, New York, NY, USA. Image source: Art Resource, NY.

Seeing the Middle Ages: Guido da Vigevano, "The Seven Cells of the Uterus" (1345). Uterus. Liber notabilium Philippi septimi francorum regis, a libris Galieni extractus. 1345. 32 x 22 cm. MS 334, fol. 267v. Photo: René-Gabriel Ojéda. Musée Condé, Chantilly, France. Copyright © RMN-Grand Palais / Art Resource, NY.

7.4 *Hours of Jeanne d'Evreux* (*c.*1325–1328). Jean Pucelle, fol. 15v, 16r. I. Walther, N. Wolf: Codices illustres; Köln 2005, S. 208.

7.5 Tomb and Effigy of Robert d'Artois (1317). Effigy (stone), Pepin, Jean (Jean Pepin de Huy) (14th century) / Basilique Saint-Denis, France / Giraudon / The Bridgeman Art Library. Reproduced by permission.

7.6 The Motet *S'Amours* (*c.*1300). *Chansons anciennes (en latin et en français) avec la musique*. MS H196, fol. 270r. Reproduced by permission of the Bibliothèque universitaire de médecine, Université Montpellier.

7.7 Saint John, "Dominican" Bible (mid-13th cent.). MS Lat. 16722m, fol. 205v. Reproduced by permission of the Bibliothèque nationale de France.

7.8 Saint John, "Aurifaber" Bible (mid-13th cent.) Reproduced by permission of Württembergische Landesbibliothek Stuttgart, Cod. bibl. qt. 8, fol. 402v.

7.9 Nicola Pisano, Pulpit (1266–1268). Siena, Baptistry, Pulpit, Adoration of the Magi, detail / De Agostini Picture Library / G. Nimatallah / The Bridgeman Art Library. Reproduced by permission.

7.10 Giotto, Scrovegni Chapel, Padua (1304–1306). Reprinted by permission of Comune di Padova–Assessorato alla Cultura.

7.11 Giotto, *Raising of Lazarus*, Scrovegni Chapel (1304–1306). Fresco (post restoration), Giotto di Bondone (*c.*1266–1337) / Scrovegni (Arena) Chapel, Padua, Italy / Alinari / The Bridgeman Art Library. Reproduced by permission.

8.1 Corpses Confront the Living (*c.*1441). Sign. XVIII B 18, fol. 542r: Alexander de Villa Dei, Hieronymus Stridonensis, Pseudo-Augustinus. Reproduced by permission of the National Museum, Prague, Czech Republic.

8.2 Donatello, *Judith and Holofernes* (*c.*1420–1430). Donatello (*c.*1386–1466). Bronze. Palazzo Vecchio, Florence, Italy. Reproduced by permission of Scala / Art Resource, NY.

8.3 Piero di Cosimo, *Venus, Cupid, and Mars* (*c.*1495–1505). Piero di Cosimo (1462–1521). Oil on poplar wood. 72 x 182 cm. Inv. 107. Reproduced by permission of bpk, Berlin / Gemaeldegalerie, Staatliche Museen, Berlin / Jörg P. Anders / Art Resource, NY.

FIGURES

5.3 Plan of Fountains Abbey (founded 1132). Adapted from Plate 70 in Wolfgang Braunfels, *Monasteries of Western Europe: The Architecture of the Orders* (Princeton: Princeton University Press, 1972), p. 84. Copyright © Dumont Buchverlag GmbH.

7.1 Single Notes and Values of Franconian Notation. From *Anthology of Medieval Music*, ed. Richard Hoppin (W.W. Norton, 1978).

INDEX

Page numbers for illustrations are in italics.

grisaille, 275
    definition of, 332
Groote, Gerhard (1340–1384), 322
Guelfs and Ghibellines, 248
    definition of, 332
Guido da Vigevano
    Seven Cells of the Uterus (1345), 263, *263*
guilds, 163–64, 192, 213, 218–21, 233, 236, 250, 286,
    300
    statutes, 218–20, 237
Guillaume de Lorris
    Romance of the Rose, 267
Guillem Guifred, bishop, 133–34
Gutenberg, Johann, 322. *See also* printing press

Habsburgs, 212, 297
hadith, 57, 92, 144. *See also* literature, Islamic
Hagia Sophia. *See* Constantinople
Haithabu, 102, 135
Hakim, al-, caliph (r.996–1021), 125
Handbook for Her Son (Dhuoda), 106
Hansa, 245
Hanseatic League, 245
Harald Bluetooth, Danish king (r.*c*.958–*c*.986), 139,
    148
Harmony of Discordant Canons. See Decretum (Gratian)
Harun al-Rashid, caliph (r.786–809), 91
Hastings, battle of (1066), 174
Hattin, battle of (1187), 198
Hebrew language, 64, 137, 214
Hebrews, 259. *See also* Jews
Henry of Anjou. *See* Henry II, king of England
Henry the Navigator, Portuguese prince (1394–
    1460), 323
Henry I, king of England (r.1100–1135), 164, 175,
    202
Henry I, king of Germany (r.919–936), 140
Henry II, king and emp., 140
Henry II, king of England (r.1154–1189), 202–5,
    207–8, 211, 219, 236
Henry III, king and emp. (r.1039–1056), 145, 148,
    165–66, 167
Henry III, king of England (r.1216–1272), 250,
    254–55
Henry IV, king and emp. (r.1056–1106), 167–69, 170
Henry V, king of England (r.1413–1422), 289, 292
Henry VI, emp. (r.1190–1197), 211
Henry VI, king of England (r.1422–1461), 295, 320
Heraclius, Byzantine emp. (r.610–641), 41
heraldry, 296

heresy, 8, 119, 211, 230, 255, 259, 265. *See also* names
    of individual heresies
heretic/heretics/heretical, 7, 231–34, 251–52, 255,
    279
    Arius, 8
    Cathars, 232
    in Church canons, 230
    Crusade against, 234
    Frederick II, emp., 211
    Hus, 303–4
    Jeanne d'Arc, 295
    Lollards, 303
Hijra (622), 52. *See also* Muhammad the Prophet
Hildebrand of Soana. *See* Gregory VII, pope
History of Alexander the Great (*c*.1459) (tapestry),
    316–17, *316–17*
Hitda, abbess of Meschede, 144
Hitda Gospels (*c*.1000–*c*.1020), 143–44
    Christ Asleep, *143*
Holy Land, 155, 170–73, 234, 236, 255. *See also*
    Crusader States; Levant; names of individual
    Crusader States
Holy Roman Empire, 212, 251, 254, 295, 297, 303.
    See also empire, definition of
homage, 131–32, 145, 172, 203, 207, 299. *See also*
    vassalage
hospices/hospitals. *See* medicine
Hours of Jeanne d'Evreux (*c*.1325–1328) (Pucelle), 264,
    264, 275–76
Hugh Capet, king of France (r.987–996), 145
Hugh of Lusignan, 132, 134
humanism, 192
Humbert of Silva Candida, 166–67
Hundred Years' War (1337–1453), 283, 289–95, 296,
    299–301, 320, 324
Hungarians, 102, 127, 130, 140, 148. *See also* Magyars
Hungary, 127, 130, 145, 148, 171, 212, 236, 242,
    247–48, 252, 257, 324
Huns, 23, 241
Hus, Jan (1369/71–1415), 303
Hussites, 303–4

Iberia, 93, 125. *See also* Andalus, al-/Andalusia;
    Spain
Ibn Rushd (Averroes) (1126–1198), 179
Ibn Sina (Avicenna) (980–1037), 126, 179
iconoclasm/iconoclastic/iconoclasts, 45, 48, 50, 56,
    75, 79–80, 83–85, 92, 106
Ifriqiya, 88–89, 130
Ile-de-France, 145, 176, 207, 220, 233, 250

Landi family, 248

languages. *See* names of individual languages

Languedoc, 233, 234, 252

Las Navas de Tolosa, battle of (1212), 198

Last Supper (1494–1497) (Leonardo da Vinci), 307, 312, *312–13*

Lateran Palace (Rome), 229

Latin Empire, 237, 243. *See also* Crusade, Fourth

Latin language, 25, 64, 72–73, 82, 109, 137, 141, 179, 215, 268, 305, 322

law/laws/lawyers
    barbarian law codes, 25, 34, 73
    Byzantine, 34, 119
    Carolingian capitularies, 98
    Castilian *fueros*, 207
    church, 134, 228–29. *See also* canon law/canons
    Codex Justinianus (529, revised in 534), 34, 179
    Digest (533), 34
    East Central Europe, 258
    English, 137–38, 164, 202–5, 236, 284
    French, 208
    Hungarian, 148
    Islamic, 91, 158
    issued by communes, 164, 286
    Novel (934), 119
    Ottoman, 288
    Roman, 7–8, 25, 34, 170, 179, 210
    schools of, 158, 179, 220
    Theodosian Code, 25, 34
    Viking, 129
    Visigothic Code, 25

layman/laywoman/laity, 6, 11, 27, 64, 99, 106, 131, 134, 165, 167, 179, 207, 229–33, 259, 270, 279, 303, 322, 324
    definition of, 332
    lay aristocrats, 27, 61, 73, 133–35, 174, 278
    lay religiosity, 261–64

Lechfeld, battle of (955), 130, 140, 144

Legnano, battle of (1176), 211

Leo the Mathematician, 83

Leo III, Byzantine emp. (r.717–741), 45, 48, 74–75, 92

Leo IV, Byzantine emp. (d.780), 80

Leo VI, Byzantine emp. (r.886–912), 80–81, 84, 130

Leo IX, pope (1049–1054), 166

León, 175, 252

Leonardo da Vinci (1452–1519)
    Last Supper, 307, 312, *312–13*

Leovigild, Visigothic king (Spain) (r.569–586), 72

lepers/leprosy, 231, 251–52, 255, 279

leprosaria, 251–52. *See also* lepers/leprosy

Leudegar, bishop of Autun (r.*c*.662–*c*.677?), 64

Levant, 158, 172–74, 197, 213, 236. *See also* Crusader States; Holy Land; names of individual Crusader States
    definition of, 333

Lewes, battle of (1264), 254

liberal arts, 178–79, 220

Libya, 41, 123, 125

Licinius, Roman emp., 6

Life of Charlemagne (Einhard), 97–99

Lille, 278, 292

Lincoln
    Cathedral, Interior (choir begun 1192, nave begun 1225), 221, 225, *225*

Lindisfarne, 66

Lindisfarne Gospels (1st third of 8th cent.?), 66, 72
    Carpet Page, *68*
    First Text Page (Gospel of Saint Luke), *69*
    Saint Luke, *67*

literature. *See also* names of individual works of literature
    Anglo-Saxon, 72, 137
    chanson de geste, 217–18
    classical, 44, 305
    courtly poetry, 214–17
    Dance of Death, 286
    fabliau/fabliaux, 216
    Islamic, 57, 91, 216
    vernacular, 267–68

Lithuania, 82, 257–58

liturgy, 28, 82, 143, 189
    Bohemian, 304
    books, 82, 103, 105
    chants, 104–5, 215, 268
    definition of, 333
    Mass, 10, 28, 33, 189, 230, 251, 261, 264, 303–4, 307
    Office/Offices/Divine Office, 8, 28, 181, 264
    prayers, 28, 165, 264
    processions, 181, 261
    Roman, 175
    vessels, 181, 259, *260*, 261
    vestments, 66, 181

Lives of the Caesars (2nd cent.) (Suetonius), 97

Lodi, Peace of (1454), 297

Lollards, 303

Lombard League, 211

Lombards, 34, 58, 73–75, 97–99, 119
    Lombard crown, 98, 140

Lombers
    Cathar meeting at (1165), 232